AF790962

Svein-Olaf Hvasshovd

Recovery in Parallel Database Systems

Database Systems

edited by Theo Haerder and Andreas Reuter

In this special book series the interested student or scholar will find leading textbooks and monographs focusing on one of the most prospective areas in the fields of computer science.

Though the classical database systems have been ranking among the most crucial EDP-applications for several years, today's development is characterized by new technical concepts of highest relevance for practical use.

The series offers sound information on both the basics and the applicational potential. Among others, the books in this series are treating subjects like open database systems, knowledge based or object oriented database systems, multimedia and CAx databases.

In German:

Hochleistungs-Transaktionssysteme
by Erhard Rahm

Datenbanken in verteilten Systemen
by Winfried Lamersdorf

In English:

Recovery in Parallel Database Systems
by Svein-Olaf Hvasshovd

Vieweg

Svein-Olaf Hvasshovd

Recovery in Parallel Database Systems

2nd Edition

vieweg

1st Edition 1996
2nd Edition 1999

All rights reserved
© Friedr. Vieweg & Sohn Verlagsgesellschaft mbH, Braunschweig/Wiesbaden, 1999

Vieweg is a subsidiary company of Bertelsmann Professional Information.

No part of this publication may be reproduced, stored in a retrieval system or transmitted, mechanical, photocopying or otherwise without prior permission of the copyright holder.

http://www.vieweg.de

Cover design: Ulrike Weigel, www.CorporateDesignGroup.de

ISBN 978-3-528-15411-0 ISBN 978-3-322-91534-4 (eBook)
DOI 10.1007/978-3-322-91534-4

Nowhere has the philosophical argument been evaded, but where it runs out into too thin a thread the Author has preferred to cut short, and fall back upon the corresponding results of experience; for in the same way as many plants only bear fruit when they do not shoot too high, so in the practical arts the theoretical leaves and flowers must not be made to sprout too far, but kept near to experience, which is their proper soil.

Carl von Clausewitz

Preface

The relational DBMS technology is a success in the commercial marketplace with respect to business data processing and related applications. This success is a result of cost effective application development combined with high data consistency. The success has led to the use of relational DBMS technology in other application environments requesting its traditional virtues, while at the same time adding new requirements. For example, the integration of relational DBMS technology with telecommunications has led to such combined requirements as transaction rates of more than 10.000 TPC-B like transactions per second, transaction service availability of certain transaction classes of 99,999%, and transaction response time under 10 milliseconds. The current trends in hardware price/performance and parallel technology make relational DBMSs which support very high transaction rates, very high availability, and soft real-time transaction response a cost effective possibility.

This book describes a recovery method supporting the traditional high DBMS data consistency while offering very high transaction rates, continuous availability, and soft real-time transaction response. It also presents high availability approaches used by commercial DBMS products.

Acknowledgements

The book is based on my doctoral (Dr.Ing.) thesis. Due to an extreme work load over a long period it has taken some time to complete the book transformation. My Dr.Ing. research and the following book transformation period clearly demonstrated to me the value of true and trustful friendship. I want to thank all good friends for their kind support and encouragement and their ability to bear with me at all times. It is a great pleasure to express deep gratitude for the help I have received in writing the thesis.

First and foremost I wish to acknowledge Prof. Dr. Andreas Reuter and Prof. Dr. Theo Haerder for giving me the opportunity to publish the result of my research. I also wish to acknowledge Prof. Kjell Bratbergsengen for his Dr.Ing. advisory.

A special thanks goes to my colleagues Dr. Øystein Torbjørnsen and Oddvar Risnes for their constructive criticism and helpful motivation. I have been fortunate to work closely with them on the HypRa project and also on the continuation TeleServe and ClustRa projects.

I also wish to thank in particular my colleagues at Telenor R&D and my former colleagues at the Database Technology Group at SINTEF DELAB for a good inspiring working environment. A special thanks to Dr. Svein Erik Bratsberg, Ole-Hj. Kristensen, Dr. Stein Dale, and Steinar Haug for their unending encouragements. I also want to thank Cindy Kandolf for her excellent proofreading.

It would be remiss not to acknowledge the support and sponsorship for my research. First of all, I express my gratitude to my employer Telenor R&D, for the support and sponsorship given during the production of this book. Secondly, I want to express my gratitude to my former employer SINTEF DELAB which was willing to carry the burden of financing me at the darkest hours and continuously sponsoring me throughout the Dr.Ing. research period. Secondly, I want to express my gratitude to my current employer TeleServe Transaction Technology AS for financing the final stage of this work and for commercialising the results from this research. I also wish to thank the Royal Norwegian Council for Scientific and Industrial Research (NFR) for granting me a two year Dr.Ing. scholarship. The generous support given by the previous director of RUNIT, Dr. Steinar Kvitsand, will never be forgotten.

I express the most sincere thanks to Telenor R&D for initiating, funding, and managing the HypRa project and for deciding to continue the research program through the TeleServe and ClustRa projects. I am happy to say that these projects provided the motivating applications, the research environment, and the application harness for my own research, without which the presented results would hardly have been obtainable.

I like to thank IBM Norge AS, Informix Software AS, TT-Technology AS, Oracle Norge AS, Sybase Norge AS, and Tandem Computers AS for all their help with supplying me with product documentation.

Plan of the Book

This book is divided into six parts. The first part introduces motivations and requirements for continuously available database management systems (DBMSs). It also presents the general basic requirements and design goals for DBMS recovery methods.

The second part of the book gives a systematic presentation and analysis of design approaches for DBMS recovery systems developed over more than fifteen years, primarily focusing on their effect on availability and transaction service response times. It starts with the older block oriented recovery approach, which represented the state of the art of the late 1970s. Recovery methods based on this approach are still in use in successful existing DBMS products. It then continues with the more modern record oriented recovery approach, which represented the state of art in the first half of the 1980s. This approach also provides the basis for the recovery methods used in successful DBMSs. It then continues with the compensation oriented recovery approach, which is the most modern of the recovery approaches implemented in commercial systems. This approach represented the state of the art in the late 1980s. The table oriented approach is the last of the presented recovery approaches. It represents an extension of the previous approaches and is only partially implemented in current commercial systems.

The third part presents the design goals and the recovery approach for the HypRa DBMS. The basic hardware and software architectures of the HypRa DBMS is outlined. A more detailed presentation of the HypRa architecture is given in [HST91a]. The HypRa recovery approach is to a large extent based on the principles from the table oriented recovery approach. To meet the response requirement from soft real-time transaction services, it supports main memory logging. To support very high availability, multiple replicas of relations are maintained online. If a primary replica fails, a hot stand-by takes over as primary without interrupting the transaction service availability. Fast automatic online recovery and repair are provided to reestablish the initial fault-tolerance level.

The fourth part of the book presents other high availability DBMS approaches than the HypRa approach. An overview of central design strategies for high availability approaches is given. Two commercial DBMS product solutions based on the shared disc and seven commercial DBMS product solutions based on the shared-nothing hardware architectures are presented. The product presentations are based on public product documentation. Some of the conclusions are deduced from information pieces obtained from multiple sources which unfortunately increases the probability of errors. The responsibility for such errors is mine. I hope they are few in number.

The fifth part of the book presents the conclusions to be drawn from this research. Directions for further work are also indicated.

The sixth part of the book introduces basic concepts relating to databases, transactions, and concurrency control in a DBMS.

Abstract

This book presents a recovery method for a distributed DBMS based on a multi-computer, with a shared-nothing hardware architecture and a high capacity and low latency inter-node communication network. The recovery method is intended to support: very high transaction service availability, 99,999% availability for simple transactions; very high simple transaction load, 10.000 TPC-B equivalent transactions per second; and soft real-time transaction response, 10 millisec. response time for single tuple transactions.

The main recovery approaches developed over the last two decades are systematically presented and analysed, in particular with respect to how well they fulfill the requirements for availability and soft real-time response. The availability aspect includes both normal operations and fast recovery. An obvious conclusion can be drawn; availability has improved markedly over these years, in particular for those systems that have been around for a while and have shown the ability to adapt to users' needs. Most elements needed in a recovery approach to provide very high availability are present in the newest main approach. The element that is particularly lacking is the ability to perform online non-blocking repair, i.e. to reestablish automatically, online, and without blocking, the initial fault-tolerance level after a recovery. The analysis of soft real-time response is mostly focused on commit processing. All the main recovery approaches analysed are still bound by the response times of disc accesses with its dire effect on transaction response times. The trend, though, is to gradually accept main memory logging.

The HypRa architecture, which supports multiple replicas of relations, i.e. one primary and one or more hot stand-by replicas is introduced. The relations are horizontally fragmented and allocated over the available nodes in the multi-computer, so that two replicas of a fragment are located to nodes with independent failure modes. Log and locks for a fragment replica are clustered to the node in which the fragment is located. The HypRa recovery approach uses main memory logging on multiple nodes with independent failure modes to avoid disc access delays during commit processing and thereby support the soft real-time response requirements. An update channel maintains the write-ahead logging properties between primary and hot stand-by logs. Operations to hot stand-by replicas are performed as redo operations based on the log. Updates to hot stand-by replicas are deferred but guaranteed to be successfully executed after the commit of a transaction. State-identifiers are connected to tuples to support non-blocking fuzzy replication of tuples.

The HypRa fault-tolerance is based on HW failure detection, and SW online failure masking, online recovery, and online non-blocking repair. The HypRa recovery approach is founded on: i) very fast take-over to preserve availability across a primary fragment failure; ii) fast recovery to recover and catch-up failed fragments to the current primary fragments; and iii) fast repair that replicates lost and unavailable replicas after a failure in order to reestablish the original fault-tolerance level. Hot stand-by fragments maintain locks to minimise unavailability during a take-over. The fast recovery utilises main memory aggregation and CPU and I/O parallelism to speed up recovery and catch-up work. Repair is performed online and is non-blocking to avoid threatening soft real-time transaction service availability, and is completed within a given time window to meet the requirements to fault-tolerance.

In order to support very high transaction service availability, novel methods for online and non-blocking DB maintenance are needed. The book introduces such novel methods for fragment replication, index production, redistribution, and transaction recompilation. Online and non-blocking methods for SW and HW maintenance are also presented, to complete the spectrum of online and non-blocking maintenance operations.

Contents

List of Figures

List of Tables

Part I

Introduction

Chapter 1

A Continuously Available, High Transaction Capacity, Soft Real-Time DBMS Server

1.1 Motivation

Large transaction processing systems, like telecommunications network service control points (SCP) ([Dou90], [WBEK91]), telecommunication operations support systems ([CMI88]), and airline ticket reservation systems ([GS84]), set very strict fault-tolerance requirements on DBMS services, particularly with respect to *availability*. Using a DBMS server as a platform for implementation of service control points leads to transaction service availability requirements similar to those for digital switching network elements, i.e. a maximum 1 hour of unavailability in 30 years ([Nor83]). Thus the need for what we call a **continuously available** fault-tolerant DBMS server. A continuously available DBMS server is termed highly available in [Kim84] and falls into the class of high-availability in [GS91]. In these types of commercial applications an unavailable DBMS server leads to serious economic problems for the operator, whether it is an airline or a telecommunications network ([Bro85]). One of the major design goals behind the HypRa DBMS server is to satisfy these system availability requirements by providing a continuously available DBMS server.

Telecommunications represents the largest online transaction processing (OLTP) opportunity in the world ([Dou90]). Every hour, over 100 million telephone calls are completed worldwide. In a busy hour about 4000 telephone calls are completed per second in Norway (with a population of 4 million people ([Ols90])). Handling these telephone calls represents a tremendous OLTP work load. Thus the need for a *scalable* DBMS server able to handle transaction work loads ranging from low to very high, i.e. a DBMS server scalable beyond 1000 transactions per second (TPS) ([Bra89c]). The second major HypRa design goal is to handle a scalable transaction work load up to 10.000 TPS.

In a telecommunication network most transaction service requests are generated by other servers like digital switches. This is different from traditional OLTP systems with its human end-user generated transaction requests. This has a dramatic influence on response time requirements to such DBMS servers. The servers requesting transaction services are bound to meet strict response times. As a consequence very demanding soft response time requirements are imposed on the transaction services provided by the DBMS server. A 10 millisec. response time may be required for 98% of the DBMS transactions mapping a logical telephone number to the corresponding routing information. This requirement causes the need for a DBMS server providing transaction services within the extreme response time constraints of a telecommunication environment, i.e.

a response time interval of 10 millisec. for a TPC-B ([GS91]) equivalent transaction. The third major HypRa design goal is to satisfy these demanding soft real-time requirements. The term soft real-time transactions are in the remainder of the book used to indicate TPC-B equivalent transactions with this type of response requirements if not explicitly stated otherwise.

The requirements for *continuous availability*, *very high transaction capacity*, and *soft response time* have had strong influence on both HypRa fault-tolerance and recovery methods and design ([SB91]), which are demonstrated in the following chapters.

1.2 Requirements for Continuously Available DBMS Servers

A DBMS server is **available** if at least the specified rate of correct transactions commit within the response time requirements (see sections 1.3 and 2.2). A DBMS server is **continuously available** if it is unavailable for less than 1 hour over 30 years.

Given the nature of DBMS operations, the availability of a DBMS server is a function of data availability. To meet the requirement of continuously available DBMS services a high level of data fault-tolerance is required by the DBMS server. In addition to masking failures, the DBMS server is required to perform fast recovery and fast online self-repair from unavailable data replicas to reestablish the initial level of fault-tolerance [HST+91b].

To maintain continuous availability, the effect on transaction commit rate and response time of *temporarily unavailable* data must be strictly time limited. Fast *take-over* by a remaining data replica to mask data failures is required. Data availability during long duration data restructuring and redistribution operations and dictionary operations are required for the same reason. Online non-blocking DBMS- and basic software maintenance is also required.

In a layered design of a DBMS server fault-tolerance must be taken into account in all hardware and software layers to achieve the required fault-tolerance level of the DBMS server. It is of the utmost importance to determine which fault-tolerance capabilities to include in hardware servers and which in the software servers to obtain a cost-effective solution with the required fault-tolerance level.

Masking hardware server failures in *hardware*, as in some current fault-tolerant hardware platforms ([Wil85], [TW89]) by duplexing hardware servers with crash failure semantics (which may in their turn be implemented by pairs of hardware server executing in lock-step) still requires the DBMS server to implement fault masking, and self-repair from unmasked hardware failures and transient software failures ([Gra86]). Hardware duplexing increases the mean time between failure from hardware servers, but the DBMS servers must provide the same fault-tolerance handling logic as when using non-masking hardware servers. Hardware duplexing is therefore an expensive hardware solution providing no software cost reductions. Thus HypRa hardware design is based on non-replicated hardware.

Hardware failures should be online masked and online self-repaired by the DBMS software levels. The basic hardware level should provide hardware fault detection and program isolation mechanisms. Compared to hardware only implemented mechanisms, fault-tolerance mechanisms implemented in the DBMS software give:

- The only way to include fault masking, recovery, and repair capabilities in the DBMS server.
- A cost-efficient implementation of a DBMS server with fault masking, recovery and repair capabilities, by reducing hardware redundancy compared to triplexed or quadrupled hardware.

- Higher fault-tolerance capabilities by adding the possibility of including a self-repairing DBMS server.

The HypRa design assumes that the hardware servers have either *crash failure semantics* or *omission failure semantics*. The software is assumed to be partially correct, i.e. the program logic is correct (see section 2.3.5). The software servers are assumed to have *performance failure semantics*.

1.3 Fault-Tolerance Concepts

The basic fault-tolerant concepts presented in this section are based primarily on [Cri89], [Cri90], [CDD90], [Lap89], and [Nel90].

1.3.1 The Service and Server Concepts

A computing **service** is a specification of a collection of operations whose execution is triggered by requests from service users or by the passage of time. For every service there exists a specification of its behaviour, i.e. the result of every service request and response time requirements. A service has an internal *service state* which is a function of the state of the resources controlled by the service.

An i486[1] is a processor service consisting of the operations and behaviour specified in its instruction set manual. An ISO-SQL service is a DBMS service consisting of the operations and behaviour defined in SQL definition report [ISO89].

A service specification consists of a *behaviour specification* and a *stochastic specification*. The **behaviour specification** of a service contains a **standard specification**, i.e. the specification of its *failure-free semantics* (standard semantics), the *real-time interval* in which the response should come, and its **failure specification**, i.e. a specification of its *failure semantics*. Specified failures are also called *controlled failures*. Failures not covered by the failure specification are *uncontrolled failures*. For example, the ISO-SQL specification contains the failure-free semantics and the failure semantics specification for an ISO-SQL service (see [ISO89]).

The **stochastic specification** of a service should specify the *minimum standard behaviour* requirements of a service, i.e. the minimum probability that the standard behaviour is observed at run time. The stochastic specification should also specify the minimum continuous run time, i.e. the *mission time*. A service is **available** when its minimum standard behaviour requirements are fulfilled, otherwise it is unavailable. This is termed a *soft* availability requirement as opposed to a *hard* availability requirement where a service is unavailable if it does not meet its standard behaviour. A debit-credit transaction service ([Gra87]) may be required to provide a minimum standard availability of 95%, 10 hours a day, 5 days a week. A telecommunication network (telecom) service control point service on the other hand may require minimum standard availability of 99.9996% continuously over 30 years. A service by these specifications is *soft real-time* because of the soft availability requirement and the real-time response interval specification.

The stochastic specification should also specify the maximum probability of an uncontrolled failure, i.e. a failure different from the specified failure behaviour. A failure is *benign* if it is specified in the service failure semantics and does not cause an available service to become unavailable, otherwise it is *malign*. An uncontrolled failure, which by definition is malign, is a *catastrophic failure*.

[1] i486 is a trademark of Intel Corporation

A **server** is an implementation of a service. Servers for a service control its resources and executes its operations. A response to a service request is either triggered by the request, by an internal state transaction, or by the passage of time. A server may either be hardware or software or a combination. An i486 processor is for example a hardware server of an i486 service.

1.3.2 The Failure Class Concept

The failure semantics of a server are defined according to one of the following **failure classes**, or a combination of two or more of them:

- **Crash failure**
  A crash failure occurs if a server after not responding to a request, never responds to any succeeding requests. A server has **atomic-crash** semantics if an operation under execution when a crash occurs either becomes completed or is not done at all. The following crash failure restart semantics are defined.
  - Amnesia-crash
    The restarted server is restarted in a predefined initial state independent of its state before the crash. An example is operating system restarts by means of re-boot.
  - Partial-amnesia-crash
    Some part of the state is the same as before the crash and the rest is reset to a predefined initial state. An example is file system restarts.
  - Pause-crash
    The crashed server restarts in the state it had before the crash.
  - Halting-crash
    The crashed server never restarts.
- **Omission failure**
  An omission failure occurs if a server omits responding to a request.
- **Timing failure**
  A timing failure occurs if a server responds to a request too early or too late. A late timing failure is called a *performance failure*.
- **Response failure**
  A response failure occurs if a server responds incorrectly, either by a wrong output or by an incorrect service state transition.

An operating system crash followed by a re-boot into a predefined initial state is an example of an amnesia-crash. A DBMS system crash, followed by a recovery of the DBMS state that reflects all committed transactions at the time of the crash, is an example of a pause-crash. A communication server occasionally losing messages, a disc drive occasionally not performing block read operations, and a transaction server aborting transactions are examples of omission failures. A transaction server not meeting the real time response-time requirements due to transaction overload, and a communication server delaying messages are examples of performance failures. A DBMS finding a deleted tuple or not finding a committed inserted tuple are both examples of response failures.

A server provides **arbitrary** failure semantics if its failure semantics are the union of all the failure classes.

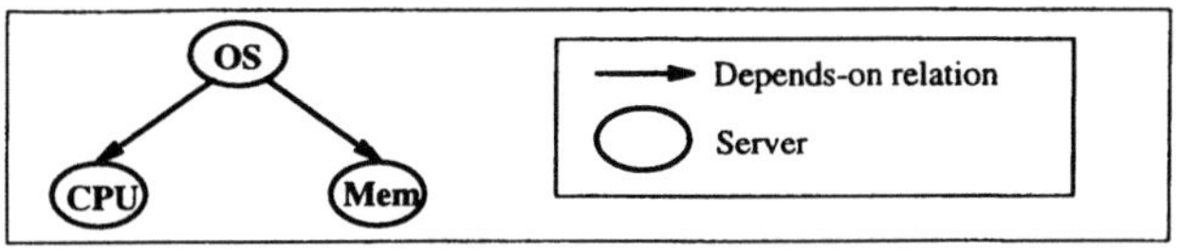

Figure 1.1: The operating system server (OS) depends-on the CPU and the memory server (Mem) to provide services according to their specification.

1.3.3 The Failure-Masking, -Recovery, and -Repair Concepts

A server S **depends-on** a server B if it relies on the correctness of B's behaviour to correctly provide its own service. The server S **uses** the server B. Figure 1.1 illustrates a basic operating system server that depends-on a CPU and memory server. The operating system server uses the CPU and the memory servers.

A server failure may be **masked** either by *hierarchical masking* or by *group masking*. Hierarchical masking is obtained if a server is still able to provide its services despite the failure of a server it uses. An hierarchical masking can for example be obtained by repeated requests in case of transient omission failures. A **server group** is a group of redundant, independent servers providing a service. A group masks the failure of a member if the group responds according to specification despite the failure. A group is **k-fault-tolerant** if it is able to mask k concurrent member failures.

Recovery of a server or server group from a failure transforms its potentially temporary inconsistent state to a consistent state. The consistent-state requirements of a service are part of the service specification.

Recovery takes place after a failure has occurred. Its task is to bring the failed server or server group from a temporary inconsistent state, that is a consequence of the failure, to a consistent state.

A group can reestablish its fault tolerance level after a failure by recovering the failed member, or by repair. A group **repairs** a failure of a member if a new member is added to the group. After a repair of a failure, a group has restored its fault-tolerance from before the failure occurred.

Exercises

1. (a) Based on the UPT service described above, give one example for each failure class. (b) Give an example of a system for each of the failure restart semantics for the crash-failure class.

2. (a) Can server groups be used by a centralised DBMS? (b) Can they be used by a distributed DBMS?

3. A mountain skier wears one wool cap and has two additional caps in his backpack. What is his wool cap fault-tolerance level?

Answers

1. (a) *Response failure*: The memory content read from RAM is incorrect and not masked by the use of memory parity. *Timing failure*: The disc drive delivers a read block too late according to its response time specification. *Omission failure*: A transaction is aborted by

the DBMS (caused by a deadlock). *Crash failure*: The CPU server gets fried by high voltage (caused by a power supply failure).

(b) *Amnesia-crash*: A UNIX operating system. *Partial-amnesia-crash*: A UNIX file system that allows a transaction to commit with the affected blocks only reflected in the cache. *Pause-crash*: A DBMS with normal recovery. *Halting crash*: The server is vapourised.

2. (a) They can. For example a centralised DBMS can maintain two replicas of the log server. (b) Yes.

3. Single fault-tolerance. The two wool caps in his backpack have obvious common failure modes.

Chapter 2

DBMS Recovery Requirements

2.1 The DBMS Service

A DBMS is assumed to be a server providing transaction services, that is, transactions according to the transaction model presented in section A.8 and to the service specification given in section 1.3.1. The standard specification of a transaction service contains the functional specification and the specification of its real-time response interval. A transaction service provided by a DBMS server has **pause-crash/omission/performance** failure semantics which is a property of DBMS servers. A DBMS server may crash (see section 2.3.2), but will recover into a consistent state and continue to provide transaction services after being recovered. A DBMS server may also omit a transaction by aborting it (see section 2.3.6). Finally, a DBMS server may respond too late, according to the service real-time specification, on some transactions, so that performance failures occur. A transaction service is as a consequence of the specification a soft real-time service.

A transaction service is **available** if the fraction of transactions being aborted, and the fraction of transactions with a too long response time, together, do not compromise the minimum standard behaviour given in the stochastic service specification. If the minimum standard behaviour is compromised the service is unavailable.

2.2 The DBMS Reliability

The **reliability** of a DBMS server describes its ability to handle failures of its resources. It is divided into its ability to preserve the **consistent DB state requirement** (see section A.8) and its ability to preserve **transaction service availability** (see section 1.3.1).

The state of a DBMS server is **consistent** if it fulfills the ACID properties stated in section A.8. It is the combined task of the concurrency control server and the recovery server to preserve the consistency of the DB. A failure may produce a temporary inconsistent DB state. Recovery brings the DB from the temporary inconsistent state to a consistent state.

Transaction service availability depends on the availability of a multitude of DBMS internal services. The availability aspect is mostly constrained to DB availability since the focus is on recovery. A DB is **fully available** if for every leaf-fragment at least one replica is available. A DB is **partially available** if for some leaf-fragments at least one replica is available, and for some leaf-fragments no replica is available. A DB is **unavailable** if for every leaf-fragment no replica is available. A leaf-fragment is available if at least one replica of all its tuples are available.

A centralised DBMS is one independent failure unit. If the node fails, the DB becomes unavailable.

Distribution of fragment replicas to independent nodes makes it possible to limit the unavailability to the fragments located at the failed node. Partial DB availability can be supported by distribution.

Replication of data on independent nodes makes it possible to mask the unavailability of a replica, caused by the failure of the node. Full DB availability is provided after a failure. Since one replica is always available, the effect of the failure may be repaired by producing another replica of the failed data.

2.3 The DBMS Failure Model

This section presents the DBMS failure hypothesis, and the classes of failure a DBMS handles.

A failure model will always represent a compromise between the probability of the occurrence of a failure and the cost of avoiding or tolerating such a failure. A failure model is therefore based on a set of failure hypotheses. The failure hypotheses presented here are quite traditional and resemble those presented in [HR84], [BHG87], [GMA89], and [Cri89].

Some of the hypotheses are explicitly modified in chapter 13.

2.3.1 CPU, Main Memory, and Bus Server Failure

CPUs, main memory, and buses are assumed to have *atomic-crash* semantics and amnesia-crash semantics. The content of, for example, main memory is therefore lost after a main memory failure. This failure semantics may be obtained by use of hardware server groups ([Cri89]) or error correction codes ([Rhe89]).

2.3.2 Node Failure

A node is an independent unit of failure containing hardware servers such as CPU, main memory, and buses.

A node has *atomic-crash* semantics, i.e. it is fail-fast. A node failure or node crash occurs if some of the hardware servers it contains fail. The failure of hardware servers may be caused by the failure of auxiliary systems like power supply or cooling fans on which they depend. All software servers on a failed node crash when a node crashes.

A node failure is assumed to destroy the content of main memory, i.e. main memory is volatile. A *block flush* operation writes a block to disc. Block flush operations are assumed to have atomic-crash semantics in the presence of a node crash when nothing else is explicitly stated. These assumptions will be modified in chapter 13.

It is indicated in [Gra81] and [HR84] that a node failure happens as often as several times a week.

2.3.3 Disc Media Failure

A disc is an independent unit of failure with *crash/omission* failure semantics. A disc drive may mask a temporary I/O failure by redoing the operation. When a disc reports a block error, this is assumed to corrupt the content of the block. A disc crash corrupts the content of the entire disc.

It is indicated in [Gra81] and [HR84] that media failures occur less frequently than node failures. Modern disc technology indicates 150.000 hours mean time to failure for a disc ([MTT91]).

To recover from a media failure at least two replicas of data are needed. Methods for masking and repairing media failure are not addressed any further in Part I or II of the book.

Media failures are returned to in chapter 13 in connection with preservation of reliability in HypRa.

2.3.4 Network Failure

The communication network is assumed to have *crash/omission/performance* failure semantics. A message may be lost, arrive at the destination out of order, or be excessively delayed. We assume that the communication network may be partitioned. A DBMS server can be implemented as a distributed DBMS. In this case at least $\frac{n}{2} + 1$ nodes must be available for the DBMS server to be available (see [ASC88], [BHG87], [Cri90]).

2.3.5 Software Server Failure

Software servers are assumed to be partially correct, i.e. the program logic is correct, but the server may suffer performance failure even if the servers are working correctly. This software quality is possible but hard to obtain with reasonable probability in practice ([Gra86]).

If a partially correct software server is using servers which have at least performance failure semantics, the software server has *performance* failure semantics ([Cri85], [Cri87]). Since the hardware servers are assumed to have at least omission failure semantics, the software servers have performance failure semantics.

2.3.6 Transaction Failure

A transaction failure occurs when a partially completed transaction is aborted. The DB has recovered from the transaction failure when all updates to the DB by the failed transaction are undone. How this recovery is actually accomplished depends on the recovery approach used by the DBMS.

If the transaction is non-dialogue, a temporary failed transaction may automatically be restarted after the recovery is completed ([HA89b]). Masking of dialogue transactions must reproduce the same values read by the user of the original transaction ([FCK87]).

It is stated that about 3% of correct transactions abort ([Gra81], [HR84]). This indicates that a low percentage of transactions actually aborts, which corresponds with our own experience.

2.4 Node and Fragment Crash Recovery, Masking and Repair

This section presents a model for node crash recovery, node and fragment failure masking, recovery catch-up, and repair of crashed fragment replicas.

2.4.1 Node Crash Recovery

The crashed node stays inactive until recovery is started. A recovery start can be performed manually or automatically. The DBMS recovery task is to reestablish a consistent DB. When recovery is completed, the node returns into normal operations. This is illustrated by figure 2.1.

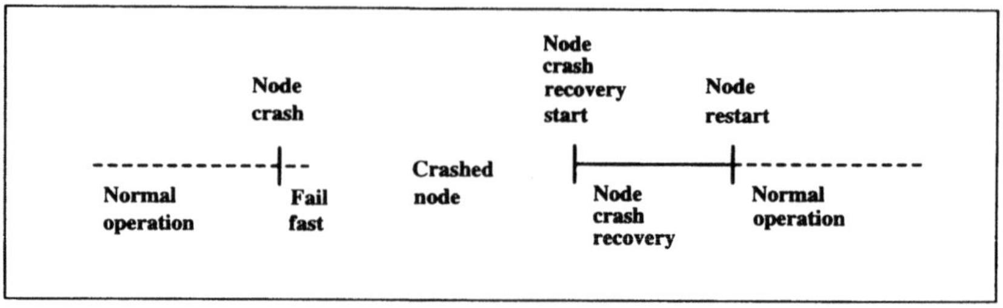

Figure 2.1: Failure model of the servers at a node.

In case of a centralised DBMS, the DB stays unavailable while the node is crashed and during the recovery processing until the node is restarted. Transaction services are unavailable during this period. If the node is part of a distributed DBMS, the fragments for which the only replica is located at the failed node are unavailable until the node has restarted.

The recovery approaches analysed in Part II are all directed towards transaction failure recovery and node crash recovery according to this model.

2.4.2 Fragment Failure Masking

If multiple replicas of a fragment exist, and the replicas are located at different nodes, a node crash can be *masked*. Masking is done to minimise fragment unavailability and minimise transaction service unavailability.

Loose synchronisation ([Cri87]) is used between the replicas of a fragment if a transaction can be committed when its DB operations are executed to the **primary replica** of a fragment, and operations are executed in deferred fashion to the other **hot stand-by replicas**. If loose synchronisation is applied and a primary replica fails, a **take-over** recovery is executed to a hot stand-by to make it the current primary. Figure 2.2 illustrates a take-over. The fragment involved stays unavailable while it is established that the node has failed and a new active node set is formed, and during the take-over recovery processing until the fragment is restarted. A take-over may involve aborting all transactions active to the fragment where the primary replica failed.

If the DB operations are executed to all replicas of a fragment when a transaction is committed, then tight synchronisation is applied between the fragment replicas and the transaction execution can remain unaffected by a node crash.

Over the last decade interest has increasingly been focused on the loose synchronisation approach in the context of fragment or DB failure masking ([Bor84], [XRF87a], [MTO91], [CAP91]).

The HypRa recovery approach, presented in Part III, is based on loose synchronisation, masking, and aborting transactions active at a crashed node.

2.4.3 Fragment Recovery Catch-Up

If a node or fragment replica failure is masked, a fragment is still available while some replica is unavailable. When a replica then recovers, operations may have been executed to the fragment in the time interval that the replica was unavailable. The recovering replica must then both perform a node crash recovery and *catch-up* with these remaining operations to be restarted.

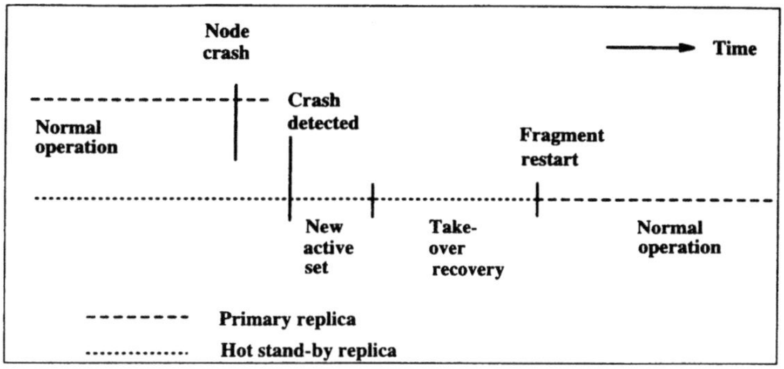

Figure 2.2: Take-over recovery to mask a failed fragment. The fragment is unavailable while the new active set of nodes is formed and while the take-over processing is performed and the fragment restarted.

Figure 2.3 illustrates a fragment recovery where both node crash recovery and catch-up are involved. The fragment replica failure is masked to provide fragment availability. The recovery and catch-up is initiated after the masking take-over recovery is completed. When the catch-up is completed the recovering fragment replica has obtained a hot stand-by role, i.e. it may take-over for the current primary in case it fails. The node crash recovery and catch-up is assumed to be completed within a time interval not compromising the transaction services availability requirements.

The HypRa recovery approach includes catch-up recovery as part of the recovery of a crashed node (see section 14.3).

2.4.4 Fragment Repair

If a crashed node is unable to start recovery processing or unable to complete recovery, then repair can be done to the fragments located at this node to reestablish the fault tolerance level. The repair is assumed to be completed within a time interval which does not compromise the availability requirement to transaction services.

A fragment repair includes production of another consistent replica of the fragment. The repair can be done either as *blocking* or *non-blocking*. A blocking policy causes the fragment to be unavailable while the replication is performed. A non-blocking approach takes a snapshot of the fragment without blocking it and then performs a catch-up to the primary replica. Figure 2.4 illustrates a non-blocking repair after a failed node crash recovery.

HypRa applies the non-blocking fragment repair policy. The non-blocking fragment replication used by HypRa is presented in [HST+91b].

2.5 The DBMS Server Architecture

In the following chapters a number of DBMS reference server architectures are presented. (See, for example, figure 10.1 or 4.1.) The analysis of transaction-recovery and node-recovery methods will be related to these reference architectures. This section presents the services from which these reference architectures are built.

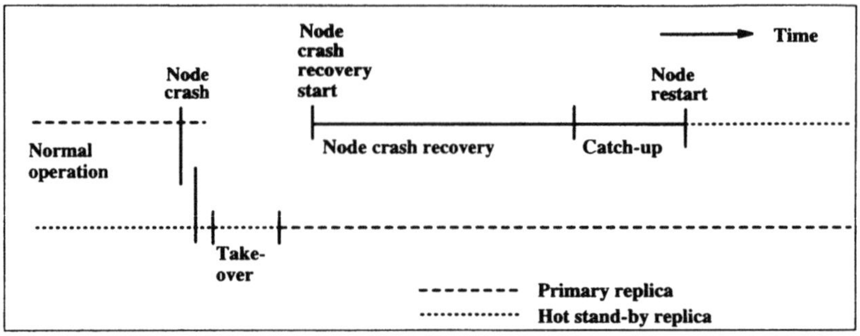

Figure 2.3: A node crash causes a primary fragment replica to fail. A take-over is performed to mask the fragment replica failure. The failed node then restarts and node crash recovery and catch-up are performed to the failed fragment replica. See figure 2.2 for take-over details.

Each layer of the DBMS mapping reference architecture (see section A.3) corresponds to a service which is implemented as either a server or server group. This gives the **relation, fragment, table, record**, and **block-service**. The mapping relations correspond either directly or indirectly to a uses relation between these services.

Each service provides the DB operations specified by the corresponding datamodel, e.g. the table service provides the table model DB operations (see section A.4). For each reference server architecture it is explicitly specified which services provide transaction operations in that context.

In addition to the services specified above, a **concurrency control-** and a **recovery-service** are defined. Concurrency control services are introduced in section A.9. The operations provided by a recovery service are defined specifically within the context of the reference architecture in which it is used.

In all of the following reference architectures, the concurrency control server uses the recovery server, i.e. the serialisation is applied before the logging is done. This guarantees the recovery server a sequence of operations that represents a serialisable execution of the transactions.

2.6 The DBMS Recovery Methods Design Goals

This section presents a collection of design and evaluation goals for DBMS recovery methods. The overall goal is to meet the *consistency* and *availability* requirements to the transaction services the DBMS server is assumed to provide ([Cod91]).

For a comparison of goals see for example [MHL$^+$89].

- **Simplicity**
  Software servers are assumed to be partially correct (see section 2.3), i.e. the program logic of the recovery server is assumed to be correct. The complexity of the recovery software is high. It is therefore necessary to keep the recovery algorithms as simple as possible.

- **Locking**
  The recovery method should allow fine granularity and semantically rich locking. These requirements are specially motivated from very high transaction rates combined with DB hot-spots.

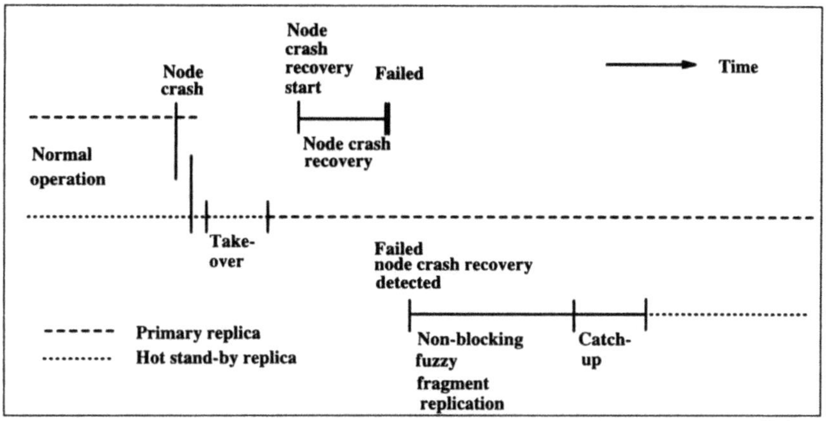

Figure 2.4: Fragment take-over recovery followed by a failed recovery. A fragment repair is needed to reestablish the fragment availability fault-tolerance level. The fragment repair is performed by a non-blocking replication of the fragment, followed by a catch-up with the current primary.

- **Low overhead and no bottlenecks during normal processing**
  The produced log volume should be low, both from a volume-cost and a management perspective. The recovery method should allow a flexible DB buffer management policy. It should avoid introducing bottlenecks between DB buffer and disc and should allow transaction execution without disc accesses. This is specially motivated by soft real-time transaction response requirements. The recovery method should be able to utilise high main memory volumes during normal processing.

- **Fast recovery from transaction failure**
  It is a design goal to be able to recover from a transaction failure within the time of the regular execution of the transaction, and faster than this for large transactions.

- **Fast node crash recovery**
  Node crash recovery should utilise large main memory and parallelism within a node. The method should support selective fragment availability during a node crash recovery. The node crash recovery disc I/O both with respect to log and DB, should be minimised.

- **Take-over**
  The recovery method should support take-over of fragment granules. A minimum of recovery work should be needed done while the fragment is unavailable. Massive transaction aborts should be avoided with a take-over.

- **Fragment repair**
  The recovery method should support non-blocking fragment replica production to automatically reestablish the fault-tolerance level after a node or fragment failure followed by a failed node recovery attempt. The replication should support distribution of the added load represented by the new replica.

These design goals will be used in the following chapters when evaluating recovery approaches, strategies, and policies.

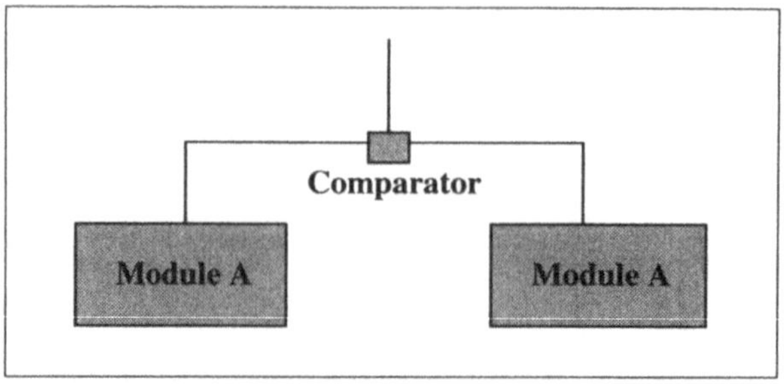

Figure 2.5: Duplexed hardware module. By using duplexed modules and a simple comparator failfast hardware modules can be built (see [GR92]).

Exercises

1. Is partial availability obtainable with a centralised DBMS?

2. How can (a) CPUs and (b) main memory be built to have atomic-crash semantics? (c) How can partial-amnesia-crash main memory be provided?

3. Characterise the following events in terms of failure classes: (a) Lost message. (b) Recoverable disc seek failure. (c) Pointer followed beyond NIL/NUL. (d) Broken disc cable. (e) A transaction responding too late.

4. (a) If the mean time to failure (MTTF) for a hardware module is 1 million hours, then what is the MTTF for a duplexed module (see figure 2.5)? Do not take the comparator into consideration. Assume no repair. (b) What is the MTTF if the mean time to repair (MTTR) is 4 hours? (See e.g. [GR92] for equations.)

5. Propose a method so that a DBMS server can be available with only $\frac{n}{2}$ nodes available.

6. What are the main tasks when recovering a centralised DBMS?

7. What are the advantages of loose synchronisation as compared to tight synchronisation?

8. (a) Why does the concurrency control server use the recovery server? (b) Develop a scenario illustrating the consequences of reversing their order. (c) Are there any conditions under which this can be done?

9. What would the effect of locking independently of the semantics of the operation and of the objects operated on be on serialisability?

Answers

1. Not according to the terminology in this book. However, it is possible if, for example, some tables are entirely stored on one disc and others are entirely stored on another disc. After a disc crash only the tables on the crashed disc become unavailable.

2. (a) By n-plexing and comparator/voter. (b) By the use of parity and checking or by the use of n-plexing and comparator/voter. (c) By dividing the memory into compartments with independent checksums.

3. (a) Omission failure. (b) Masked failure or timing failure depending on the length of the delay. (c) Arbitrary failure. (d) Crash failure of the disc server. (e) Performance failure.

4. (a) With two operational units, the mean time to first failure is $\frac{MTTF}{2}$. So the mean time to failure for the remaining module is MTTF. This gives $MTTF\frac{3}{2}$

   (b) The probability that one unit is unavailable is $\frac{MTTR}{MTTF+MTTF} \approx \frac{MTTR}{MTTF}$ with $MTTF \gg MTTR$. The probability that one unit will fail while the other is unavailable is approximately $\frac{1}{MTTF} \cdot \frac{MTTR}{MTTF}$. With two independent units, this can happen in two ways. The probability of this happening is $2\frac{MTTR}{MTTF^2}$. The mean time to this event is $\frac{1}{2\frac{MTTR}{MTTF^2}} = \frac{MTTF^2}{2MTTR}$

5. One of the nodes is marked and this fact is known by every node in the group. The group of nodes with the marked node as a member is available if it consists of at least half of the nodes.

6. The task is to reestablish a consistent DBMS. This is accomplished by removing the effects of partially completed and aborted transactions to the database and installing the missing effects of committed transactions to the database.

7. Less load on the stand-by. Fewer deadlocks. Less delay during transaction commit processing.

8. (a) The concurrency control server determines the sequence of operation execution. When the concurrency control server is using the log server, the operations are logged in their executed sequence. Redo can then be executed in the same order as the original do operations and undo in the reverse order.

   (b) The logged sequence of two write operations to the same tuple is the inverse of the actual execution sequence. The transactions also begin to commit before a node crash. Redo will then execute the operations in reverse order to the original execution. The resulting DB state is not consistent because this tuple does not reflect the last committed state before the crash.

   (c) If serial execution of transactions is applied, the concurrency control server can use the recovery server or vice versa. The reason for this is that only one transaction is active at a time. The transactions are executed in the sequence determined by the arrival of their first operation.

9. Each transaction locks the entire DB in write mode. The effect is serial execution of transactions.

Part II

Analysis of Centralised DBMS Transaction and Node Crash Recovery Approaches

Chapter 3

Introduction

This part presents an analysis of four recovery approaches developed over the last two decades. The analysis includes the first four of the recovery design goals specified in section 2.6, with the emphasis on locking, overhead and bottlenecks during normal processing, transaction recovery speed, and node crash recovery speed. The approaches are evaluated according to how they meet the HypRa design goals (see section 1.1).

The **block oriented recovery approach** is the oldest of the recovery approaches analysed. It represents the state of the art from the late 1970s. It is also the recovery approach that least meets the HypRa design goals with respect to locking, low overhead, and no bottlenecks during normal processing. Only coarse grained and traditional locking are supported instead of a fine grained and semantically rich locking model (see section A.9). The produced log volume is high as a consequence of the use of block logging instead of record logging. The block oriented approach does, on the other hand, introduce flexible DB buffer policies which allows for large DB buffers. It also introduces flexible checkpointing policies constraining node crash recovery work with an acceptable overhead during normal operations.

The **record oriented recovery approach** represents the state of the art for the first half of the 1980s. This approach removes one of the main obstacles of the block oriented approach. Record logging is used instead of block logging with a significant reduction in the produced log volume and comparable reduced log I/O load. A bottleneck on concurrent committing transactions caused by one disc access per commit is also prevented. Node crash recovery speed up is provided both through the reduced log volume and by avoiding redoing operations already reflected in the stable DB by use of block state-identifiers.

The **compensation oriented recovery approach** is the newest of the presented approaches which is in use in commercial systems. It stems mainly from the late 1980s. This approach removes the other main obstacle inherent in the older approaches. Fine grained and semantically rich locking is supported. This is done at the expense of a slightly higher log volume than the record oriented approach and some increased node crash recovery work load.

The **table oriented recovery approach** is only partially in use in commercial systems. This approach provides fast node crash recovery and fast recovery of large failed transactions. In addition, it supports fine grained and semantically rich locking together with low log volumes. Policies have also been introduced to remove secondary DB management activities from time critical transaction path in order to meet soft real-time response requirements. This is therefore the approach which most fully supports the recovery design goals stated in section 1.1.

All the recovery approaches analysed in this part have deficiencies making them unsuitable for HypRa. The block state-identifier policy is incompatible with online non-blocking repair combined with subfragmentation (see section 10.7). This deficiency is removed in Part III by introducing the multi-level state-identifier policy. All the analysed recovery approaches require a committed transaction to have been involved in at least one disc access. Therefore they do not meet the soft real-time response requirement. The neighbour write ahead logging strategy presented in Part III removes this bottleneck.

Chapter 4

The Block Oriented Approach

This chapter presents the **block oriented recovery approach**. A block oriented recovery approach is applied if concurrency control and recovery is done at the block datamodel level, i.e. blocks are the units of locking and logging.

Recovery methods based on the block oriented approach are fully or partially used by commercial DBMS products, for example RA2 ([BJWK+76]), SIBAS ([Ref86]), TORNADO ([MET88]), Oracle ([Dea87]), and Sybase ([DP88]).

4.1 The Block Oriented DBMS Server Architecture

This section presents the block oriented server architecture illustrated in figure 4.1. The architecture is compatible with the DBMS architecture presented in [BHG87]. The server architecture does not illustrate the module architecture of any particular implemented DBMS. To gain efficiency and to handle aspects not included in the presented architecture, the module architecture of implemented DBMSs is less clean with respect to functionality and layering (see for example [HA89b]).

The relational, table, and record servers perform mapping between the respective datamodels (see section A.3); receiving DB and transaction requests and requesting DB and transaction services from the servers they use (see section 2.5). These servers are not investigated further in this chapter because they are not involved in recovery related tasks.

The particular aspects of the presented server architecture are the uses relations between the *record-*, *concurrency control-*, *recovery-*, and *block servers*. The concurrency control server receives block DB and transaction operation requests from the table server. It serialises the DB operation requests according to the specifications given in section A.9 and requests the same services from the recovery server.

The recovery server receives a sequence of serialised block DB and transaction operations. From the block server, the recovery server requests block DB operations and operations for controlling the transfer of blocks between the volatile main memory DB buffer and stable disc. The block server transfers blocks from disc to DB buffer. The transfer is controlled by the recovery server as defined by the chosen DB buffer strategy. The block server may in turn request the recovery server to transfer a particular block from the DB buffer to disc (*Flush*(B_i)). Transaction and node failures are recovered by the recovery manager. To support node crash recovery the recovery server provides a restart operation.

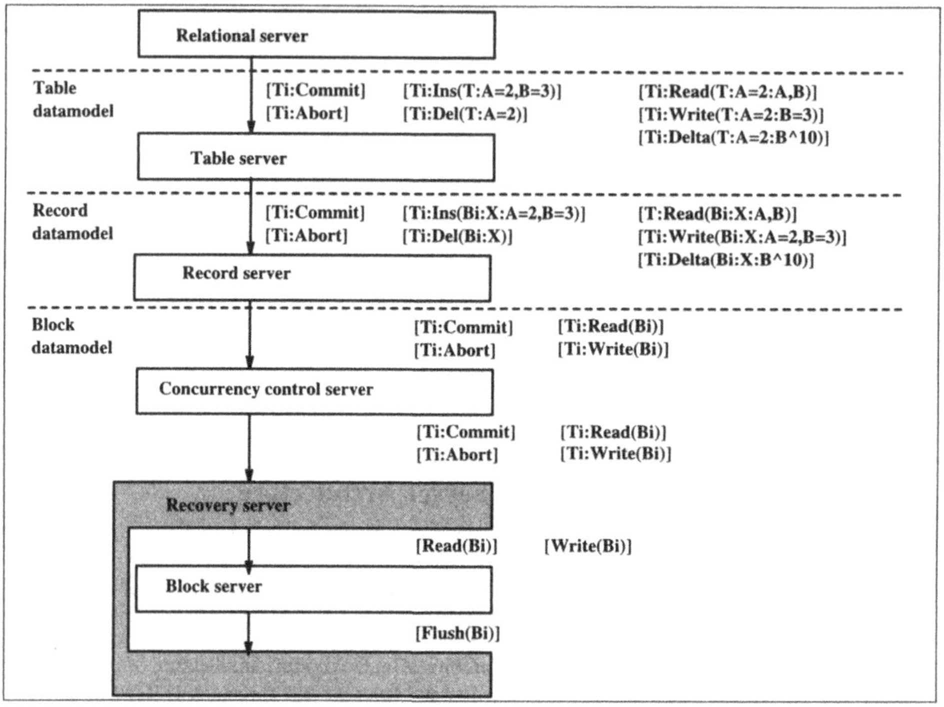

Figure 4.1: The block oriented DBMS server architecture. The layered DBMS architecture corresponds to the architecture presented in figure A.3. The concurrency control and recovery servers are included in the block datamodel layer. Operations are marked when required by the transaction identifier (T_i) of the transaction to which they belong. See section A.5, A.6, and A.7 for table, record and block datamodel operations, respectively. See section A.8 for transaction operations. See also section 2.5 for an introduction to the DBMS server architecture. The record datamodel is assumed to use the record index policy (see section A.6). The *Flush(B_i)* operation is a request by the block server to flush the block with the block identifier B_i, see section 2.3.2.

4.2 The Block Oriented Recovery Classification Scheme

This section presents the classification scheme for the block oriented approach. The classification scheme is based on a collection of recovery related DBMS strategies. Each of these strategies and its inherent policies is outlined in more detail in the following sections. The proposed classification scheme is closely related to the classification scheme presented in [HR84] and [Reu84], which also is the basic classification scheme used in [BHG87].

- **The log strategy**
  A log represents the history of DB and transaction operations executed towards the DB. Logging is done according to the write ahead log protocol. The log strategy determines the log garbage collection policy, state oriented versus state transition logging, and the granularity of the logged data item.

- **The block propagation strategy**
  The propagation strategy determines how consistency synchronisation is carried out between the stable DB blocks. The need for synchronisation is a consequence of the fact that only one block at a time can be written to disc. Since a transaction may involve more than one block, the DB may reflect an inconsistent state. The propagation policy is **atomic** if the stable DB is at any time allowed to reflect only consistent DB states. The propagation policy is **non-atomic** if the stable database is allowed to reflect inconsistent states.

- **The DB buffer strategy**
  The DB buffer strategy determines which updates to DB buffer blocks are reflected in stable storage to preserve transaction and node recovery, and when they are so reflected. If updates are reflected before the transaction producing them has committed, we must be able to undo the updates in case of transaction abort. On the other hand, a committed value must be preserved in stable storage before a transaction commits, else a node failure may lose the value.

- **The checkpoint strategy**
  The primary goal of the checkpoint strategy is to limit the work to be done during recovery restart after a node failure, to recover a consistent DB state. At periodic intervals a checkpoint is produced, so that all DB operations preceding the checkpoint are guaranteed to be reflected in the stable DB.

A consequence of performing concurrency control at the block datamodel level is that blocks are the unit of locking. A transaction locks the blocks it reads and writes until it terminates (see section A.9). A block is a coarse locking unit (see section A.9), as opposed to the fine granularity locking as stated as a design goal (see section 2.6). Write locks are exclusive, allowing only one transaction at a time to perform updates on a block. Fine granularity locking is primarily motivated by the desire to avoid DB hot-spot bottlenecks ([PRS88], [Gaw85]).

4.3 The Impact of Volatile DB Buffer on Transaction and Node Recoverability

The DB buffer is a collection of fixed size units composed of volatile main memory. A DB buffer replica of a DB block may temporarily exist, storing a block replica in addition to the stable storage replicas. A disc replica of a block may be outdated with respect to its DB buffer replica due to operations done in-place to the DB buffer block, but not yet reflected in the stable storage replica(s). Since the DB buffer is volatile, some synchronisation restrictions have to be imposed between a

DB buffer and stable disc replica of a block to ensure recoverability from transaction and node failures.

If, for example, an aborted transaction has written the only stable storage replica of a block, the previous committed value of the block is lost. The DBMS is then unable to recover from the transaction failure because of the loss of the last committed value. The intention of the **undo rule** is to avoid overwriting the last replica of the last committed value of a data item.

The last committed value may also be lost if it is only present in volatile storage. If for example the volatile replica of a block is written by a committed transaction, but the operation is not reflected in any stable storage replica, and the node fails, the last committed value is lost. The DBMS is not able to recover from the node failure because of the loss of the last committed value of the block. The reason for introducing the **redo rule** is to avoid not writing a committed value to stable storage before commit.

- **The undo rule**
  Before the last stable storage replica containing the last committed value of a data item X is allowed to be updated by an uncommitted transaction, sufficient information has to be stored in stable storage to be able to reproduce the last committed value of X.

- **The redo rule**
  Before a transaction is allowed to commit, sufficient information has to be stably stored to be able to reproduce the committed values of the transaction.

The undo- and redo-rules ensure recoverability from transaction failures. They also ensure recoverability from single or multiple concurrent node failures, since a node failure causes main memory amnesia at the node, but it does not corrupt the content of stable storage, i.e. the state of the stable DB at the node.

It is assumed that the main memory connected to a node does not have the capacity of the DB discs connected to the node so that some part of the DB stored at a node will not concurrently have a stable and a volatile replica. To ensure recoverability from a single disc crash affecting either the stable DB or the additional information needed by the redo and undo rules, at least two stable storage replicas of data items and the additional information must be kept. To provide single fault-tolerance from media failure, two replicas of both the DB and the additional information needed by the undo- and redo-rules are required.

4.4 The Log Strategy

The log strategy is composed of policies that determine how logging is done in combination with the block oriented recovery approach. In addition, basic information about logs, log records, and write ahead log rules are provided.

4.4.1 The Log

A **log** is a stable and/or volatile representation of a set of log sequences maintained by the recovery server. A **log sequence** is composed of log records that represent operations and where the sequence of the log records corresponds to the sequence the recovery server received the corresponding operation requests. The union of logs maintained by a recovery server contains, at any time, at least those log records needed to recover a consistent DB from any transaction failure or node crash.

A **node global** log sequence contains the log records representing state changing DB operations and log records representing transaction operations at a node. A **transaction local** log sequence is the subset of a node global log sequence relating to a particular transaction. A **block global** log sequence is the subset of a node global log sequence containing the state changing DB operations relating to a particular block. A **tuple global** log sequence is the subset of a node global log sequence containing the state changing DB operations relating to a particular tuple. A **checkpoint** log sequence contains the checkpoint log records at a node.

A block oriented recovery server may maintain a node global log sequence represented by one log at the node, the **node global log**. A record oriented recovery server may maintain multiple log sequences, e.g. a node global log sequence, a transaction local sequence for each transaction, a block global log sequence for each block and a checkpoint log sequence. They can be represented by multiple logs, for example one log for the checkpoint log sequence and one log for all the other log sequences.

4.4.2 Log Record Identification

A **log record identifier** identifies a log record uniquely within the log it is part of. A **physical** log record identification policy identifies a log record relative to its physical position, or *log address* ([MHL+89]), within the log. A **logical** log record identification policy identifies a log record by a log record identifier field containing a surrogate key value, i.e. by a *log sequence number* (**LSN**) ([Dat83], [HL86], [BHG87]) (see section A.4). The physical log record identification policy cannot be used in combination with a replicated log policy, where multiple replicas may exist of a log record, since the replicas will have different log addresses.

The recovery server is required to detect the last log record in a log when recovering from a node crash. A simple policy supporting this requirement is to let the LSN be monotonously increasing, i.e. an explicit total ordering of the log ([Gra78], [HL86], [MHL+89]). If node crash recovery work starts from the last log record, the log must be searched for a break in the LSN values to establish the last log record. This can be accomplished by an inexpensive search ([Hag90]). It is in the following assumed that a monotonously increasing LSN policy is adopted to identify log records in a log.

In addition to a unique identification of log records within a log and a representation of the total ordering of the log, a log record must be uniquely identified within the log sequences it belongs to, and the ordering in the log sequences must be represented. Policies for this are presented with the policies using the various log sequences.

4.4.3 The Log Record

A **log record** contains a **generic** and a **specific** part. The generic part related to the block oriented approach contains the following fields:

- **Log record identifier**
  A unique log record identifier based on the LSN policy (see section 4.4.2).

- **Transaction identifier**
  A unique transaction identifier in the context of the DB. This identifies the transaction of the logged operation. The transaction identifier tells which transaction the logged operation belongs to. Since the transaction model is flat (see section A.8), the transaction identifier is a unique number.

- **Operation identifier**
  A unique operation identifier in the context of the datamodel of the DB. The operation identifier tells which operation is executed. If the datamodel contains only one state changing DB operation, the operation identifier can be omitted. In the block datamodel context the only DB state changing operation is the *write* operation.

The specific part of the DB operation log records contains the block identifier and the before- and/or after-image of the block. Log records representing transaction operations contain only the generic log record part.

4.4.4 The Write Ahead Log Rules

The **write ahead log** (WAL) protocol is a log oriented interpretation of the undo and redo rules defined in section 4.3. It consists of the following rules:

- **Undo WAL rule**
  An undo log record must be written to stable storage before the effect of a do-operation is allowed in the stable storage DB. An undo log record is a log record representing an undo operation.
- **Redo WAL rule**
  A redo log record must be written to stable storage before the transaction the do operation belongs to is allowed to commit. A redo log record is a log record representing a redo operation.

Some presentations of WAL include only the undo WAL rule in the WAL concept ([BHG87]).

4.4.5 The Log Garbage Collection Rules

The WAL rules specify the log production rules. They do not determine the valid lifespan of a log record, i.e. when it becomes log record garbage. A before-image log record of a block, for example, is garbage after the transaction that produced it has committed.

The garbage collection rules presented here are explicitly related to the block datamodel and relate only to transaction and node failures. It is assumed that for each written block both one before- and one after-image log record are produced, as specified in section 4.4.6. The garbage collection rules states the *earliest time* a log record can be removed as garbage.

- An *after-image log record* for a block X by transaction T_i can be removed if:
  1. T_i aborted; or
  2. T_i committed and some later transaction T_j wrote X; or
  3. T_i committed, and the after-image value is the last committed value of X, and this value is the stable storage value of X and no other log records exists for X.
- A *before-image log record* for a block X by transaction T_i can be removed if:
  1. T_i committed; or
  2. T_i aborted and some later transaction T_j wrote X; or
  3. T_i aborted and the before-image value is the last committed value of X, and this value is the stable storage value of X, and no other log records exists for X.

The third garbage rule, with respect to both the after- and before-images, states that a log record is outdated when the stable storage block reflects its content. The third rule is of particular interest concerning checkpoints.

4.4.6 Before- and After-image Log Records

The write operations are the only DB state changing operations related to the block datamodel. The operation identifier may therefore be left out of the log entries (see section 4.3).

The **after-image** value of a write operation is the value of the block after the operation is executed. The **before-image** value of a write operation is the value of the block before the operation is executed. The redo WAL rule requires that a log record with the after-image value of the block is written before the transaction commits. The before-image is not required to be written since the after-image log record of the last committed transaction that wrote the block is the before-image log record of this operation. There is a serious disadvantage of using the previous after-image log record as before-image. The log record containing the before-image may be anywhere on the log before the current position, i.e. there are no limitations on how far away the before-image log record can be. If a transaction aborts, the recovery server must scan the log until all before-images for the write operations of the transaction are found. This may result in painfully slow transaction rollbacks, which runs counter to the fast transaction recovery design goal (see section 2.6). To avoid this slow transaction rollback, both the before- and after-images of a written block are logged by the DBMS systems based on block oriented WAL ([BJWK+76], [Dea87]).

When a DB block is written, two log blocks are written to disc: the before- and the after-image log entries. This produces a large log volume and a high log disc I/O load, which are one of the main disadvantages during normal operations of block logging.

4.4.7 State Transition Logging

State logging is applied when the before- and the after-images of a block write operation are logged. The alternative is **state transition logging** and is applied if the "xor" between the before- and after-images are logged.

By state logging, an undo or redo write operation does not need to be applied to the same block state as the original write operation was applied to. All log records except the one producing the last committed value may also be removed as garbage (see section 4.4.5).

When logging is based on state transition, redo has to be applied to the before-image value of the block and undo has to be applied to the after-image value of the block to produce a correct result. In addition state transition logging induces other garbage collection rules than state logging.

4.4.8 Partial Block Logging

The I/O caused by block logging can partially be compensated by **partial block logging**. Instead of logging complete blocks, only the part of a block modified by a write operation is logged ([Gra78]), starting with the first written byte and ending with the last written byte.

Some terminology confusion exist in the literature as to whether partial block logging is to be regarded as record logging ([Hag90]), or a type of block logging. In this book partial block logging is regarded as a particular type of block logging.

There are some disadvantages limiting the effect of this approach (see [GR88]). First of all most DBMSs have a header as part of every block. This header may be updated as a result of writing a

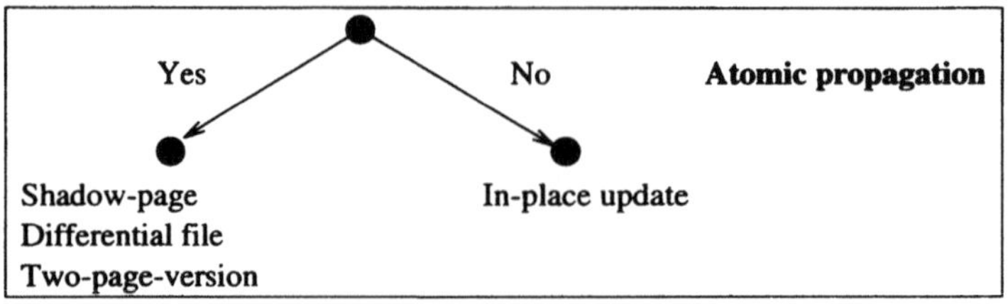

Figure 4.2: Illustration of the DB propagation strategies and policies implementing the strategies.

record further down in the block. If a record is inserted in the block, a new pointer is inserted in the header and the record itself may be inserted in the far opposite part of the block. The result is that most of the block must be logged. Secondly, the content of a DB block is often relocated due to variable length fields which again require most of the block being logged.

4.5 The DB Block Propagation Strategy

The DB propagation strategy is related to the consistency requirements imposed on the stable DB. If the stable DB is allowed at any given time to reflect only consistent DB states, the **atomic** DB propagation strategy is adopted. If the stable DB is allowed to reflect inconsistent DB states, the **non-atomic** propagation strategy is adopted.

The problems concerning propagation strategies arise from the fact that transactions may update more than one block, while only one block at a time can be transferred to disc. This mismatch may be handled by introducing stable blocks not part of the stable DB, so that blocks may be transferred to stable storage without being part of the stable DB. This illustrates the difference between the DB **write policy** and **propagation policy**. The write policy determines when a block is written to stable storage. The propagation policy determines when it becomes part of the stable DB.

The propagation action of including written blocks into the stable DB may be done atomically by a single disc block write operation. A number of atomic propagation policies are developed and documented in the literature. Examples of such policies are shadow-page ([Lor77]), differential file ([Sev82]), and two-page-versions ([Reu80]).

All policies providing atomic propagation are based on *multiple stable block replicas*. A non-atomic propagation policy on the other hand may provide a single block replica where all updates are done to that block, i.e. providing an **in-place** update policy.

A recoverable non-atomic propagation alternative is the combination of an in-place update policy and a WAL log policy. This alternative will need recovery work done during restart since the stable DB may reflect an inconsistent state. Figure 4.2 illustrates propagation strategies with implementation policies.

The main advantage of the atomic propagation policies is their *very simple recovery logic* due to the fact that the DB represents a consistent state when restart is initiated after a node failure. If propagation is connected to every transaction commit, the DB is consistent at restart. Every block contains the last committed value.

There are also some fundamental disadvantages related to the atomic propagation policies if applied to DBMSs designed for high transaction rates, large DBs, and high DB availability due to inherent bottlenecks. The shadow-page policy is used to illustrate these disadvantages, because most evaluations are related to that policy. This is a result of its use in System R ([CGY81], [CAB+81],

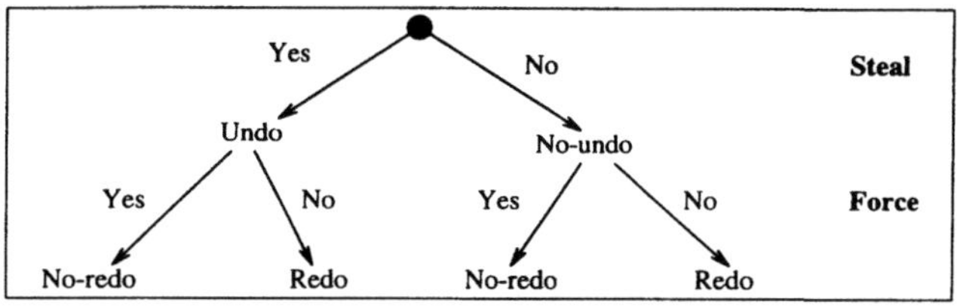

Figure 4.3: Classification of recovery algorithms based on the DB buffer strategy.

[GMB+81], [Tra82], [MHL+89], [KGMC85]).

The shadow-page policy serialises *commit* operations, since transaction commit is based entirely on propagation. The reason for this is that only one commit operation is allowed to update the shadow-page directory at a time. The probability of a transaction requesting more than one disc I/O during commit processing grows with the size of the DB and the number of blocks accessed by the transaction. As the time spent in commit processing grows, fewer transactions may commit per second.

If propagation is used as a checkpoint mechanism, the checkpointing may take seconds with a large DB, which makes the DB unavailable for ongoing transactions during checkpoint production ([Gra81]). Allocating a new stable replica each time a block is written, corrupts data clustering intended by physical DB design.

Comparing disc I/O during normal processing in DBMSs using the shadow-page policy with the combination of the in-place and the WAL policy both analytic ([Reu84]) and simulated ([KGMC85]) results show that the combination of in-place update and WAL is to be preferred. The evaluation of System R ([Gra81]) concludes that the choice of the shadow-page policy was a mistake, even though its overall performance was not unacceptable.

4.6 The DB Buffer Strategy

The DB buffer strategy controls the stable storage write policy. There are many different buffer management policies ([HB84], [EH84]), but it is not the intention of this section to present a survey of these policies. The following policies determine the DB buffer strategy ([HR84]):

- **Steal**
  The **steal** policy is applied if DB buffer blocks containing uncommitted values are allowed to be transferred to disc. The **no-steal** policy is applied if DB buffer blocks containing uncommitted values are only allowed to stay in the DB buffer.

- **Force**
  The **force** policy is applied if all DB buffer blocks updated by a transaction have to be transferred to disc and propagated at the termination of its abort or commit operation. A **no-force** policy is applied if propagation is not required as part of commit and abort processing.

Combinations of these policies with the in-place update policy, give rise to the following classification of recovery algorithms ([BHG87]). (The classification is illustrated in figure 4.3.)

- **Undo/redo**
  DB buffer blocks with uncommitted values are allowed to be written to disc. DB buffer

blocks containing committed values are allowed to be unreflected in the disc block replicas. As a consequence a WAL based log with sufficient information to perform both undo and redo work has to be produced. At node crash recovery both undo and redo work may have to be done.

- **Undo/no-redo**
  DB buffer blocks with uncommitted values are allowed to be written to disc. Before abort or commit processing of a transaction terminates, all DB buffer blocks written by the transaction must have been transferred to disc. As a consequence of this policy only before-images of written blocks have to be logged to recover from node failures. At node crash recovery, only undo work need to be done. Redo work is guaranteed to be unnecessary since all results of all terminated transactions are reflected in the stable DB.

- **No-undo/redo**
  DB buffer blocks with uncommitted values are not allowed written to disc. DB buffer blocks containing committed values are allowed to be unreflected in the disc block. As a consequence only after-images need be logged. At restart no undo work is done. Redo work may be needed.

- **No-undo/no-redo**
  This combination of policies represents a contradiction in the non-atomic propagation context.

The force policy requires all blocks written by a transaction to be reflected in stable storage at transaction termination time. The blocks must be written to disc during the execution time of the transaction but not necessarily during commit or abort processing. Using this policy leads to unnecessary block writes for hot-spot blocks compared to the no-force policy. On the other hand, the force policy induces a transaction oriented checkpoint. Redo work is not required for the transaction at restart. Therefore after-images do not need to be logged for recovery from node crashes, which saves log I/O during normal operations.

If recovery from media failures is taken into account in addition to transaction and node failure recovery, after-image log records are needed by most centralised systems in combination with an off-line archive-DB. Therefore after-image log records have to be produced. The overall effect is that the force policy requires more disc I/O during normal operations than the no-force policy. The same amount of log records, and more block writes are produced when compared to the no-force policy. This result corresponds to the results presented in [Reu84].

The force policy may require less work to be done during restart than the no-force policy, since no redo work is required. The force policy provides simpler recovery algorithms than the no-force policy because the redo sections can be left out.

The no-steal policy requires all written blocks to stay in the DB buffer during the transaction lifetime. This induces severe demands on main memory especially with long lived transactions performing many updates. Additional DB buffer overflow mechanisms must be added to handle overflow in the DB buffer caused by concurrent transactions updating more blocks than available DB buffer block slots ([EB84]).

The undo/redo policy allows the block server most freedom with respect to how long a block may stay in the DB buffer and which block to choose as victim when flushing a block to disc. The only requirement this policy has concerning block buffer management is that the undo and redo rules introduced in section 4.3 have to be obeyed.

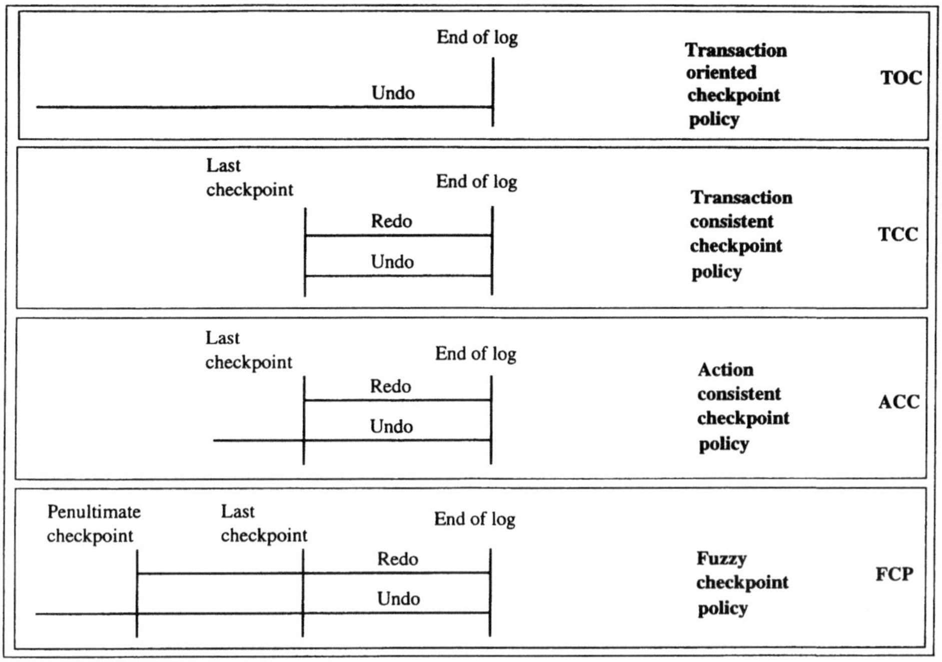

Figure 4.4: Illustration of checkpoint limitation on redo and undo node crash recovery work.

4.7 The Checkpoint Strategy

Checkpoints are produced periodically for two reasons: to support fast node crash recovery by limiting the node crash recovery undo and/or redo work load; and to support efficient log garbage collection by limiting the log volume required to perform node crash recovery. Four checkpoint policies are presented ([HR84]), **the transaction oriented-**, **the transaction consistent-**, **the action consistent-**, and **the fuzzy checkpoint policy**. The checkpoint policies are evaluated by their impact on normal transaction processing; especially regarding service availability for soft real-time transactions and their impact on node crash recovery work load. The policies are divided into two groups: checkpoint policies producing *transaction local checkpoints*, i.e. limitations on the redo and/or undo node crash recovery work local to individual transactions; and checkpoint policies producing *node global checkpoints*, i.e. limitations on the undo and/or redo node crash recovery work among all transactions at the node.

4.7.1 The Transaction Oriented Checkpoint Policy

The **transaction oriented checkpoint** (**TOC**) policy is a consequence of the force DB buffer policy and imposes *transaction local checkpoints*. When the force policy is applied, all blocks updated by terminated transactions are reflected on disc. Redo work and undo work for terminated transactions are therefore not needed during node crash recovery. Each transaction termination represents a local redo and undo checkpoint to the transaction. The recovery work includes only undoing the active transactions at the crash time (see figure 4.4).

The main disadvantage of the TOC policy is its lack of imposed undo work limitations. No stable active transaction lists are produced by the policy. The complete log must be scanned during the undo recovery pass to ensure that all active transactions are undone. This can result in a long recovery time if the log garbage collection is lagging behind.

The TOC policy allows log records to be garbage collected with respect to node crash recovery as soon as the transaction they belong to are terminated. When a transaction is terminated, it is reflected in the stable DB and its log records are not needed by any later node crash recovery.

4.7.2 The Transaction Consistent Checkpoint Policy

The **transaction consistent checkpoint (TCC)** policy produces node global checkpoints. It received its name because a checkpoint transaction under this policy produces a transaction consistent DB, i.e. a DB reflecting the last committed value before the checkpoint. The TCC checkpoints limit both the undo and redo node crash recovery work. The TCC policy is called *commit consistent checkpointing* in [BHG87].

A node global checkpoint is related to all transactions at a node. A node global checkpoint introduces a position in the log sequence of a node in which it is guaranteed that all results of operations reflected by previous DB log records up to this position are reflected on stable storage. The concept expressing the log record sequence, i.e. the log record identifier (see section 4.4.2), is used to identify a node global checkpoint position. If the log sequence at a node is split, either dedicated checkpoints per log sequence must be produced or a checkpoint containing the checkpoint position of every log sequence have to be produced. If node global checkpoints are combined with a block local sequence log record identification policy, a checkpoint must contain the checkpoint position for every block of the node, which is too costly an alternative.

The TCC policy involves the following activities when a checkpoint transaction is executed:

- **Write lock the DB**
  A write lock for the entire DB is requested and consequently no new transactions are started. The system can then either wait for the currently active transactions to terminate (*waiting termination policy*) or coerce them to terminate (*coerced termination policy*).
- **Flush dirty blocks**
  Every block reflecting logged state changing DB operations not reflected on stable storage, i.e. *dirty blocks*, is flushed to disc.
- **Checkpoint log record**
  A checkpoint log record is written to the log.
- **Unlock the DB**
  The checkpoint transaction is terminated by releasing the DB write lock.

The checkpoint log record contains the generic part in which the operation identifier indicates a checkpoint operation. The log record identifier, in addition to uniquely identifying the checkpoint log record, indicates the checkpoint position in the log sequence. That is, every log record in the log sequence with a lower log record identifier is reflected on stable storage.

A checkpoint transaction is well-formed and atomic. The checkpoint log record represents the transaction commit of the checkpoint transaction. If the checkpoint transaction aborts before its log record is on disc, the effect is as though the checkpoint transaction had not been done at all. The log record must therefore be logged after all the dirty blocks are flushed.

The TCC policy produces a consistent DB at each checkpoint, i.e. each block reflects the result of the last committed transaction. The node crash recovery undo and redo work is node globally limited by this checkpoint policy since every transaction started before a checkpoint is terminated before the checkpoint and is never involved in any node crash recovery work. No transactions are started before and terminated after a checkpoint as a result of the checkpoint transaction locking policy. The only transactions involved in node crash recovery work are those started after the last TCC checkpoint (see figure 4.4).

Transaction T_1 and T_2 of figure 4.5 are not involved in the recovery work since they were started and terminated before the last checkpoint. Transactions T_3, T_4, and T_5 do not exist in the TCC context, since all active transactions are terminated before a checkpoint is produced. Transaction T_7 is redone since it was started after the last checkpoint and committed before the node crash. Transaction T_6 and T_8 are undone since they were started after the last checkpoint and are either active or aborted at the node crash.

An advantage of the TCC policy is the simple log garbage collection policy it provides. Each TCC checkpoint is a node global garbage collection point with respect to node crash recovery. Since the checkpoint produces a consistent DB, all log records prior to the checkpoint can be garbaged.

The main disadvantage of the TCC checkpoint policy is that it threatens soft real-time transaction service availability caused by its omission rate. The omissions are caused by its long duration, coarse locking, and/or possible coerced transaction termination policy. A checkpoint transaction write locks the entire DB over its lifetime which can take several seconds. All new transactions must wait until the checkpoint transaction terminates before being allowed to execute.

There are two main sources for the long execution time of TCC checkpoint transactions. First, it may take time to wait for active transactions to terminate if the waiting termination policy is used. If, on the other hand, the coerced termination policy is used, the active transactions must be rolled back. If a long transaction is active, the rollback work can also take time. Secondly, for large DB buffers, e.g. 64 megabyte, the number of updated blocks that must be flushed to disc can be large, thereby introducing seconds of elapsed time to perform disc I/O. The block flushing time may alone threaten soft real-time transaction response time.

Use of the coerced termination policy to terminate active transactions may threaten the acceptable omission rate of transactions because all active transactions are aborted.

The write DB lock used by the TCC checkpoint transactions can be substituted with a read DB lock which gives a somewhat less restricting TCC policy with respect to terminating active and not accepting new transactions. Read transaction can stay active while the checkpoint transaction is executing, and new read transactions can be accepted.

4.7.3 The Action Consistent Checkpoint Policy

The **action consistent checkpoint** (**ACC**) policy produces node global checkpoints. The policy received its name because the DB resulting from an ACC checkpoint is DB operation or action consistent, i.e. all logged DB state changing operations prior to the checkpoint are reflected in the stable DB and none logged state changing DB operations after the checkpoint are reflected in the stable DB resulting from the checkpoint transaction. The ACC policy is called *cache consistent checkpointing* in [BHG87] which also refers to the ACC checkpoint definition.

The ACC policy involves the following activities when a checkpoint transaction is executed:

- **Write latch the DB buffer**
  The checkpoint transaction requests a write latch on the entire DB buffer and waits until all current block latches are released before serviced, i.e. a waiting termination policy for the active block DB operations is assumed.
- **Flush dirty blocks**

All DB buffer block replicas are inspected and all dirty DB buffer blocks are flushed to disc.

- **Checkpoint log record**
  A checkpoint log record is written containing the *active transaction table*.
- **Unlatch the DB buffer**
  The checkpoint transaction is terminated by releasing the write latch on the entire DB buffer.

The checkpoint log record is composed of a generic part and a specific part containing the *active transaction table* of the transactions active when the checkpoint was taken. The active transaction table contains, for each transaction, the transaction identifier and the log record identifier of the most recent log record of the transaction. The log record identifier of an ACC checkpoint log record identifies the checkpoint position in the log sequence. When an ACC checkpoint log record is reflected on stable storage, the locking policy used by the ACC checkpoint transactions guarantees that all DB operations represented by preceding log records are reflected on stable storage, and that none of the DB operation represented by log records following an ACC checkpoint log record, are reflected in the stable DB resulting from an ACC checkpoint transaction.

ACC checkpoints impose node global redo node crash recovery work limits, but they do not impose node global undo node crash recovery work limits (see figure 4.4). Since no logged DB operations preceding the checkpoint position ever need to be redone, an ACC checkpoint imposes a node global redo crash recovery work limit. In the example of figure 4.5, transaction T_1, T_2 and that part of transaction T_3 preceding the checkpoint are not redone during the node recovery since the operations were logged before the checkpoint. Redo node crash recovery work is restricted to transactions that started after the last ACC checkpoint and committed before the node crash. Transaction T_7 of figure 4.5 illustrates this.

Transactions that started before an ACC checkpoint, and either aborted after the checkpoint or were active at the node crash, need to be undone during the node crash recovery work also for their logged DB operations prior to the checkpoint. Therefore undo node crash recovery work is not node globally limited by the last ACC checkpoint. Transactions T_4 and T_5 of figure 4.5 illustrate this since they both started before the last checkpoint and need to be undone. Transactions started after the last checkpoint which either aborted or were active at the node crash need to be undone. In the example of figure 4.5, transactions T_6 and T_8 illustrate this.

The last ACC checkpoint represents a node global garbage collection point for every redo log record part. The checkpoint does not represent a node global garbage collection point for the undo log record parts, since undo log record parts for active transactions at the checkpoint are required if the transaction aborts.

The main disadvantage of the ACC checkpoint policy is its service availability threat to soft real-time transactions. This threat is caused by its latching of the entire DB buffer during the lifetime of a checkpoint transaction, i.e. while dirty blocks are flushed. With a large DB buffer, for example 64 megabyte, the dirty block flushing may take seconds. The flushing time is added to the normal execution time of all transactions active concurrently with the checkpoint transaction resulting in performance failures for transactions with soft real-time requirements.

If an ACC checkpoint is to be produced according to its definition, and the checkpoint transaction is required to produce only one checkpoint log record, and the position of the checkpoint log record implicitly indicates the checkpoint position in the log sequence, each ACC transaction must latch the entire DB buffer during its lifetime. If some of these requirements are lifted, checkpoints according to the ACC definition can be produced with some reduced unavailability threat to soft real-time transaction services.

The write latch on the entire DB buffer can be substituted by a read DB buffer latch, since no state changing logged DB operations can then be performed concurrently with the checkpoint

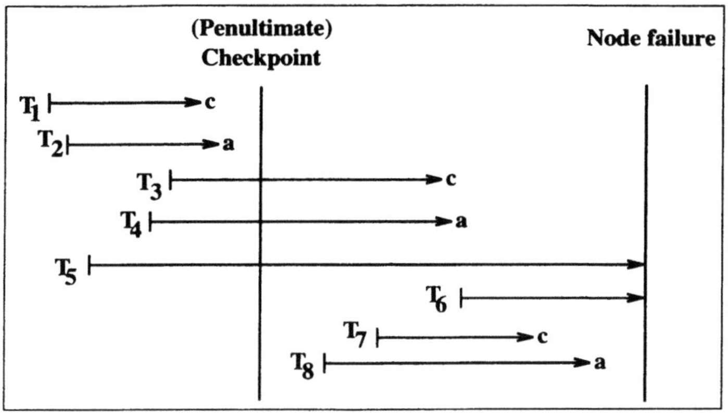

Figure 4.5: Start and termination of transactions related to the last checkpoint (Checkpoint) and node crash (Node failure). If the checkpoints are produced by the fuzzy checkpoint policy, the last checkpoint is replaced by the penultimate checkpoint (Penultimate). A transaction is represented by an arrow, where the transaction identifier is given at the beginning, e.g. T_1, and the termination is indicated by either a commit (c), an abort (a), or by an indication that the transaction was active at the node crash.

transaction. The use of a read latch allows read DB operations to be performed concurrently with the checkpoint transaction, and thereby lessen the service availability problems imposed.

If the checkpoint log record is divided into a begin-checkpoint and an end-checkpoint log record, a block can be unlatched after being inspected and possibly flushed. The begin-checkpoint log record is composed of the same fields as the checkpoint log record presented above and has a similar function. The function of the end-checkpoint log record is to confirm the commit of the checkpoint transaction. The pair of begin- and end-checkpoint log records represents the checkpoint. The log must be scanned to the begin-checkpoint log record since concurrent operations on unlatched blocks can be logged between the begin- and the end-checkpoint log record.

The following case illustrates a possible inconsistency that might result if the checkpoint log record was not split and blocks were unlatched after being inspected and flushed. The checkpoint transaction has flushed a block and unlatched it. A write operation is then performed (by another transaction) on the block before the checkpoint transaction commits. Its log record precedes the checkpoint log record, indicating that the effect of the operation is reflected in the stable DB produced by the checkpoint, which is not the case. During a possible restart this operation might not be redone, producing an inconsistent DB. See section 4.7.4 for more details of two log record based checkpointing.

An alternative policy to splitting the checkpoint log record to allow unlatching of inspected blocks is to include an additional log position field into the checkpoint log record explicitly stating the log stream position of the checkpoint, since it does not necessarily correspond to the checkpoint log record position. If this policy is used, the log must be scanned to that position, and not only to the checkpoint log record position.

If checkpoint log records are written into a separate log stream instead of into the ordinary log stream, only one checkpoint log record has to be produced per checkpoint in order to allow blocks to be unlatched after being inspected and possibly flushed. In this case, the checkpoint log record must contain the log record identifier of the last log record reflected in the produced stable DB. See section 4.7.5 for more details.

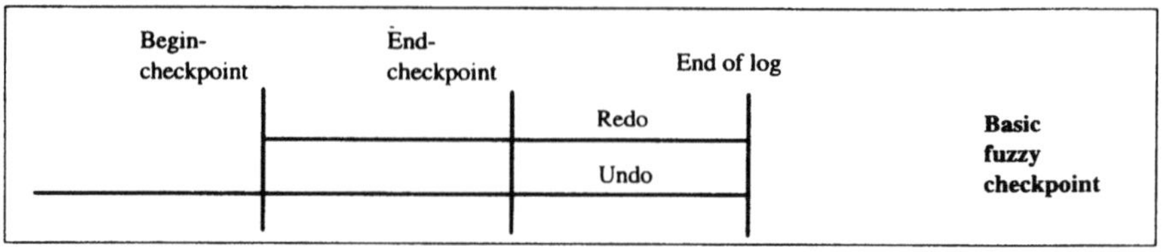

Figure 4.6: The basic fuzzy checkpoint policy.

4.7.4 The Fuzzy Checkpoint Policy

The **fuzzy checkpoint (FCP)** policy produces node global checkpoints. Its imposed node crash recovery work limitations are similar to the ACC policy, i.e. the redo node recovery work is globally limited, while the undo recovery work is not globally limited but limited to the active transactions at the checkpoint. The main advantage of the FCP policy compared to the TCC and ACC policies is that it allows transactions to be executed without interruption and concurrently with a checkpoint transaction and therefore does not represent a threat to service availability of soft real-time transactions.

A fuzzy checkpoint produces a stable DB that is guaranteed to reflect all logged DB operations prior to the checkpoint. The stable DB may also reflect some logged DB operations executed concurrently with the checkpoint transaction. The stable DB reflects no logged DB operations performed after the commit of the checkpoint transaction. The definition of an FCP checkpoint differs from the definition of an ACC checkpoint with respect to operations performed concurrently with the checkpoint transaction. While the ACC policy guarantees that none of these are reflected, no such guarantee is provided by the FCP policy.

Different variants of the FCP policy which exploit the potential in the policy to a variable degree are proposed in the literature. The variant proposed in [BHG87] read latches the entire DB buffer over the checkpoint transaction lifetime, thereby imposing comparable service availability threats to soft real-time transactions as ACC checkpoint transactions. The variant proposed in [LSG$^+$79] and [GR88] avoids this unnecessary coarse latching.

The **basic FCP** policy is followed if each checkpoint transaction produces a begin- and an end-checkpoint log record. The **penultimate FCP** policy is followed if one log record is produced by each checkpoint transaction and if it is guaranteed that all logged DB operations before the penultimate checkpoint are reflected in the stable DB when a FCP checkpoint transaction is committed.

The following actions take place when producing a basic fuzzy checkpoint:

- **Begin-checkpoint log record**
  Write a begin-checkpoint log record containing the *active transaction table* to the log. See section 4.7.3 for the active transaction table.
- **Flush dirty blocks**
  Inspect every DB buffer block replica once. Read latch a block while it is inspected and possibly flushed. If a block is dirty it is flushed to disc.
- **End-checkpoint log record**
  Write an end-checkpoint log record.

The basic FCP policy illustrates that only one block is read latched at a time while a checkpoint transaction is executed. This is sufficient to guarantee the fulfillment of the FCP checkpoint definition that at least all logged DB operations preceding the checkpoint are reflected in the checkpoint produced stable DB. During node crash recovery, the redo log pass must include every log record from the begin-checkpoint log record since concurrent operations may have been executed with the checkpoint transaction. Of these operations the FCP policy guarantees no stabilisation (see figure 4.6). The active transaction table can be included in the end-checkpoint log record instead of in the begin-checkpoint log record.

The **penultimate FCP** policy produces only one log record per checkpoint by letting the penultimate checkpoint log record take the role of the begin-checkpoint log record. That is, commit of one checkpoint transaction also represents the start of the succeeding checkpoint transaction. A consequence of this policy is that a checkpoint transaction flushes only those blocks that both are dirty and have not been flushed since before the previous checkpoint. This reduces the block flush work load of a checkpoint transaction and makes better use of the DB buffer policy. On the other hand, more node crash recovery work is normally needed because the redo pass must scan a larger part of the log than is needed if the basic FCP policy is used, i.e. the log from the penultimate checkpoint, depending on the checkpointing intervals.

The penultimate FCP policy can be combined with the **dirty block table** policy if a table containing the block identifiers of every dirty block as after the block flushing done by the checkpoint transaction. The dirty block table will be used to further restrict the node crash redo and undo recovery work (see sections 5.7.5 and 5.7.6).

The following actions are involved in a penultimate checkpoint transaction:

- **Flush dirty blocks**
  Inspect every DB buffer block replica. Read latch a block while it is inspected and possibly flushed. If the block is dirty, and has not been flushed to disc since before the last checkpoint, flush it to disc.

- **Checkpoint log record**
  Write a checkpoint log record containing the *active transaction table*, and the *dirty block table* if the dirty block table policy is used.

Since a penultimate FCP checkpoint only guarantees that all operations performed before the second last checkpoint are written to disc, no flush-synchronisation is needed, i.e. the blocks can be flushed in any sequence as long as they are write operation consistent, which is guaranteed by the read latch. An FCP checkpoint transaction server can therefore execute continuously at a lower priority level, asynchronously to transaction servers ([GR88]). The checkpoint transaction server determines the blocks to be flushed and requests the disc server to flush the blocks in any order to minimise the disc access work ([BHW74]). This checkpoint algorithm utilises spare disc I/O capacity to perform checkpointing because the checkpoint server and the involved block accesses run at low priority. The checkpoint I/O is taken out of the critical path of transaction processing, and the disc I/O can be optimised.

4.7.5 Separate Checkpoint Log Streams

Checkpoint log records can either be written to a dedicated checkpoint log or included in the standard node log. The **checkpoint log policy** is followed if checkpoint log records are written to a dedicated log. The checkpoint log policy is only relevant in combination with any of the node global checkpoint policies, since only these policies produce checkpoint log records.

If node crash recovery work is required to begin by scanning the log from the appropriate checkpoint, it is necessary to provide fast access to the checkpoint log position. Stable information of checkpoint log positions must therefore be supported outside the log to provide this access method. This is provided by use of the checkpoint log policy since a checkpoint log is small. In this case writing the complete checkpoint log record to a dedicated log represents no significant added disc I/O work.

The checkpoint log policy combined with the TCC policy produces log records similar to those documented in section 4.7.2. Since checkpoint transactions are executed strictly sequentially, their transaction identifier uniquely identifies both the checkpoint log record and the log sequence in the checkpoint log. The log record identifier of the checkpoint log records indicates the checkpoint position in the standard node log. A TCC checkpoint transaction is committed when its log record is written to the stable checkpoint log. A TCC checkpoint log record can be garbage collected when a succeeding checkpoint log record exists.

The checkpoint log policy combined with any of the ACC policies requires only one log record produced per checkpoint since the log record identifier indicates the checkpoint log position. The combination corresponds to the combination with the TCC policy.

The checkpoint log policy combined with any of the FCP policies also requires only one log record per checkpoint of the same reason as with the ACC policy. The active transaction table is, if basic FCPs are used, assumed to be included, as in the end-checkpoint log record. A penultimate FCP checkpoint log record can be garbage collected when two succeeding log records exist. Since a block must be written to commit a checkpoint transaction, the addition of the dirty block table will normally represent no additional disc I/O work.

4.8 The Combined Block Oriented Classification Scheme

This section presents the combined block oriented classification scheme. The combined scheme tells which combinations of DB block propagation, DB buffer, and checkpoint policies that are possible. The set of policies is restricted to those included in the previous analysis. The combined classification scheme is presented in figure 4.7.

It is assumed as part of the block oriented model that blocks are the unit of locking. It is further assumed that logging is based on complete blocks, is state oriented, and includes both before- and after-images.

The atomic block propagation policy chosen is the shadow-page policy. Transaction commit is then based entirely on the propagation policy, which requires no logging. When the shadow-page policy is combined with logging, transaction commits are not based on the propagation policy. DBMSs combining the shadow-page policy with logging include the recovery server in the record layer and are not included in this classification. As a consequence of the shadow-page based transaction commits, a TCC is implicitly produced by each transaction commit. The transaction commits do also produce TOCs, which are also a consequence of the atomic propagation policy.

The combination of the in-place update policy with the force policy implies TOCs. No restart work is needed for committed transactions, since all updated blocks are reflected on disc. The combination of the no-undo steal policy with the ACC policy induces a global limit on restart undo work. This is a result of the no-undo policy. Any combination of in-place update, steal, and force policies can be combined with the TCC, the ACC, or the FCP policy.

A recovery method based on the shadow-page policy is evaluated to impose the highest recovery cost under normal operations. It may, for small DBs and low update transaction rates, be as good as an in-place update based recovery method. For large DBs and high update transaction loads, the normal operations recovery cost exceeds those of in-place based recovery methods. For large DBs and high update transactions loads, the inherent potential bottlenecks of the shadow page recovery

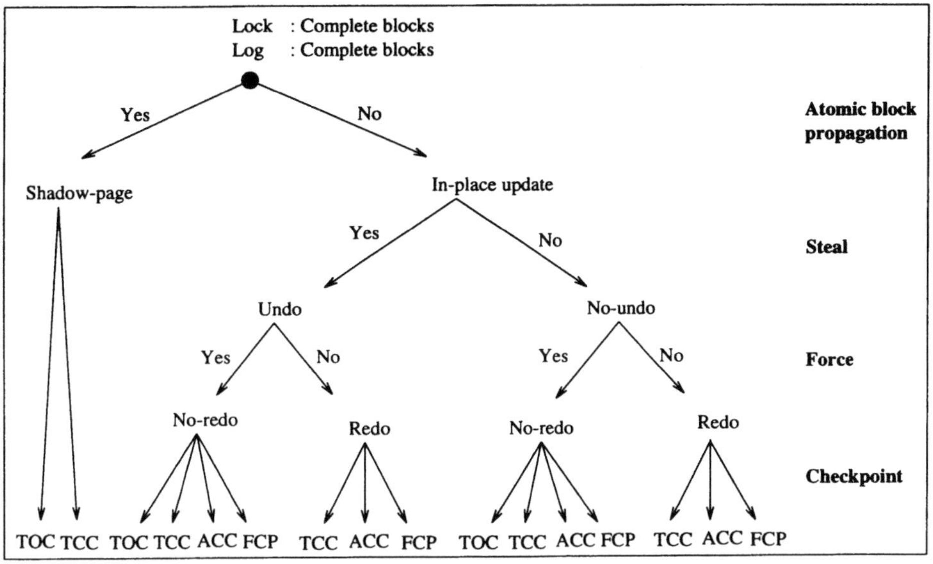

Figure 4.7: Illustration of which combinations of DB propagation policies (atomic/non-atomic), DB buffer policies (steal/no-steal, force/no-force), and checkpoint policies (TOC, TCC, ACC, FCP) are possible.

policy will constrain the transaction throughput of the DBMS.

Of the non-atomic block propagation based recovery methods, those based on a no-redo policy induce higher recovery costs during normal operations than those based on a redo policy. The recovery methods based on no-undo impose more constraints on the DB buffer management than those based on the undo policy. The fuzzy checkpoint policy induces lower recovery costs during normal operations than the other checkpoint policies. The recovery method based on the combination of the in-place update, the undo, the redo policy, and the fuzzy checkpoint policy is evaluated to represent the best combination in regard to low recovery cost during normal operations and few bottlenecks.

A recovery method based on the shadow-page policy represents the simplest recovery algorithm. A recovery method based on the combination of in-place update, undo, redo, and fuzzy checkpoint represents the most complex recovery algorithm of those evaluated in this chapter. In this evaluation of complexity, the inherent higher complexity of the shadow-page policy compared to the in-place update policy is not included.

The recovery component of the System R reprerests 10% of the system code lines ([Gra81]). The recovery component of DB2 represents 11% of the code lines ([Cru84]), and finally, the recovery component of TechRa constitute approximately 10% of the code lines ([KVA89], [HL86]). The recovery methods of the three systems differ greatly, however.

4.9 Conclusion

The design goals behind the recovery methods classified as block oriented are focused more on algorithmic simplicity and midrange performance requirements than on avoiding bottlenecks emerging from performance stress. Coarse grained locking and block logging are inherent in all these methods.

None of the block oriented recovery methods satisfies the stated recovery design requirements in section 2.6. They represent the recovery design requirements of another age or widely different systems than those required by continuously available DBMSs (see chapter III).

Exercises

1. (a) Would the use of stable main memory influence the undo and the redo rules? (b) How many replicas of a data item would be needed to recover from a stable main memory crash?

2. (a) Why are log records uniquely identified? (b) How can the last log record produced before a node crash be found if the physical log record identification policy is used? (c) What are the problems caused by extending a log file dynamically? (d) Propose a method to deal with these problems.

3. (a) What is the advantage of state transition logging based on "xor" as opposed to state logging? (b) What would be the effect on undo processing of state transition logging based on "xor" operations? (c) What would be the effect on redo processing?

4. (a) What are the advantages of partial block logging? (b) A block has a pointer array pointing to its contained records. The pointer array is located from the block's lowest address. How much needs to be logged when a record is deleted? (c) How much needs to be logged when a record is inserted in free space by the pointer array? (d) How much needs to be logged when the record is inserted at the highest addresses of the block?

5. (a) Which DB propagation policy and DB buffer policy are used if only undo log records are produced? (b) Assume the logging policy in a. How far back does the log need to be scanned during a node crash in this case if no other explicit checkpoint policy is used?

6. Assume the DB fits into one block, the transactions perform one write operation each, and a block flush and a block read operation take 10 milliseconds each. (a) What is the maximum transaction rate for a shadow-page based DBMS? (b) Assume one logging disc is used. What is the maximum transaction rate for an undo logging DBMS, and (c) for an undo/redo logging DBMS?

7. (a) Why can the transaction rate of b above not be increased by applying two log discs? (b) How can the transaction rate of c in the previous exercise be increased?

8. (a) Which checkpointing policy is implicitly followed in exercise 5? (b) What would be the effect of using the action consistent checkpoint policy on the node crash recovery work?

9. (a) How is a transaction in the prepare-to-commit state at a node crash recovered? (b) Include this in figure 4.5 and show how this influences the action consistent checkpoint policy.

10. Let the checkpoint log records contain the oldest log sequence number of the active transactions. (a) Could this be used to to limit the undo recovery work? (b) Could it be used to log less information per checkpoint?

11. Under which conditions can the combination of the in-place update policy, the no-undo policy, and the no-redo policy appear? See figure 4.7.

Answers

1. (a) No. The rules are independent of the type of stable memory. (b) Two replicas with independent failure modes.

2. (a) To uniquely refer to one log record from another and to uniquely identify an operation based on its log record identifier. (b) If log records are linked, then follow the log record sequence until the equivalent of a NIL pointer is found. There are many ways to implement the equivalent of a NIL pointer. (c) The dynamical extensions must be atomical operations implemented without the support of logging. (d) See chapter 14 where a method is proposed. Alternatively, use multiple fixed length log files. Log the allocation of another log file in the previous one. Start redo recovery based on that file before starting redo recovery based on the next one.

3. (a) A log record is only one block larger compared to two blocks if the state based logging is used; one before-image and one after-image. (b) No effect on the undo logic. "xor"-operations are executed instead of write operations. (c) A redo write operation is stateless, i.e. the result is independent of the original value of the block. During state based redo recovery, it must be determined which "xor" operations are actually reflected in the block, otherwise inconsistency may occur.

4. (a) Reduced log volume compared to block logging. (b) The before and after value of the pointer to the deleted record and the start address of the pointer within the block. (c) The before- and after-image of the bytes from the pointer to the inserted record up to and including the inserted record. (d) As in c, but it will encompass a record size of approximately two blocks. The partial block logging did not give reduced log volume.

5. (a) Steal and force. (b) To the beginning of the log, because we do not know when all active transactions are recovered before the end of the log is encountered. Note that the log does not need to be longer than the log records produced over the lifetime of the oldest active transaction at the crash time.

6. (a) A shadow based transaction performs two block writes in which the DB block is the first accessed and is write locked over the duration of the transaction. This gives a maximum of approximately 50 tps. (b) Each transaction causes one flush operation to the log disc. The force operation causes one flush operation to the DB disc. Since the log flush must be done before the DB flush, they will be done in sequence. This gives a maximum of approximately 50 tps. (c) This gives one flush to the log disc which gives a maximum of approximately 100 tps.

7. (a) You are still dependent on the access rate of the single DB disc. (b) Log round robin to multiple log discs. One transaction writes to just one log disc. The transaction capacity is increased by the number of discs without increasing the transaction response time.

8. (a) Transaction oriented checkpointing (TOC). If every dirty block is flushed as part of a transaction commit, the action consistent checkpoint (ACC) policy is also followed. (b) The redo work is limited, which is not the case if only the TOC policy is used.

9. (a) The transaction is redone. It can not be undone because its outcome is uncertain. If the DB is made available before the outcome is established, the locks held by the transaction must have been reset.

10. (a) The oldest log record of the transactions active when the checkpoint was produced restricts the undo work. (b) It can be substituted for the active transaction table in the checkpoint log records. It is obviously normally smaller than the active transaction table.

11. The DB consists of one block, and the in-place, no-steal, and force policies are applied.

Chapter 5

The Record Oriented Approach

This chapter presents and classifies recovery methods using **record logging** related to the **restricted record datamodel** (see section A.6) combined with concurrency control based on **block locking** (see section A.9) and the non-atomic **in-place** block propagation policy (see section 4.5).

The design goals behind the record oriented recovery methods are mainly focused on removing one of the main deficiencies of the block oriented approach. The produced log volume during normal operations is significantly reduced when compared with the block oriented approach.

The record oriented approach provides the foundation for the more elaborate compensation oriented approach presented in chapter 6. The record oriented approach represents a combination of policies not used by modern DBMSs given its inherent limitations. Thus it represents a stepping stone toward chapter 6, in which the restrictions imposed by coarse granularity locking and the restricted record datamodel are solved. Policies of chapter 6 are more easily explained when introduced and analysed in context of the record oriented approach than directly in the context of the compensation oriented approach.

5.1 The Record Oriented DBMS Server Architecture

This section presents the record oriented DBMS server architecture, which is illustrated in figure 5.1. The server architecture shown here does not represent the module architecture of any particular DBMS. The example is biased more towards a clean and simple structure than towards making a foundation for efficient DBMS implementations.

The relational and table servers perform mapping between the relational and the table datamodel, and the table and the record datamodel (see section A.3) by receiving DB and transaction requests and by requesting DB and transaction requests according to the server used. (See section 2.5 for a general presentation of the server architecture.) Since the relational and the table servers are not specificly involved in recovery related tasks, they are not investigated further in this chapter.

The servers specifically involved in recovery related tasks are the concurrency control, the recovery, the record, and the block servers. The *concurrency control server* receives DB operations according to the restricted record datamodel and transaction operations from the table server. The concurrency control server serialises the DB operations according to the specifications given in section A.9, by performing *coarse granularity* locking according to the *traditional locking model*, thereby performing concurrency control related to blocks.

Since a record is fully contained in a block, the record the operation is intended for becomes locked when the block it is contained in is locked. A read record operation read locks the block the record is contained in. A write, delete, or insert record operation write locks the block in which

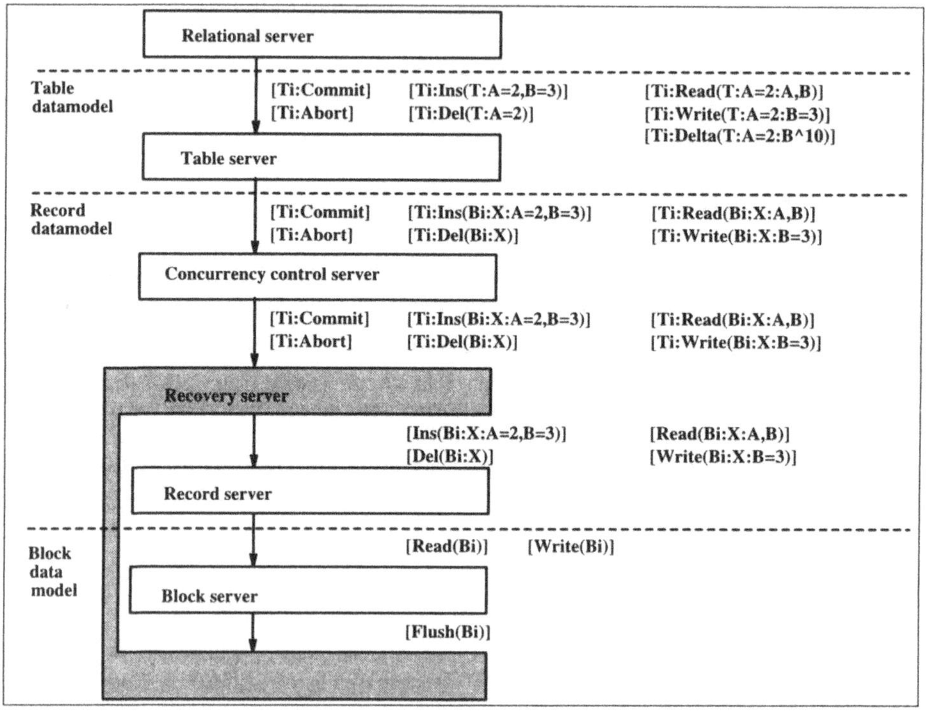

Figure 5.1: The record oriented DBMS server architecture. The layered DBMS architecture corresponds to the architecture presented in figure A.3, and section 2.5. The concurrency control and the recovery servers are included in the record datamodel layer. See figure 4.1 for introduction to the operation syntax used. The restricted record datamodel is used with the record index identification policy.

the record is, or is to be, contained. The locking is assumed to be well formed (see section A.9). An effect of the combination of coarse granularity locks with the traditional locking model is that multiple transactions that perform state changing DB operations are never concurrent to a block. If a transaction aborts the consistent state of a block operated on by the transaction is obtained by restoring the state of the block before the first of the operations by the transaction executed to it.

The *recovery server* receives a sequence of serialised DB and transaction operation requests from the concurrency control server. It logs both the state changing DB operations and the transaction operations. Record logging is applied to the DB operations. The logging is done according to the WAL protocol (see section 4.4.4).

The *record server* receives DB operations according to the restricted record datamodel from the recovery server, and requests block DB operations from the block server. The recovery server controls the transfer of blocks between the DB buffer and disc to ensure that the WAL rules and the DB buffer strategy (see section 4.6) are obeyed.

A consequence of record oriented logging is that the recovery server is involved in two distinct datamodel layers: the record datamodel layer for the logging of DB and transaction operations and ensuring that the redo WAL rule is preserved; and the block datamodel layer for ensuring that the undo WAL rule is followed.

5.1.1 Log Volume Reduction

The main motivation for record logging instead of block logging is the reduction of log volume produced during normal operations. If logging of complete blocks is applied and a write record operation is executed, both the before- and the after-image of the block containing the record are logged. This produces a log volume of two blocks. Given a block size of 2Kbytes, this gives a log volume of 4K bytes for each write operation. If on the other hand record logging of complete records is applied, and the size of the written record is for example 100 bytes, the produced log volume of the same operation by record logging is approximately 220 bytes. The produced log volume by record logging is in this case only 5.5% of the log volume produced by complete block logging, which illustrates the main advantage for record logging over complete block logging.

If record logging is compared to partial block logging, the produced log volume of the two are comparable as long as no physical relocation within the block is required, or the header part of a block is updated. Partial block logging requires logging of the part of a block involved in relocation. This is not the case for record logging, as will be shown. Inserting a record, compacting a block, or writing a variable length field in a record frequently involves physical relocation within the block or update of the block header. In these cases partial block logging produces a higher log volume than record logging (see section 4.4.8). This illustrates one of the advantages of record logging over partial block logging.

5.2 The Record Oriented Classification Scheme

This section presents the classification scheme for the record oriented approach. The classification scheme is based on a collection of recovery related DBMS strategies. Each strategy and its related policies are outlined in the following sections. The presented classification scheme is somewhat influenced by the structure of [BHG87].

- **The record logging strategy**
  The record logging strategy determines how the logging is actually done during normal operations to comply with the requirements of the WAL rules and gain the potentials of

reduced log volume compared to block logging. The record logging is operational, state oriented, and follows the single-block policy. A group commit policy is presented to let multiple commit operations share a log block access.

- **The record access strategy**
  The record access strategy determines how consistent record access based on the log record record-identification concepts is obtained within a block and between blocks when blocks are split during the lifetime of a transaction. The record access policies are chosen to give low log volume together with few restrictions on record relocations within blocks.

- **The transaction failure recovery strategy**
  The transaction failure recovery strategy determines how the effects of a failed transaction are removed from the DB by undoing the state changing DB operations of the transaction. The reset state recovery policy resets a block back to the last committed state. It will be shown that this is a possible policy to combine with coarse granularity locking and block or record logging.

- **The node crash recovery strategy**
  The node crash recovery strategy determines how node crash recovery transforms a partial-amnesia DB to the last commit consistent DB by minimising the necessary log scan and DB access work load.

5.3 The Record Logging Strategy

The record logging strategy is composed of a collection of policies that determine how the record logging is actually done. The record logging of state changing DB operations is assumed to be *state logging* oriented, i.e. based on before- and after-images of the records. It is assumed that a **one log record** policy is used so that the all log information for an operation is kept in one log record.

5.3.1 The Single-Block Policy

A logged DB operation may in general operate on one or more blocks. A **single-block policy** is followed if a logged DB operation is allowed to operate on only one block, otherwise a **multi-block policy** is followed.

It is a property of the single-block policy that a logged operation is either completely reflected in the stable DB or not reflected in the stable DB at all during a node crash recovery. This property is preserved by the atomic block transfer operations (see section 2.3.2). If on the other hand, the multi-block policy is adopted, a logged operation may be *partially reflected* in the stable DB during node crash recovery. A multi-block policy requires more complex node crash recovery algorithms than a single-block policy, since partially done operations must be recovered in addition to the recovery requirements by operations completely done or not done at all. An example of the adoption of the multi-block policy is to avoid logging index-record operations as in System R ([MHL+89]).

The record oriented approach applies the single-block policy. Every record is fully contained in a block and every record DB operation is related to a single record.

5.3.2 The Log Record

A log record contains a *generic* and a *specific part*. A log record according to the record oriented approach contains the following generic fields (see section 4.4.3 for comparison with the block logging approach):

- **Log record identifier**
  A unique log record identifier based on the monotonously increasing LSN policy (see section 4.4.2).

- **Operation identifier**
  Since more than one type of DB operations are logged, a specific operation identifier have to be part of every log record. The transaction operations Commit and Abort are logged. The DB state changing record operations Write, Insert, and Delete are logged.

- **Transaction identifier**
  The unique identifier of the transaction to which the logged operation belongs.

- **Transaction previous log record identifier**
  The log record identifier of the previous log record of the transaction.

The log record for every transaction operation contains the generic fields as given above.

A log record for a write operation contains the following specific fields:

- **Data item identifier**
  The data item identifier identifies a record uniquely within a block and is used to access a record during both transaction and node crash recovery. The data item identifier is composed of the *block identifier* of the block containing the record, and the *record identifier* according to the record identifier policy identifying the record uniquely within the block (see section A.6).

- **Stable block state**
  If a node global block state policy is used, the block state after the operation is executed is expressed by the log record identifier. The undo block state is stored in this field since it cannot be calculated from the state-identifier.

- **Before-image**
  The before-image of the record operated upon by the logged write operation.

- **After-image**
  The after-image of the record operated upon by the logged write operation.

The specific log record part for an insert operation does not contain any before-image since no before-image exists for an inserted record. The specific log record part for a delete operation does not contain any after-image of the record since no after-image exists for a deleted record. (See section 4.7 for presentation of checkpoint log records.)

The undo part of a log record for a state changing DB operation contains the complete log record except for the after-image. The redo part of a log record for a state changing DB operation contains the complete log record except for the before-image and the previous transaction log record identifier.

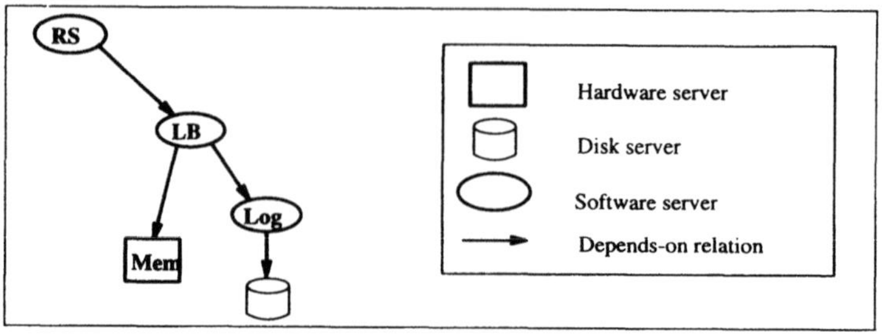

Figure 5.2: The recovery server (RS) depends-on the log-buffer server (LB). The log-buffer server depends-on the hardware main memory server (Mem) and the log server (Log). The log server depends-on the disc server.

5.3.3 Partial Record Logging

Partial record logging is a method to further reduce the log volume compared to complete record logging. The intention behind partial record logging is to log only fields that are involved in the DB state changing record operation. The reduction is logical to log record fields.

With respect to the restricted record datamodel, partial record logging only applies to write operations. If for example record relocation within a block is logged, and done by use of write record operations, a log record for such an operation may contain only the generic log record part since the before- and after-image of the record is the same and kept within the same block.

Partial record logging does not apply to insert and delete record operations, since the complete record is involved in these operations.

5.3.4 The Log Buffering Policy

Compared to block logging, production of log records that are fractions of a block requires a main memory log-buffer server to reduce the disc I/O load proportional to the produced log volume. Since record logging and partial block logging produce log records that are fractions of blocks, a log-buffer server is required with both these policies. When a log-buffer server is introduced, precautions must be taken with respect to the WAL rules, since log-buffers are volatile (see section 4.4.4).

The depends-on relations between a recovery server, a log-buffer server, and a log server are illustrated in figure 5.2. The log-buffer server is assumed to have amnesia-crash semantics, i.e. the content of the log-buffer is lost after a node crash.

A log record produced by the recovery server is appended to the main memory log-buffer. When the log-buffer contains a log record volume of at least a block, these log records are appended to the log file so that their production order is preserved. The log-buffer is assumed to apply a double buffering policy to avoid delaying a transaction while a block is appended to the block file ([BHW74]). See for example [HL86] for an actual design.

5.3.5 Conforming to the Undo WAL Rule

The undo WAL rule requires that the undo log record part for a state changing DB operation must have been written to stable storage before the DB buffer block reflecting the corresponding operation is written to disc. To obey the undo WAL rule, at least the undo part of all log records up to and including the last DB state changing operation in the block's block global log sequence are written to disc before the block is written to disc (see section 4.4.1). This policy is called the **block undo rule** policy.

Since the block global log sequence for a block is a subset of the node global log sequence, a stricter but correct requirement would be to require all log records up to and including the last DB state changing log record in the node global log sequence to be written to disc before the block. Since the log identifiers identify and express the sequence in the node global log sequence, the undo rule is obeyed if all log records with a less or equal log record identifier to the log record of the last state changing DB operation executed to a block are written to disc before the block is written to disc. This policy is called the **global undo rule** policy. The following assumes that the global undo rule is obeyed. It will be shown that the consequences of the global undo rule policy compared to the block undo rule policy are negligible when a node global log is used.

The log record identifier of the last state changing DB operation executed to a buffer block replica is either included in the block replica, or connected to the block buffer replica to conform to the undo WAL rule ([BHG87]). Such a field is called a "*high water mark*" ([Gra78]) or *state-identifier* when it is included in every block replica since it expresses the block state with respect to executed logged operations to it.

To guarantee the global undo rule policy, the recovery server ensures that all log records with log record identifiers less than or equal to the state-identifier value of the block requested to be flushed are already written to the stable log or become forced to the stable log before the block is flushed. This leads to very simple management. The log-buffer server must only keep track of the largest log record identifier written to disc. To guarantee the block undo rule policy, the log-buffer server must test if any log record with a lesser log record identifier is contained in the log buffer. If so, the log buffer is flushed before the block is flushed.

The log records for a block are normally written to disc already when a block is requested to be flushed because a DB block will stay in the DB buffer longer than a log record will stay in the log buffer when all log records are written to a node global log. A log record stays in main memory no longer than it takes to fill a log block. A DB block normally stays in main memory until the DB buffer manager picks it to be flushed after having stayed in main memory a long time without being referred to. The undo rule does therefore not normally impose additional log disc accesses nor additional transaction response time. Since all log records go through one log buffer the block undo rule policy and the global undo rule policy behave similarly.

5.3.6 Conforming to the Redo WAL Rule

The redo WAL rule requires that all redo log record parts for a transaction log sequence are written to stable storage before the transaction commits. This requirement is obtained by appending the commit log record to the log buffer and then *forcing* the log-buffer to be appended to the stable log. Since all log records for the transaction precede the commit record, they have either already been appended to the stable log or are appended to the stable log by the force action.

If more than one log-buffer manager is used at a node, e.g. one per fragment replica, the forcing must be done to each of the log-buffers. The forcing can be done in parallel but requires one disc access per log-buffer needed to be forced.

5.3.7 The Group Commit Policy

An inherent bottleneck in the record based WAL protocol is the need to force the log-buffer when committing a transaction to ensure the redo rule. This introduces at least one log disc write per committed transaction. Since the log write operations involves the log disc, this represents a commit bottleneck, i.e. the transaction commit rate cannot exceed the block write capacity of the log disc.

In addition to representing a bottleneck to the transaction commit rate, the log write operation introduces a lower real-time bound on transaction response time. A transaction response time will always exceed the disc write access time.

The **group commit** policy avoids the commit disc write imposed transaction commit rate bottleneck by grouping together transactions to commit and force the log-buffer only once for the group. The time span in which a commit group is collected is a tuning parameter for the method ([GR88]). The smallest time span for collecting a commit group is a disc access, i.e. as soon as the disc has written a log block it is requested to write the next log block.

The group commit policy circumvents the commit rate bottleneck by adding to the transaction response time. The largest response time added to a transaction corresponds to the time span where a commit group is formed. Therefore the smallest worst case added response time is one disc access. This is acceptable as long as the response time is within the transaction service real-time requirement. If the response time requirement cannot be met by the grouping time, as it is with soft real-time transaction services, the group commit policy is not applicable.

Soft real-time transaction services require lower response time than is possible to provide by either the non-group commit or the group commit policy. To avoid the disc access imposed response time limit, discs must be substituted by fault-tolerant main memory logging. Main memory based logging policies are presented in Part III.

5.4 The State-Identifier Strategy

A **state-identifier** policy is adopted if a state-identifier is included in a data item, for example blocks or tuples, to precisely tell which operations have been executed to the data item. A state-identifier connected to a data item is also called its "high water mark" ([Gra78]). A **non-state-identifier** policy is adopted if state-identifiers are not included in data items.

5.4.1 The Block State-Identifier Policy

A **block state-identifier policy** is used if state-identifiers are connected to every block.

DB state changing operations are assumed to be executed in a strict sequence to a block. The log record identifiers reflect the execution sequence and are monotonously increasing. Therefore, during recovery it can be deduced from the value of a block state-identifier that every operation with a less or equal log record identifier value to the block state-identifier is reflected in the stable block replica. The state-identifier can therefore be used to reduce the redo work. No operation with a lesser or equal log identifier needs to be redone. By making redo follow the same sequence of operations as the do execution, a redo operation is executed to the same state of the data-item as the do operation. Block overflow during redo processing can then be avoided.

The block state-identifier can also be used to avoid undo work. If a resetting state-identifier policy is used (see section 5.6), operations are not to be undone if their log record identifiers are greater than the block state-identifier. The operation is then not reflected in the block.

A block is the largest data-item a state-identifier can be connected to since a block is the largest unit of atomic transfer between disc and main memory. Since connecting a state-identifier to a data-item requires some data volume, the block state-identifier policy requires least space. The block state-identifier policy can be combined with both a coarse and fine locking model (see chapter 6). The block state-identifier policy can also be combined with any checkpoint policy.

5.4.2 The Non-State-Identifier Policy

When a non-state-identifier policy is used it cannot necessarily be deduced from the data item itself which operations have been executed to it. To limit the recovery work, a non-state-identifier policy must be combined with other policies.

The non-state-identifier policy has been used by some DBMSs like IBM System R ([MHL$^+$89]) and TechRa version 2 ([HL86]). To limit the node crash recovery work, these systems have used other policies than the state-identifier policy. IBM System R used the action consistent checkpoint policy with the shadow policy to produce at each checkpoint a consistent image of the DB ([MHL$^+$89]). Redo recovery after a node crash could start from this version of the database. Since two replicas of the DB exist, this solution is disc volume expensive. The use of the action consistent policy to produce action consistent checkpoints may for large DBs represent a threat to transaction service availability (see section 4.7.2).

TechRa version 2 uses a DB buffer force policy so that only undo work is required to be done during a node crash recovery. The use of the force policy limits the transaction commit rate which may threaten the transaction service availability.

5.5 The Record Access Strategy

It is a basic requirement to provide consistent access to records both during transaction failure recovery and node crash recovery based on the *data item identifier* concept of the log record (see section 5.3.2). The access consistency requirement both contains consistent access to given records and preservation of the ordering of records within blocks. The main topics when evaluating record access policies are: their induced log volume; minimal logging of record relocation within blocks; and their restrictions on record relocations within a block during the lifetime of a transaction.

The data item identifier of a log record is split into two parts, the block identifier and the record identifier (see section 5.3.2). The access to a record during transaction rollback or node crash recovery is based on both of these parts. The block identifier provides direct access to the block requested during transaction and node crash recovery since block access is independent of index structures maintained by the table layer and media failure is not taken into consideration. Therefore consistent access to the block determined by the logged block identifier is guaranteed.

The record identifier part of a log record data item identifier identifies a record within a block. Even though only one transaction at a time may perform state changing DB operations to a block, transactions may perform several operations to one block over the lifetime of a transaction. That may cause record relocations within the block or a block split and thereby threaten record access based on the logged record identifier.

The record access strategy within a block is based on a combination of the following policies and the record identification policies presented in section A.6: the **logical logging policy**, the **structure preserving locking policy**, and the **relocation marker policy**.

The **logical logging policy** (LLP) ([GR88]) determines whether a record relocation operation is to be logged or not. The relocation of a record is assumed to be done by a write record operation. If

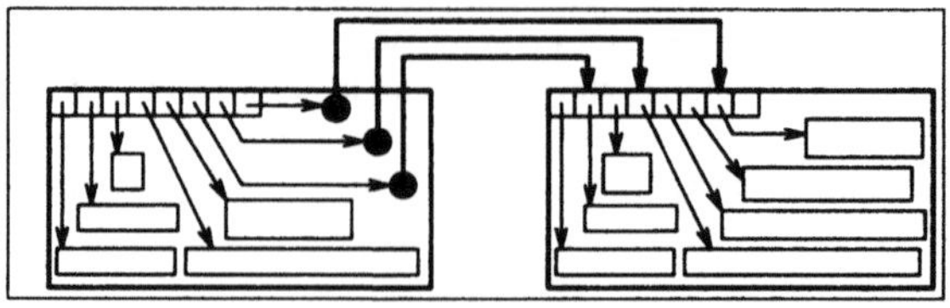

Figure 5.3: Use of the relocation marker policy is illustrated in combination with the record index based record identification policy. Each block contains a record index table containing pointers to the actual records in the block. A block has been split in two. Some records are moved to the new block. The move operations are logged by a delete record operation followed by an insert record operation to the new block. For each moved record, a pointer record (bullet) is left in the original block and is consistent with the original record identification.

no relocation operations are logged, the logical logging policy is used. If the logging of relocation operations is done according to the partial record logging policy (see section 5.3.3), the log record contains no specific part, i.e. a tiny log record is produced. If, on the other hand, complete logging of a write record is used, the produced log record is more than twice the size of the relocated record, which represents a significant log volume. Relocation operations may be logged either within the transaction requesting the relocation operation or in a subtransaction (see section 10.4). If the relocation operations are logged within the transaction, they are undone if the transaction aborts. If a record relocation operation is executed in a subtransaction, its effect survives if the subtransaction is committed, independently of the commit or abort termination of the transaction.

The **structure preserving locking policy** (SPL) determines if a record is fixed to a particular location in a block during the lifetime of a transaction to preserve consistent access to it in case of transaction failure recovery or node crash recovery. The use of structure preservation locking constrains record relocation and reduces the effect of compacting within a block. The use of SPL is therefore undesirable.

The **relocation marker policy** (RMP) determines if a pointer record is left at the original location of a record when the record is relocated. The policy may be used within a block and when records are moved between blocks (e.g. when splitting a block) (see figure 5.3). Since a pointer record is small compared to a record, the additional space requirement is negligible. Use of the marker policy introduces the need for rules determining when a record pointer becomes obsolete and can be removed as garbage.

5.5.1 The Record Address Policy

The record address record identification policy identifies a record by its physical address within a block (see section A.6). The combination of the record address policy with variable length records requires either the use of the LLP, the SPL, or the RMP policy to preserve consistent access to records in case of transaction rollback. This is because the record identifier is modified whenever the record is relocated. Given its disadvantages, the record address policy is not used by modern DBMSs.

5.5.2 The Record Index Policy

The *record index* record identification policy is independent of the actual physical location of a record within a block. Record relocation within a block does not modify the record identifier or the sequence of records within the block. Therefore neither the LLP, the SPL, nor the RMP policy are needed when relocating records within a block. The record index identification policy can be combined with logical logging within a block, i.e. record relocation is not logged within a block. This fulfills one of the stated goals for the strategy. Relocation restrictions on records within a block are also avoided which comply with the second strategy goal.

Consistent access preservation to record indexes during transaction lifetimes is maintained without use of the LLP, the SPL, or the RMP policy if the following record index method is used. The record index must maintain two structures, a unique index to each record and the ordering of the records within the block. The index value of a record can be kept unchanged over the lifetime of a record by avoiding relocating the index record. This can be accomplished by introducing a list among the index records which maintains the ordering of the records. Log records for insert and delete record operations must be modified to contain the updates to the index record list so that the original list can be recreated if the transaction aborts. An index record for a deleted record can be used by an inserted record before the transaction that deleted the record is committed since both operations belong to the same transaction and the insert operation will be undone before the delete operation. If tuple or any finer granularity locking is used instead of block locking, an SPL policy must be introduced to preserve stable access to the record indexes of deleted records to guarantee that they are not used by inserted records of any other transaction before the transaction that deleted it is terminated (see section 6.5.3).

Block splitting operations must be logged (see section 5.3.1). They can either be logged within the transaction that requests the block split, or be done by a subtransaction ([ML89], [HSAG90]). If operations related to the block splitting are logged within the transaction, they have to be undone with the transaction if it aborts.

The RMP policy must be used if record identification from outside the block is based on the similar data item identifier as the log records (see section 5.3.2). The RMP policy must therefore be used if for example secondary indexes refer to records based on these data item identifiers. The application of the RMP policy is illustrated in figure 5.3 where a pointer record is left for each moved record. If external references to records are based on tuple oriented data identifiers, e.g. primary key, the RMP policy is not required ([ML89], [HSAG90]). If the block splitting operation is logged by a subtransaction, the undoing of a block split operation as part of undoing the transaction requesting the split is avoided if the transaction aborts and the subtransaction commits.

5.6 The Transaction Failure Recovery Strategy

The transaction recovery strategy determines how a failed transaction is recovered by undoing its record state changing operations. The **resetting state policy** is followed, i.e. the internal DB state is reset to its state before the transaction was executed for every block operated on by DB state changing record operations. It is assumed that the block state-identifier policy is used, i.e. a block state identifier is connected to every block.

It will be shown that the resetting state policy can be used in combination with the coarse grained, traditional locking model (see section A.9), and block or record logging.

5.6.1 The Undo- and Redo- Record Oriented DB Operations

For each state changing record oriented DB operation the recovery server provides a do, an undo, and a redo entry-point ([Gra78]) (see section A.6). The do entry point is used during normal execution of the operation.

When an operation is undone, the undo version of the operation is activated with parameters from the undo part of the log record. Since the resetting state policy is used, the block state-identifier is reset as if the operation, that is undone, had not been executed at all.

When an operation is redone, the redo version of the operation is activated with parameters from the redo part of the log record.

5.6.2 The Undo Work Order Policy

The **work order** policy determines the sequence in which undo and redo operations are executed relative to the sequence of the corresponding do operations. The **forward** work order is adopted if the operations are executed in the same sequence as the corresponding do operations. The **reverse** work order is adopted if the operations are executed in reverse sequence of the corresponding do operations.

Undo operations must be executed in *reverse work order* to a block when the combination of traditional and coarse granularity locking, record logging, and block state-identifier policies is used. One transaction may execute more than one operation to a block. If the operations to a block are undone in the forward work order, an inconsistent DB state may result, as shown by the case below. The reverse work order preserves the consistency between the actual block state and the block state as indicated by the state-identifier. There are no requirement of work order synchronisation between undo operations that relate to different blocks.

The following case illustrates possible inconsistencies that can occur if undo operations are executed in a forward work order to a block in the given policy context. Two distinct records identified by record index 1 and 2 are stored in the same block. The two last operations to that block are write operations to record 1 followed by a write operation to record 2, both by the same transaction. After performing the write operations, the transaction aborts. If the write operations are undone in forward order, the write operation to record 1 is undone first, resetting the state-identifier of the block to the value it had before the operation was executed. That state-identifier value indicates that the other operation is also undone. The undo of the write to record 2 is not undone. The effect is an inconsistent DB state.

If block logging is used instead of record logging, the possibility of inconsistencies between block state and state-identifier caused by record logging is removed. If the block state is tested before an undo operation is executed, and it is only done if the state-identifier is larger or equal to the state-identifier value of the log record, the undo operations can be executed without work order synchronisation.

5.6.3 The Transaction Roll Back

The recovery server keeps a table in main memory that contains an entry for each active transaction with the log record identifier of the most recently produced log record by the transaction (see figure 5.4). Each log record contains the log record identifier of the previous log record produced by the transaction. This list represents the reverse transaction log sequence and is called **the transaction log chain**.

A transaction is recovered by following the list and activating the corresponding undo-entry point for each of the logged DB operations with parameters from the undo part of the log record. When all the undo operations are executed, an abort log record is produced that points to the last DB state changing log record of the transaction. Then an abort response is signaled to the DB service requester.

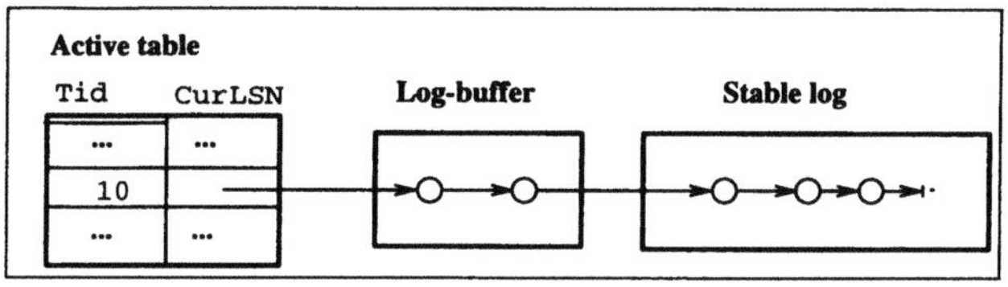

Figure 5.4: The active transaction table (Active table) contains one tuple per active transaction. Each tuple contains the unique transaction identifier (Tid) and the log record identifier of the most recent log record (CurLSN). The list of log records represents the reverse transaction log called the transaction log chain.

5.7 The Node Crash Recovery Strategy

The node crash recovery strategy is analysed with respect to the complexity of the recovery logic and the recovery work load. The recovery logic must produce a consistent DB at node restart. Fast recovery from a node crash is one of the stated recovery design goals in section 2.6 and is as such the most important criterion used to evaluate possible node crash recovery strategies.

5.7.1 The Node Crash Recovery Logic

The node crash recovery logic is composed of the following main components ([Gra78]), in which the content of each component is dependent on a collection of policies:

- **The log analysis work logic**
  The log analysis work determines the redo and the undo transaction sets. The term *analysis* for this work was introduced in [MHL+89].

- **Redo work logic**
  The redo work is composed of the redo log reading pass and execution of the redo DB record operations.

- **Undo work logic**
  The undo work is composed of the undo log reading pass and execution of the undo DB record operations.

When performing redo work the **log pass policy** determines the number of times the relevant log part is read. Restart methods may use a separate log pass for each logic component, i.e. three log passes. At least one of the log passes is a **scan**, i.e. access of the stable log block replicas. The other passes may be performed in main memory if the relevant part of the log is read into main memory as part of the scan, thereby reducing the disc accesses compared to scanning the log file during each pass. This aspect of reduced node crash recovery work is returned to in chapter 7. Here, on the other hand, each pass is assumed to involve block accesses.

The **sequentialisation policy** determines if the redo work is done before the undo work (**redo-undo**) or the undo work before the redo work (**undo-redo**). The sequentialisation of redo and undo work does not influence the correctness of the node crash recovery in the context of the record oriented approach because the traditional block locking policy allows at most one transaction requiring recovery to be active to a block at a node failure.

The **redo policy** determines if a **complete redo** or a **selective redo** is done. A complete redo *repeats history* so that all operations done before the failure are redone, also operations belonging to transactions in the undo set. Selective redo only redoes operations for transactions in the redo set.

5.7.2 The Redo and Undo Sets

To determine the redo and undo sets, the log file must be read. The reading may either start from the appropriate checkpoint and end with the last log record, or start with the last log record and end at the appropriate checkpoint. If the penultimate fuzzy checkpoint policy is adopted, the appropriate checkpoint is the second-last checkpoint. If the basic FCP policy is used, the appropriate starting point is the begin-checkpoint log record of the last checkpoint. If the ACC or TCC policy is adopted, it is the last checkpoint. If the TOC policy is adopted, it is the beginning of the log.

If the TCC or ACC checkpoint policy is used, the redo set contains all committed transactions since the last checkpoint, and the undo set contains all transactions aborted after the last checkpoint and the active transactions. The redo and undo set of the penultimate fuzzy checkpoint policy corresponds to the TCC and ACC policies with the penultimate checkpoint substituted for the last checkpoint. The redo and undo set of the basic FCP policy corresponds to the TCC and ACC policies with the begin-checkpoint log record of the last checkpoint substituted for the last checkpoint log record. If the TOC checkpoint policy is used, the redo set is empty, since all blocks written by a transaction is flushed before the transaction terminates. The undo set contains only the active transactions since the aborted transactions are also flushed before the abort log record is written. If the TOC or no checkpoint policy is used, the beginning of the log is used as the checkpoint.

5.7.3 The Redo Work Order Policy

The combination of state oriented record logging with the restricted record datamodel, traditional coarse locking, and block state-identifiers requires redo DB operations to be executed in forward order relative to each block. Since a transaction can execute multiple operations to a block, some operations can be forgotten to be redone if the reverse order is used.

The following case illustrates that DB inconsistencies may result if redo work is done in reverse order (see figure 5.5). Two distinct records identified by record index 1 and 2 are stored in the same block. The two last operations to that block are a write operation to record 1, followed by a write operation to record 2, contained in two distinct transactions that both committed before a node crash occurred. The effect is that none of these write operations were reflected in the stable block replica at the node crash. If the latter write operation is redone first, which would happen if the redo work is done in reverse order, the block state-identifier of the block would indicate that both operations was reflected in the block. The first of the operations would not be redone for this reason. The result is an inconsistent DB. The redo execution must be done in forward order.

It is verified in section 5.6.2 that the undo work at transaction recovery must be done in reverse order. Undo work at node crash recovery must therefore also be done in reverse order. Since the redo work must be done in forward order, at least two log passes are needed if both redo and undo recovery work are required (see figure 5.6).

The combination of state oriented *block* logging, traditional block locking, and block state-identifiers allow redo work to be processed in any work order. This is a result of the equal logging, locking, and state-identifier scopes. It is verified in section 5.6.2 that the undo work with this combination of policies can also be performed in any work order. Therefore the entire node crash recovery work can be combined into one log pass (see figure 5.6).

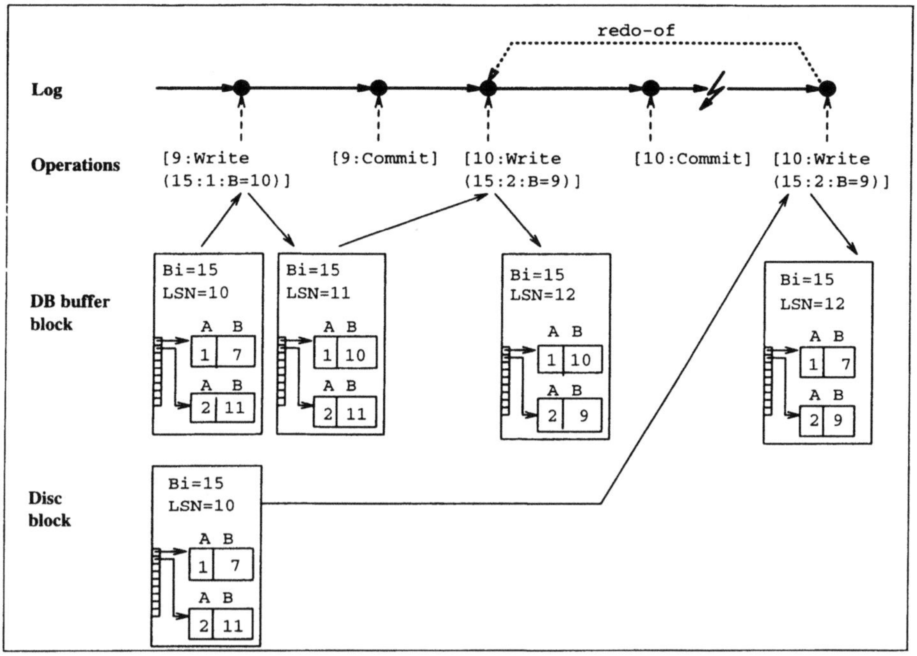

Figure 5.5: Case documentation of DB inconsistency during node crash recovery resulting from reverse redo work order used in combination with traditional block locking, state oriented record logging to the restricted record datamodel, and block state-identifiers. Two committed transactions with transaction identifiers 9 and 10 perform one write operation each to two different records in block 15. The stable disc replica of the block does not reflect the write operations at the node crash (lightning symbol).

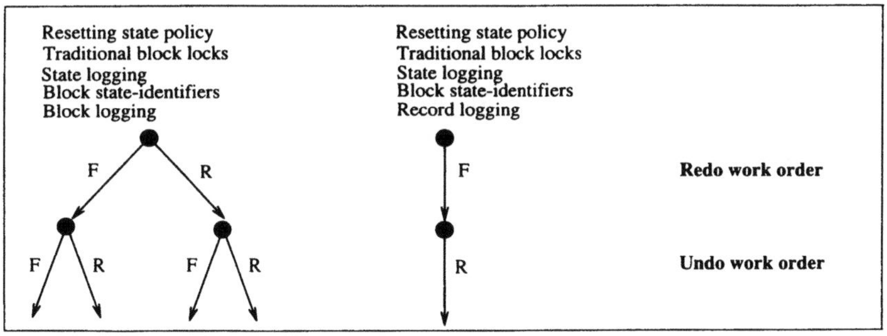

Figure 5.6: Illustration of the work order restrictions in combination with the block oriented and the record oriented recovery approaches. The block logging approach allows redo and undo work to be done in either forward (F) or reverse (R) order. The record oriented approach requires redo work to be done in forward- and undo work in reverse order.

5.7.4 The Node Crash Recovery Work Load Policies

The node crash recovery work is managed by the recovery server after receiving a *restart* request. The recovery work load is calculated from the involved disc I/O. The design goal is to minimise the node crash recovery disc work load:

- **Log scanning**
  Reading log blocks by scanning the part of the log involved in the restart.
- **DB block read**
  The minimalisation is both with respect to the total number of distinct blocks read and the number of rereads of the same block.
- **DB blocks written**
  The minimalisation is to restrict the overall number of written blocks, and to restrict the number of times the same block is written.

A node performing node crash recovery has almost all its resources available to be dedicated to the recovery task since no transaction load is active at the node. This is unlike when transaction recovery is performed, since the ordinary transaction load is done concurrently with the transaction recovery. When designing a node crash recovery strategy it should be taken into consideration that most CPU, main memory and disc I/O capacity is available for the recovery activities, and that dedicated recovery policies based on these facts should be evaluated.

The two main policies determining the involved recovery disc I/O are the **log scanning** policy and the **DB buffer recovery** policy. The log scanning policy determines the number of times the redo restricted part of the log is scanned. The recovery buffer policy determines if the standard log buffering and DB buffering policies are used during the node crash recovery or if a dedicated node crash recovery log buffering and a dedicated DB buffering policy are used.

The **single log scan** policy reads the required log blocks once from disc into main memory, and performs subsequent log passes in main memory. The **multiple log scan** policy reads the relevant log part from disc in every log pass. The single log scan policy requires enough main memory to contain the relevant log part during the node crash recovery. The single log scan policy produces less disc accesses than the multiple log scan policy when more than one log pass is required. It is assumed in the following that the multiple log scan policy is used.

The **standard DB buffer recovery** policy implies no changes of buffer policy during node crash recovery compared to normal operations. The **dedicated DB buffer recovery** policy uses a log buffer large enough to hold the part of the log involved in the node crash recovery so that the log is scanned only once, and it uses a dedicated DB buffer policy to avoid rereading and rewriting the blocks. It is assumed in the remainder of this chapter and in chapter 6 that the standard DB buffer policy is used. Recovery methods using the **dedicated** DB buffer policy are presented in chapter 7.

5.7.5 Node Crash Recovery Undo Work Load Reduction Policies

The dirty block table that can be included in fuzzy checkpoints (see section 4.7.4), can be used to reduce the DB block read work load during the undo node crash recovery work ([BHG87]).

The following rules can be used to avoid reading a DB block to analyse whether an operation needs to be undone. The rule requires that if the redo-undo sequentialisation policy is used, then this sequentialisation policy is combined with selective redo. If the complete redo is used, then the operations this rule determines can be avoided, have been redone during the redo work. To apply selective redo with the redo-undo sequentialisation policy without a preceding analysis pass, an active transaction table must be included in the checkpoints. The active transaction table can be located in either the begin- or the end-checkpoint log record if the basic FCP policy is used.

- **U1**
  A DB state changing log record does not need to be undone if the abort log record for the transaction is written between the two last checkpoints and if the dirty block table of the last checkpoint does not contain the block.
- **U2**
  A DB state changing log record does not need to be undone if the abort log record for the transaction is written between the two last checkpoints and the dirty block table of the last checkpoint indicates that the stable state value of the block is larger than the state identifier of the abort log record.

Since the abort record is located between the checkpoints, all undo operations for the transaction are done before the last checkpoint. Therefore the undo operations for state changing DB log record that are referred to, must have been executed before the last checkpoint. If the block the operated on record is located to, is not in the dirty table at the last checkpoint, as by rule U1, it must have been flushed. The stable DB therefore reflects the effect of the undo operation.

The well-formed, strict two-phased, traditional, coarse locking policy results in the fact that only one transaction can concurrently execute state changing DB operations to a block. Locks held by an aborting transaction are released after every undo operation is executed and the abort log record written. A state changing log record of another transaction to the same block as the state changing log record must have been executed after the abort operation (since the abort operation released the block lock). Consequently its log record is logged after the abort log record. If such an operation is reflected in the stable block replica, the undo operation is also reflected.

5.7.6 Node Crash Recovery Redo Work Load Reduction Policies

The dirty block table that can be included in fuzzy checkpoints (see section 4.7.4), can be used to reduce the DB block read work load during the redo node crash recovery work ([BHG87]).

The following rules prevent reading a DB block to analyse if an operation needs to be redone. The rules can be combined with both selective and complete redo, and with both the redo-undo and undo-redo sequentialisation policies.

- **R1**
  A DB state changing log record between the two last checkpoints does not need to be redone if the dirty block table of the last checkpoint does not contain the block.
- **R2**
  A DB state changing log record between the two last checkpoints does not need to be redone if the dirty block table of the last checkpoint does contain the block with a larger stable state-identifier value.

The DB state changing operation is executed after the penultimate and before the last checkpoint. If the block is not in the dirty table after the next checkpoint it must have been flushed in the meantime. The effect of this DB state changing operation is therefore reflected in the stable DB and does not need to be redone. If the block is dirty at the next checkpoint and the block state-identifier is larger, the block has been flushed and some new operation has been executed to it.

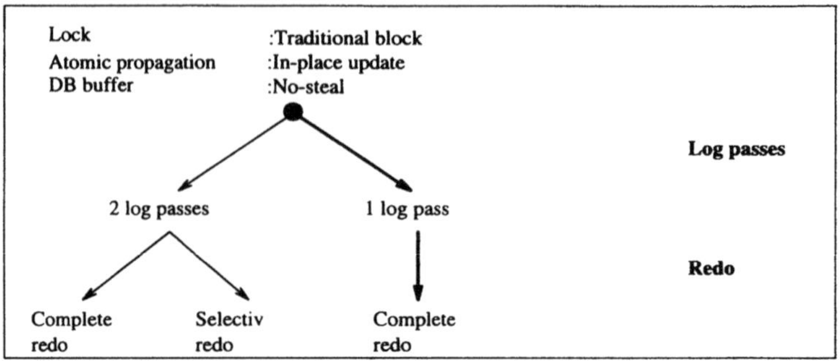

Figure 5.7: Node crash recovery methods combined with the no-steal DB buffer policy.

5.8 The Node Crash Recovery Methods

This section combines the node crash recovery strategy with the DB buffer strategy. The various resulting node crash recovery methods are presented and evaluated on the design goals presented in section 5.7.4.

5.8.1 Node Crash Recovery Methods Combined with the No-Steal DB Buffer Policy

The no-steal DB buffer policy eliminates undo recovery work, because no uncommitted values are written to disc. Therefore if the no-steal buffer policy is used, only redo work might be done during a node crash recovery. These recovery strategies require using the no-steal buffer policy also during the node crash recovery to provide idempotent recovery from node crashes, i.e. the effect of transactions that might be undone must be avoided introduced in the stable DB also during the recovery work. Figure 5.7 illustrates the classification of node crash recovery strategies with the no-steal buffer policy.

The log analysis and the redo work can be done in two separate passes. This alternative allows for either the selective or the complete redo policy. Since the selective redo policy involves less redo work because operations to be undone are never redone before being undone, this is the preferred of these two alternatives.

The log analysis pass and the redo work pass can be combined since the log analysis can be done in any work order. By combining these passes, the log file can be scanned once. This combination requires the complete redo policy since it is not known when performing the redo operations if the transaction belongs to the redo or the undo set.

If the multiple log scanning policy is used, the combination of one log pass with complete redo policies is preferred with respect to recovery work load compared to the two log pass alternatives, because of reduced number of disc accesses. The one log pass and complete redo policy combination is used by the IMS DBMS ([IBM86b], [Chr86], [Obe80], [PS83], [SUW82], [MHL+89]) in combination with fine granularity locking.

5.8.2 Node Crash Recovery Methods Combined with the Force DB Buffer Policy

The TOC policy, which is a consequence of the force DB buffer policy, eliminates the need for redo work, because the result of all terminated transactions is reflected in stable storage. Only

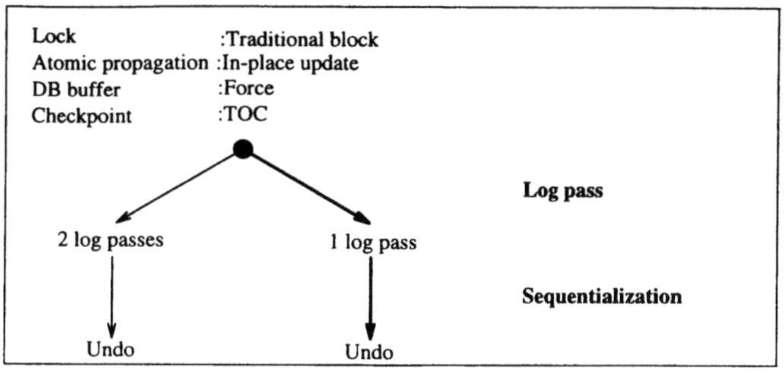

Figure 5.8: Node crash recovery methods combined with the force DB buffer policy.

undo work might be needed to recover from node crashes.

Log analysis and undo work can also be done in two separate passes. On the other hand, the log analysis and undo work can be combined in one log pass in reverse work order. If the multiple log scanning policy is used, the combination of log analysis and undo work in one pass is preferred, with respect to recovery work load, compared to the two log passes alternatives. The preferred alternative involves the less log file disc accesses. The preferred node crash recovery method is used both by the RA2 ([BJWK+76]) and the TechRa version 2 ([HL86]) DBMSs.

5.8.3 Node Crash Recovery Methods Combined with the Steal and No-Force DB Buffer Policy

The combination of the steal and no-force DB buffer policies may require both redo and undo work when recovering from a node crash since stable block replicas may reflect operations of aborted transactions and because operations of committed transactions may not be reflected in the stable block replicas. The classification of node crash recovery methods given the steal and no-force DB buffer policy is illustrated by figure 5.9.

When the node recovery needs both redo and undo work to be done, at least two log passes are required, since the redo work requires forward and the undo work reverse work order. The log analysis pass can either be done in a separate pass or be combined with the undo or the redo pass.

The redo and undo work may be performed in any sequence, i.e. redo-undo or undo-redo sequentialisation. This is possible because of the traditional block locking (see section 5.7.1).

If the undo-redo sequentialisation policy is used, the selective redo policy must be adopted. The transactions to be undone are already undone before the redo work is done. Redoing the transactions to be undone may produce an inconsistent DB state. Selective redo can be combined with redo-undo sequentialisation if a separate log analysis pass is done before the redo work. Complete redo can therefore only be combined with the redo-undo sequentialisation policy.

If the multiple log scanning policy is used, the two log pass policies are preferred rather than the three log passes policies, since fewer log block accesses are needed. The undo-redo policy is preferred to the redo-undo policy since the redo-undo policy is redoing the operations later to be undone which might cause blocks to be reread and rewritten. The combination of policies that produce the least node crash recovery work load is two log passes, undo-redo sequentialisation, combined with selective redo.

The node crash recovery method presented in [Gra78] uses the combination of three log passes,

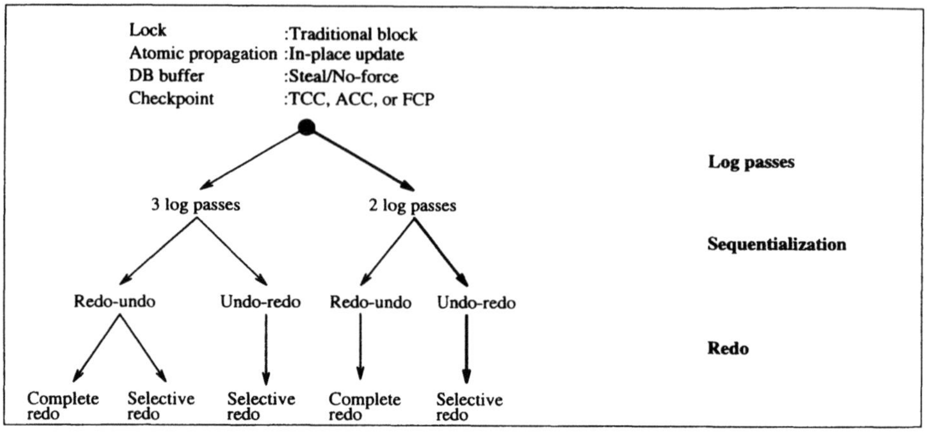

Figure 5.9: Node crash recovery methods combined with the steal/no-force DB buffer policy.

undo-redo sequentialisation, and selective redo policies. The node crash recovery method based on LSNs presented in [BHG87] uses the combination of two log passes, undo-redo sequentialisation, and selective redo.

5.9 Conclusion

The record oriented recovery approach satisfies a larger set of recovery design goals (see section 2.6) than the block oriented recovery approach (see chapter 4). The disc I/O overhead during normal operations due to logging is significantly reduced due to the reduced log volume compared to block logging.

The inherent commit processing bottleneck present in the block oriented approach is reduced by making commit operations share one disc access, in other words group commit. Node crash recovery based on the record oriented approach is faster than recovery based on the block oriented approach primarily since less disc I/O are done during the recovery, again as a function of the reduced log volume produced compared to block logging.

The two main disadvantages of the record oriented recovery approach are the coarse locking granularity imposed by block locking and the restrictions on record DB operations imposed by the restricted record datamodel. The coarse locking policy and the restricted set of record operations impose bottlenecks with respect to high transaction rates to hot-spot blocks. The record oriented recovery approach provides the foundation for the more elaborated compensation oriented recovery approach presented in chapter 6.

Exercises

1. Assume a record size of 100 bytes and a block size of 16 Kbytes. 60% of the record operations are read, 30% are write, 5% are insert, and 5% are delete. The size of the primary key is 10 bytes. What is the approximate log volume reduction compared to block logging when the steal/no-force policy is used?

2. What is the approximate log volume reduction in exercise 1 if the no-steal/no-force policy is used?

3. The write operations in exercise 1 update one field. The size of the field is 10 bytes. What is the log volume reduction of partial record logging compared to record logging when the steal/no-force policy is applied?

4. Assume a record can span multiple blocks. (a) What are the consequences during a node crash recovery of logging a multi-block record write operation as one operation? (b) What might a log record for a multi-block record write operation look like?

5. Why can logging of record operations on secondary index tables be avoided in combination with the TCC checkpointing policy based on the shadow-page policy?

6. Assume that record operations on index tables are logged as part of the log record produced by the record operations on primary tables. What might such a log record look like?

7. Make the same assumption as in exercise 6 and assume the same log record structure. How can block state-identifier based recovery be combined with no separate logging of record operations on secondary index tables, if the in-place block propagation policy is used?

8. What might a log record for partial record logging look like?

9. (a) What is the intention behind "high water marks" or state-identifiers? (b) What are the effects of block local state-identifiers as opposed to block global state-identifiers?

10. (a) Propose a scheme that allows block global state-identifiers to wrap around. (b) What are the consequences of such a scheme? (c) How can it be administrated?

11. (a) Why is the global undo rule policy assumed not to slow down transaction execution? (b) Why is the redo WAL rule expected to slow down transaction execution? (c) How can this slow down be avoided?

12. (a) How can the group commit policy be adapted to handle a higher log record production rate than the access rate of a single log disc? (b) Which consequences will multiple log discs combined with group commit have on transaction response time?

13. How does IBM System R obtain consistent redo recovery without the use of state-identifiers?

14. How does the TechRa DBMS obtain consistent redo recovery without the use of state-identifiers?

15. (a) Under which conditions is index position stability of a record not required? (b) Under which conditions must the sequence among records within a block be maintained?

16. Propose a method for the record index policy that maintains the index position of a record over its lifetime, and at the same time maintains the sequence among the records as records are inserted and deleted from the block.

17. (a) When can a pointer record be deleted? (b) Propose a method for splitting a block by use of the relocation marker policy (RMP) and subtransactions. (c) Propose compact logging of a block split subtransaction.

18. (a) What is the primary purpose of transaction log chains? (b) What would the effect of dropping transaction log chains be on checkpointing? (c) How would the active table be influenced by maintaining the oldest log record of each transaction?

19. (a) Can block logging based recovery be done by one log pass, with redo and undo work executed in reverse order? (b) Can forward order be used instead?

20. How is a subtransaction recovered compared to its parent transaction?

Answers

1. Block logging will produce log records of size two blocks plus a little overhead. This gives log records of approximately 32 Kbytes each. Record logging for write record operations gives log records that are twice the size of the record plus an overhead of about 20 bytes, depending on the chosen policy. This gives a log volume for a write record operation of about 220 bytes. The insert and delete record operations give log records the size of a record and the same overhead as the write log records, which gives approximately 120 bytes per log record.

2. The no-steal/no-force policies reduce the block log records by the size of one block copy. The resulting block log records are approximately 16 Kbytes. The log records from the write record operations when record logging is applied are approximately 120 bytes since one record copy is removed. The size of insert log records is unchanged when redoing the insert, i.e. they are approximately 120 bytes. A delete log record only needs the primary key to redo the delete operation. The size of delete log records is therefore the size of the primary key plus the overhead, i.e. approximately 30 bytes.

3. The partial log records produced by the write record operations contain the primary key, the before- and after-image of the updated field, and the log record overhead. The log record overhead is extended by at least a byte to indicate which fields are present in the partial log record. This gives a size of approximately 40 bytes. The size of insert and delete log records are unchanged.

4. (a) The write operation can be partially reflected during recovery from a node crash. The redo and undo of a multi-block write must be able to handle such situations. (b) The generic and specific parts of a multi-block write log record are as presented in section 5.3.2. The before- and after-images contain the part of the record contained in the first block. In addition, a sequence of block identifier, before-, and after-image triples follows, one per additionally involved block.

5. Recovery will then start from a transaction consistent version of the DB where it is known exactly which record operations are and which are not reflected. Do redo-undo recovery. A consistent dictionary can then be read during the redo recovery to obtain information of which secondary tables exists and their structure.

6. The generic and specific parts of the log record will remain the same. In addition, a set of specific log record parts will follow, one per index record operation. Each of these parts will contain a data item identifier to uniquely identify the index record within a block, and a field vector indicating which fields of the primary record is contained in the index record and the sequence of the fields.

7. The sequence of record operations to every index table block must be the same as the sequence of the corresponding primary table record operations. The following illustrates an inconsistency which may occur if this is not followed. The block state-identifiers of both primary and secondary index table blocks must reflect the log record identifiers of the log records produced by the operations to the primary index tables. If two record operations, R1 and R2, are executed in that sequence, the log record identifier of R1 is less than the log record identifier of R2. The corresponding secondary index record operations are I1 and I2. If I2 is executed before I1, the secondary index records operated on by these operations are stored in the same block, and a crash occurs after I2 is reflected on stable storage and before I1 is reflected on stable storage, then the block state-identifier will express that I1 is reflected on stable storage. I1 will not be redone during recovery and an inconsistency has occurred.

8. The specific part for write record operations contain a field vector indicating which of the fields are logged. The sequence of the logged fields is assumed to correspond with their sequence in the record.

9. (a) Its intention is to reflect the state of the object it is connected to with respect to logged operations executed to the object. (b) The stable block state field in the log records will contain the after-image of the block state-identifier. The before-image of the block state-identifier is not logged because it is the after-image value decremented by one. Before flushing a block the log buffer must be searched to determine if the log records with a smaller or equal log record identifiers for the particular block have been flushed to stable storage.

10. (a) Divide the value range of the log sequence numbers into three intervals A, B, and C. Let $i \in A$ and $j \in B$ with $i < j$. Let $j \in B$ and $k \in C$ with $j < k$. Let $k \in C$ and $i \in A$ with $k < i$. The scheme can be extended to handle any larger number of value intervals. (b) Modifications as follows: 1) Comparison of log sequence numbers given by the rule in a. 2) During generation of log sequence numbers, it must be verified that no blocks have a state-identifier value in the interval when they start being reused. (c) A low priority transaction is run periodically in background, reading every block to determine if a block has a state-identifier of the next value interval to be used. In that case a dummy state changing record operation is executed to the block. When the transaction commits, no blocks exist with a state-identifier in the next value interval. Further optimisations are left to the reader.

11. (a) A block normally stays longer in the DB buffer after the last record operation executed to it than the corresponding log record produced by that record operation stays in the log buffer before it is flushed. (b) The commit log record by a transaction is produced immediately before the transaction terminates. It therefore causes log block flush which causes the termination to wait for the flush to complete. (c) It can be obtained by logging to a stable medium with more favourable access times than discs, e.g. RAM with battery backup.

12. (a) Use multiple log discs and multiple log buffers. Write round robin to the buffers and flush log buffers round robin to the log discs. (b) The maximum delay is determined by the last log record produced because of the round robin policy. The maximum added wait time for the last log record is one disc access.

13. System R performs redo recovery from a transaction consistent DB state (see exercise 5). It thereby avoids the problem of determining which operations are and which are not reflected in the stable DB at node crash time. State-identifiers are, as a consequence, not needed. System R does a complete redo recovery followed by undo of all active and not in-doubt transactions at crash time.

14. Because of the force policy applied by TechRa, no redo recovery is needed.

15. (a) When a reference to a record external to the block in which it is contained is based on the record identifier. This would be, for example, from index tables and log records. (b) When the access method requires a sequence maintained, e.g. an index sequential access method.

16. The sequence can be maintained by an additional linked list between the index entries. The sequence can also be maintained by an additional tree structure instead of a linked list.

17. (a) A pointer record can be deleted when no references to the moved record should use its old record index. (b) Delete records from the original block, insert records in the new block, and insert pointer records in the original block in one subtransaction. (c) Produce one log record from the subtransaction containing a generic part where the transaction previous log record identifier can be omitted. The specific part contains the block identifiers of the two involved blocks, the smallest record identifier of the moved records, and all the moved records.

18. (a) Speed up transaction rollback as compared to following the node global log sequence in reverse order and testing every log record produced during the life time of the transaction during a transaction rollback. (b) If transaction log chains were not maintained, the active transaction table would not contain a CurLSN field (see figure 5.4). If the (begin-)checkpoint log records contained the active transaction table, they would as a consequence not contain references to the last log record produced by the active transaction before the checkpoint. (c) The log sequence number of the first log record produced by a transaction would be kept in the active transaction table instead of the CurLSN. It would therefore be included in the (begin-)checkpoint records and be used to restrict the necessary undo recovery work during a node crash recovery.

19. (a) Yes, see figure 5.6. (b) Yes, see figure 5.6.

20. A subtransaction is recovered independently of its parent transaction since it is a nested top-level transaction.

Chapter 6

The Compensation Oriented Approach

This chapter presents and classifies recovery methods that use **record logging** (section 5.3) and are related to the **complete record datamodel** (section A.6). Concurrency control is based on the **fine grained, semantically rich locking model** described in section A.9.

The compensation oriented approach provides the foundation for recovery methods adopted by modern DBMSs such as: IBM DB2 ([Dat84], [IBM89b], [IBM89a], [Cru84], [HJ84]), Tandem Non-Stop SQL ([Dim85]), VAX DBMS ([RS89]), and VAX Rdb/VMS ([JR89]) and by older DBMSs such as IMS ([IBM86c], [McG77], [Obe80], [PS83], [SUW82], [GK85a], [SR84]).

6.1 The Compensation Oriented DBMS Server Architecture

The layering of the compensation oriented DBMS server architecture (see figure 6.1) corresponds to the layering of the record oriented DBMS server architecture presented in section 5.1 (see also figure 5.1). The differences between these architectures stem from the use of the complete record datamodel, and the fine grained, semantically rich locking model by the compensation oriented DBMS server architecture compared to the restricted record datamodel and coarse grained, traditional locking model used by the record oriented DBMS server architecture.

The servers and the uses relations of the compensation oriented DBMS server architecture correspond to those of the record oriented architecture and are therefore not repeated here (see section 5.1). The concurrency control server serialises the record DB operations according to the fine grained, semantically rich locking model. A read record lock is set for each record that is read by a read record operation. A write record lock is used for each record operated on by a write, delete, or insert record operation. A delta lock is used for each record operated on by a delta record operation. Locking is assumed to be well-formed and strict two-phased (see section A.9).

To preserve block consistency over the duration of each single record operation, a particular scheduler is used which is included in the block server. This scheduler uses block **latches** that lock a block over the duration of a record operation ([ABC+76], [Wei91]). See also section 4.7 for use of latches when checkpointing.

The semantically rich locking model can also be combined with coarse grained locking. A separate DBMS server architecture based on this combination is not explicitly presented. In the following sections the combination of coarse grained, semantically rich locking is infrequently referred to. However, the IBM DB2 system uses coarse grained locking.

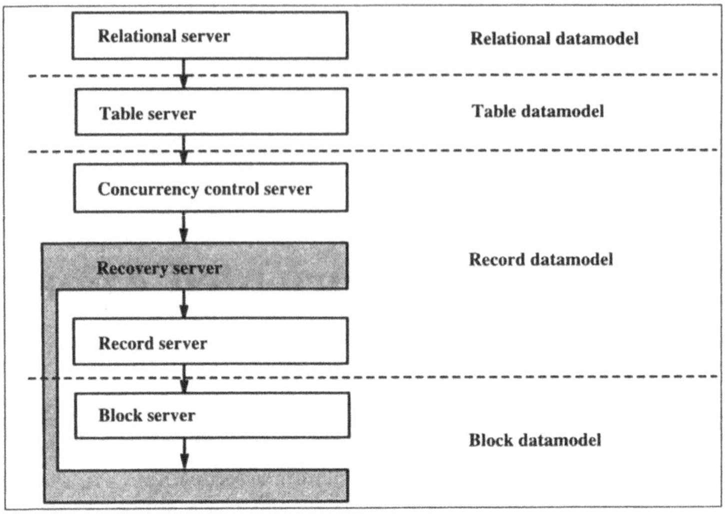

Figure 6.1: The compensation oriented DBMS server architecture. The layered architecture corresponds to the server architecture presented in figure 5.1. The architecture supports the complete record datamodel (see section A.6), and the fine grained, semantically rich locking model (see section A.9).

6.2 The Compensation Oriented Classification Scheme

This section presents the recovery classification scheme for compensation oriented centralised DBMSs. The classification scheme is based on a collection of recovery related DBMS strategies. The record logging-, the record access-, the transaction recovery-, and the node crash recovery strategies are adaptations of the similar strategies from the context of the record oriented approach (see chapter 5). The compensation recovery strategy is a particular result of the fine grained and semantically rich locking model.

- **The record logging strategy**
  The record logging strategy determines how log record production is performed during normal operations to fulfill the WAL rules. It also determines the log record structure, for example, complete versus partial record logging policy. The presented policies are supplementary to those presented in section 5.3. The use of block state-identifiers connected to every block is assumed. The semantically rich locking model requires state-transition based logging of delta record operations. The compensation strategy requires logging of undo operations by compensation log records (CLRs).

- **The compensation recovery strategy**
  The compensation recovery strategy recovers a DB state that is equivalent to, but not necessarily the same as, the consistent DB state. This is opposed to the resetting recovery policy where recovery produces a DB state that equals the consistent DB state. The resetting recovery strategy does not capture the requirements from fine grained or semantically rich locking models. The compensation logging policy determines the logging of undo operations during both transaction and node crash recovery processing, i.e. the log production and the CLR structuring policies. The compensation state policy determines how to preserve consistency between the different representations of a block state: the actual block state; the

block state-identifier; and the logged block state.

- **The record access strategy**
The record access strategy determines how consistent record access is obtained by undo record operations based on the record-identifiers contained in the log records. The record access policies to be presented are supplementary to those presented in section 5.5 and are based on the record datamodel. The transaction consistent and action consistent block split policies are presented.

- **The transaction failure recovery strategy**
A failed transaction is recovered according to the compensation recovery strategy. This yields a DB state at the record datamodel level that is equivalent to, but not necessarily identical to, the state that would have existed if the failed transaction had not been executed. At the relational datamodel level, the DB state that is produced is equal to the state which would have existed if the transaction had not been executed.

- **The node crash recovery strategy**
A node crash is recovered according to the compensation recovery strategy if the DB state at the record datamodel level is equivalent to the last committed DB state and the DB state at the relational level is equal to the last committed DB state. The work order and sequentialisation policies of redo and undo work in the context of the compensating strategy are determined. The selective redo policy determines how to avoid executing redo operations which later will be undone.

6.3 The Record Logging Strategy

The record logging strategy determines the log record production, the log record structuring, and the log buffering policies to fulfill the WAL rules. The policies presented in this section are supplementary to the policies presented in section 5.3. The emphasis is on logging of delta record operations in combination with the semantically rich locking model. See section 6.4 for compensation logging.

6.3.1 Delta Record Operation Logging

The semantically rich locking model requires *state transition logging* of delta record operations (see section 4.4.7). This is required because multiple concurrent transactions can perform delta record operations to the same data item when the semantically rich locking model is used. The requirement is independent of the locking granularity. If one of a set of concurrent transactions fail, and is rolled back by resetting a data item's value to the value it had prior to the delta record operation was executed, the effect of some other delta record operations by transactions already committed to the same data item can be lost.

The following case illustrates inconsistencies resulting from using state based logging of delta record operations. (See figure 6.2 for illustration.) Transaction T_{10} sets a delta lock and performs a delta record operation incrementing a field from 8 to 18. This is followed by transaction T_{12} performing a delta record operation to the same field increasing its value by 5. Transaction T_{12} then commits followed by an abort of transaction T_{10}. The delta operation performed by T_{10} is undone by resetting the value of the field to its before-image value 8 as before the delta record operation was executed according to state based logging. The resulting DB state is inconsistent. The total effect of the two transactions should have been to increase the field by 5 from 8 to 13. The effect of the committed transaction T_{12} is lost.

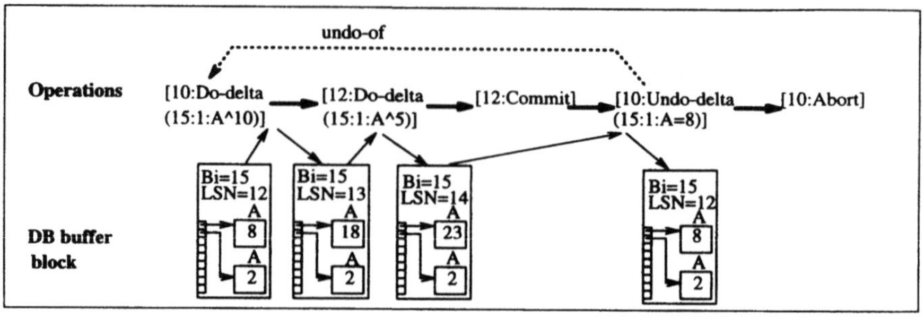

Figure 6.2: Case which illustrates inconsistent undo of delta record operation when using state based logging of delta record operations.

If, on the other hand, the undo delta record operation by transaction T_{10} compensated for the state transition done by its original delta record operation by decrementing the field by 10, a consistent state would have been the result.

The previous case shows that delta operations, in combination with the semantically rich locking model, have to use state transition logging. If the fine grained record locking had been replaced with coarse grained block locking, the same inconsistency would have occurred. This illustrates that the requirement of using state transition logging in combination with the semantically rich locking model is independent of the locking granularity. The consequences of using state transition logging in combination with the compensation logging- and compensation state policies are analysed in section 6.4.

6.3.2 The Delta Log Record

A log record for a delta record operation contains the following specific part in addition to the generic part (see section 5.3.2):

- **Data item identifier**
  The data item identifier that identifies a record uniquely within a block (see section 5.3.2).
- **Stable block state**
  If a node global block state policy is used, the field contains the previous block state-identifier value of the block.
- **Delta image**
  The delta-image of the record operated on by the logged delta operation.

The delta-image is based on either complete- or partial record logging (see section 5.3.3). If complete logging is used, policies for expressing a null delta value are required, i.e. a value indicating that the field is not involved in the delta operation. See [IBM89b] for documentation of such a policy.

6.4 The Compensation Recovery Strategy

The compensation recovery strategy is used to recover from both failed transactions and node crashes. It recovers a consistent DB state at the relational datamodel level (see figure 6.1), while at internal DBMS levels it recovers a DB state that is equivalent to but not necessarily the same as the consistent DB state ([Lyn83]). This is as opposed to the resetting recovery strategy where the DB state after a transaction or node crash recovery is required to equal the consistent DB state. It will be shown that the compensation recovery strategy is able to cope with a larger set of recovery approaches than the resetting recovery strategy. The resetting recovery strategy does not capture the requirements from fine grained and semantically rich locking models. Since the recovery server is located at the record datamodel level, the recovery processing is done to the record datamodel.

The following case illustrates the resetting recovery policy applied to a transaction recovery. A transaction that has performed a successful block split aborts without undoing the block split executed by a subtransaction. If the block split had been undone, a DB state identical to the original state would have been established. The DB state at the record level is, after the recovery, equivalent to that state because the table datamodel DB state is independent of which block a tuple is contained in as long as it is contained in one and only one block. The DB state at the relational level therefore equals the consistently recovered DB state while the state at the record datamodel level is equivalent to the consistently recovered state.

The compensation recovery strategy is composed of the compensation log structure policies, the compensation log record production policies, and the compensation state policies. The compensation log structure and log record production policies are also termed the compensation logging policies when referred to collectively. The **compensation log structure** policies determine the structure of the compensation log records and the relationships between the compensation log records and the non-compensation log records. The **compensation log production** policies determine how compensation log records are produced during transaction failure recovery, node crash recovery, and multiple node crash recoveries. The **compensation state** policy determines how the block state-identifier value is updated to maintain consistency between the block state, its block state-identifier, and the block state as expressed in the log.

The following sections illustrate that the compensation recovery policy is required in combination with record logging, block state-identifiers, and a fine grained, semantically rich locking model. The presented analysis is primarily based on the extensive case analysis presented in [Hva90] but is also influenced by the analysis presented in [MHL$^+$89] and [MP90].

6.4.1 The Compensation Log Record Structure Policies

A **compensation log record (CLR)** represents an undo state changing DB operation compensating for a previously executed do or undo state changing DB operation, e.g. a CLR may represent an undo-write record operation compensating for a previously executed write record operation. By logging undo operations, the log expresses explicitly which undo operations have been executed and their execution sequence relative to each other and to non-undo log records. A log record representing the do version of a DB state changing operation is termed a non-CLR in the context of the compensation recovery strategy.

The combination of the following policies determines the CLR structure. The **redo CLR** policy is followed if the CLRs contain a redo part, otherwise the **no-redo CLR** policy is followed. The redo CLR part is required to redo an undo operation during a potential node crash recovery. An **undo CLR** policy is followed if CLRs contain an undo part, otherwise a **no-undo CLR** policy is followed. The undo CLR part is required to undo an undo operation which are potentially required by some compensation log production policies to handle multiple node crashes (see section 6.4.5).

A **log-backchain CLR** policy is followed if the CLRs indicate which log record they are compensating for, otherwise a **no-log-backchain CLR** policy is followed. The log-backchain is used to explicitly state the log records that are compensated for and those that have to be compensated for during the node crash recovery processing. It also determines where to find the potentially

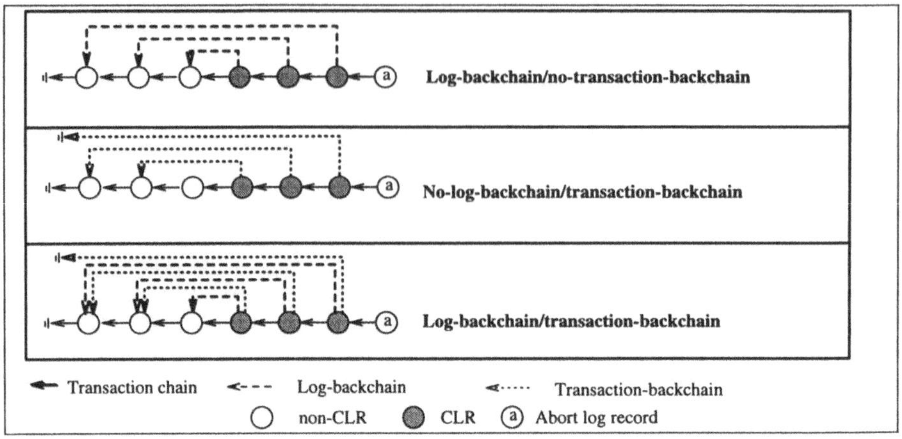

Figure 6.3: The log-backchain and transaction-backchain CLR policy combinations are illustrated by a failed transaction that is rolled back according to the compensation recovery strategy.

necessary redo and undo information.

The **counting CLR** policy is applied if the relation between a CLR and the log record it is compensating for is maintained only during node crash recovery processing, otherwise a **no-counting CLR** policy is applied. The counting CLR policy is an alternative to the log-backchain CLR policy. If CLRs are produced in reverse order within each transaction sequence to the log records they are compensating for, it can, during node crash recovery processing, be determined which log record each particular CLR is compensating for.

A **transaction-backchain CLR** policy is adopted if each CLR indicates the next log record to be undone in the transaction log sequence, otherwise a **no-transaction-backchain** policy is adopted. The transaction-backchain policy can be used during node crash recovery to skip reading the log records within the transaction log sequence that are already compensated for and their corresponding CLRs. It is assumed that a backchain pointer is implemented by use of log record identifiers.

A CLR is independent of the log record it is compensating for if the no-log-backchain and no-counting CLR policies are adopted. As a consequence, each CLRs must itself contain all information required to possibly redo and undo a compensation operation. The log-backchain and counting CLR policies can be combined with any of the redo and undo CLR policies, since the redo and undo parts required to redo or undo the undo operation can be interpreted from the log record which the CLR is compensating for. The no-redo/no-undo/counting/no-transaction-backchain/no-log-backchain CLR policy combination produces the smallest CLR log volume since each CLR only contains the generic log record fields. It will be shown in section 6.5 that this policy combination introduces requirements for record identification stabilisation since undo operations relies on the record identification of the log record to be compensated. This policy combination also introduces additional log garbage requirements since a log record cannot be deleted before it is certain that it will not be required by any CLR.

At least one of the counting, log-backchain or transaction-backchain policies are required to be used to determine which log records belonging to a transaction that are already compensated for at the occurrence of a node crash. The single CLR policy (see section 6.4.5) is therefore required to be combined with at least one of these policies. Figure 6.3 illustrates the different combinations of the log- and transaction-backchain policies. The no-log-backchain/transaction-backchain combination is used by the ARIES recovery method ([MHL+89]). The log-backchain/transaction-backchain combination is used by the ARIES-RRH recovery method ([MP90]).

The following describes the fields contained in the specific part of a write CLR if the redo/undo/log-backchain/transaction-backchain CLR policy combination is applied. See the paragraphs above to determine which fields are left out by other CLR policy combinations.

- **Data item identifier**
  The data item identifier of the record operated on by the compensation operation producing the CLR. The data item identifier identifies a record uniquely within a block (see section 5.3.2).
- **Log-backchain**
  The log record identifier of the log record compensated by the CLR.
- **Transaction-backchain**
  The log record identifier of the previous log record in the transaction log sequence to the log record compensated by the CLR.
- **Before-image**
  If the CLR compensates for a write or delete record operation this field contains the before-image of the record relative to the undo operation. If the CLR compensates for a delta record operation the field contains the delta-image relative to the undo operation.
- **After-image**
  If the CLR compensates for a write or a insert record operation this field contains the after-image of the record relative to the undo operation.

The before-image block state-identifier value is not logged when the global block state-identifier policy is used. This is a consequence of the compensation state policy. The block will never be reset to this previous state in case of a roll back.

6.4.2 The Compensation State Policy Combined with The Semantically Rich Locking Model

This section focuses on how to preserve consistency between the actual block state and the block state as indicated by the block state-identifier in the context of the semantically rich locking model. The block state-identifier value is determined by either the *resetting state* policy (see section 5.6), or the *compensating state* policy. The presented analysis shows that the semantically rich locking model requires the compensation state policy used.

The following case illustrates that the resetting state policy can cause inconsistencies when combined with delta operations and the semantically rich locking model. The case is similar to that of section 6.3.1 which was illustrated by figure 6.2. Transaction T_{10} sets a delta lock and performs a delta record operation which increases the block state-identifier value of the involved block from 12 to 13. This is followed by transaction T_{12}, which also performs a delta record operation to the same record, increasing the state-identifier value to 14. Transaction T_{12} then commits followed by an abort of transaction T_{10}. The delta operation performed by T_{10} is undone by resetting the before-image of the operation and the state-identifier value is reset to its original value 12 according to the resetting state policy. The consequence is an inconsistency because the effect of the committed transaction T_{12} is lost. If another transaction T_{13} reads this record it will not get the last committed value to this record, which is an inconsistent result.

If the compensation policy had been applied to the undo operation by T_{10}, i.e. if an undo-delta operation had been performed, and the resetting policy had been restricted to the block state-identifier value, i.e. if the block state-identifier was reset to 12, then an inconsistency between the actual block state and the block state as indicated by the block state-identifier had occurred. The block state-identifier would not have reflected that the delta operation by T_{12} was reflected in the block. Assume that the block is written to disc and followed by an immediate node crash. A node crash recovery of the node is performed. Since the state-identifier does not indicate that delta operation by T_{12} is reflected in the block, it is redone. The result is an inconsistent DB. This DB inconsistency is a result of the inconsistency between the actual block state and the state indicated by its state-identifier.

If the compensation state policy had been used for both the delta operation and the block state-identifier instead of the resetting state policy, the undo operation of transaction T_{10} would have increased the state-identifier value to 15. As a consequence, the actual block state and the state indicated by the state-identifier would have coincided and the node crash recovery would have produced a consistent DB. The inconsistencies documented would not have been removed by moving the state-identifiers from blocks to records. If the resetting policy was applied to both the delta operation and the record state-identifier the same inconsistency as documented would be the result. If the compensation policy was applied to the delta operation and the resetting policy to the record state-identifier the actual record state and the record state as expressed by the record state-identifier would be inconsistent after undoing the delta operation by transaction T_{10}.

The previous case shows that the resetting state policy can never be combined with the semantically rich locking model because the semantically rich locking model allows multiple concurrent transactions to perform state changing DB operations to the same locked data-item. The resetting state policy is able to handle consistently state changing DB operations from only one concurrent transaction to each locked data-item.

6.4.3 The Compensation State Policy Combined with The Fine Grained Locking Model

This section focuses on how to preserve consistency between the actual block state and the block state as indicated by the block state-identifier in combination with the fine grained locking model. The use of fine grained locking lets multiple concurrent transactions perform state changing DB operations to different records within the same block. If the resetting state policy is used, abort of a transaction can produce inconsistency between the block state and the state-identifier indicated block state. The analysis will document that the compensation state policy is required.

The following case illustrates that the resetting policy can cause inconsistent DB states when combined with block connected state-identifiers and fine grained locking. The case is illustrated by figure 6.4. Transaction T_{10} writes a record and the block state-identifier is increased from 12 to 13. Transaction T_{12} writes another record in the same block which increases the state-identifier to 14. Transaction T_{10} then aborts. Its write operation is undone, and the state-identifier is reset to 12 as before the undone write operation was executed according to the resetting state policy. This introduces an inconsistency between the actual block state and the state as indicated by the state-identifier since the write operation by transaction T_{12} is reflected in the block but not by the state-identifier. The block is written to disc. A node crash occurs. Since the write operation by transaction T_{12} is not reflected by the state-identifier it is not undone, leaving an inconsistent DB state.

The inconsistency would not have occurred if the compensation state policy had been used instead of the resetting state policy. The undo operation of transaction T_{10} would have increased the state-identifier value from 14 to 15. The node crash recovery would have undone the write by transaction T_{12} since the state-identifier would have indicated that the write operation was reflected

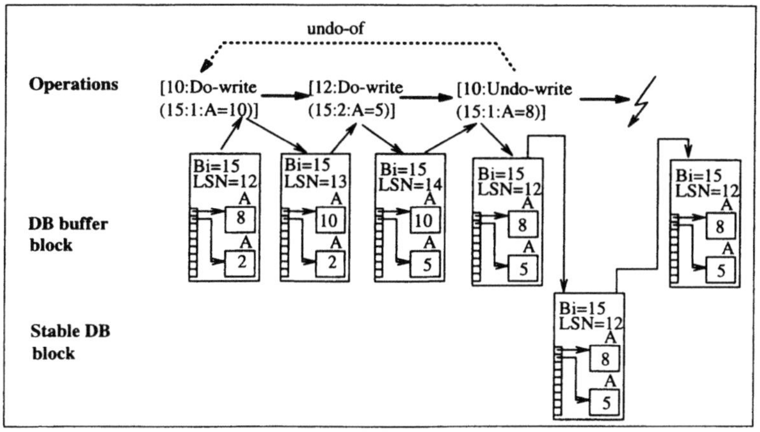

Figure 6.4: Case which illustrates an inconsistent DB state resulting from the combination of block state-identifiers, with the resetting state policy and the traditional fine granularity locking model.

in the stable block. If the state-identifiers were connected to records instead of to blocks, the inconsistencies documented above would not have occurred since only one transaction would concurrently be active to a record.

The previous case shows that the resetting state policy cannot be applied in combination with the traditional locking model when the locked data-items are of finer granularity than the data-items the state-identifiers are connected to. In the previous case, records are the locked data-items and blocks are the data-items state-identifiers are connected to. A record is always contained in a block so the locking granularity is finer than the state-identifier granularity. The resetting state policy can be applied when state-identifiers are connected to blocks and the traditional locking model is applied to blocks or more coarse data-items such as files, tables or fragment replicas because the locked granules are equal to or more coarse than the granules the state-identifiers are connected to. The resetting state policy can also be used if state-identifiers are connected to tuples and the traditional locking model is applied to tuples since the state identifier covered data-items equals the locked data-items. The compensation state policy on the other hand can be applied in all these combinations.

6.4.4 The Compensation State Policy Combined with the Compensating Logging Policy

This section focuses on how to preserve consistency between the block state as expressed by the block state-identifier and the block state as expressed by the log. It is assumed that the compensation state policy is used (see section 6.4.3). The analysis shows that the compensation logging policy must also be used when the state compensation policy is used, otherwise inconsistent DB states can occur.

The following case illustrates that inconsistencies can occur if the compensation state policy is used without logging undo operations, i.e. by applying the no-compensation logging policy. The case is illustrated by figure 6.5. Transaction T_{10} performs a delta record operation. Transaction T_{12} then performs a delta record operation to the same block. Transaction T_{12} aborts, and a compensating undo-delta operation is executed. The undo-delta operation increases the state-identifier value according to the compensation state policy so that the state-identifier expresses that the undo

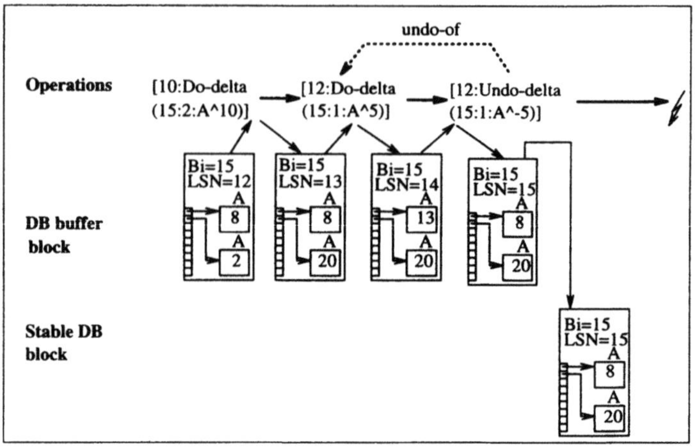

Figure 6.5: Case which illustrates an inconsistent DB resulting from combining the compensation state policy with a non-compensation logging policy.

operation has been executed. The undo-delta operation is not logged since the no-compensation logging policy is applied. The block is flushed to disc. A node crash occurs after the block is flushed. An inconsistency exists between the stable block state as expressed by its state-identifier and the log. One of the active transactions has executed an undo operation. The log does not reveal which one of the transactions the undo operation belongs to since it is not logged and both transactions were active when the node crash occurred. The node crash recovery is not able to distinguish which one of the two delta operations has been undone from the log, and is therefore not able to guarantee producing a consistent DB state.

If the compensation logging policy had been used, the confusion would have been avoided. The CLR would have stated precisely which undo operation was reflected in the stable block.

The previous case shows that the compensation state policy requires the use of the compensation logging policy. The compensation logging and the compensation state policies must be combined.

6.4.5 The Compensation Log Production Policy

This section analyses the compensation log production policies to be used during both transaction recovery and node crash recovery. It is assumed that the compensation logging policy is combined with the compensation state policy to preserve consistency between block state-identifiers and the log (see section 6.4.4). A node crash that occurs during node crash recovery processing is termed a **multiple node crash**.

The compensation log production policy, during transaction recovery, produces one CLR per undo operation executed (see section 6.4.1). The logging is assumed to obey the WAL rules. An undo operation compensates for one and only one do operation. The number of CLRs produced during transaction recovery therefore equals the number of non-CLRs they compensate for. Figure 6.6 illustrates the production of CLRs during transaction recovery.

The following three node crash compensation log production policies are evaluated: the **single CLR** policy; the **repeating CLR** policy; and the **recursive CLR** policy. The following analysis includes only transactions that are in the active state when a node crash occurs. Figure 6.6 illustrates

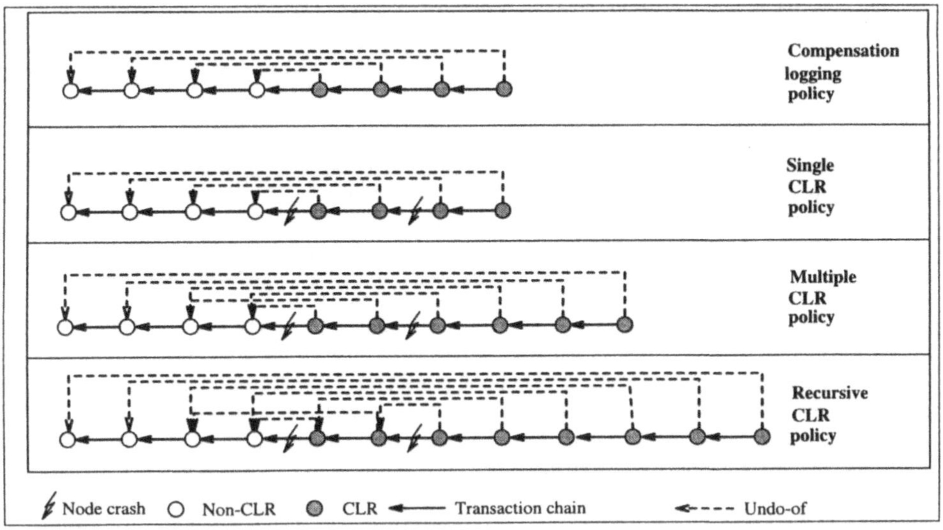

Figure 6.6: Case which illustrates transaction failure recovery and multiple node crash recovery by the single-, repeating-, and recursive CLR policies.

each of the compensation log policies.

The **single CLR** policy produces one CLR per non-CLR independently of a node crash during a transaction or node crash recovery. Compensating undo operations are never undone but may be redone. The no-undo CLR policy is therefore always adopted because the undo part of CLRs is only needed when an undo operation needs to be undone. The number of CLRs produced during a node crash recovery is limited to the number of non-CLRs of the transaction to be compensated. This is the smaller number of CLRs to be produced when applying the compensation logging and compensation state policies.

The single CLR policy requires that, after a node crash, it can be determined exactly which log records the existing CLRs are compensating for, and which are still to be compensated for, to avoid multiple CLRs and missing CLRs. This information can be obtained through the log-backchain CLR policy, the transaction-backchain CLR policy, or the counting CLR policy (see section 5.6.3). The log-backchain CLR policy provides the information since each log-backchain pointer determines which log record a CLR is compensating for. From this, the set of missing CLRs can be determined. The information is provided by the transaction-backchain CLR policy because a transaction-backchain implies that all the non-CLRs it spans are compensated (see figure 6.3). The counting CLR policy provides the information since both non-CLR and CLRs for a transaction are linked into the transaction log chain and CLRs are produced in reverse order to the log records they are compensating for. By following the transaction log chain it can be determined which non-CLR each CLR is compensating for and which CLRs are missing.

The **repeating CLR** policy produces a CLR for every non-CLR irrespective of any CLRs produced before the node crash. A non-CLR can be compensated for by more than one CLR if multiple node crashes occur. A consequence of this is that the repeating CLR policy requires undo operations of every state changing DB operation to be *idempotent* because an undo operation compensating for a state changing DB operation can be repeatedly executed even though the effect of the undo operation is contained in the stable block. Undo-delta operations are not idempotent. The repeating CLR policy can therefore not be combined with the semantically rich locking model. Since undo operations are never undone, the no-undo CLR policy can always be applied. The repeating CLR policy is used by the IMS DBMS ([SUW82]).

The **recursive CLR** policy undoes all log records, i.e. both non-CLRs and CLRs, during a node crash recovery. An undo operation executed before the node crash will first be undone. This produces a state equivalent to when the do operation was executed. The do operation is then undone which produces a state that is equivalent to the recovery consistent state. The number of log records related to an original state changing DB operation will be doubled for each node crash in case of multiple node crashes. This is illustrated in figure 6.6. The recursive CLR policy requires that the do and undo versions of the state changing DB operations are *complementary*. This requirement works in the combination with the semantically rich locking model.

The transaction log chain is used during the undo processing since all log records belonging to the transaction are undone. The recursive CLR policy will usually be combined with the no-log-backchain/no-transaction-backchain/no-counting CLR policy combination since these policies provide no additional information to what the transaction log chain already provides. The redo/undo CLR policy combination must be used in this case since an undo operation can have to be both redone and undone. Compared to the single CLR policy, the recursive CLR policy produces more CLRs in the case of multiple node crashes. The number of log records can grow exponentially ([MHL+89]) in case of frequent multiple node crashes because of the doubling effect described above. The risk of outgrowing the available log space during the critical phase of a node crash recovery is therefore higher than when the single CLR policy is used.

6.5 The Record Access Strategy

The requirements of record access stability based on the record identification concept contained in log records correspond to those presented in section 5.5, i.e. the preservation of consistent record access and the preservation of the record sequence within a block in case of transaction or node failure.

6.5.1 The Semantically Rich Locking Model

The combination of the *semantically rich* locking model, instead of the traditional locking model, with coarse granularity locking represents no alterations to the analysis presented in section 5.5. Delta record operations require the same record access stability as for example write record operations. No particular analysis is therefore presented.

6.5.2 The Record Address Policy

The *record address* record identification policy is not included in this analysis because of the disadvantages documented in section 5.5.1. Also in the context of fine granularity locking, the combination of the record address policy with variable length records require the LLP, SPL, or RMP policies (see section 6.5) to preserve consistent record access.

6.5.3 The Record Index Policy

The analysis presented in this section is based on the record index policy documented in section 5.5.2. The fine granularity locking model requires unconditional use of the SPL policy, unlike when the coarse grained locking model is used.

The SPL policy is needed to preserve the record identifier of a deleted record so that the identifier is not reused by a concurrent transaction inserting a record. If the transaction deleting the record aborts, it will require the same record identifier in the undo operation. The SPL policy locks the record index of a deleted record over the lifetime of the transaction that deleted it.

The following case illustrates a possible inconsistency resulting from allowing an inserted record to take the record index of a record deleted by a non-terminated transaction. Transaction T_{10} deletes a record in block 109 with record index value 12. Transaction T_{21} then inserts a record into the same block. This is allowed in the context of the fine granularity locking model. The inserted record is assigned the record index value of the deleted record, i.e. record index value 12. Transaction T_{10} then fails and an undo-delete operation must be executed to recreate the deleted record. The undo-delete operation must create a record with the record index value of the original record since the record index is the only information the recovery server has available to preserve unique record identification and record sequencing within a block. An inconsistency has occurred because the record identifier is taken by another record.

If the SPL policy had been used, the index value of the deleted record would have been locked so that the inserted record would have been allocated another index value and the inconsistency would have been avoided. The previous case shows the unconditional requirement of the SPL policy in the context of the fine grained locking policy.

6.5.4 Block Split and Merge

A block split can affect multiple concurrent transactions in combination with fine granularity locking. Transactions that are concurrent with the transaction that requests a block split may have performed state changing DB operations to the records that were moved to another block by the block split. If some of these transactions abort, consistent record access to the moved records must be preserved based on the record identifier of the log records.

A block split can be done **transaction consistent** or **action consistent**. The transaction consistent block split policy requires the transaction requesting the block split to obtain a block write lock before splitting the block. The transaction keeps the block write lock over its lifetime to prevent other transactions from seeing the block split before it is committed, otherwise non-serialisable situations could occur.

The transaction consistent block split policy preserves the disadvantages of the coarse locking model when performing block splitting. Thus the advantage of fine granularity locking of record operations are reduced. Several transactions may have to wait because the transaction requesting a block split is waiting to obtain an exclusive block write lock on the block to be split and because the transaction performing the block split keeps the block locked for the rest of its lifetime. This may threaten the availability of soft real-time transaction services because of performance failures caused by prolonged transaction response times. This is especially the case when hot-spot blocks are split.

The consequence to record access consistency of the transaction consistent block split policy is that the SPL policy must be used to preserve the record indexes of deleted records over the lifetime of the transactions that deleted the records (see section 6.5.3). If the transaction that deleted the tuple aborts, the index is required again by the deleted record.

Problems occurring during transaction failure recovery that stem from not enough free space in a block to undo deleted records must be avoided. If a transaction that deleted a record from a block aborts, and enough records have been inserted by committed transactions in the meantime, so that there is not enough free space within the block for reinserting the deleted record, such a problem has occurred. This can be avoided by a **block space lock (BSL)** policy that guarantees that a block always keeps enough free space for deleted records of active transactions. Block splits during a transaction abort cannot be allowed because this could lead to deadlocks. If two transactions had deleted tuples from the same block and both decide to abort and there is not enough space to reinsert these tuples, the first will request a write lock for the block. It will never get that lock because of the other aborting transaction. A deadlock has occurred which can not be solved by aborting some of the involved transactions because the deadlock occurs among rollback processing transactions.

The *action consistent* block split policy write locks the block being split only during the splitting to obtain an action consistent image of the block as it was when the splitting took place. This locking policy guarantees a short duration write lock to a split block. The action consistent block split policy therefore avoids the disadvantages of the transaction consistent block split policy. The action consistent block split policy requires the SPL to be used for the same reason as the transaction consistent block split policy.

The RMP policy must be used to compensate for the possible inconsistent accesses to the moved records by transactions that performed state changing DB operations to moved records before the split, then aborted, and performed undo operations to moved records after the split. This required use of the RMP policy is as opposed to when the coarse locking model was applied. The RMP policy is then only required to be used if references to records based on the record identifier are used from external to a block, e.g. by secondary indexes ([ABC+76]).

Since the action consistent block split policy only locks the block to be split during the splitting, the effect of the split can be seen by other transactions before the split requester transaction terminates. Action consistent block splitting can therefore not be done within the transaction requesting the split since the split then would have been undone if the transaction aborted. The block split can be done by a subtransaction (see section 10.4) of the transaction requesting the splitting. This transaction policy assure that the split is independent of the requester transaction, i.e. the block split is not undone if the requester transaction fails. See [ML89] and [HRA+90] for a more detailed introduction to fine grained block splitting policies, particularly for concurrent B-tree access methods.

6.6 The Transaction Failure Recovery Strategy

The transaction failure recovery strategy determines how a failed transaction is recovered by undoing its record state changing DB operations based on the compensation recovery strategy. It is assumed that the transaction recovery strategy is combined with block state-identifiers, the compensation recovery strategy, and the record index based record access strategy.

6.6.1 The Undo Work Order Policy

This section discusses the work order requirements of the transaction recovery processing relative to the transaction local log sequence. It will be shown that undo processing must be done in reverse work order relative to the transaction local log sequence. To compensate for the effects of multiple write record operations by one transaction to the same record, undo operations must be executed in reverse order relative to the operations they are compensating for. The CLRs are therefore produced in reverse order relative to the non-CLRs they are compensating for.

The following case illustrates that inconsistencies can occur if multiple write operations by a transaction to the same record are undone in forward work order. Transaction T_{10} performs two write operations to the same record. The original value of the written field is 2. The first operation writes 10, and the second 5 to the same field. If the undo operations are executed in the same order

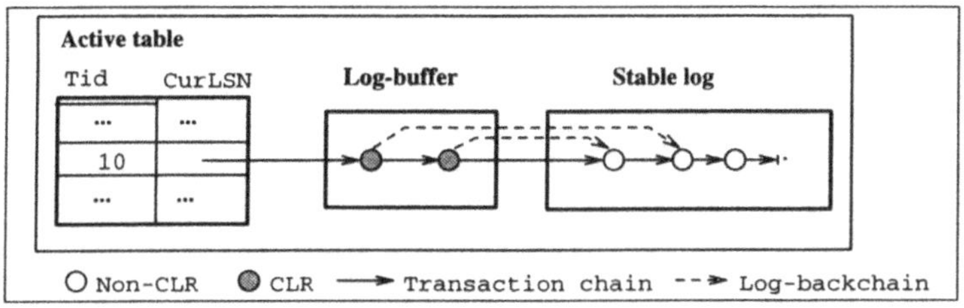

Figure 6.7: Transaction T_{10} is in the process of being rolled back. Two of its state changing DB operations are undone and one should be, but is not yet, undone. The log-backchain policy is assumed to be used, so that a CLR points to the log record it compensates for.

as the do operations, the value of 10 would be the result because it is the before-image value of the second write operation. The result is an inconsistent DB. If the undo operations had been executed in reverse work order, the value of 2 would have been the result (because it is the before-image value of the first write operation), which is a consistent result.

The case above shows that undo operations must be executed in reverse order relative to the do operations they are compensating for to a record within a transaction local log sequence. This requirement would not be obeyed if undo is done in forward work order to each transaction local log sequence. Therefore to obey the requirement, all undo operations are executed in reverse work order relative to the do operations they are compensating for within each transaction local log sequence.

6.6.2 The Transaction Roll Back

The transaction failure recovery uses the same main memory active transaction table as presented in section 5.6.3 to keep track of the log record identifier of the most recently produced log record of every transaction. This information is used to maintain each transaction chain.

A transaction is rolled back in reverse work order by following the transaction log chain and for each non-CLR performing a compensation operation and producing a CLR. The CLR is linked into the transaction log chain. If the log-backchain policy is adopted, the log record identifier of the compensated non-CLR is included in the CLR. If the transaction-backchain policy is adopted, the log record identifier of the previous field (see section 5.3.2) of the compensated non-CLR is included in the CLR. Figure 6.7 illustrates a failed transaction in the process of being rolled back where two operations of its DB state changing operation are compensated for and one is still not compensated for. The log-backchain policy is used.

If the action consistent block split policy is adopted, a record can have been moved to another block after the state changing DB operation was executed and before the compensating undo operation is executed. In this case, the undo operation uses the marker pointer to access the record (see section 6.5.4). If multiple block splits have occurred, multiple marker records must be followed to access the record. The state-identifier value contained in the produced CLR is the state-identifier value of the block in which the record is actually stored. If the redo CLR policy is used, it is the record's actual block identifier and record index that is included in the CLR. In this case the record identifiers of the non-CLR and the CLR differ as a result of the block split.

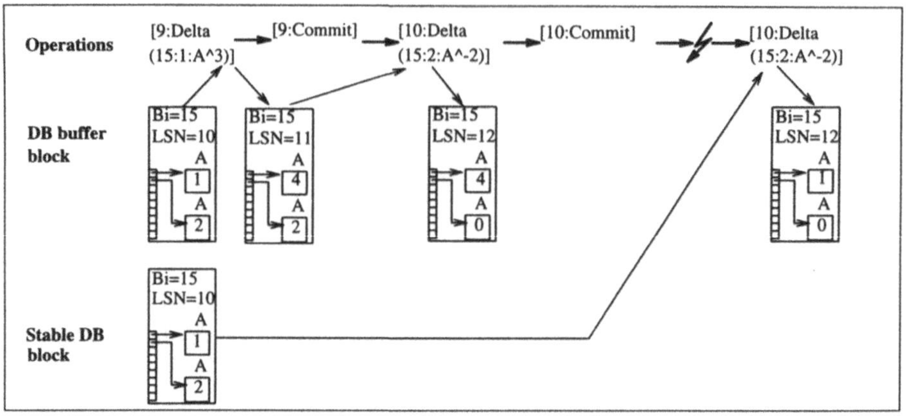

Figure 6.8: Case which illustrates inconsistency during node crash recovery resulting from redo work done in reverse work order in combination with the fine granularity, semantically rich locking model.

6.7 The Node Crash Recovery Strategy

The node crash recovery strategy presented in this section is based on the compensation recovery strategy. The structure of the analysis corresponds to the structure of the node crash recovery strategy analysis based, on the resetting recovery strategy presented in section 5.7. It will be shown that the redo work of the node crash recovery must be done in forward work order to a block log sequence or a log sequence containing the block log sequence. It will also be documented that the redo-undo sequentialisation policy must be used to the global node sequence so that, if both redo and undo work have to be done, the redo work must be done before the undo work. The selective redo policy in combination with the compensating recovery strategy is presented. The selective redo policy avoids redoing operations which will be undone later during the node crash recovery.

6.7.1 The Redo Work Order Policy

This section analyses the node crash recovery redo work order in the context of the compensation recovery strategy. It will be shown that the redo work must be done in forward work order relative to each block log sequence or in forward work order relative to a log sequence for a union of block log sequences, to preserve consistency between the block state as expressed by a block state-identifier and the actual block state during the redo processing.

The following case illustrates that inconsistencies can occur if redo work is done in reverse work order to a block. The case is illustrated in figure 6.8. Transactions T_9 and T_{10} perform one delta operation each to two different records within the same block. Both transactions commit. A node crash occurs. The stable block replica contains no effect of the two committed transactions. If the reverse work order is applied, the delta operation of transaction T_{10} is redone first. The block state-identifier is set to its value as after the delta operation. An inconsistency between the actual block state and the block state as indicated by the block state-identifier has occurred. The state-identifier indicates that the effect of both the committed transactions are reflected in the block. The effect of the delta operation by transaction T_9 is actually missing. When the delta operation by transaction T_9 is attempted to be redone, the state-identifier indicates that it is already reflected

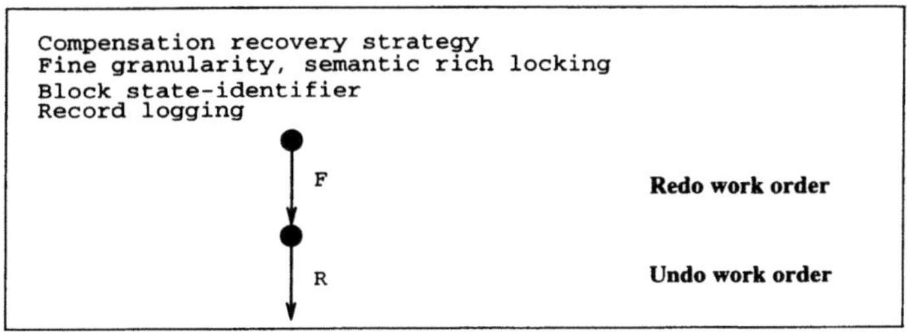

Figure 6.9: Work order restrictions in the context of the compensation strategy.

in the block because the state-identifier value is greater than the state-identifier in the log record. The result is an inconsistent DB.

If, on the other hand, the redo processing was executed in the forward work order, a consistent DB would be the result since both the committed delta operations would have been redone.

The previous case shows that the redo work must be done in forward work order relative to a block. Since the node global log sequence is a union of the block log sequences, the redo work must also be performed in forward work order relative to the node global log sequence. This result is similar to when the resetting recovery strategy is applied in combination with record logging (see section 5.7.3). The similarity is a result of the fact that the log records are only reflecting partially the state of the blocks the state-identifiers are connected to.

It was concluded in section 6.6.1 that the undo work must be done in reverse work order relative to each transaction local log sequence. Since the union of transaction log sequences are included in the node global log sequence, the undo work must also be done in reverse order relative to the node global log sequence. Redo and undo work therefore can not be performed in combination with one log scan. If a node crash recovery method requires both redo and undo work, at least two log scans must be used (see figure 6.9). The work order restrictions are similar to those imposed when the resetting state policy is combined with record logging (see figure 5.6).

6.7.2 The Sequentialisation Policy

The sequentialisation policy determines if the node crash recovery redo work is done before the undo work (**redo-undo**), or the undo work before the redo work (**undo-redo**) (see section 5.7.1). It will be shown that only the redo-undo sequentialisation policy can be used in combination with the compensation recovery strategy. This contrasts with the resetting strategy where both the redo-undo and the undo-redo sequentialisation policies can be used (see section 5.7.1).

The following case shows that inconsistencies can occur if the undo-redo sequentialisation policy is adopted in combination with the compensation recovery strategy. The case is illustrated in figure 6.10. Transaction T_7 performs a write record operation and then commits. Transaction T_{11} then performs a write record operation to the same block before a node crash occurs. None of the write operations of the two transactions are reflected in the stable block replica. The node crash recovery processing performs the undo work before the redo work according to the undo-redo policy. The undo work is performed in reverse work order and the redo work in forward work order (see section 6.7.1). The undo work therefore compensates for the write operation of transaction T_{11} by an undo-write operation. The execution of this undo-write operation increases the block state-identifier value so that it indicates that the DB operations of all the preceding log records have been executed, which is inconsistent with the actual block state. The redo work therefore does not

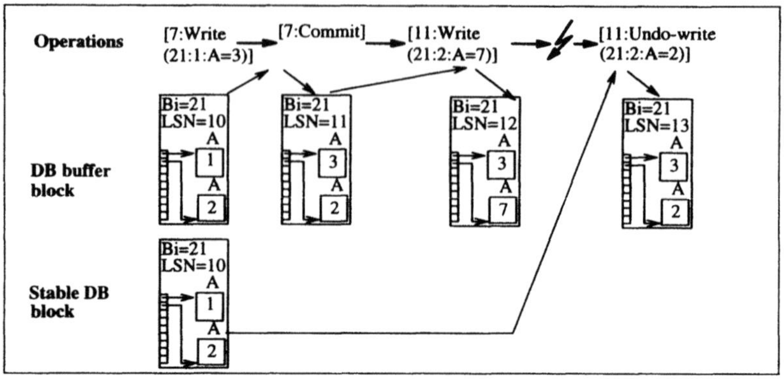

Figure 6.10: Case which illustrates inconsistency resulting from combining the compensation recovery strategy and block state-identifiers with the undo-redo sequentialisation policy.

redo the write operation of transaction T_7 since the block state indicates that it is already executed. The result is an inconsistent DB state.

The inconsistency would not have occurred if the redo-undo policy had been used. The redo-undo policy would first have redone the write operation by transaction T_7 since it is missing. Then, if the complete redo policy had been used, the write operation of T_{11} would have been redone. Finally the write operation by transaction T_{11} would have been undone. The result would be a consistent DB.

The inconsistency of applying the undo-redo sequentialisation policy which is illustrated in the previous case is independent of the chosen lock granularity policy. The use of either block or record locks in the previous case gives the same inconsistent DB. A similar inconsistent DB would also be the result if the write operations were exchanged by delta operations and the semantically rich locking model used. This shows that the required undo-redo sequentialisation policy is neither a result of the fine granularity locking nor a result of the semantically rich locking model. It is a result of using the compensation logging and compensation state policies. The compensation recovery strategy therefore imposes a stricter sequentialisation requirement on the node crash recovery methods than the resetting recovery strategy. The effect of this on the node crash recovery work load is returned to in section 6.8.

6.7.3 The Selective Redo Policy

The selective redo policy avoids redoing operations that are later to be undone because they belong to loser transactions, i.e. transactions that are to be rolled back in the node crash recovery processing. By avoiding redoing such operations, a node crash recovery may involve fewer disc accesses because fewer blocks may be read, dirtied and possibly written. The selective redo policy thereby reduces the disc I/O work load component which is the most significant component of node crash recovery work load (see section 6.7).

Avoiding the redoing of an operation of a loser transaction depends on the sequence of loser and non-loser operations to a block. Avoiding the execution of redo and undo operations also depends on which compensation log production policy is used. Since the repeating CLR policy cannot be combined with the semantically rich locking model, it is not included in the analysis (see section 6.4.5).

If a state changing DB operation of a loser transaction that is not reflected in a stable block replica is followed by a state changing operation to the same block by a non-loser transaction, the operation of the loser transaction must be redone. Since the operation of the loser transaction is not reflected in the stable block, the operation of the non-loser transaction is not reflected in the block either. The operation of the non-loser transaction must therefore be redone. It is assumed that the standard DB buffer policy is used, in which case a block flush operation can take place between any redo or undo operations during a node crash recovery (see section 5.7.4). If the loser operation is not redone before the non-loser operation, an inconsistency between the actual block state and the block state as expressed by the block state-identifier is the result. The block state-identifier indicates that all operations preceding the non-loser operation, which includes the loser operation, is reflected in the block. If a block flush occurs, followed by a second node crash, the recovery processing after the second node crash will deduce that the loser operation is reflected in the block which can result in an inconsistently recovered DB (see sections 6.4.2 and 6.4.3). It is therefore necessary to redo an operation of a loser transaction if it is followed by an operation of a non-loser transaction that must be redone. To avoid redoing an operation of a loser transaction, all later operations to the same block must also belong to loser transactions. The consequences of applying a dedicated DB buffer policy so that a block is guaranteed not to be flushed before it has been completely recovered are presented in section 7.9.2.

If the *single CLR* policy is used, an undo operation must be redone if the operation it is compensating for is reflected in the stable DB and the undo operation is not reflected in the stable DB. This is a sufficient requirement since it is assumed that the redo work is done to the node global log sequence so that the undo operation will never be reflected in the stable block without the operation it compensates for being reflected in the stable block. This requirement also holds when the action consistent block split policy is used. An (undo) operation is required to be redone if it is followed by another (undo) operation that is required to be redone or itself must be redone. This requirement preserves the consistency between the actual block state and the block state as indicated by the block state-identifier.

An undo operation can be avoided if the operation it compensates for is not reflected in the stable DB. A CLR must be produced independently of the execution of the undo operation to preserve the consistency between the block state and the log (see section 6.4.4). If a state changing DB operation is later executed to the block, and the block is flushed before a second node crash occurs, the block state indicates that the original operation is reflected in the block and that the undo operation is not reflected because it is not logged. During the recovery from the second node crash the operation is undone another time which can result in an inconsistent DB for non-idempotent DB state operations. If the CLR had been produced, the block state would have indicated that both the operation and its compensating undo operation were reflected in the block, which is a state equivalent to the consistent DB state.

If the *recursive CLR* policy is used, CLRs are treated similar to non-CLRs. Therefore an operation belonging to a loser transaction does not need to be redone if it is not followed by operations belonging to non-loser transactions to the same block. An undo operation can be avoided if the operation it compensates for is not reflected in the stable DB. As with the single CLR policy, a CLR is required to be produced even if the undo operation is not executed.

The **selective redo point** is the log sequence number where all the following log records in a block log sequence belong to loser transactions. The selective redo point must be determined for every block to which redo work is potentially required before redo work is done in order to apply the selective redo policy. To store the set of selective redo points a main memory *selective redo point table* is used. To determine the selective redo points, the recovery status of the involved transactions must be known. It can therefore not be combined with the analysis pass if the log is scanned in forward order. Nor can it be combined with the redo pass since the redo work must also be performed in forward order. It can be combined with the analysis pass if the log is scanned in

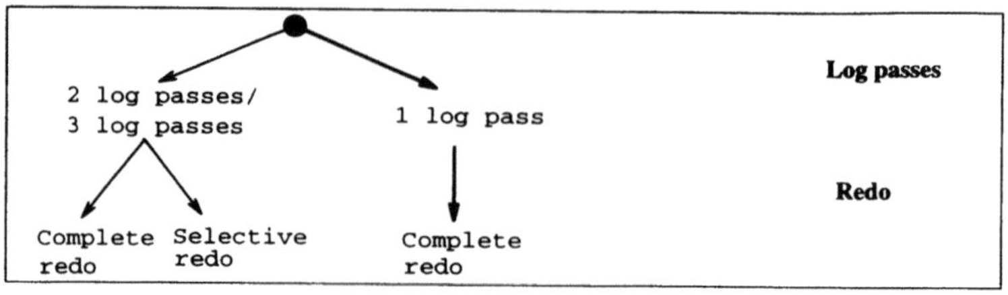

Figure 6.11: Classification of node crash recovery methods combined with the no-steal and no-force DB buffer policy.

reverse order, i.e. starting from the log crash point. It can also be done in an additional log pass after the analysis pass and before the redo pass. Reduced versions of the selective redo policy which require less main memory for storing the selective redo point table are presented in [MP90].

If the single CLR policy is used, a table of the log record identifier values of the CLRs following the selective redo point with their associated log-backchain pointer values must be determined for each block. This can be combined with determining the selective redo points for every block. Since these tables require additional space, an alternative is to assume that the operations compensated for by every CLR are reflected in the stable blocks. This policy avoids the need for more than one selective redo point per block since every CLR is treated similarly to the log records belonging to non-loser transactions.

The selective redo policy can also be combined with the coarse granularity, traditional locking model. In that case, a log record belonging to a transaction which is active at the crash will never be followed by a log record of a non-loser transaction within its block log sequence, which is a result of the block write locks. This removes the analysis needed to determine the selective redo points. It can be done as part of the redo pass if it is preceded by an analysis pass determining the transaction recovery status. This policy is used by DB2 ([IBM86a]).

6.8 The Node Crash Recovery Methods

This section presents and evaluates the node crash recovery methods based on a combination of the node crash recovery strategy presented in section 6.7 and the DB buffer strategy presented in section 4.6. The evaluation criteria are given in section 5.7.4.

6.8.1 Node Crash Recovery Methods Combined with the No-Steal DB Buffer Policy

The no-steal policy does not require any undo work to be performed during node crash recovery because no effects of uncommitted transactions are ever reflected in the stable DB. The no-force policy may require redo work to be performed because a node crash can occur without all effects of the committed transactions being reflected in the stable DB.

The no-steal policy in combination with the fine granularity or the semantically rich locking model requires a DB buffering policy which will ensure that blocks written to disc do not contain effects other than those from committed transactions. The **deferred update** policy ensures this requirement. Transactions do not update to records in-place in the DB buffer during the transaction execution, but to *pending lists*. The DB buffer updates are done as part of transaction commit processing. If a transaction aborts, its pending list is deleted. The deferred update policy is used by Ingres ([RS86], [BHG87]) and IMS Fast Path ([IBM86b]). The use of the compensation recovery

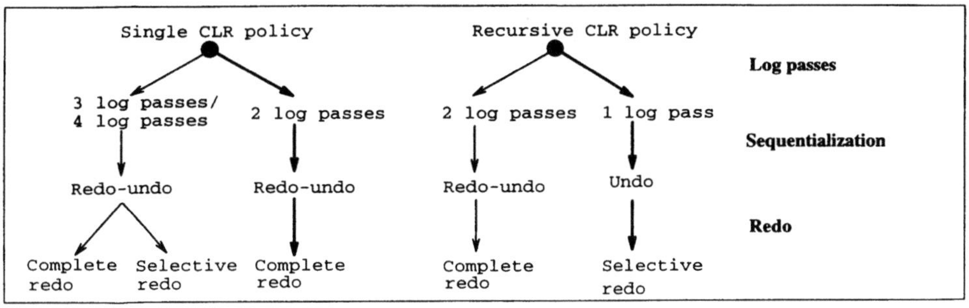

Figure 6.12: Classification of node crash recovery methods combined with the force and steal DB buffer policy.

strategy is not relevant in this context because no operations ever need to be compensated for since they are not reflected in any DB block before a transaction is committed.

A node crash can occur before all effects of a committed transaction are reflected in stable storage, in which case redo work is required. The DB state changing operations must therefore be logged, but the log records only need the redo part to perform the redo processing. It is assumed that the no-steal DB buffer policy is applied during node crash recovery processing to avoid uncommitted effects being introduced into the stable DB, also during the recovery processing.

The node crash recovery can be done with one log pass to perform the redo work. This node crash recovery method can only use the complete redo policy since selective redo requires at least one additional log pass to establish the selective redo point (see section 6.7.3). If a two or three log pass node crash recovery method is used, the selective redo policy can be applied (see figure 6.11). The selective redo policy is of limited interest in the context of the no-steal DB buffer policy because it does not reduce the involved recovery disc I/O work load, which is its main objective. The deferred update policy does not access DB blocks before a transaction has committed. The one log pass node crash recovery method will for this reason be preferred, since it involves fewer log block accesses and the same number of DB block accesses as the node crash recovery method using the selective redo policy.

The no-steal based node crash recovery methods presented in this section can be compared with the node crash recovery work load of the similar methods combined with the resetting recovery policy (see section 5.8.1). The preferred node crash recovery method presented in this section is work load compatible with the preferred resetting strategy based node crash recovery method, i.e. they both use one log pass and complete redo recovery.

6.8.2 Node Crash Recovery Methods Combined with the Force DB Buffer Policy

The force DB buffer policy requires all operations of a transaction to be reflected in the stable DB before a transaction commits. The steal DB buffer policy allows operations to be reflected in the stable DB before a transaction terminates. Given the combination of the force and steal DB buffer policies, the state-identifier of every stable block replica is greater than or equal to the last committed operation executed to the block. Every operation which is logged but not reflected in a stable block replica belongs to a loser transaction, since every operation of non-loser transactions is reflected in the stable DB. Operations belonging to loser transactions may also be reflected in the stable DB. The node crash recovery methods may therefore require undo work to be performed. The transactions that are active when a node crash occurs have to be undone.

A node crash recovery may require redo work to be performed in combination with the *single CLR policy*. This requirement is independent of the use of the complete or the selective redo policy. A transaction that has failed can be in the process of being rolled back when a node crash occurs. Some but not all of its operations are compensated for by undo operations. Some of the operations that are compensated for are reflected in the stable DB but their compensation operation is not reflected in the stable DB. These missing compensation operations must be redone if either the complete or the selective redo policy is used (see section 6.7.3). If the selective redo policy is used, one or two analysis passes must be performed before the redo pass to establish the selective redo points (see section 6.7.3). The node crash recovery methods may therefore require at least two log passes to perform both the redo and undo work (see figure 6.12). Three or four log passes are needed altogether if selective redo is to be applied.

No redo work is required to be performed at all during node crash recovery if the *recursive CLR policy* is combined with the selective redo policy. No undo operations of transactions in the process of being rolled back and not reflected in the stable DB are required to be redone, unlike when the single CLR policy is applied (see section 6.7.3). Since all operations of non-loser transactions are guaranteed to be reflected in the stable DB by the force policy, no redo processing is needed. The analysis pass can be combined with the undo pass to establish the set of loser and non-loser transactions (see section 5.7). The node crash recovery processing can therefore be done in one pass (see figure 6.12). A node crash recovery method applying complete redo requires two log passes.

The node crash recovery method which involves the smallest recovery work load when multiple node crashes are infrequent is the combination of the recursive CLR policy with selective redo policy since only one log pass is required and only undo work is performed. The involved node crash recovery work load by this node crash recovery method is compatible to the preferred node crash recovery method presented in section 5.8.2 where only one log scan was required and only undo work performed.

6.8.3 Node Crash Recovery Methods Combined with the Steal and No-Force DB Buffer Policy

The steal and no-force DB buffer policy may require both redo and undo work to be performed when recovering from a node crash. The stable DB may reflect operations belonging to loser transactions which have to be compensated for. The effect of operations belonging to non-loser transactions may be missing from the stable DB and the operations have to be redone. The classification of node crash recovery methods given the steal and no-force policy are illustrated in figure 6.13.

Since a node crash recovery may require both redo and undo work, the node crash recovery methods require at least two log passes. This applies regardless of the compensation log production policy used. Since the redo work must be done before the undo work, the two log pass based node crash recovery method can only be combined with the complete redo policy. This node crash recovery method corresponds to the ARIES recovery method ([MHL+89]).

The selective redo policy requires either one analysis pass performed in reverse log order or two analysis passes to establish the transaction recovery status and the selective redo points per block. The analysis passes must be done before the redo pass. A node crash recovery method using the selective redo policy will therefore use altogether three or four log passes. The node crash recovery method using four log passes and the selective redo policy corresponds to the ARIES-RRH recovery method ([MP90]).

The node crash recovery methods presented in this section can be compared to the resetting recovery strategy node crash recovery methods for the same DB buffer policy (see section 5.8.3).

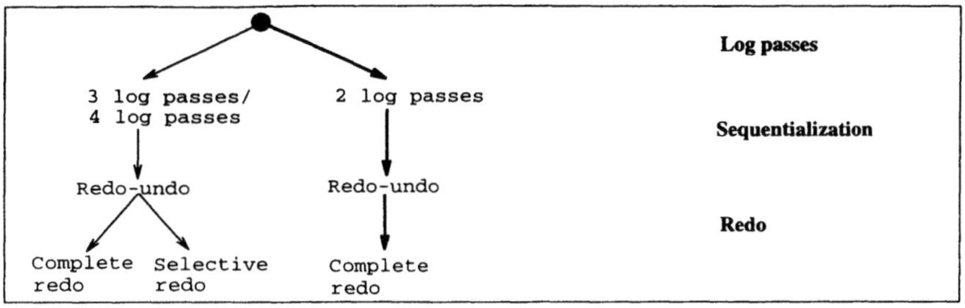

Figure 6.13: Classification of node crash recovery methods combined with the steal and no-force DB buffer policy.

The resetting recovery based node crash recovery method involving the smallest recovery work load uses two log passes in combination with selective redo. All the node crash recovery methods presented in this section involve a higher node crash recovery work load, since two log passes can only be combined with the complete redo policy and the selective redo policy cannot be combined with less than three log passes. The reason for this is that the compensation recovery strategy requires redo work to be done before undo work, as opposed to the resetting recovery policy which allows both the redo-undo and the undo-redo sequentialisation policies.

6.9 Conclusion

The compensation oriented recovery approach satisfies a larger set of design goals than the record oriented approach (see chapter 5). The fine grained record locking model removes the block write hot-spot bottleneck. Multiple concurrent transactions can perform write operations to different records within the same block, which is the consequence of fine (record) versus coarse (block) granularity locking. The semantically rich locking model reduces the hot-spot bottleneck effect further by allowing multiple concurrent transactions to perform delta record operations even to the same record.

The logging overhead during normal operations by the compensation oriented approach is approximately equal to the logging overhead by the record oriented approach. Both approaches log record operations. The added load by the compensation oriented approach of logging undo operations for failed transactions are negligible, because of the low percentage of failed transactions (see section 2.3.6).

The main disadvantages of the compensation oriented recovery approach are: the redo and undo operations are based on the record datamodel record identification policies (see section A.6); the record identification policies are neither block nor location independent; redo access stability to a tuple based on a record identifier is not preserved if the tuple is moved to another block; replication transparency is lacking so that a log record cannot be applied to another replica of the same tuple than the one the original state changing DB operation was applied to. The other tuple replica may have another record identifier. The table oriented approach (see chapter 7) provides block independency to undo tuple operations. The HypRa recovery approach (see Part III) provides location and replication transparency to both undo and redo tuple operations.

Exercises

1. (a) Why do delta record operations combined with semantically rich locking require state transition logging? (b) Would the inclusion of range tests with delta operations change this?

2. (a) Describe a delta log record for partial record logging. (b) Why is data type information not needed in the log records? (c) Which advantages would be obtained by including basic data types with log records?

3. (a) What would a log record for a multiply operation look like when locks making multiply operations commute? (b) What might a log record for a divide operation look like when multiply and divide operations commute?

4. A transaction consists of four write operations on records of size 100 bytes each. The transaction rate is 1000 transactions per second. Approximately 3% of the transactions abort. What is the difference in produced log volume between the resetting based record logging policy and the compensation logging combined with (a) redo/undo/transaction-backchain CLR policy and (b) no-redo/no-undo/counting CLR policy?

5. Assume undo logging is done by writing the log sequence numbers of CLRs into a dedicated field in the non-CLRs. (a) What would be the effect of this policy on the undo WAL rule? (b) What would be the effect on the redo WAL rule? (c) Why can this method not be used with the repeating or the recursive CLR policies?

6. Based on the case in exercise 4, would the policy presented in exercise 5 save log volume compared to the redo/no-undo/transaction-backchain CLR policy, if we assume an LSN takes 6 bytes?

7. A transaction consists of a sequence of two write record operations to two different records followed by a sequence of two delta record operations to the same record. Four such transactions were active at a node crash. They were executed in strict sequence. (a) Illustrate node crash recovery based on the compensation logging policy.

   The node crashes during recovery just as all the undo operations are done. Illustrate the following node crash recovery based on (b) the single CLR policy and (c) the recursive CLR policy. (d) Why can the repeating CLR policy not be used?

8. Assume that a block has 10 block state-identifiers, that a maximum of 10 DB state changing transactions are allowed to execute concurrently, and that fine granularity and traditional locking are applied. (a) Why can undo-redo recovery then be done in combination with the resetting logging policy? (b) Why can this method also be used with the rich locking policy in combination with the block global LSN policy? (c) How could the transaction rate be increased beyond 10 without increasing the number of block state identifiers per block?

9. (a) How can the original space by a deleted record, a "tomb-stone", be used to represent its structure preservation lock and its part of the block space lock? (b) Assume that the action consistent block split policy is used. What is the effect on available space after a block split by use of tomb-stones?

10. Assume that the record indexes of deleted records do not need to be preserved over the lifetime of a transaction. Assume that block space locks are used. (a) What are the conditions for splitting a block under the transaction consistent block split policy? (b) If the action consistent block split policy is used, what will be the value of the block split locks of the blocks involved in a block split? (c) Which effects does this have?

11. (a) When, at the earliest, can the space kept by a tomb-stone be released? (b) How can the oldest log record identifier of the current active transactions be used to simplify management of when to release space held by tomb-stones?

12. Assume reference to records by record indexes are only by log records. Assume that the action consistent block split policy is used. (a) When can a relocation pointer record be removed? (b) Why must the undo CLR policy be used?

13. Would writing the oldest LSN of the currently active transactions in a block when it is flushed help in determining the selective redo point after a node crash for a block?

14. How could the log be scanned only once?

Answers

1. (a) The use of the state resetting policy may cause inconsistencies between the state as expressed by the block state-identifier and the actual block state. See section 6.4.2. (b) No.

2. (a) The generic part of the log record is unchanged. The specific part is unchanged except for a delta image vector which is added to indicate which fields are included and which are not included in the delta image.

   (b) Redo and undo write operations do not need type information because the content of the after- or before-image is copied into the corresponding fields. The same arguments applies to insert and delete operations. A delta image without type information requires one and only one data type to be involved in delta operations or that, in case of multiple types, the type can be deduced from the size or structure of the delta image.

   (c) The DBMS would be able to support a richer set of basic data types.

3. (a) The generic log part would be unaltered. The operation identifier would take another value indicating a multiply operation. The specific part would look like the specific part of a delta log record. The equivalent of a delta image would indicate the value of the multiplier for the fields involved in the operation.

   (b) The same as a log record for a multiply operation.

4. (a) We assume a generic log record part for non-CLRs takes approximately 20 bytes. The resetting recovery policy would produce approximately $1000 \cdot (20 + 2 \cdot 100) = 220000$ bytes per second. We have not included the terminating log record for a transaction in these figures. The generic log record part plus the data item identifier and the transaction backchain for the redo/undo/transaction-backchain CLR policy take approximately 30 bytes. The non-CLRs produce the same log volume per second as with the resetting log policy. The CLRs produce $1000 \cdot \frac{3}{100} \cdot (30 + 2 \cdot 100) = 6900$ bytes per second. This gives an increase in log volume of 1% compared to the resetting log policy.

   (b) The CLRs under the no-redo/no-undo/counting policy consist only of the generic part, so the size of the CLRs is approximately 20 bytes. The CLRs produce $1000 \cdot \frac{3}{100} \cdot 20 = 600$ bytes per second. This gives an increase in log volume of 0.1% compared to the resetting log policy.

5. (a) The policy presented requires log blocks to be read and updated to include the compensation information. When a block is flushed, the log buffer is checked to determine that all log records relating to operations reflected in the block are stably stored. In addition it must be determined that all updated log records referring to compensation operations reflected in the block are stably stored.

   (b) The effect on the redo WAL rule is that all log records updated with compensation information by a transaction must be stably stored before the transaction terminates.

   (c) A non-CLR could not be allowed to expand in the process. The method would only tolerate one CLR per non-CLR because it leaves space for only one compensating LSN per non-CLR. Both the repeating and the recursive CLR policies may, in the event of multiple node crashes, produce multiple CLRs for a non-CLR. A more complex method would produce CLRs only in the event of multiple node failures by bypassing this restriction.

6. The method presented in exercise 5 would produce approximately $1000 \cdot (26 + 2100) =$ 226000 bytes. The redo/no-undo/transaction-backchain CLR policy would produce approximately $220000 + 1000 \cdot \frac{3}{100} \cdot (30 + 100) = 223900$ bytes.

7. (a) The recovery will be based on redo-undo sequentialisation policy. The CLRs will be produced in reverse order relative to the non-CLRs they refer to. (b) The single CLR policy will, during the next node crash recovery, produce no more log records because a CLR is already produced for each of the non-CLRs. (c) The recursive CLR policy will produce one CLR for every log record belonging to an active transaction. So the number of log records belonging to these four transactions will be doubled. (d) A delta operation is not idempotent.

8. (a) A transaction uses a designated block state-identifier location to reflect the resulting block state of its record operations. The location can be determined from the transaction identifier. The transaction separate block state-identifiers makes it possible to reset the block state identifier belonging to the actual transaction during undo processing without causing inconsistency between the actual block state and the state expressed by its state-identifiers.

   (b) The delta operations will not cause inconsistencies because the block state is represented by the combination of the transaction identifier and the LSN. This avoids the inconsistencies documented in section 6.4.2.

   (c) This could be obtained by including the transaction identifier with the corresponding state-identifier. Still no more than 10 transactions can concurrently be active to a block, but there are no restrictions on the total number of active transactions. Including the transaction identifiers in a locking structure would not be sufficient because it would not be possible under node crash recovery to determine which state identifier location a transaction uses.

9. (a) A simple method is to mark the deleted record with a unique tomb-stone marker. The space for this marker is taken from the record itself. This reserves the record index because there exists a record to which it points. Since the size of the actual record is unchanged, sufficient space is implicitly reserved.

   (b) The tomb-stones are moved as ordinary records. The new available space corresponds to one block minus the space taken by the pointer records needed. A pointer record is needed for every moved tomb-stone.

10. (a) No other transaction is active that has performed state changing operations which are active to the block.

    (b) The same space must be reserved in both the blocks after a split as in the original block before the split because it is not known how the reserved space should be divided between the two blocks. To be safe we must assume that all space could be required from either of them.

    (c) This may mean that sufficient space is still not available for insertion of a record even after a block split.

11. (a) When the transaction causing the tomb-stone has committed. (b) Assume that the tomb-stone marker includes the LSN of the delete record operation producing the tomb-stone. A tomb-stone can definitely be removed when the oldest LSN of the active transactions is larger than the LSN in the tomb-stone marker.

12. (a) It can be removed when the last transaction that was active to the split block is terminated, if CLRs are independent of the relocation pointers. If CLRs depend on relocation pointers to

locate the record, the relocation pointers can not be removed before the last undo operation based on these CLRs is reflected in the block.

(b) The undo operation is executed to another block than the do operation. To maintain the single block policy for CLRs, the data item identifier of the CLRs should refer to the actual block the record is located in when the undo operation is executed. Including the after-image in the CLRs makes it possible to garbage collect the non-CLR independently of the CLRs when applying the single CLR policy.

13. No, because a transaction that was active when the block was flushed may have committed before the node crash.

14. Scan the log and build a main memory copy. Do the remaining log reading in main memory.

Chapter 7

The Table Oriented Approach

This chapter presents recovery strategies relating to the **table layer** (see section A.4), using **tuple logging** combined with concurrency control supporting **fine granularity** and **semantically rich tuple locking** (see section A.9). The table oriented recovery approach satisfies a larger set of recovery design goals (see section 2.6) than the compensation oriented approach, which is the other of the previously presented recovery approaches that supports fine grained and semantically rich locking (see chapter 6).

The table oriented recovery approach is not fully used in any commercial DBMS, to our knowledge. Policies from this approach are on the other hand used in some modern DBMSs such as Encompass ([Bor81], [Hel85a], [Hel85b]), Tandem Non-Stop SQL ([BP88], [Gro88]), and TechRa ([HL86]).

7.1 The Table Oriented DBMS Server Architecture

This section presents the table oriented DBMS server architecture (see figure 7.1). The presented architecture does not correspond to any particular implemented DBMS and is used to describe and analyse recovery capabilities of the table oriented approach. The main difference between the table oriented DBMS server architecture and the compensation oriented DBMS server architecture (see section 6.1) is that concurrency control and recovery services are performed at the table layer instead of to the record and block layers. In addition, a separate access method server is introduced at the table layer.

The *concurrency control server* receives transactions (see section A.8) and tuple DB operations (see section A.5) from the relational server. The concurrency control server serialises the tuple DB operations by using fine grained, semantically rich tuple locks according to the specifications given in section A.9. It is assumed that for every table a primary key or (for those relations where a primary key is not defined) a surrogate key is defined (see section A.4). The term primary key is, in this chapter, also used for a surrogate key. The primary key specification is part of the dictionary representation of the table.

A write, insert, or delete tuple operation write locks the involved tuple on its primary key value. A delta operation delta locks the involved tuple on its primary key value. A read operation read locks the involved tuple on its primary key value. The locks are well-formed strict two-phased (see section A.9).

The *access method server* maps a tuple to its record representation. A tuple is assumed to be mapped to one record and is therefore contained within one block (see section 6.3.1). The access method scheduler supports block granularity traditional locking, i.e. **access method block (AM)** locks. An AM read lock is kept over the duration of a tuple operation to a block, i.e. the duration

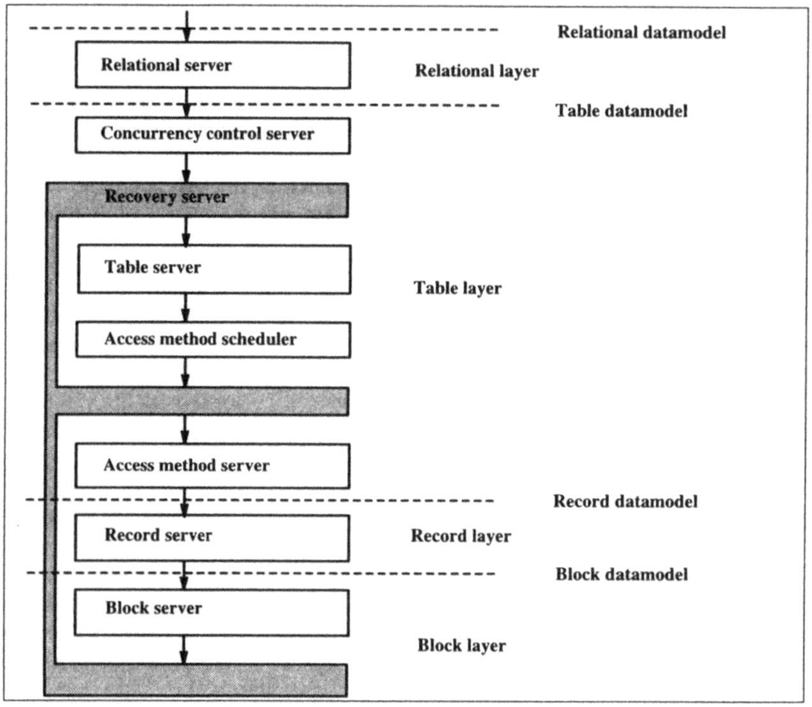

Figure 7.1: The table oriented DBMS server architecture. The layered DBMS architecture corresponds to the architecture presented in section A.3 and figure A.3. The concurrency control server is included in the table layer. The access method server included in the table layer maps a tuple to its record representation. The access method scheduler serialises access method operations.

of a search for and reading of a tuple or index-tuple within a block. An AM write lock is kept for the duration of a tuple operation to a block if no block split/merge is involved. The duration of an AM write lock for a index-tuple operation or a tuple operation where a block split/merge is involved depends on whether the transaction consistent or the action consistent block split/merge policy is used. An AM lock is independent of tuple locks so that tuple locks to tuples contained in an AM locked block can exist.

The *recovery server* logs tuple and top-level transaction operations as they are received from the concurrency control server and index-tuple, block split/merge, and subtransaction operations as they are received from the access method scheduler. The logging is done according to the WAL rules (see section 4.4.4). The top-level transaction concept is used in this chapter for all transaction operations received from the relational level. A subtransaction is a nested top-level transaction.

7.2 The Table Oriented Classification Scheme

This section presents the classification scheme for table oriented centralised DBMSs. The classification scheme is based on a collection of recovery related DBMS strategies. Each strategy is composed of a collection of policies (see also section 6.2). The new strategies introduced are presented below. In addition, extensions and adaptations of strategies presented in previous chapters are presented.

- **The logging strategy**
  The DB state changing tuple operations are logged according to the tuple logging policy (see section 7.3.1). Block split/merge operations are logged physically to blocks so that the block and primary key (BPK) combined undo and redo identification (BPK/BPK) policy must be used for tuples and index-tuples moved between blocks. The transaction consistent block split/merge policy uses the BPK/BPK policy. The action consistent block split/merge policy uses the BPK/BPK policy for operations by subtransactions and the BPK undo and the table and primary key (TPK) redo combined identification (BPK/TPK) policy for tuple operations by top-level transactions.

- **The checkpoint strategy**
  Block flush operations are logged to establish block local checkpoints to limit the node crash recovery redo work to a block. The block local checkpoint strategy is supplementary to the node global checkpoint and the transaction local checkpoint policies presented in section 4.7. A policy that detects potentially damaged stable block replicas after a node crash in case of non-atomic block flush operations is also presented.

- **The tuple access strategy**
  The tuple access strategy is composed of policies used to provide consistent tuple access during normal transaction and transaction failure processing. It is focused on policies preserving tuple access stability in combination with block split/merge policies, since the TPK undo identification policy may require the primary key based tuple access methods to be used during the undo processing. A zombie locking policy is presented, preserving primary key uniqueness for tuples deleted by active transactions.

- **The non-sequential recovery strategy**
  Node crash and transaction failure recovery work load reduction and speed up are obtained through: single log scans, main memory log-aggregation, block complete and block autonomous recovery, and I/O and CPU parallelism between blocks. Redo and undo log record parts are aggregated to blocks given the BPK/BPK combined identification policy. Redo log record parts are aggregated to blocks and undo log record parts are aggregated

to tables and tuples given the BPK/TPK identification policy. The action consistent block split/merge policy requires undo operations by access method subtransactions to be executed before undo operations by top-level transactions to a block.

- **The transaction failure recovery strategy**
  A failed transaction is recovered according to the compensation recovery strategy (see section 6.4). A conditional non-sequential transaction failure recovery policy is presented.

- **The node crash recovery strategy**
  A node crash is recovered according to the compensation recovery strategy (see section 6.4). Non-sequential node crash recovery is presented to obtain recovery work load reduction and speed up. Selective redo policies are adapted to block complete recovery. Partial DB availability through a node crash recovery is provided.

7.3 The Logging Strategy

The policies presented in this section are related to logging of tuple-, index-tuple-, and block split/merge operations. The log production policy for DB state changing tuple and index-tuple operations corresponds to the compensation recovery strategy presented in section 6.4 and is not repeated here. Both tuple- and index-tuple operations are in this section termed tuple operations.

7.3.1 The Identification Concept Polices

This section focuses on identification concepts used in log records produced by DB state changing tuple operations, i.e. how a tuple operated on by a DB state changing operation is uniquely referred to in the produced log record. A **block independent** policy is followed if the identification concepts for log record parts are both *logical to blocks*, i.e. the block identifier is not used in the identification concept, and *logical to tuples within blocks*, i.e. the physical location of a tuple within a block is not used in the identification concept, otherwise a block non-independent policy is used. A block independent redo (undo) policy is followed if the block independent policy is used by redo (undo) log record parts. A **combined identification** policy is composed of a redo and an undo identification policy.

The **block and primary key identification (BPK)** policy identifies the tuple referred to in a log record part by the combination of the block identifier of the block in which the tuple was contained when the operation producing the log record part was executed, and the primary key of the tuple. The block identifier is used to access the block. The primary key is used to access the tuple or tuple position within a block. Since the BPK policy uses the block identifier to access the block, it is independent of primary key based tuple access methods. The BPK policy is block non-independent.

The **table and primary key identification (TPK)** policy identifies a tuple referred to in a log record part by the combination of the table identifier and the primary key. The table identifier is used to obtain the base reference to the access method for the table. The primary key is used to access the tuple in the primary key based access method. The TPK policy is block independent since the tuple access is independent of the block identifier of the block the tuple was contained in when the do operation was executed and the access to the tuple within a block is based on the primary key.

The combined identification policies analysed in this chapter are the BPK/BPK and the BPK/TPK policies (see figure 7.2). The redo processing is therefore block non-independent. Analysis of block independent redo processing is presented in Part III. Analysis of the undo identification

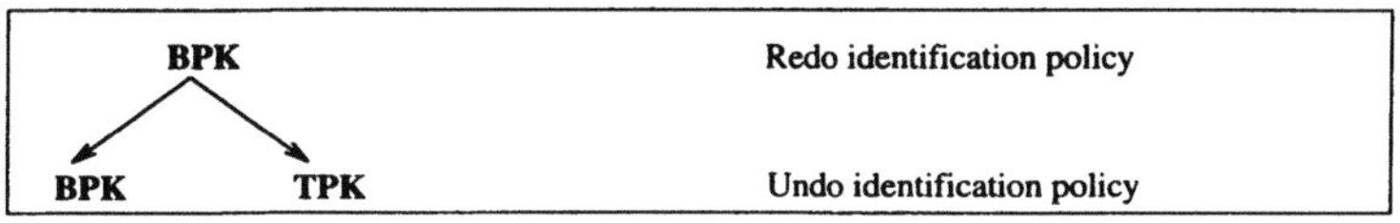

Figure 7.2: The BPK/BPK and BPK/TPK combined identification polices.

policies are presented in section 7.5. The BPK/BPK combined identification policy is for example used by the TechRa DBMS ([HL86]).

Redo processing accesses a block on its block identifier. A block state-identifier is contained in every block. The block state-identifier value of the block determines if the operation is reflected in the stable block replica, i.e. the operation is reflected if the state-identifier of the block is larger or equal to the log record's log record identifier (see section 5.4). Redo is performed in forward block log sequence order so that a redo operation is executed to the same logical block state as the original tuple operation was executed to. The primary key uniqueness (see section A.4) guarantees that within a given block state, multiple tuples with equal primary key values will not occur. Therefore a redo operation is provided with consistent tuple access within a block. Since a redo operation is executed to the same tuple logical block state as the do operation, a block will, when a redo operation is executed, contain the same free space as when the do operation was executed. Block splits and block merges during the redo processing will therefore not be different from those during the normal processing.

7.3.2 Dictionary Independence Policies

This section addresses **dictionary independent** recovery processing of tuple operations. A recovery operation is dictionary independent if access to the data dictionary is not required in order to execute it. The data dictionary is assumed to be implemented as a collection of tables called the **dictionary tables**. It is assumed that tuple operations are applied also to the dictionary tables and that it cannot be determined from the table identifier that a table is a dictionary table. Tables that are mappings of relations are called **data tables** when distinction from dictionary tables is required. A transaction may include operations to both dictionary tables and data tables ([IBM89b]), e.g. a transaction may both create a table and insert tuples into the table.

The **primary key log vector** policy is adopted if log records produced by DB state changing tuple operations have included information stating explicitly which of the logged fields the primary key is composed of and their ordering, else a non-primary key log vector policy is applied. If the non-primary key log vector policy is adopted together with a tuple logging policy (see section 7.3.1) the data dictionary must be accessed during recovery processing to obtain the primary key information that is contained in a primary key log vector. This requires synchronisation between dictionary recovery and data recovery during a node crash recovery. A non-primary key log vector policy cannot be combined with the no-force DB buffer policy. If a no-force policy is used, during a possible redo after a node crash, a tuple operation may request deleted dictionary information. This is illustrated by the following case. A committed DB state-changing operation to a tuple $P1$ of table T is not reflected in the stable DB when a node crash occurs. A later committed transaction deleted the table T so that the dictionary representation of the table is not reflected in the stable DB at the node crash. The tuple operation cannot be redone since the dictionary information is unobtainable. The TechRa DBMS uses the non-primary log vector policy with the force DB buffer policy ([HL86], [Lys86b], [Lys86a], [KVA89]).

If non-sequential recovery is performed (see section 7.6), and both dictionary and data operations can occur within a transaction, then similar synchronisation problems between dictionary and data recovery may occur independently of the DB buffer policy. If a transaction that creates a table, inserts tuples into the table, and finally deletes the table, fails, then the recovery of the dictionary must be synchronised to provide the tuple undo operations with dictionary information.

By adopting the primary key log vector policy, transaction- and node crash recovery processing becomes dictionary independent. Sufficient dictionary information is kept with the log records to perform the redo or undo operations (see also section 5.3.1 for comparison). It will in the following be assumed that the primary key policy is used.

If a DBMS supports multiple basic field types, a similar **field type log vector** policy can be adopted to provide dictionary independent field type information during transaction- and node crash recovery processing. This is not analysed further in this book.

7.3.3 Partial Tuple Logging

Log records produced according to the tuple logging policy (see section 7.3.1) contain the same generic log record fields as log records produced according to the record logging policy (see section 5.3.2).

The **complete tuple logging** policy is followed if the log records produced by DB state changing tuple operations contain all the fields of the involved tuple (see section 5.3.2). The **partial tuple logging** policy is followed if only the fields operated on and the fields included in the primary key are logged. The primary key fields are required to access the tuple. This is different from the partial record logging policy (see section 5.3.3), in which only the fields being operated on had to be logged since record access is based on the block identifier and record index. The log volume reduction effect of the partial tuple logging policy is therefore less than the reduction effect of the partial record logging policy, since more fields are required to be logged.

Both the BPK/BPK and the BPK/TPK combined identification policies use the primary key to identify a tuple or tuple position during redo and undo processing. To access a tuple or tuple position during undo processing, the log record must contain the values of the non-operated-on fields that are contained in the primary key and the after-image values of the primary key fields that are operated on. To compensate for the operation, the undo log record parts must include the before-image values of every operated-on field.

If the operation to be redone is not reflected in the block (see section 7.3.1), the tuple is accessed on its primary key value as it was before the do operation was executed. To access a tuple or tuple position, the log record must contain the value of the fields contained in the primary key but not operated on and the before-image values of the fields contained in the primary key and operated on. To redo the operation, the after-image value of every operated on field is required.

7.3.4 The Split/Merge Log Records

The split/merge log record is used to log a split/merge operation to a block. A split/merge operation updates the block's border records and link pointer. The operation is used both in connection with the transaction consistent and action consistent split/merge policies (see section 7.5).

A split/merge log record contains the generic log record fields and the following specific fields. It is assumed that the upper/lower border policy is followed (see section 7.5.2).

- **Block identifier**
  The block identifier of the involved block. One split/merge log record is produced for each of the blocks involved in a block split or block merge.

- **Link pointer**
  The before- and after-image value of the link pointer of the merged or split block. See section 7.5.2.

- **Lower border record**
  The before- and after-image value of the border record containing the lower value of the block. See section 7.5.2.

- **Upper border record**
  The before- and after-image value of the border record containing the upper value of the block. See section 7.5.2.

If the upper border policy is applied instead of the upper/lower, the lower border field is removed.

7.3.5 The Block Flush Log Record

A block flush log record (BFR) is used to log a block flush operation produced according to the SBF policy (see section 7.4.1). A BFR is not contained in any transaction log sequence since it is produced by an internal block level transaction. A BFR therefore requires only a reduced generic log record part (see section 5.3.2).

A BFR contains the following fields:

- **Log record identifier**
  The unique log record identifier.

- **Operation identifier**
  The operation identifier of the block flush operation.

- **Block identifier**
  The unique block identifier of the flushed block.

- **Stable block state**
  The state-identifier value of the flushed block.

A start-BFR, according to the DBF policy (see section 7.4.1), contains the same fields as a BFR but with a different operation identifier value. A commit-BFR may contain either the same fields as a BFR, or a previous log record identifier field instead of the block identifier and the block state-identifier (see section 5.3.2). A previous log record identifier of a commit-BFR will contain the log record identifier of the corresponding start-BFR log record.

7.4 The Checkpoint Strategy

The checkpointing policies presented in this section are supplementary to the transaction local and node global checkpointing policies presented in section 4.7. The block checkpoints limit the redo node crash recovery work to a block. The hot-spot checkpoint policy logs the set of hot-spot block identifiers to quickly regain the DB cache effect after restart from a node crash.

7.4.1 The Block Checkpoint Policy

To reduce the node crash recovery work, checkpoints can be introduced into the block global log sequences by logging block flush operations with the block state-identifier value of the flushed block (see section 4.7, [GR88], and [Hag90]). A block flush operation is in this context an internal transaction initiated from within the block layer with a particular logging protocol and garbage collection rules (see sections 4.4.4 and 4.4.5 for comparison).

A block local checkpoint limits the redo node crash work to the block so that no operations to the block preceding a block checkpoint need to be redone. The block checkpoints limit the undo node crash work to a block if the block checkpoint policy is combined with the no-steal DB buffer policy (see sections 4.6 and 6.8). In this case the effect of a block checkpoint to a block corresponds to that of a transaction consistent checkpoint (TCC) to a node, since both the redo and undo node crash recovery work to the block is limited. If the block checkpoint policy is combined with the steal DB buffer policy, no undo limits are imposed on the block since a flushed block may contain effects of uncommitted transactions. In this case, the effect of a block checkpoint to a block corresponds to an action consistent checkpoint (ACC) to a node, since it limits the redo node crash recovery work but not the undo recovery work.

Two block flush logging policies are presented, the **single block flush logging** (**SBF**) policy and the **double block flush logging** (**DBF**) policy. The SBF policy writes a block flush log record (BFR) (see section 7.3.5) to the log when a block flush operation is acknowledged as done. The BFR is not required to be forced to the stable log.

A BFR ensures that the effect of all logged state changing DB operations with a lesser or equal state-identifier value than contained in the BFR, and executed to a data-item contained in the block are reflected in the stable block replica. These operations are therefore never to be redone since they are reflected in the stable block replica. This can be checked by analysing the log alone without reading the DB block. A block flush logging policy can therefore reduce the node crash recovery I/O work load.

If a BFR is written before the corresponding flush operation is acknowledged, a failure can occur after the BFR is included in the stable log and before the block flush operation is done. This gives as result an inconsistency between the checkpointed stable block state and the actual stable block state. This can lead to inconsistent node crash recovery, since operations are not being redone because the BFR states that they are reflected in the stable block replica but they are actually missing from the block. The BFR must therefore be written after the flush operation is acknowledged.

The actual state-identifier value of a stable block replica can be greater than the state-identifier value contained in the last BFR for the block. A stable block replica can therefore reflect the effect of operations logged to the block after the last block checkpoint. A BFR is written after the corresponding flush operation is done so that, until the corresponding BFR is written, the state-identifier of the stable block replica is greater than the state-identifier value of the last BFR. Multiple block flush operations can have been executed before the BFR corresponding to the first of them is reflected in the stable log, so that even when this BFR is reflected in the stable log, the state-identifier value of the stable block can be larger than the state-identifier of the last BFR for the block. Forcing BFRs to the stable log instead of writing them and not allowing multiple outstanding block flushes would not remove the problem that the state-identifier value of the stable block replica can be larger than the state-identifier value of the last BFR. There is still a delay from when the flush operation is done until the BFR is reflected in the stable log. Operations done after the last BFR can therefore be reflected in the stable block replica.

The DBF policy forces a start flush block log record (start-BFR) to the stable log before the flush operation is requested and writes a commit-BFR to the log when the flush operation is acknowledged. The DBF policy determines precisely which flush block operations are in progress when a node crash occurs, i.e. the start-BFRs written without a matching commit-BFR. For every block not in a flush when a node crash occurs, the state-identifier value equals the state identifier value of the last start-BFR. No operations executed after the last start-BFR is therefore reflected in the stable block replica. It is known without reading the block which operations are missing from the stable block replica, for blocks not in flushing when the node crash occurred. The effect of this on selective redo is analysed in section 7.9.2. The DBF policy induces more log disc accesses during normal operations than the SBF policy resulting from forcing the start-BFRs. The DBF policy also produces a larger log volume of the same reason.

If a block flush operation is not atomic, the set of blocks in the flushing process equals the set of possibly crashed stable blocks resulting from the node crash. This information cannot be deduced if the SBF policy is used, since the start of a flush operation is not logged.

7.4.2 Hot-Spot Block Checkpoints

When restarting a node after recovering from a node crash, it is important to avoid threatening the availability of soft real-time transaction services caused by prolonged initial transaction response times. It is therefore important to regain the effect of the DB cache to avoid unnecessarily long transaction response times caused by disc accesses to hot-spot blocks.

To obtain fast DB cache effect after a node crash restart, a *hot-spot table* containing the block identifiers of hot-spot blocks can be included in the node checkpoints. A block is a hot-spot if it has stayed continuously in the DB buffer over a given number of checkpoints. The hot-spot blocks are read into main memory by a transaction based on the hot-spot table of the last checkpoint, if they are not already contained in the DB buffer after the recovery processing.

7.5 The Tuple Access Strategy

Tuple access stability is required during transaction failure recovery and node crash recovery undo processing based on the tuple and index tuple undo identification policy (see section 7.3.1). A new aspect of access stability is introduced by the TPK undo identification policy since the tuple access methods are used during the node crash undo processing.

7.5.1 Access Method Policies

A table maps a tuple to its record representation and is implemented by an access method (see section 7.1). An access method can be single- or multi-leveled. The records representing tuples are contained in the bottom level blocks. Index-tuples are contained in higher level blocks. The tuple access methods are based on the primary key defined on a table ([Lys86a], [HRL89], [HA89b], [HSAG90]). The primary key interval stored in one block is not overlapped by the primary key interval of other blocks at the same level. A B-tree access method, for example, obeys these requirements ([BM72], [PLL81], [BHG87], [ML89], [HRA+90], [SC91]). The searching at any level is based on the primary key. A hash table access method with a separate B-tree or a linked block list per hash table entry also satisfies these requirements ([BHW74], [Moh90]). The hash key is calculated from the primary key, and the primary key is used in the searching.

Access method maintenance is subtransaction oriented and uses AM block locks (see section 7.1). Block split/merge uses either the transaction consistent or the action consistent block split/merge policy (see section 6.5.4). A **recursive action consistent block split/merge** policy is used if a subtransaction is used for each level requiring a block split/merge or an index-tuple inserted or

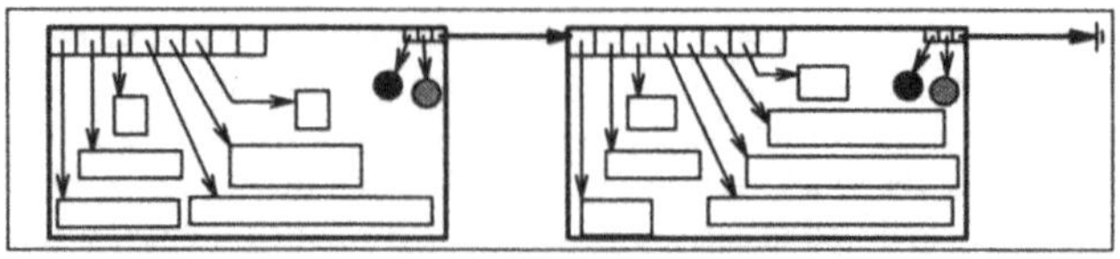

Figure 7.3: The link- and the upper/lower border policies. Each block contains an upper border record (black bullet) indicating that the primary key value of every tuple in the block is less than its primary key. The block also contains a lower border record (gray bullet) indicating that the primary key values of every tuple contained in the block is greater than or equal to its value. A link pointer exists between the two blocks so that the block pointed to contains tuples with the next largest primary key values within the same level.

deleted, as a result of a split/merge at the bottom level in a multi leveled access method ([HRA+ 90]). Every higher level subtransaction is an independent top-level transaction (see section 10.4).

An **action consistent access method** occurs if the recursive action consistent policy is used. A subtransaction that splits a block is committed without the index-tuple at the next higher level being inserted. An action consistent access method requires consistent tuple access. It must therefore be combined with other policies (see section 7.5.2) to provide tuple access.

7.5.2 The Link and Border Policies

The link and border policies are used to compensate for action consistent access methods so that consistent tuple access is provided during normal transaction and transaction failure recovery processing (see section 7.5.1).

The **link** policy is followed if a block contains a pointer referring to the block with the immediate larger primary key value interval within the same level. (See figure 7.3.) A double link policy, in which a block contains pointers referring to the block with the immediately larger and the block with the immediately smaller primary key value intervals within the level, is not analysed since it is not required to compensate for the action consistent access method or to obtain block autonomous recovery (see section 7.6.4).

An access method follows the **upper border** policy if a block contains a primary key value border record so that the primary key value of every tuple or index-tuple contained in the block is less than the primary key value of its upper border record. The **upper/lower border** policy is followed if a block contains both a lower and an upper border record. The lower border record indicates that the primary key of every tuple or index-tuple contained in the block is greater than or equal to its primary key value.

The link and upper border policies are used with the action consistent block split/merge policy to compensate for an action consistent access method. Tuples or index-tuples moved as a result of a block split/merge are always moved in the direction of the link pointer. If a block split subtransaction to a level is committed and no subtransaction inserting an index-tuple at the next level has yet been committed, consistent access to the moved tuples is based on the use of the link and upper border policies. The upper border policy indicates that if the primary key value of the requested tuple is larger than the primary key value of the upper border record, the requested tuple is within a block in the direction pointed to by the link pointer. The link pointer is therefore followed.

If a block merge subtransaction to a level is committed and no subtransaction has removed the index-tuple referring to the empty block and the empty block itself, consistent access to the moved tuples through the index-tuple is based on the upper border record of the empty block. Its primary key value indicates that every tuple is contained in a block in the direction indicated by the link pointer. The link pointer is followed.

It will be shown that the upper/lower border policy can be used to obtain block complete recovery when the action consistent block split/merge policy is used (see section 7.6.4).

7.5.3 Block Split and Merge

The presentation of block split and merge in this section is supplementary to the presentation given in section 6.5.4. A split/merge operation is physical to a block since it updates the border records and link pointer of the block. The BPK/BPK combined identification policy must therefore be used by split/merge log records, with a NONE primary key part. Operations moving a tuple or index-tuple from one block to another as a result of a block split/merge are physical to each of the involved blocks, i.e. a tuple is deleted from the original block by a delete tuple operation and inserted into the other block by an insert tuple operation.

A block merge is activated either when a block becomes empty or when the filling degree of adjacent blocks becomes too low, depending on the policy adapted by the actual access method. The TechRa DBMS, for example, merges blocks when they become empty ([Lys86a]). The block that is removed from an access method by a block merge is released when the transaction containing the split/merge commits, if the transaction consistent block split/merge policy is used.

The action consistent block split/merge policy can either release a block that is removed by a block merge when the subtransaction commits, or adopt a late block release policy. A block is released under the **late block release** policy if the block cannot be reused again until all the transactions that were active to the tuples or index-tuples that are moved, or that would have been moved if they were not deleted by an active transaction, are terminated. If some of these transactions require undo access to some moved tuples based on the BPK undo identification policy, the late release policy combined with the link and upper border policies will provide tuple consistent access. Even if block merge is activated to empty blocks, multiple transactions can be active to the released block since multiple concurrent active transactions can have deleted the last tuples from the block. It is assumed that every reference to a tuple from external to the block is based on the its primary key (see section 7.5.5).

7.5.4 DB Buffer Policies for Block Split/Merge Subtransactions

The action consistent block split policy can be combined with any of the DB buffer policies (see section 4.6). The choice of DB buffer policies influences the access method consistency at a node crash recovery and the response time delay of a split/merge subtransaction.

The following case illustrates an access method inconsistency and lost tuples occurring as a result of a committed block split subtransaction being incompletely reflected in the stable DB when a node crash occurs.

Block $B1$ is split by the subtransaction T_1 so that the tuple P that was contained in $B1$ is moved to the block $B2$. T_1 commits. Block $B1$ is flushed after the commit. The tuple P is therefore not contained in the stable replica of $B1$. A node crash occurs before $B2$ is flushed. $B2$ therefore neither reflects the border and link pointer values of T_1 nor contains P. The access method is inconsistent since the link pointer and border values of $B2$ do not reflect the last committed transaction and P is lost. Node crash recovery is required to redo the update to its border record and link pointer, and redo the insert of P into $B2$.

The inconsistency documented in the previous case would not have been removed by use of the no-steal DB buffer policy for the two blocks involved in a split/merge subtransaction. The original block ($B1$) may still reflect the result of the subtransaction while the other block ($B2$) reflects no effects of the subtransaction at the node crash. A similar inconsistency could occur if the force DB buffer policy was adopted since a node crash could occur during the commit processing of T_1 after $B1$ is flushed, but before $B2$ is flushed.

The combination of the force and no-steal policy with the semantics of the split/merge transaction can prevent inconsistent access methods from occurring at node crash recovery. The no-steal policy prevents the original block from being flushed during the split/merge. If the original block is *flushed last* of the blocks involved in the subtransaction, this block flush atomically introduces all the effects of the subtransaction into the stable DB. The forcing prolongs the execution time of a split/merge subtransaction because of the block flushes done. The force and no-steal policy combination is used by the TechRa DBMS ([HL86]).

7.5.5 Tuple Access

This section shows that neither the SPL nor the RMP policies (see section 5.5 and 6.5) are required in the context of the table oriented recovery approach. This represents a simplification compared to the compensation recovery approach, in which these policies were required (see section 6.5.4).

The logical position of a tuple within a block is determined by its primary key value. There is therefore no need to preserve the index position of a deleted tuple within a block over the lifetime of the transaction as was required by the compensation oriented recovery approach. The requirement for application of the SPL policy is therefore eliminated (see sections 5.5 and 6.5.3).

The use of the transaction consistent block split/merge policy or the action consistent block split/merge policy, together with the link and upper border policies, removes the need for the RMP policy to provide consistent tuple access during normal transaction and transaction failure recovery processing. Consistent information concerning where a tuple has been moved to is given as part of the access method instead of being connected to the records. To remove the use of the RMP policy, every internal reference to a tuple within the DBMS must be based on its primary key. Every secondary index to a relation is an index table (see section A.3). Inclusion of the primary key of the primary tuple as primary tuple reference in secondary index tuples removes the requirement of using the RMP policy (see [Tec84] and [HRA+90]).

7.5.6 The Zombie Policies

The zombie policies are concerned with preservation of primary key uniqueness in the context of a dynamic database. To preserve primary key uniqueness, care must be taken when inserting and deleting tuples and updating primary keys of existing tuples. This is termed the *zombie problem* and is part of the phantom problem ([BHG87]). A "zombie" is a deleted tuple or an updated primary key reappearing as a consequence of a transaction abort.

When a tuple is deleted its primary key value must be avoided reused by another transaction before the transaction deleting the tuple is committed. If this is not obeyed inconsistencies may occur. An inconsistency is caused if the transaction deleting the tuple aborts after the transaction reusing the primary key value committed. The primary key is no longer unique since two tuples have the same primary key value (see section A.4). Similar inconsistencies may occur if write operations are allowed on primary key fields. An abort may cause a tuple to acquire its old primary key value again.

A **zombie locking** policy locks the primary key value of a deleted tuple ([HRA+90]). A zombie lock conflicts with an insert operation inserting a tuple with the locked primary key value. A zombie lock may also conflict with a write operation if write operations are allowed to update primary key fields. A zombie locking policy locks also both the old and the new primary key value when write operations are allowed on primary key fields. This avoids insert and write operations by other transactions on both the affected primary key values. A zombie locking scheme allows insert, delete, and write operations to be performed on primary keys.

If delta operations are allowed on primary key fields, a locking scheme must be provided to preserve unique primary keys independently of transaction termination combinations. The following case illustrates this. Two different tuples $P1$ and $P2$ exist in the same table. Their primary key values are 10 and 12. Transaction T_8 performs a delta operation to $P1$ increasing its primary key by 5 from 10 to 15. Transaction T_9 then performs a delta operation to $P1$ increasing its primary key by 2 from 15 to 17. Then transaction T_8 fails and the primary key value of $P1$ is decreased by 5 from 17 to 12. The result is an inconsistent DB since $P1$ and $P2$ have the same primary key values.

To provide primary key uniqueness, the locking scheme must lock all possible commit and abort primary key combinations for the concurrent transactions performing primary key delta operation on a tuple. A primary key delta operation is not allowed if any possible resulting primary key value conflicts with any existing or any locked primary key. The number of primary key delta locks may grow exponentially with the number of transactions performing primary key delta operations to the tuple. An alternative to such a locking scheme is to disallow delta operations on primary key fields. In the remainder of this book, this alternative is assumed to be used.

Undo of a tuple delete operation requires free space to reinsert the tuple. This free space must be located such that the reinserted tuple becomes correctly located given its primary key value. Similar problems occur during undo processing if write or delta operations are allowed on primary key fields and updating a primary key may cause a tuple to move. A **zombie space lock (ZSL)** policy can be used to lock free space for zombies over the lifetime of a transaction. The locked space is connected to the primary key value and is therefore managed independently of the actual block the zombie tuple is to be inserted into. The BSL policy connects locked space to block (see section 6.5.4). An alternative to using a ZSL policy is allowing for block splits even during transaction recovery processing, which will be returned to in section 13.12.

7.5.7 The Transaction Consistent Block Split/Merge Policy

The transaction consistent block split/merge policy compromises the fine granularity tuple locking model since split/merged blocks are AM write locked over the lifetime of the transaction performing the split/merge (see section 6.5.4).

The transaction consistent block split/merge policy is simpler than the recursive action consistent policy. Since the transaction consistent block split/merge policy transforms an access method from one consistent state to another consistent state, there is no need to use either the link or any border policies to preserve consistent tuple access. The late block release policy is also not needed (see section 7.5.3).

The transaction consistent block split/merge policy can use the BPK undo identification policy, since a tuple or index-tuple will be found in the same block as it was when the do operation was executed. The transaction consistent block split/merge policy cannot be combined with the TPK undo identification policy to the moved tuples, since a consistent access method may not exist during a transaction failure recovery. If for example a transaction fails while it is splitting a block and before it has inserted an index-tuple into a block at the next level, no primary key based access path exist to the tuples in the new block. Therefore the transaction recovery cannot use the access method to provide undo tuple access.

7.5.8 The Recursive Action Consistent Block Split/Merge Policy

The recursive action consistent block split/merge policy concurrently locks at the most two blocks per split/merge subtransaction. A block is AM locked only for the duration of the subtransaction (see section 7.1). The top-level transaction requesting a block split/merge is delayed only for the duration of the bottom level split/merge subtransaction ([HRA+90]). The recursive action consistent block split/merge policy therefore removes the soft real-time transaction service availability threat which is inherent in the transaction consistent split/merge policy.

The action consistent block split/merge policy allows top-level transactions to be active to tuples moved by a split/merge subtransaction. A tuple can therefore be contained in a different block when a top-level transaction performs an undo tuple operation than when the corresponding do operation was executed. If the sequential undo policy is followed, DB state changing tuple operations by top-level transactions can use the BPK undo identification policies if it is combined with the late block release policy. If a block merge subtransaction releases a block before all transactions that may access it to perform undo processing of a moved tuple are terminated, inconsistencies can occur. The late block release policy must therefore be used to keep the border record and link pointer of a released block consistent until all transactions that were active to the moved tuples and to the deleted tuples that should have been moved are terminated.

It will be shown in section 7.6.7 that if the non-sequential undo policy is used, the BPK undo identification policy cannot be used. Since subtransactions use block granularity locks to higher access method levels, no concurrent subtransactions will be active to a block locked by a block split/merge subtransaction. Therefore the use of the late block release policy is not required to these higher level blocks.

The TPK undo identification policy can be used by top-level DB state changing tuple operations. A transaction that was active to a tuple before it was moved accesses the tuple by its primary key also during the transaction failure recovery processing. The late block release policy is therefore not required since undo processing is independent of the block in which the tuple originally was contained. Since the access method is used to access the tuple during node crash recovery undo processing, an action consistent access path to a tuple must have been recovered before the undo processing is done to the tuple. This can be accomplished by using the no-steal and force DB buffer policy for split/merge involved blocks (see section 7.5.4) or by recovering the access method before recovery processing of the tuple operations by top-level transactions.

The TPK undo identification policy can also be used by DB state changing index-tuple operations that are not involved in a block split/merge, when it is extended with a level indicator. Since the block is not involved in any split/merge, consistent access within the block is provided when the corresponding undo operation is executed. An action consistent access path to the tuple must be recovered before the index-tuple undo processing is done during a node crash recovery. The TPKK policy must in this case be extended by including a level indicator in each block. This alternative is not further investigated, because block independent recovery to index-tuple or split/merge operations are not required since an access method is local to a node (see chapter 14).

If the action consistent block split/merge policy is used, the split/merge operation must be executed to the block into which the tuples are inserted before any of the moved tuples are inserted, and the split/merge operation must be executed to the block from which the tuples are deleted after all the moved tuples are deleted. If these requirements are not met, a block may contain tuples with primary key values outside its primary key range which may cause an inconsistent DB after a subtransaction failure recovery. If a block split/merge subtransaction fails after inserting a moved tuple and without having updated the border record, and the sequential transaction failure recovery policy and the BPK undo identification policy are used, then the block is accessed on its block identifier but the insert operations are not undone because the upper border record value does not indicate that the tuple is contained in the block. If these requirements are met and the sequential transaction failure recovery policy is used, the BPK undo identification policy can be used. The TPK undo identification policy cannot be used, because the access method is not action consistent. If a split/merge subtransaction fails after inserting a moved tuple into the other block but before the split/merge operation is executed to the original block, there exists no consistent access path to the other block.

If the action consistent block split/merge and the non-sequential transaction failure recovery policies are used (see section 7.8), the BPK/BPK combined identification policy must be used by the log records produced by the operations inserting moved tuples or index-tuples into the block. The undo split/merge log record parts are aggregated on the involved block identifiers. If the BPK/TPK identification policy is used for the tuple operations, they are aggregated on the primary key within each table. If the block aggregated split/merge operation to a block is undone before undoing the tuple operations, inconsistencies may occur because insert operations are not undone. If the tuple aggregated operations are undone before the block aggregated operations, inconsistencies may occur because some delete tuple operations will not be undone. If the BPK/BPK policy is used by both the split/merge and the tuple moving operations, the undo is executed in reverse order to each block, which removes these inconsistencies.

Splitting and merging blocks involves redistribution of primary key intervals between blocks. As a consequence, the block into which a zombie tuple will be reinserted can also be different from the original block in which it was contained. The BSL policy can therefore not be used since it is assumed that a zombie tuple will require space from the same block from which it was deleted if the transaction fails and the tuple is reinserted. The ZSL policy can, on the other hand, be used, since the required space is connected to the primary key of the tuple so that the block into which the zombie potentially will be reinserted keeps enough space free for it.

7.6 The Non-Sequential Recovery Strategy

Fast node crash recovery and fast transaction failure recovery are stated design goals (see section 2.6). The non-sequential recovery strategy provides recovery *work load reduction* and *speed up* compared to the sequential recovery methods presented in the compensation oriented recovery approach (see sections 6.6, 6.7, and 6.8). The fast recovery is obtained through: i) single log scan, the log part involved in the recovery is scanned only once; ii) log-aggregation, log records are aggregated to data items in main memory; iii) complete and autonomous block recovery, a block is at most read once during a recovery and the recovery of a block is independent of other blocks; and iv) CPU and I/O parallelism, multiple blocks and tuples can concurrently be under recovery and multiple blocks can concurrently be accessed from disc.

This section analyses the restrictions to the aggregation of log record parts and the synchronisation requirements between tuple and index-tuple recovery. In the previous recovery approaches, transaction failure recovery and node crash recovery have been done sequentially, i.e. done by following the transaction local and node global log sequences. The **non-sequential node crash recovery** policy is followed if the node crash recovery work is not done according to the node global log sequence. The **non-sequential transaction failure recovery** policy is followed if the transaction failure recovery work is not done according to the transaction local log sequence.

7.6.1 The Single Log Scan Policy

The **single log scan** policy is used if the log records involved in recovery processing are read into main memory by a single log scan and further log passes are done in main memory (see section 5.7.4). Main memory overflow polices are not presented in this chapter but will be included in chapter 14.

The single log scan policy reduces the node crash recovery disc access work load for the restart methods requiring multiple log passes. All log passes except the first are done in main memory. To indicate what is gained, the redo log part is scanned at least twice when a sequential node crash recovery policy is combined with the steal/no-force DB buffer policies (see section 6.8.3). Since transaction failure recovery requires only one log pass, no log disc access work load reduction is obtained.

The single log scan policy gives recovery speed up to node crash recovery methods requiring multiple log scans as compared to the standard DB buffer policy. Main memory accesses to log records are faster than accesses through a log-buffer server (see section 5.3.4). No speed up is gained for transaction failure recovery by this policy since only one log pass is required.

7.6.2 The Log-Aggregation Policy

The **log-aggregation** policy is followed if log records or log record parts involved in a recovery are aggregated to their contained identification concepts so that the log sequence is preserved for each identifier. The log-aggregation policy must be combined with the dedicated DB buffer policy so that the log records involved in the recovery are read and aggregated in main memory. The **non-log-aggregation** policy is followed if the log required to perform recovery is read into main memory without any aggregation being done.

The dedicated DB buffer policy is assumed to be used. The log-aggregation policy splits the node log sequence into a collection of log sequences. Since the BPK redo identification policy is used, redo log record parts are aggregated to blocks identifiers. The log sequence is preserved for each block. If the BPK undo identification policy is used, undo log record parts are aggregated to the block identifier and the log sequence is preserved to the block. If the TPK undo identification policy is used, the undo log record parts are aggregated to a table and to a tuple within the table preserving the log sequence to the tuple.

The log-aggregation policy can reduce the DB disc access recovery work load. By aggregating redo and undo operations to data items, rereading and rewriting of a DB block can be avoided during the recovery processing. If a non-aggregation policy is used, a block can have been removed from the DB buffer between two succeeding recovery operations to the block. In these cases block reread and possibly rewrite occurs. The log-aggregation policy can also speed up the recovery processing. By eliminating DB block reread and rewrite, the recovery processing has to wait for fewer disc accesses.

The dedicated DB buffer policy can also be combined with a non-log-aggregation policy. The recovery work load reduction and speed up effects of the dedicated DB buffer policy of multiple log scans done in main memory are obtained, but not the work load and speed up effects of the log-aggregation policy. The node crash recovery methods presented with the compensation recovery approach (see section 6.8) can be used with a non-log-aggregation policy independently of redo and undo identification policies used.

The evaluation of the node crash recovery methods based on the number of log scans involved (see section 6.8) are not relevant when a dedicated DB buffer policy is used.

7.6.3 Asynchronous Recovery Policies

The **CPU asynchronous recovery** policy is followed if multiple undo or redo operations can concurrently be executed during a node crash or transaction failure recovery. The CPU asynchronous recovery policy is used to obtain recovery speed up. The CPU asynchronous recovery policy is combined with the log-aggregation policy so that multiple aggregates are recovered concurrently, i.e. no more than one redo or undo operation is active concurrently to each aggregate, but multiple redo or undo operations from different aggregates can be active concurrently. If for example redo and undo log record parts are aggregated to block identifiers CPU asynchronous recovery processing can be done to blocks.

The **I/O asynchronous recovery** policy is followed if multiple disc I/O operations can be active concurrently. An optimised block access policy is used if the blocks involved in the redo or undo recovery work are grouped to give reduced block access work load. If log records are aggregated to blocks, the block identifiers can be sorted on discs and physical properties of the disc to reduce the load per disc access ([GR88]).

The CPU asynchronous recovery policy can also be used to obtain transaction concurrent undo processing during node crash recoveries. In this case multiple transactions are undone asynchronously. This combination will not be investigated further in this book (but see [MHL+89], [Moh91], and section 14.1).

7.6.4 The Block Complete and Block Autonomous Recovery Policies

The **block complete recovery** policy is followed if all recovery processing to a block and the tuples or index-tuples it contains is performed so that the block is guaranteed never to be reread during the recovery processing. The block complete recovery policy exploits the work load reduction and speed up potential in the log-aggregation policy since all the aggregates related to a block are recovered at one time. The redo-undo sequentialisation and synchronisation between block and tuple undo aggregates are done to a block.

The **block autonomous recovery** policy is followed if no other blocks need to be read to recover the block. To obtain block autonomous recovery, synchronisation between blocks during the recovery processing must be avoided. Recovery processing that requires information not kept in the log record or block, from for example the data dictionary, must also be avoided.

7.6.5 Aggregation of Redo Log Record parts

This section shows that, because state-identifiers are connected to block granules, log-aggregation of redo log record parts must be done to granules no finer than blocks. Since the BPK redo identification policy is used, the redo log record parts will be aggregated to blocks so that the block log sequence is preserved.

If log-aggregation is done to granules finer than blocks, for example tuples, inconsistencies may occur between the actual block state and the block state as expressed by the block state-identifier. This is illustrated by the following case. Transaction T_{10} performs a write operation on the tuple $P1$ contained in block $B1$, increasing the block state-identifier from 100 to 101. The transaction then performs a write operation to the tuple $P2$, which is also contained in the block $B1$ increasing the block state-identifier to 102. The transaction then commits. The node crashes before $B1$ is flushed so that none of the write operations are reflected in the stable block replica. At node crash recovery the redo log record parts are aggregated to the involved tuples. The recovery server chooses to recover $P2$ before $P1$. The operation to $P2$ is redone, increasing the block state-identifier to 102. The operation to $P1$ is then attempted to be redone, but is not since the block state-identifier value tells that it is already reflected in the block. The result is an inconsistent DB.

The previous case shows that if state-identifiers are connected to block granules, aggregation cannot be done to granules finer than blocks. If redo log record parts are to be aggregated to tuples, state-identifiers have to be connected to tuples or fractions of tuples (see chapter 11). The previous case also shows that if state-identifiers are connected to blocks and non-sequential redo recovery is used, the TPK redo identification cannot be used since redo log record parts would be aggregated to tuples.

7.6.6 Aggregation of Undo Log Record Parts with the Transaction Consistent Block Split/Merge Policy

This section analyses the aggregation of undo log record parts combined with the use of the transaction consistent block split/merge policy. It will be shown that aggregation can be done to blocks if the BPK undo identification policy is used. It will also be shown that the TPK undo identification policy cannot be used.

A transaction that has performed a DB state changing operation to a tuple or index-tuple without later moving the tuple will, during a transaction failure recovery, find the tuple in the same block as when the do operation was executed. This is a consequence of the fact that a transaction that performs a split/merge obtains exclusive locks on the moved tuples. The BSL or ZSL policy will ensure that enough free space exists so that a deleted tuple can be reinserted into its original block. The BPK undo identification can therefore be used for non-moved tuple and index-tuples. The move of a tuple or index-tuple is assumed to be logged physically to the involved blocks by a delete from the original block and an insert into the new block (see section 7.5.3). The undo of the move can therefore be done physically to the involved blocks without synchronisation between the blocks. The BPK undo identification policy can therefore also be used for moved tuple and index-tuples. Non-sequential undo processing can be done autonomously to each block since no synchronisation is required between the blocks. Undo operations to a tuple must be done in reverse order relative to the tuple log sequence (see section 6.6.1). This requirement is met if undo operations are done in reverse order relative to each block sequence.

Since moving a tuple from one block to another is logged physically to the involved blocks (see section 7.5.3), the BPK undo identification policy must be used to these operations (see section 7.5.7). If the TPK policy is used for non-moving tuple and index tuple operations, problems occur with performing the undo in reverse order to a tuple. The tuple operations representing the move are aggregated to the blocks and the non-moving operations to the tuples. Non-moving tuple operations can have been done to a moved tuple both before and after the move within the same transaction. If the block aggregated operations are undone before the tuple aggregated operations to a block, inconsistencies may result. Inconsistencies may also result if the tuple aggregated operations are undone before the block aggregated operations. This is illustrated by the following case:

A transaction performs a delta operation to a tuple. The transaction splits the block containing the tuple so that the tuple is moved. As a consequence the tuple is deleted from its original block and inserted into the new block. Then the transaction performs another delta operation to the tuple before a node crash occurs. If during the node crash recovery of the original block, the block aggregated operations are undone first, followed by the tuple aggregated operations, the tuple is first reinserted into the original block. The reinserted tuple reflects the effect of the first delta operation. If the tuple aggregated operations are then undone, both the delta operations are undone which gives an inconsistent result since the last delta operation was not reflected in the block. If the tuple aggregated operations are undone first and the block aggregated last, the tuple is reinserted into the original block but the effect of the delta operation is not undone, which also is inconsistent.

7.6.7 Aggregation of Undo Log Record Parts with the Action Consistent Block Split/Merge Policy

This section analyses the aggregation of undo log record parts combined with the action consistent block split/merge policy. It will be shown that aggregation of tuple undo log record parts by top-level transactions must be done to tuples. It will also be shown that block aggregation of subtransaction operations can be combined with tuple aggregation of top-level transaction operations if the block aggregated undo processing is performed before the tuple aggregated undo processing.

Aggregation of undo log record parts produced by top-level transactions cannot be done to blocks. A block split/merge subtransaction can have moved a tuple between the do and the undo operation. Aggregation to blocks will therefore not guarantee that undo to a tuple is done in reverse order which is required to guarantee a consistent DB (see section 6.6.1). The following case illustrates an inconsistency occurring if aggregation is done to blocks.

Transaction T_{10} performs a do-write operation to a tuple P which is contained in block $B1$. $B1$ is then merged by a subtransaction with block $B2$. P is deleted from $B1$ and inserted into $B2$. T_{10} performs another do-write to P which is now contained in $B2$. T_{10} then fails and its transaction log sequence is read into main memory and aggregated to the involved blocks. CPU asynchronous recovery processing is done to the blocks. $B1$ happens to be recovered before $B2$ so that the operations performed to $B1$ are undone before the operations to $B2$. The two write operations to P are as a result of this undone in forward order. An inconsistent DB is the result.

The inconsistency discussed above is caused by the non-sequential recovery processing combined with block aggregation. The inconsistency is independent of the use of the late block release policy since that policy only provides consistent tuple access but does not influence the sequence of undo operations to a tuple. The inconsistency would have been avoided if the undo log record parts had been aggregated to the tuples to which the operations were executed, instead of to the blocks in which the tuples were contained.

Operations by top-level transactions are not executed to tuples after an active split/merge subtransaction has AM locked the block in which they are contained. A consistent recovery is therefore obtained if undo processing of all subtransaction operations are done before undo processing of any top-level operations to tuples contained in the block.

7.6.8 Block Complete Recovery

To obtain block complete recovery (see section 7.6.4), undo processing to all tuples contained in a block must be done before the block is released. Since a block can be accessed by its block identifier during redo processing or undo processing of subtransaction operations, it must be determined based on information within the block itself which primary key interval is contained in the block. The upper border policy is not sufficient to determine this since the lower border value is not known. The following case illustrates this.

Block $B1$ contains three tuples $P1$, $P2$, and $P3$ where the primary key value of $P1$ is the smallest and the primary key of $P3$ the greatest. Transaction T_1 deletes $P1$ and then deletes $P3$. Transaction T_2 then writes $P2$ and commits. The block is flushed before a node crash occurs. Node crash redo reads the block and finds that no redo is needed since all operations are reflected in the block. The undo processing is reinserting the $P3$ tuple into the block since the upper border and the primary key value of $P2$ determines that the tuple is to be contained in the block. The undo processing on the other hand cannot decide if $P1$ is to be contained in the block since its primary key is smaller than any of the primary key values in the block. The upper border value of the block containing the next non-overlapping smaller primary key interval (block to the left of $B1$) could be larger than the primary key value of $P1$. To determine if $P1$ belongs to $B1$ or to some block to the left of $B1$, the block to the left of $B1$ must be read, which compromises the block autonomous requirement.

The uncertainty of whether a tuple belongs to a block or not is removed if the upper/lower border policy is used instead of the upper border policy. During normal processing the lower border is known from either the upper border of the block containing the next smaller primary key interval or from the index-tuple of the next higher level. By using the block identifier to access the block, the lower border is not known. By applying the upper/lower border policy it is possible to perform block complete recovery.

7.7 The Compensation Recovery Strategy

This section analyses the consequences of the non-sequential recovery policy on the compensation recovery strategy. The non-sequential recovery policy does not necessarily undo a transaction by producing CLRs in reverse order relative to the node global transaction-chain of the non-CLRs for which they are compensating. That is the case with sequential transaction failure recovery. The non-sequential recovery policy produces CLRs in reverse order to the log-aggregate transaction-chain.

The log-backchain and transaction-backchain CLR policies indicate explicitly which non-CLR a CLR compensates for. These policies allow any sequence of sequential and non-sequential incomplete transaction recovery and node crash recoveries. The counting CLR on the other hand does not explicitly state which non-CLR a CLR compensates for. It therefore requires that an incomplete (non-)sequential transaction recovery is followed by (non-)sequential node crash recoveries.

The log-backchain and transaction-backchain CLR policy can also be used to indicate that all non-CLRs spanned by the backchain pointer in the log-aggregate or node sequence transaction-chain are compensated for. Inconsistencies may occur if a non-sequential incomplete transaction recovery is followed by a sequential node crash recovery or if it is interpreted as an incomplete sequential transaction recovery by a non-sequential node crash recovery.

7.8 The Transaction Failure Recovery Strategy

The transaction failure recovery strategy determines how a failed transaction is recovered by undoing its DB state changing operations. Conditional use of the non-sequential recovery strategy is applied to transaction failure recovery. The non-sequential undo policy is used to recover long transactions where significant work load reduction and speed up can be gained as compared to using the sequential transaction recovery policy. The "midnight rider" ([GR88]) and "multi log tape" transactions ([Moh91]) illustrate the existence of such long transactions in production environments. The sequential recovery strategy is used to recover small transactions where the overhead of the non-sequential policy is not compensated for by the load reduction and speed up gained. Heuristics are assumed to be used based on the transaction log volume when deciding if the sequential or the non-sequential recovery policy is to be used.

Only non-sequential transaction failure recovery methods are presented in this section since the sequential alternative corresponds to the transaction failure recovery strategy presented in section 6.6. Two different non-sequential transaction failure recovery methods are presented depending on if the transaction consistent or the action consistent block split/merge policy is used.

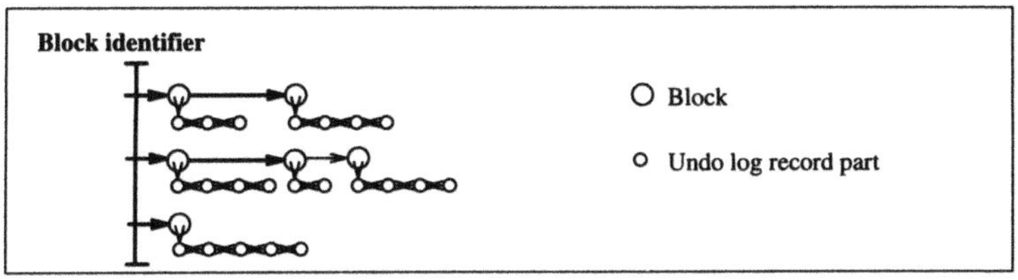

Figure 7.4: Case data structure for log aggregation when the transaction consistent block split/merge policy is used. The undo log record parts are aggregated to blocks.

7.8.1 Non-Sequential Transaction Failure Recovery Method with The Transaction Consistent Block Split/Merge Policy

It was shown in section 7.5.3 that split/merge operations are physical to blocks. The BPK undo identification policy must therefore be used to split/merge log records. In section 7.5.7 it was shown that the primary key access method cannot be used to access the tuples involved in a split/merge during undo processing when the move is done physically to the involved blocks. The access path to the involved tuples is not necessarily consistent as a result of the split/merge. The BPK undo identification policy is therefore used by the log records for these tuple operations. In section 7.6.6, it was shown that tuple operations not involved in moving the tuple between blocks cannot be aggregated to tuples. The undo processing to tuples involved in both move and non-move operations is not guaranteed to be done in reverse order. Therefore the BPK undo identification policy must be used to all log records.

The undo log record parts are aggregated to their contained block identifier. The log records are read into main memory by following the transaction log chain and the undo log record parts are aggregated to the block identifier value contained in the log record so that the transaction log chain is maintained for each block. The undo processing is done in reverse order relative to each block aggregate producing a CLR per undone operation. The CLRs are therefore produced in reverse order to the non-CLRs per block aggregate. Figure 7.4 illustrates a case log-aggregation data structure. A hash table is supported for the block identifiers with a list or tree structure for each entry. A linked structure preserving the block log chain is maintained for each aggregate.

Block autonomous recovery (see section 7.6.4) is obtained the following way: since the tuple move operations are physical to each of the involved blocks, there are no synchronisation requirements between blocks. The primary key log vector policy is used to obtain dictionary independence so that no dictionary blocks need to be read to recover a block (see sections 7.3.2 and 7.3.2).

Block complete recovery (see section 7.6.4) is obtained by reading a block into main memory and then executing all recovery operations to it. This ensures that the block is not reread in the recovery processing which is a consequence of aggregating undo log record parts to the blocks. The ZSL policy is used to prevent new block split/merges from occurring during the transaction roll back (see section 7.5.6).

The CPU asynchronous recovery policy is used to a block so that multiple block aggregates can concurrently be recovered (see section 7.6.3). The concurrency degree is determined by the resources dedicated to the transaction roll back. The complete set of blocks involved in the recovery is known when the log-aggregation is completed since the log records are aggregated to blocks. The I/O asynchronous optimised block access policy (see section 7.6.3) can be used when reading the blocks to be recovered.

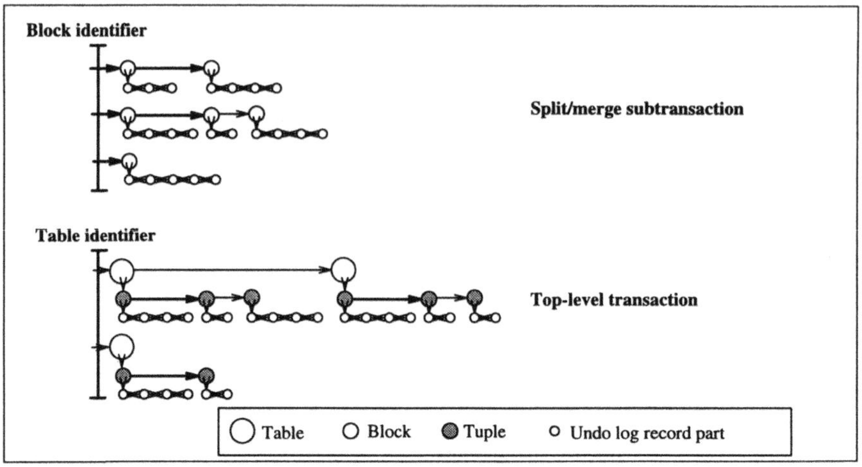

Figure 7.5: Case transaction failure recovery log-aggregation combined with the action consistent block split/merge policy. Undo log record parts by top-level transactions are aggregated to tables and, within a table, to tuples. Undo log record parts by subtransactions are aggregated to blocks.

7.8.2 Non-Sequential Transaction Failure Recovery Method with The Action Consistent Block Split/Merge Policy

Split/merge operations are physical to blocks (see section 7.5.3), so that the BPK undo identification policy must be used to split/merge log records. An access method is also temporarily inconsistent during a split/merge subtransaction when the link and border policies are used. During a block split/merge subtransaction the border values of the two adjacent blocks may temporarily overlap and action consistent access paths are temporarily not necessarily provided to tuples or index-tuples contained in the block they are moved to (see section 7.5.7). To access the tuples or index-tuples involved in a split/merge subtransaction during undo recovery processing, the primary key access method cannot be used. The BPK undo identification policy must be used instead. Block granularity AM locks are used to index-tuple operations. The BPK undo identification policy can therefore be used for these operations (see section 7.6.7). Block transparency is not required for index-tuple operations since they are local to an access method at a node. The BPK undo identification policy is used to all operations by subtransactions.

Tuple operations by top-level transactions cannot be aggregated to blocks as a result of the action consistent block split/merge policy (see section 7.6.7). The TPK undo identification policy is therefore used to every log record produced by top-level transaction DB state changing operations.

The log records are read into main memory by following the transaction log chain. The undo log record parts produced by a subtransaction are aggregated to the block identifier contained in the log record as presented in section 7.8.1. The undo log record parts by a top-level transaction are aggregated to the table identifier contained in the log record and within the table to the tuple aggregate by the primary key value contained in the log record (see section 5.3.2). Recovery of a failed top-level transaction will only involve tuple aggregated undo log record parts. Recovery of a failed higher access method level subtransaction will only involve block aggregated undo log record parts. Recovery of a bottom level split/merge subtransaction will involve both block and tuple aggregated undo log record parts since the top-level transaction initiating the subtransaction will be undone along with the subtransaction (see section 10.4).

Figure 7.5 illustrates a case log-aggregation data structure. The log-aggregation to blocks is identical to the log-aggregation presented in section 7.8.1. The log-aggregation to tables is supported by a hash table based on the table identifier with a list or tree structure for each entry. A list or tree structure is maintained for each table over the tuples involved in the recovery. A linked structure preserving the tuple log chain is maintained for each tuple aggregate.

Block autonomous recovery is obtained by use of the primary key log vector policy and by the fact that tuple move operations are physical to blocks (see section 7.8.1). Undo synchronisation is done to a block by completing the block aggregated undo processing to the block before performing any tuple aggregated undo processing to tuples contained in the block. Block complete recovery is obtained for a block requiring both block and tuple aggregated recovery by using this undo synchronisation to the block. Block complete recovery for every tuple contained in the block is obtained by using the upper/lower border policy. A block is the unit of CPU asynchronous recovery of the block aggregated log record parts. A tuple is the unit of CPU asynchronous recovery of the tuple aggregated log record parts. The I/O asynchronous recovery and optimised block access policies are used (see sections 7.6.3 and 7.8.1) to the blocks which are aggregated.

The AM lock to a block and the tuple locks to the tuples contained in a block are released when the block is completely recovered. This provides fast access to recovered blocks and tuples compared to the situation if all locks are released only when the transaction recovery is completed.

A top-level transaction may have to recover tuples with primary key values outside the primary key intervals of the aggregated split/merge operations. Recovery of these tuples is done concurrently with the block aggregated recovery. The tuple aggregated recovery avoids accessing blocks contained in the block aggregated recovery since the tuples contained in these blocks will be recovered with the block aggregated recovery. The primary key based tuple access methods are used to access these tuples and tuple positions. Optimised tuple access, specific to each tuple access method, to the blocks containing tuples to be recovered can be used to obtain recovery work load reduction and speed up, e.g. skip-scan read for B-trees ([HSAG90]).

7.9 The Node Crash Recovery Strategy

The node crash recovery strategy presented in this section is based on the non-sequential recovery strategy. The selective redo policy is adapted in combination with the block complete recovery policy. The selective aggregation policy avoids aggregation of log record parts not required in the recovery processing. Partially and gradually increased data availability during recovery processing is provided by locking the data-items requiring recovery processing and making the remainder available to transaction processing.

7.9.1 Redo and Undo Work Synchronisation

The BPK redo identification policy is used by all redo log record parts (see section 7.5). The redo log record parts are therefore aggregated to the block identifiers contained in the log record so that the block log chain is maintained. Redo operations are executed to a tuple logical block state equivalent to the state the do operation was executed to. Redo recovery work is done in forward work order to each block, which is required when state-identifiers are connected to the blocks (see section 7.6).

The redo-undo sequentialisation policy is followed to a block so that redo operations are done to the block before any undo operations are done to the block or to the tuples contained in the block. Since redo-undo synchronisation is done locally to a block, block complete recovery is obtained during node crash recovery. If global redo-undo synchronisation had been used instead, i.e. redo had been

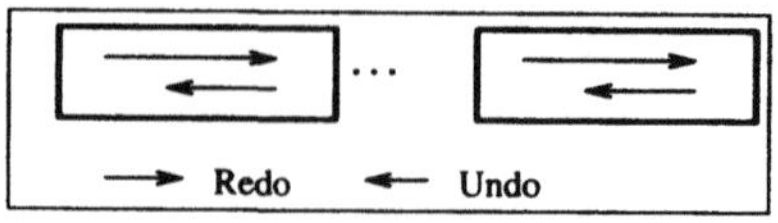

Figure 7.6: Synchronisation of redo and undo work with the transaction consistent block split/merge policy.

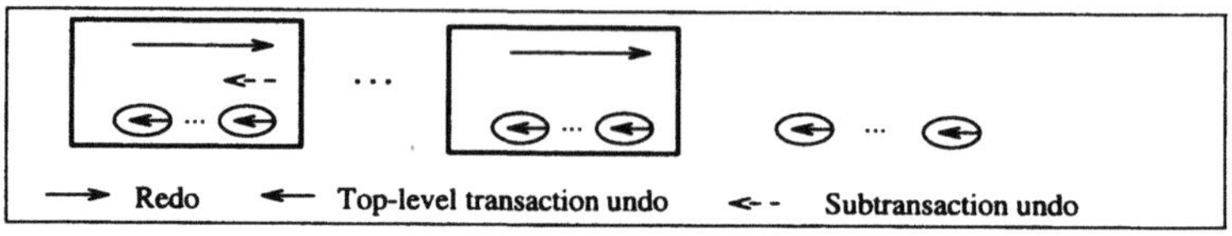

Figure 7.7: Synchronisation of redo and undo work with the action consistent block split/merge policy.

completed to the node before any undo operations had been allowed, block complete recovery would not have been obtained since a block could have been reread during the undo processing. The log-aggregation of undo log record parts and the synchronisation of undo recovery work is similar to that presented in section 7.8.1 if the transaction consistent block split/merge policy is used, or to that presented in section 7.8.2 if the action consistent block split/merge policy is used.

A case log-aggregation data structure for the redo log record parts can be the same as the data structure presented in section 7.8.1, and illustrated by figure 7.4, where the undo log record parts are substituted with redo log record parts.

The undoing of a tuple operation may hit a block involved neither in block aggregated redo nor in block aggregated undo processing if the action consistent block split/merge policy is used. This happens if a loser transaction has executed some operations to a tuple but no operations are executed to the block the tuple is contained in after the last block- or global checkpoint. If the fuzzy global checkpoint policy is used, no operations have been done to the block after the penultimate checkpoint. The block identifier cannot be used to access these tuples because the tuple can have been moved by a split/merge subtransaction before the checkpoint.

To obtain access to these tuples, the primary key based access method must have been recovered. It can not be determined which tuples have to be accessed through the primary key based access method before all blocks to be involved in the block oriented recovery have been read. The primary key interval of a block requiring redo recovery work but not requiring recovery processing of a split/merge operation is not known before the block is read. This is an effect of not including the upper/lower records in the block flush log records and dirty block tables (see section 4.7.4) and is removed in chapter 14. The set of tuples in this group is assumed to be small given the requirement to be fulfilled to be a member of the group. These tuples are therefore recovered after all the block accessed recovery has been completed for each table if AM locks are not used during the recovery.

Figure 7.6 illustrates node crash recovery work synchronisation when the transaction consistent block split/merge policy is used. The recovery is block autonomous so that no synchronisation is done between blocks. To each block the redo aggregated recovery is done before the undo aggregated recovery.

Figure 7.7 illustrates node crash recovery work synchronisation when the action consistent block split/merge policy is used. The recovery is autonomous to blocks. Within a block the redo work precedes the undo work and the subtransaction undo work precedes the top-level transaction induced undo work.

7.9.2 The Selective Redo Policy

The selective redo policy prevents redoing operations that later need to be undone because they belong to loser transactions (see section 6.7.3). The selective redo policy is analysed below in the context of the transaction consistent and the action consistent block split/merge policies. It is assumed that the log-aggregation and the block complete recovery policies are used.

If the single CLR policy is used with the transaction consistent block split/merge policy, an undo operation must be redone if the operation it compensates for is reflected in the block but the undo operation is not reflected in the block. Since the transaction consistent block split/merge policy is used, both a do and its compensating undo operation are done to the same block. Therefore an undo operations cannot be reflected in a stable block without the corresponding do operation being reflected in the block. A do operation by a loser transaction is not required to be redone. This is a consequence of the complete recovery policy, i.e. a block is never flushed until it has been completely recovered.

An undo operation does not need to be redone if the operation it is compensating for is not reflected in the block. CLRs are not required produced if a block-undo-checkpoint (BUC) log record is produced after all undo processing is completed to the block so that the block state-identifier value equals the block-undo-checkpoint log record identifier. This is a consequence of the block complete recovery policy. In this way the block state-identifier indicates that all the recovery is done. If BUCs are not used, CLRs must be produced.

If the DBF policy is used (see section 7.4.1), for every block not in the process of being flushed when a node crash occurs, it can be determined which log records are reflected in the block without reading the block. If no redo or undo operations have to be executed to the block, the block does not need to be read at all during the recovery processing.

If the recursive CLR policy is used, CLRs are treated similar to non-CLRs. Therefore an operation belonging to a loser transaction is not redone. An undo operation is not executed if the operation it compensates for is not reflected in the stable block. A BUC is produced when the block is completely recovered or CLRs are produced during the recovery.

Since redo log record parts are aggregated to blocks, the selective redo point to a block (see section 6.7.3) can be determined by scanning its redo aggregate in main memory in reverse production order.

The single CLR policy combined with the action consistent block split/merge policy has close similarities to the single CLR policy presented in section 6.7.3, which is a consequence of the fact that a do and an undo operation can be executed to different blocks. An undo operation must be redone if the block state-identifier is larger than or equal to the log record identifier of the operation it compensates for. An undo operation to a tuple that has been moved between the time that the do operation was executed and the time that the undo was executed must be preceded by a committed insert operation to the same block. Since this operation is therefore reflected in the block when the undo operation is executed, the block state value is greater than the log record identifier of the compensated operation. An (undo) operation by a loser transaction must be redone if it is followed by an operation that must be redone. A do operation to a tuple that is moved before the compensating undo operation is executed must therefore be followed by a committed delete operation to the same block. The do operation will therefore be redone.

An undo operation is not executed if the operation it is compensating for has a log record identifier value that is greater than the state-identifier value of the block. In this case, the do operation is not reflected in the block and the tuple has not been moved because in that case a preceding committed insert operation would have been executed to the block. A BUC can be produced when the block recovery is completed as an alternative to producing CLRs.

The recursive CLR policy, when combined with the action consistent block split/merge policy, is the same as the recursive CLR policy presented in section 6.7.3. This is a consequence of the fact that the recursive CLR policy is undoing both do and undo operations belonging to a loser transaction. Instead of logging CLRs, a BUC log record can be produced when a block is completely recovered.

7.9.3 The Selective Aggregation Policy

The **selective aggregation** policy is used if only the log record parts required by redo and undo operations are aggregated into main memory. The selective aggregation policy prevents main memory from being wasted by not keeping in main memory the log record parts which are not required to perform the recovery. The selective aggregation policy also avoids extensive garbage collection to remove log record parts during the aggregation.

The part of the log required to be scanned in order to perform a node crash recovery is limited to the blocks containing log records produced *after* the last or penultimate node global checkpoint, and the blocks containing log records produced *before* this checkpoint by loser transactions.

The redo selective aggregation policy depends on the use of the block state-identifier value of the last checkpoint to the block a DB state changing operation is executed to (see sections 5.7.6 and 7.4). This block state-identifier value is contained in either the dirty table of the last node global checkpoint (see section 4.7) or the last block local checkpoint to a block if the block local checkpoint is produced after the last node global checkpoint. The block state-identifier value of the last checkpoint to a block must therefore be known before aggregation of the log record parts preceding the checkpoint to obtain redo selective aggregation.

The undo selective aggregation policy depends on the use of the transaction status at the node crash time. The transaction status is determined from the last log record produced by the transaction. If the log is read in reverse production order from the last log record produced before the node crash, both the redo and undo selective aggregation conditions are met.

Fast access to the last node global checkpoint log position is provided by the checkpoint log policy (see section 4.7.5). At node crash recovery, the location of the last log record produced before the node crash can be determined by scanning the log in forward order from the log position of the last node global checkpoint, until the end of the log is found. The read log blocks are buffered in main memory. This policy determines the last log record without introducing additional recovery I/O work load, i.e. only one log scan is required. If the fuzzy checkpointing policy is used, no additional space is required since buffer space will be used to aggregate the log records preceding the last checkpoint. An alternative policy to determine the last log record which requires some additional block accesses, but no main memory buffering, is presented in [Hag90].

The selective log-aggregation reads the log in reverse order from the last log record from the buffered block replicas. A main memory block replica is released when the aggregation of its contained log records are completed. The remaining log blocks to be read to perform the log-aggregation are read in reverse production order.

7.9.4 Early Partial DB Availability During Node Crash Recovery

Partial DB availability during the node crash recovery can be provided by locking only those data items that need recovery processing and making the others available to normal transaction processing ([Moh91]).

If the transaction consistent block split/merge policy is used, the blocks requiring either redo or undo processing are known when the log-aggregation is done. By AM write locking these blocks, all data items involved in recovery processing are made unavailable. The DB can be opened for ordinary transaction processing when the log-aggregation is performed and the blocks requiring recovery are AM locked. An AM lock is kept on until the block recovery is completed for the block. In this way the DB gradually becomes more available during the recovery. Tuple locks by in-doubt transactions are set during the aggregation.

If the action consistent block split/merge policy is used, blocks requiring redo processing or block aggregated undo processing are AM write locked. The selective redo policy can be used to determine if redo processing is required to a block. A block where redo processing is not required but block aggregated undo processing is, is AM write locked. A write tuple lock is set to a tuple if a write, insert or delete tuple operation is to be undone. A delete tuple operation or a write tuple operation modifying the primary key sets a zombie lock to the tuple. Tuple locks are set for both loser and in-doubt transactions. The DB is opened for normal transaction processing when all the AM and tuple locks are set. AM block locks are released when the redo and block aggregated undo work is completed to a block. Tuple locks by loser transactions are released when the tuples contained in a block have completely recovered. A gradually increased availability is thereby provided.

7.10 Conclusion

The table oriented recovery approach supports tuple logging and fine granularity and semantically rich logging. In addition this approach supports block independent undo processing of DB state-changing tuple operations, i.e. the undo processing is logical to blocks and logical within blocks. This recovery design must be supported if non-blocking fragment replica production is to be provided ([HST+91b]). The table oriented approach therefore removes one major disadvantage when compared to the compensation oriented approach since the compensation oriented approach only supports undo processing that is block non-independent. Its undo processing is physical to blocks and logical within blocks (see section 6). To provide block independent undo processing, the tuple access methods may be used during the undo processing which is not required by block non-independent strategies.

The table oriented approach provides fast node crash recovery and fast transaction failure recovery. The fast recovery is obtained through scanning the log only once, aggregating the log in main memory, and applying I/O and CPU parallelism in both redo and undo recovery processing. The effect is recovery speed up and work load reduction compared to the sequential recovery strategy applied by the block and the record oriented recovery approaches. Conditional non-sequential transaction failure recovery is supported to obtain recovery work load reduction and to speed up the recovery of large transactions. Partial DB availability during a node crash recovery is also supported to provide fast restart after a node crash.

The main disadvantage of the table oriented approach is that redo recovery processing is block non-independent. The table oriented recovery approach can therefore not be used by DBMSs providing non-blocking production of fragment replicas with subfragmentation since both redo and undo block transparency are required. This disadvantage is removed in the HypRa recovery approach (see Part III). Another disadvantage of the table oriented recovery approach is its usage of disc based logging (see section 5.3.7), which imposes a minimum response time limit on transaction services (see section 5.3.7). This disadvantage is removed by the nWAL logging strategy presented in section 13.

Exercises

1. Why is only one recovery server used in the table oriented DBMS server architecture (see figure 7.1), as opposed to one independent recovery server per concurrency/scheduler server?

2. What are the advantages of applying the block and primary key identification (BPK) policy to log records as compared to (a) the block and record index identification policy and (b) the block and record address identification policy?

3. (a) What are the consequences of using the tuple and primary key (TPK) identification policy for the undo part of tuple log records? (b) Illustrate some problems of using the TPK identification policy for redo log record parts?

4. (a) What is the primary key log vector policy used for? (b) When can the non-primary key policy be used in combination with the TPK identification policy?

5. (a) What would be the effect on log records of including primary key vector and field type vector information in the tuples? (b) How can the (index) tuples be accessed during redo and undo recovery when the primary key vectors and field vectors are included in the (index) tuples? (c) What constraints do you see in including the primary key vectors and field vectors in the (index) tuples or log records compared to in both (index) tuples and log records? (d) What are the restrictions on adding new fields when primary key vectors and field type vectors are used? (e) What is the effect on partial record logging?

6. Compare the data volume and log volume of including primary key vectors and field type vectors in the tuples and in the log records. Assume that 70% of the DB state changing operations are a write operation, 10% are delta operations, 10% are delete operations, and 10% are insert operations. (a) What would be the break-even point between the two approaches? (b) Would the break-even point have been changed if partial tuple logging had been applied?

7. Make the same assumptions as in exercise 6. Further assume a transaction rate of 1000 transactions per second and 4 write tuple operations per transaction. Database archive copies are taken once per day and redo log record parts are maintained to go with the copies. The database is 1G byte and populated by 100 byte tuples. (a) Should the primary key vector and field vector be included in the log records? (b) What would the effect be of producing a database archive copy once every hour?

8. What would be the log volume reduction caused by partial tuple logging as compared to complete tuple logging when the BPK/TPK combined identification policy is used in the following case? The tuples are 100 bytes each and composed of 10 fields of equal size. The primary key includes 1 field. All operations are tuple writes updating 1 field each.

9. (a) Why should both lower and upper border records be included in the blocks? (b) What would be the effect of applying the upper border policy, (c) the lower border policy, and (d) the no border policy?

10. (a) What are the differences between the single block flush logging policy and the double block flush logging policy with respect to flushing the log? (b) Would you consider the double block flushing policy realistic when disc is the stable logging medium?

11. Assume a node has six discs, running at approximately half capacity, performing block flush operations. What log volume is produced by (a) the single block flush logging policy and (b) the double block flush logging policy? (c) What sort of log disc accesses does the policies cause?

12. (a) Estimate the effect of hot-spot tables on log volume based on the TPC-B benchmark (see [Gra91] and [CKS91]). (b) Develop a node crash recovery method using hot-spot tables. (c) How can the method produced in b be used to reduce unavailability caused by a node crash?

13. (a) What is the purpose of action consistent access methods? (b) How can sufficient consistency be maintained if tuples are moved in the opposite direction of the link pointer? (c) Propose a method to traverse a B-tree in the opposite direction of the link pointers.

14. Develop a "simple" hash based action consistent access method.

15. How can the oldest log sequence number of the currently active transactions be used to simplify management under the late release policy?

16. (a) Compare the log volume of the action consistent block split policy when the steal/no-force policy is applied and when the no-steal/force policy is applied. (b) Assume DB blocks and log blocks are of equal size. Compare the worst-case disc accesses induced by each of the two policies in the time critical path of the transactions. (c) Compare the best case. (d) How would the use of stable main memory logging influence the comparison?

17. (a) Would the use of write locks based on primary keys solve the zombie problem? (b) Would write locks based on a surrogate key solve the zombie problem?

18. Describe log records for delta operations on primary key fields.

19. Describe a zombie space lock method.

20. (a) The use of the zombie space lock policy or the block space lock policy may require more management than is desirable. Propose a simpler method requiring less management than the method in exercise 20. (b) Propose a method that uses single or higher level fault-tolerance to stay available also after running out of free space at a node.

21. (a) Give examples illustrating the reduced delaying effect of the recursive action consistent block split/merge policy. (b) Give transaction load examples where the delaying effect of the transaction consistent block split/merge policy and the recursive action consistent block split/merge policy are indistinguishable.

22. Propose a block split policy which implies less transaction delays than the recursive action consistent block split policy.

23. One often-executed operation is searching a block to find a tuple on its primary key value. New processors have large on-board caches and long cache lines. Assume 8 Kbyte blocks and 128 byte cache lines. (a) Propose a modification of the record index policy that clusters information in such a way that the cache structure gives significant speed-up during a tuple search within a block. (b) Give an approximate calculation of the speed-up effect.

24. Another often-executed operation is searching a block to find a tuple on its primary key value. New processors have large on-board caches and long cache lines, which make an assumption of a flat main memory unrealistic. Assume 8 K byte DB blocks, 100 byte tuples, and 64 byte cache lines. (a) Propose a modification of the record index policy that clusters information in such a way that the cache structure gives significant speed-up during a tuple search within a block. (b) What would be the effect of including the 4 most significant bytes of the primary keys in the index records? (See, e.g. [NBC+93].) (c) Give an approximate calculation of the speed-up effect of the modified index record policy and inclusion of primary key parts in the record index.

25. Propose a logging method for a combined create table followed by massive insert of tuples. The goal is minimum log volume.

26. How can production of log records from index tuple operations be avoided when splitting a block?

Answers

1. All recovery methods proposed in this chapter require that the sequence between logged operations scheduled by different servers is maintained in the log. (See, e.g. section 7.6.6 and 7.6.7.) The recovery methods proposed in chapter 14 remove this constraint and make it possible to have independent recovery servers for each concurrency controller.

2. (a) There is no need to maintain the stability of the index of a tuple over its lifetime if the BPK policy is used. (b) The record can be relocated within a block independently of the references to the record.

3. (a) Transaction recovery uses the access methods. The access method must also be action consistent or transaction consistent when undo processing takes place during node crash recovery. (b) The access methods must be (action) consistent during node crash tuple redo recovery. Problems concerning use of the TPK redo identification policy for index tuple operations are discussed in section 7.5.8.

4. (a) The primary key log vector policy is used to identify which fields are included in the primary key and their internal sequence. (b) If the number of fields in the primary key and their internal sequence is the same for every table in the DBMS, the non-primary key policy can be used in combination with the TPK identification policy. This is the case if, for example, the primary key consists of the first field in the tuple. The TPK identification policy can also be used if the information kept in the primary key log sequences are kept in every tuple. For more details, see the answer to exercise 5.

5. (a) The effect of including primary key vectors and field vectors in the tuples is that they do not explicitly need to be logged. They are therefore not part of the log records for write tuple operations as long as the write operations are not adding or deleting fields from the tuple. They are never included in the log records by delta tuple operations. They are implicitly part of the log records for delete and insert tuple operations.

   (b) The sequence of the tuple fields in the log records is the same as in the corresponding tuple when the do operation was executed. The ordering and sequence of the primary key fields in an index tuple corresponds to the ordering and sequence of the primary key fields in the non-index tuples for the table. The primary key vector information found in any tuple and index tuple of the corresponding table can therefore be used both during redo and undo recovery processing.

   (c) If the primary key vector and field vectors are included in either the tuples or the log records, the structure of the tuples must be the same during undo and redo as during the original do processing. By including primary key vectors in both tuples and log records, the position of primary key fields in the tuples can have changed from the point when the original operation was executed until the undo or redo operation was executed. If the field vector is included in both tuples and log records, the basic type of primary key field is allowed to change from the point when the do operation was executed until the undo or redo operation was executed as long as type conversion functions are available. The above also applies to index tuples.

   (d) A field cannot be added in such a way that the position of the primary key fields is modified. With respect to primary keys, a field can therefore be added after the last field in the primary key. A field which modifies the position of any non-primary key fields cannot be added. To be safe, new fields should be added to the end of the tuple.

(e) A log record with a partially logged tuple contains information corresponding to the vector indicating the position of the logged fields. There is therefore no effect on partial logging by the primary key vector policy or the field type vector policy.

6. (a) The write and delta tuple operations would contain a primary key vector and a field type if the primary key log vector policy and field type policy were applied and no such vectors if the vectors were included in the tuples. The vectors would be included in the delete and insert tuple log records regardless of the chosen policy. We assume that if the vector information is included in the tuples, it requires the same data volume as in the log records. It is therefore the number of write and delta log records being stored compared to the number of tuples stored which decides which of these two policies is preferable. If, therefore, the number of stored tuples is less than 80% of the number of stored log records, keep the vectors in the tuples. Otherwise, keep them in the log records.

   (b) Since the results in (a) are independent of the actual log record sizes, the use of partial tuple logging would not change the result.

7. (a) The number of log records to be maintained per DB copy is $1000 \cdot 4 \cdot 24 \cdot 60 \cdot 60 \approx 346M$. The number of tuples is $\frac{10G}{100} = 10M$. It is preferable to keep the vectors in the tuples. (b) The number of log records per DB copy is $1000 \cdot 4 \cdot 60 \cdot 60 \approx 14M$. It is preferable to keep the vectors in the tuples.

8. The generic log record headers are the same except for the vector needed by partial tuple logging to represent the position of the logged fields, and they are therefore not included in the calculations. The vector needed by partial logging to represent the position of the logged fields does not need more than 2 bytes given 10 fields per tuple. A partial tuple logging record will contain the primary key field, i.e. 10 bytes, and the before- and after-image of the updated field, i.e. 20 bytes, which gives a total of 32 bytes. A full tuple logging record will contain the before- and after-image of the tuple, i.e. 200 bytes. The reduction is 168 bytes per log record.

9. (a) Both lower and upper borders are needed for each block to obtain block independent recovery. (b) Block independent recovery becomes impossible. (c) The action consistent block split/merge policy, as presented, becomes impossible. If the link pointer is turned, a policy with similar effect could be developed based on the lower border record. (d) The action consistent block split/merge policy becomes impossible.

10. (a) The single block flush logging policy imposes no flush operations on the log buffer. The double block flush operation, on the other hand, imposes one flush operation on the log buffer per flushed DB block. (b) No, because of the imposed log flush operation rate.

11. (a) Half capacity gives about 25 flush operations per second per disc. The total number of flush operations to log is $6 \cdot 25 = 150$ per second. The size of each block flush log record (BFR) is approximately 22 bytes. The single logging (SBF) policy produces $150 \cdot 22 = 3300$ bytes of log per second. (b) The start-BFRs of the double logging (DBF) policy produce about the same log volume as the BFRs of the SBF policy. The size of the commit-BRFs is approximately 17 bytes when the previous log record option is used. This gives a total log volume by the DBF policy of $3300 + 150 \cdot 17 = 5850$ bytes of log per second. (c) If the log block size is 4K bytes, the SBF policy induces approximately one log disc access per second. The DBF policy, on the other hand, induces another 150 disc accesses per second, which requires at least 3 additional log discs to be handled.

12. (a) An entry in a hot-spot table contains the block identifiers of a hot-spot block, which are estimated at 5 bytes each. Since the TPC-B data volume increases linearly with the transaction rate, we use a 20 transactions per second system as our basis. An 8 K byte block size is assumed. The blocks of the Branch and Teller tables are accessed often enough

to be hot-spots. The hot-spot table will contain 28 entries of 5 bytes each and a header of approximately 25 bytes, giving a total of 165 bytes. A TPC-B transaction produces a log volume of approximately 100 bytes for each of the 4 operations,, a start-transaction log record of approximately 75 bytes, and a commit log record of approximately 25 bytes. This gives a log volume of approximately 500 bytes per transaction, which gives a log volume of 600 K bytes per minute. With a 1 minute checkpoint interval the log volume of a hot-spot table is negligible.

(b) Hints! If the checkpoint log policy is followed, the hot-spot table can be accessed from the start of the node crash. If sufficient main memory is available, the hot-spot blocks can be start to be read into main memory in parallel with reading the log into main memory. This will use the available disc access capacity which will not otherwise be used in this recovery phase. Hot-spot blocks can also be read in parallel with the block recovery. It is necessary to check if a block which needs to be recovered is already read and to check if a block belongs to the hot-spot set to determine if it is due to be flushed after recovery.

(c) If the lack of hot-spot blocks in main memory causes unavailability because of too long transaction response time, the DBMS is unavailable until hot-spot blocks are read into main memory. By doing this in parallel with the recovery work, the unavailability time becomes reduced compared to reading the hot-spot blocks after the recovery work is completed, see (b).

13. (a) High availability through fine granularity and short duration locking. (b) By use of a lower border record. If the searched tuple has a smaller primary key value than the primary key of the lower border, the searched tuple has been moved in the opposite direction of the link pointer. (c) Maintain a stack for each cursor indicating its current position on each level. The block identifier on each level is sufficient to give the BPK identification policy. Update these stacks when blocks are merged. An alternative method is to access the B-tree from the top each time, going to the next block in the opposite direction of the link pointer at the bottom level.

14. A "simple" hash based method performs hashing based on primary key to a bucket and organises the bucket as an recursive action consistent B-tree.

15. The block can be released when its block state identifier is older than the oldest log sequence number of the currently active transactions.

16. (a) The least possible log volume is produced by the steal/no-force block split policy when one log record is produced for the original block and one for the new block. The log record for the original block contains, in addition to the generic part, the before- and after-image of the high border tuple and the before- and after-image of the number of record index entries in the block. The log record for the new block contains, in addition to the generic part, the tuples inserted into the block. The volume of the log record relating to the original block depends on the size of the primary key. We estimate a typical volume of approximately 100 to 200 bytes. The volume of the log record relating to the new block is approximately half the block size as a result of splitting the block into two approximately equal sized parts. With typical block sizes of 4 K bytes or 8 K bytes, this log volume will be dominant. With a 4 K byte block size, the approximate log volume per block split is 2 K bytes. The no-steal/force policy produces no log records and therefore no volume at all.

    (b) The steal/no-force policy produces one log flush operation per split block, because the log buffer must be flushed before the split transaction commits. An additional block flush operation may occur in the worst case in the critical path of the split block transaction, because the log buffer may fill up during the transaction. The flush operation during the split transaction can be performed outside of the critical transaction path, depending on the log buffer method. This gives a worst case of 2 block accesses. The no-steal/force policy requires the original block to be flushed before the splitting starts if the block is dirty. The new block must be flushed within the critical path of the transaction, and so must the original block after the splitting is done. This gives a worst case of 3 block accesses.

(c) The least number of disc accesses for the steal/no-force policy is one disc access in the critical path of the transaction. The number of disc accesses for the no-steal/force policy is 2.

(d) The use of stable main memory logging avoids any disc accesses at all in the critical path of the transaction when the steal/no-force policy is used.

17. (a) Yes, because the deleted tuple is write locked during the transaction lifetime and will conflict with inserted tuples, because they will try to obtain a write lock on the same primary key. (b) No, because a deleted tuple and a conflicting inserted tuple will have different surrogate keys.

18. To be able to access a tuple during redo and undo recovery, it is necessary to know not only the primary key state transition but also the primary key before- and after-image state. It is therefore necessary to log sufficient information to calculate both the before- and after-images of the primary key from information kept in the log records. If the do, redo, or undo execution of the delta operation causes the tuple to be moved to another block, sufficient information to produce the before- and after-image of the complete tuple needs to be logged. If the tuple is moved to another block during the original execution of the delta operation, the block identifier and before-images of both the involved blocks are needed.

19. Write locks are assumed to use primary keys to identify the tuples they are referring to. The size of the tuple is included in the write lock record for each deleted tuple. It is assumed that the lock records for tuples belonging to a table are kept sorted. By keeping upper and lower border records in the blocks, it can be determined each time an attempt is made to insert a tuple into a block if sufficient space is available, by comparing the required space with the what is physically available in the block and required by zombie tuples.

20. (a) When a tuple is deleted, convert it into a zombie by keeping its primary key, keeping the size of the tuple, marking it as a zombie, and including the log sequence number of the operation in the zombie. The primary key will determine which block the zombie is placed in after a block split. Zombies are handled as normal tuples during both block split and block merge. The zombie can safely be removed when its log sequence number is less than the oldest log sequence number of all currently active transactions.

(b) Start out with a reasonable level of unused blocks. Do no management of zombie space at tuple level, i.e. release space in a block when a tuple is deleted and do not keep track of zombie space in the lock records. Use recursive action consistent block split/merge. Allow blocks to be split when rolling back a transaction. Associate priorities with tables. When a node runs empty of free blocks, request maintenance, and release all the blocks kept by a hot stand-by fragment replica of a table at the lowest priority level. Keep on doing this until all hot stand-by replicas are consumed. In this way the availability is maintained by reducing the fault-tolerance level. Running out of free blocks is handled as any other failure. When all hot stand-by replicas are consumed, depending on the chosen policy, either the system can be shut down, or the same policy can be applied to the primary replicas, thereby causing a partially available system.

21. (a) The following is a simple case illustrating the effect of the recursive action consistent block split policy. A transaction inserts a tuple, causing a block to split in the beginning of its execution. The total execution time of the transaction is 2 seconds. Another transaction with a normal response time of 100 milliseconds reads one tuple from the same table as the other transaction is inserting tuples into. When the read hits a block which is locked to be

split, the execution time is extended by about 2 seconds, which threatens the availability of the transactions.

(b) The delaying effects of the recursive action consistent block split policy and the transaction consistent block split policy are the same if the following conditions are fulfilled when the transaction consistent block split policy is used. The tuple operation causing the block split operation must be the last operation by the transaction. The commit must not have to wait for any other parties. The block split must not be propagated upwards.

22. Move the block splits entirely out of the critical path of the transactions. (The following assumes that the tuple state-identifier policy is applied.) A block overflow area is used to keep the spill-over tuples for a block until the block is split. The block to be split and the spill-over tuples are fuzzy copied into two new blocks. Then redo catch-up is applied to the copied tuples to apply the remaining tuple operations to the tuples. Then the new blocks are linked into the access method to take the place of the old block. An interesting alternative in case of a main memory DB is not to use the block concept at all.

23. (a) A flexible organisation of the record indexes is the same as a B-tree with cache lines as blocks.

    (b) Including the 4 most significant bytes of the primary key of the tuples in the record indexes will support early discrimination of a tuple without an additional cache miss by accessing the tuple itself.

    (c) Each record index is assumed to consist of a 2 byte pointer to the tuple and a 4 byte primary key part, i.e. 6 bytes per record index. We assume a filling degree of 75% per cache line which gives 8 bottom level cache lines and a root cache line. The root cache line is assumed to be at a fixed position in the block. Two cache misses are expected to get the pointer to the right tuple when it is assumed that the primary key part will determine the tuple. If, on the other hand, a traditional binary search is used instead of a B-tree, 3 cache misses must be expected, i.e. 1 cache miss to get the number of record indexes and 2 cache misses during the binary search to get record index cache lines. In addition, approximately 6 cache misses occur when tuples are checked.

24. To keep the produced log volume down, apply a steal/force policy. The force policy is followed by flushing the remaining blocks which stay in main memory and belong to the table before committing the transaction. Redo is therefore never needed. To undo the inserts, it is sufficient to log only the allocation of the blocks belonging to the table into which the tuples are inserted. Undo will follow the transaction log chain in reverse order and release the blocks without accessing them.

25. Cluster the logging of all the moved tuples into one log record. See section 13.11.

Part III

The HypRa Recovery Approach

Chapter 8

Introduction

The following chapters describe the recovery strategies developed to meet those of the HypRa recovery requirements not met by the existing recovery approaches: very high transaction service availability and soft real-time transaction response.

A HypRa DBMS server combines hardware and software to provide **reliable, continuously available, soft real-time** DBMS services according to the ISO SQL standard ([ISO89]). The HypRa DBMS server is based on a *shared-nothing* ([RS86]) multi-computer hardware architecture with powerful and highly isolated nodes. The nodes are interconnected by a high capacity, multi-path, *hypercubic* communication network ([BLRA80]). HypRa DBMS servers provide multi-fault-tolerance and graceful degradation with respect to data availability by online failure masking, recovery, and online self-repair of unavailable fragment replicas (see sections A.2 and 2.1). A HypRa DBMS server has crash/omission/performance failure semantics (see section 1.3).

This presentation of the HypRa DBMS server focuses on the hardware architecture, basic software, and DBMS aspects primarily influencing the HypRa recovery design. The HypRa recovery approach is presented in Part III. The presentation of hardware architecture and fault-tolerance aspects is based on [HST91a]. The presentations of DBMS aspects include elements from the HypRa DBMS overall design ([HA89b], [HA89a], [Hva89b], [HA89c], [Ask89b]) and the HypRa DBMS detailed design ([HSAG90], [ARH$^+$90], [HS90]). An introduction to the HypRa project history and prehistory is given in [Bra90]. Particular aspects of the development of hypercubic shared-nothing hardware platforms are given in [BG89], [Bra89a], and [Bra89b]. See [Fri90] for a survey of hypercube based relational DBMS systems.

The **location- and replication independent tuple recovery** strategy provides redo and undo tuple recovery that is independent of which block, fragment replica, table, or node a tuple is located in at recovery time compared to the tuple's location when the original operations were executed. The strategy also provides recovery to any replicas of a tuple regardless of which replica the original operations were executed to. The location and replication policy therefore removes the redo block non-transparency which was inherent in the table oriented recovery approach (see chapter 7). The location and replication independent tuple recovery is required to perform non-blocking fragment replication with subfragmentation.

The **log distribution** strategy supports the distribution and replication of logs. The distribution is based on the application of stable main memory logging. One tuple log fragment with two replicas exists per fragment. Tuple log records for one fragment is therefore located to one log. Fragment global monotonously increasing tuple state-identifier values are used to avoid unnecessary redo recovery work.

The **neighbour write-ahead logging** strategy supports policies for logging in main memory at two different nodes located in two different disaster units. Logs at a node are kept partially in stable volatile media and partially in stable non-volatile media. The neighbour write-ahead log protocol determines the rules concerning when a log record part must be written to stable storage at the node and to a node in another disaster unit. The nWAL log garbage collection rules present the set of rules used to determine when undo and redo log record parts can be removed. Before a log record is allowed to be entered into a primary log replica, sufficient space is required to be available in both the primary and the hot stand-by log replica for the log record, and its potential CLR. Sufficient space must be allocated to a transaction so that its deferred operations are guaranteed to be executed.

The **HypRa recovery** strategy supports take-over policies, transaction failure recovery policies, and fast node crash recovery policies. The take-over policies supports a primary take-over policy allowing a hot stand-by fragment replica to change its role to a primary fragment replica very fast to obtain minimum fragment unavailability as caused by a primary fragment replica failure or a node crash. The transaction failure recovery policies support sequential, asynchronous and non-sequential fragment recovery. The fast node crash recovery is intended used to restart a node before another replica have been produced of the fragments located at the node. The fast restart is non-sequential to obtain speed up and minimum recovery work load.

8.1 The HypRa DBMS Server Architecture

This section presents the parts of the HypRa DBMS server architecture required in addition to what was already presented in chapter 10 and section 7.1. Every relation is horizontally fragmented and replicated (see section A.2). It is assumed throughout this part that two replicas exist of each fragment. Two replicas document the principles of the involved policies and are used to restrict the complexity of the presentation. (When more than two existing replicas per fragment are referred to in the following, this is explicitly mentioned.)

As a result of the automatic corrective online repair policy (see section 10.7), multi-level fragmentation may occur after node or fragment failure repair (see section A.2). A leaf fragment or subfragment involved in the failure can be further subfragmented to distribute the additional load represented by additional data to a node over multiple nodes. To keep the number of subfragments within a manageable number, non-blocking subfragment concatenation is also provided when fragments are relocated to the fragments original node.

Each fragment or subfragment replica is implemented by one and only one table (see section A.4). A consequence of this policy is that all tuples contained in a table belong to the same fragment replica. Multiple fragment replicas belonging to the same relation can be located to the same node (see section 10.7). This may occur during and after a fragment repair, following a node or fragment replica failure, when a fragment is subfragmented and the subfragment replicas are allocated to different nodes. No more than one replica of a leaf-fragment (see section A.2) is ever stored at a node.

Tables, in addition to implementing relations, are used to implement fragments supporting data management that is local to a node, such as disc-block allocation bit maps and table directories. These fragments are termed **node internal fragments**. Two replicas exist for the node internal fragments to support maintenance in case of media failure. The primary replica of an internal fragment is allocated to the node itself and the hot stand-by replica is allocated to a node in another disaster unit. The fine grained and semantically rich tuple locking model is used when accessing the node internal fragments to provide very high tuple concurrency also to the node internal fragment replicas.

The HypRa DBMS is organised as a server group (see section 10.1). The architecture of each of the DBMS servers in the server group is composed of the *node internal layers* and the *global*

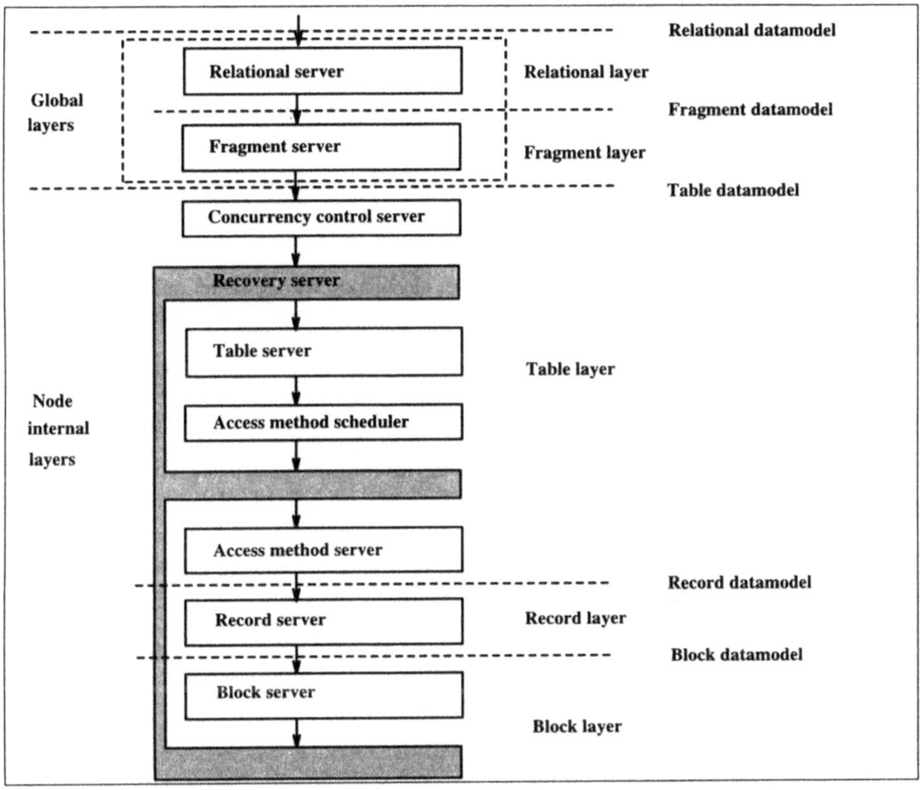

Figure 8.1: The HypRa DBMS server architecture. The layered DBMS server architecture corresponds to the architecture presented in section 7.1 and figure 7.1, but is extended with the fragment layer as a consequence of the distributed DBMS architecture (see section A.3 and figure A.3). The block, record, and table layers are the node internal layers. The fragment and relational layers are the global layers. The fragment and relational servers are included in the HypRa DBMS server group (see figure 10.1).

layers (see figure 8.1). The node internal layers are the table, record, and block layers with the corresponding architecture as the *table oriented server architecture* (see section 7.1). The global layers are the fragment and the relational layers which contain the servers included in the DBMS server group.

Exercises

1. Come up with at least three transaction services, in addition to those mentioned in this chapter, that require continuous availability.
2. What are the main causes of unavailability?
3. (a) How many disc accesses can be included if the response time of a TPC-B transaction is 10 milliseconds? (b) Do you see any immediate implications of this to the DBMS?

Answers

1. Air traffic control, anti-missile surveillance, emergency services (fire, ambulance, police, maternity ward), car rental services. Especially for Americans: Pizza delivery.
2. From [GR92]: Software failures (approximate 60%), operations failures (approximate 15%), hardware failures (approximate 5%), maintenance failures (approximate 5%), environmental failures (approximate 10%), unknown failures (approximate 5%).
3. (a) A disc access takes about 10 milliseconds. Therefore none can be included in the critical path of the transaction.

   (b) Logging is part of the critical path of a transaction and is normally done to disc. The DBMS must support stable logging without using discs. This can be done by RAM with battery backup or by logging in RAM on multiple nodes.

Chapter 9

The Hardware and Basic Software Design

9.1 The Hardware Architecture

The HypRa hardware design is based on a multi-computer with homogeneous and powerful nodes with a high degree of node isolation, interconnected by a multipath symmetric communication network. The nodes are built from inexpensive, commercially available, standard components instead of specially designed technology. The nodes are interconnected into a hypercubic topology. Most of the error detection, masking and repair are done in the software servers. The HypRa design philosophy gives the advantage of low hardware cost and high degree of scalability.

HypRa is based on the **shared-nothing** hardware architecture, i.e. there is no shared memory or discs between nodes. This is as opposed to the **shared discs** hardware architecture of Tandem ([Kat78], [Bar78], [Bar81]), where discs are shared between nodes and also as opposed to the **shared main memory** hardware architecture where main memory are shared between nodes. Figure 9.1 illustrates the shared-nothing, shared discs and shared memory hardware architectures.

The *shared main memory* architecture cannot be used to provide a DBMS server with fault masking capabilities since the shared memory is a critical component used by servers at all nodes. Shared main memory makes the DBMS server crash when a node crashes since all nodes rely on the correctness of the shared memory. Therefore a continuously available DBMS server as required by HypRa cannot be based on a shared memory hardware platform.

The *shared-nothing* hardware architecture is cost-effective compared to the shared disc architecture if data distribution, masking and self-repair of unavailable fragment replicas are capabilities required by the DBMS, which is the case for HypRa. In this case the shared-nothing and the shared disc architectures both require high internode network capacity to *online* produce new replacement replicas for unavailable data replicas. The shared-nothing architecture utilises off-the-shelf single ported disc controllers as opposed to the more expensive dual ported disc controllers.

The internode network may have a lower capacity if none of the following capabilities are required by the DBMS ([Dim85]):

- Self-repair from unavailable data replicas by dynamic data reproduction.
- High capacity complex query processing.
- Data distribution dictated by the shared disc interconnection topology.

The HypRa nodes are *homogeneous*, i.e. equipped with similar hardware servers, to avoid critical

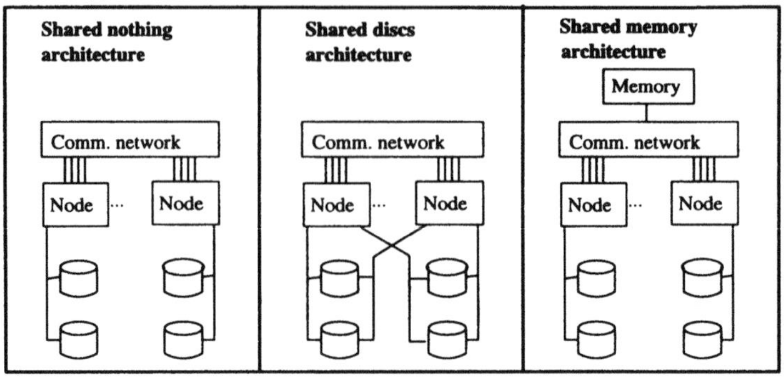

Figure 9.1: The shared-nothing architecture connects the nodes only through the communication network (Comm. network). The shared disc architecture connects the nodes through both the communication network and the disc to node connections. In the shared memory architecture the nodes share global main memory.

hardware servers. If a node crashes, its processing power is lost and the discs connected to it are unaccessible. The hardware services lost by a crashed node are also provided by every other available node. The crashed node is masked in software and the fragment replicas located at the unaccessible discs are masked and repaired by the DBMS servers.

The nodes are *powerful* or coarse-grained to handle uneven transaction or query work loads and to handle additional work load as a result of failed nodes. A high degree of *node isolation* is achieved since the nodes are only communicating through designated communication channels.

A node is equipped with the following: CPU, for example the Intel i486[1] processor; main memory, for example 32MByte of dynamic RAM; disc channels, for example 4 SCSI bus controllers; and $d + 1$ communication channels, where d is the dimension of the hypercube. A communication channel can for example be implemented by a 4 Kbyte dual ported RAM chip or a fibre optic link to obtain an even higher degree of physical node isolation. See figure 9.2 for illustration of the hardware architecture of a node in a 4-dimensional hypercube.

The hardware policy of using off-the-shelf commercially available hardware components is adopted to take advantage of the low hardware cost per node. This policy excludes the use of special hardware components dedicated to log and recovery tasks, and a recovery design based on the use of such special hardware.

9.2 The External Communication

The HypRa client-server communication uses the Remote Database Access (RDA) ([ISO88]) protocol. The client-server communication is scalable with respect to both fault-tolerance and communication capacity. Communication co-processors can be connected to any node to provide hardware platforms for communication protocols between a HypRa server and a HypRa client at an application platform. The multiplicity of communication co-processors allows for multi-level fault-tolerant client-server protocol implementations. To provide triple client-server communication fault-tolerance at least four nodes must be equipped with one communication co-processor each. See figure 9.3.

[1] i486 is a trademark of Intel Corporation

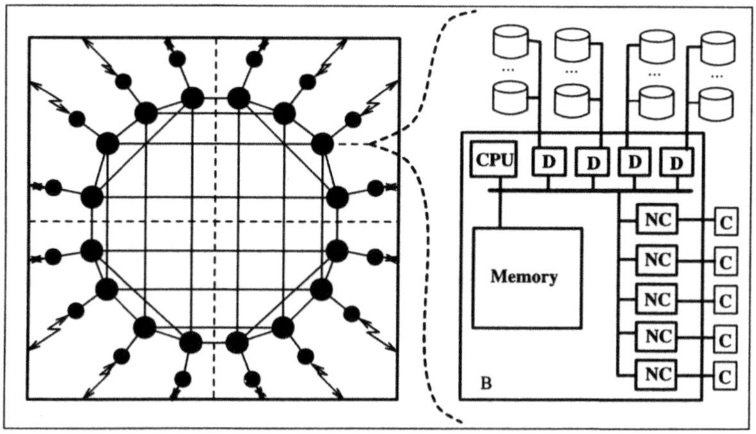

Figure 9.2: The HypRa DBMS server internal hardware architecture. A simplified 16-node (4-dimensions) HypRa server is illustrated. The hardware is based on off-the-shelf components. The CPU (Central Processing Unit) is a processor of, for example, the Intel family; the RAM (Random Access Memory) is, for example, 32 MByte of dynamic RAM; the boxes labeled D (Disc channel) can be SCSI bus controllers; and the boxes labeled (Neighbour Communication channel) can be implemented by fiber optic links. The CPU, memory, disc channels, and communication channel servers can be contained on a single node board (B). A cabling unit (C) connects a neighbour communication channel of one node to a neighbour communication channel of its neighbour node. A communication co-processor for external communication, for example, can be connected to each node. For a hypercube, the following definitions are given: d is the number of dimensions ($d = 4$ in the figure); $n = 2^d$ is the number of nodes ($n = 16$ in the figure); $c = \frac{d \cdot n}{2}$ is the total number of communication channels; and $l = d$ is the longest optimal path from a node to any other in a perfect hypercube. Fire-walls are provided along two hypercube dimensions (dashed) to divide the server into four hardware disaster-units.

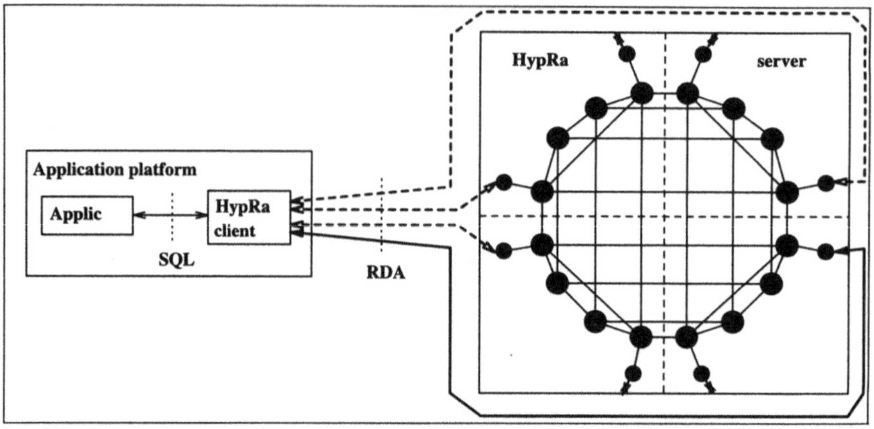

Figure 9.3: The HypRa DBMS client-server architecture. A simplified 16-node (4-dimensions) HypRa server is connected to a HypRa client at an application platform by a Remote Database Access (RDA) ([ISO88]) client-server communication protocol. Communication co-processors are connected to half of the HypRa nodes. The RDA protocol uses four sessions to obtain client-server communication fault-tolerance. The interface between a HypRa client and an application (Applic) uses the SQL language ([ISO89]).

The external communication capacity is scalable independently of the number of nodes of the HypRa server since the number of communication co-processors can be varied online from one co-processor for an entire HypRa server up to multiple co-processors per HypRa node. There is a shared-nothing hardware relation between a node and its connected communication co-processors. Figure 9.2 illustrates a configuration where one communication co-processor is connected to each node and figure 9.3 illustrates a configuration where communication co-processors are connected to half of the nodes.

9.3 Replaceable Hardware Units

HypRa is composed of fine granularity hardware replaceable units as opposed to coarse granularity hardware replaceable units typical of a complete computer ([XRF87a]). All replaceable hardware units are customer replaceable, i.e. personnel from a customer organisation may perform the replacement operations. All replacements can be done online, i.e. when the HypRa server is online, to support continuous availability.

Each *node board* with the hardware servers it contains (CPU, memory, neighbour communication channels, and disc channels) is an online customer replaceable unit. Each *disc, cabling unit, power supply unit,* and *cooling fan* is an online customer replaceable unit. This is illustrated in figure 9.4.

9.4 Depends-On Relations Between Hardware Servers

The disc servers are assumed to have omission failure semantics and atomic-crash semantics, i.e. a physical disc operation is either completely done or not done at all if a disc crash occurs (see section 2.3.3). A disc channel server is dependent on the discs it provides access to (see figure

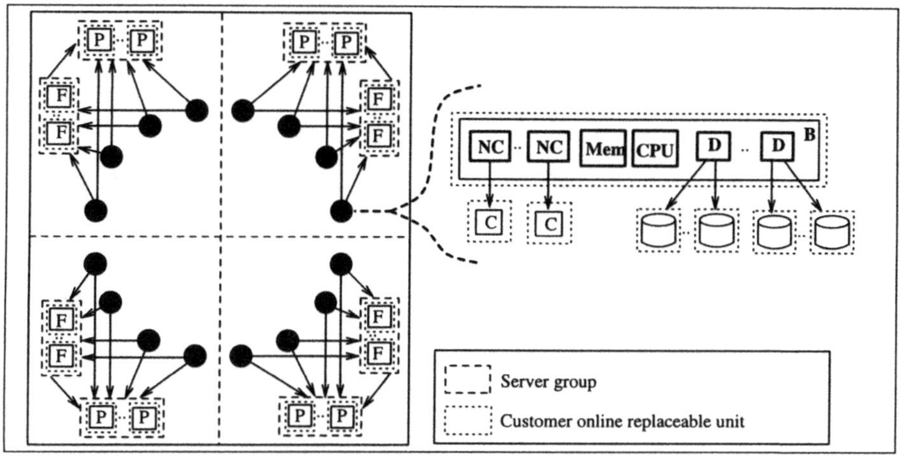

Figure 9.4: Individual node boards (B), discs, cabling units (C), power supply units (P), and cooling fans (F) are online customer replaceable hardware units. The server is divided by fire-walls along two dimensions into four independent disaster-units. Cooling fans are organised into groups with single fault-tolerance within each distaster-unit. All servers on a node and the discs connected to a node are powered from the same power supply group. The nodes within a disaster-unit are powered and fanned by the groups of the disaster-unit.

9.4). The disc channel servers are assumed to have omission failure semantics and atomic-crash semantics. If a disc channel server fails all its connected disc servers become unaccessible.

The CPU server is assumed to have crash failure semantics and atomic crash semantics (see section 2.3.3). Memory errors are detected through parity checking. The memory server is assumed to have crash failure semantics (see section 2.3.3).

A cabling unit is assumed to have crash failure semantics. A neighbour communication channel server provides a data and a reset channel. The data channel is supported by a hardware checksum generator to detect data communication errors. The data channels have omission failure semantics. Masking of data channel failures is done by the software communication servers. The reset channels are not supported by failure detection mechanisms and have therefore *arbitrary failure semantics*. The arbitrary failure semantics of reset channels are masked in software by cooperation between multiple software servers when recovery restarting a node.

A power supply unit is assumed to have crash failure semantics. The power supply units are organised into power supply unit groups with single fault-tolerance. A power supply is a uninterruptible power supply (see section 13.1). A cooling fan is assumed to have crash failure semantics. The cooling fans are also organised into groups with single fault-tolerance. See figure 9.4 for illustration of power supply unit groups and cooling fan groups.

All hardware servers of a node, including the discs connected to the node, are powered from the same power supply unit group. When a node crashes, all data stored at the discs connected to the node becomes unavailable because of the shared-nothing architecture. Therefore there is no need for independent powering of the discs from the node they are connected to.

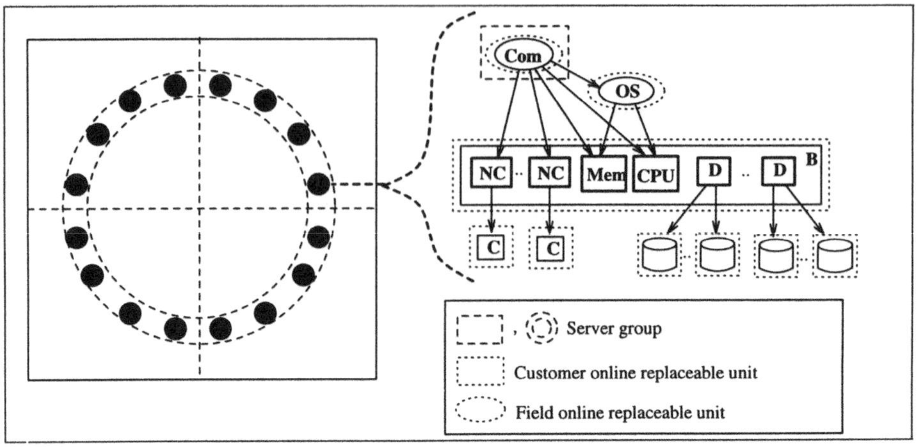

Figure 9.5: The depends-on relations between the operating system server (OS), communication server (Com) and hardware servers at a node. The communication servers at all nodes constitute a server group with $d-1$ fault-tolerance. See figure 9.2 for definition of terminology.

9.5 Disaster-Tolerant Hardware Design

A HypRa server is divided by two or more *fire-walls* along hypercube dimensions into a group of hardware disaster-units. The disaster-units are independent with respect to physical disaster failures such as flood, fire, and power outage. The independence is obtained at the hardware level through the organisation of power supply and cooling fan services to nodes. See both figures 9.2 and 9.4 for illustration. The nodes of a disaster-unit are powered from the same power supply unit group and share the same cooling fan group. The cooling fan group is powered from the same power supply group as the nodes it serves. Nodes from different disaster-units are never powered or fanned from the same power supply unit group or cooling fan group.

9.6 The Communication Server

The hypercubic communication topology is regular and symmetric. It provides multiple paths between nodes, scalable capacity with the number of nodes, and low communication latency. The hypercube is a frequently used interconnection topology for parallel shared-nothing multicomputers ([Nug88], [TPP88], [BG89], [DGS+90]). The communication server provides end-to-end ([Tan81]) packet-switching based transport protocols with crash/omission/performance failure semantics.

The *multi-path* capability of the hypercubic interconnection topology is given by the fact that each node is connected by a neighbour communication channel to a neighbour node in each of the hypercube dimensions. This gives both communication capacity and communication fault-tolerance with respect to communication channel and node crash.

The *communications capacity* scales with the number of nodes in the hypercube as opposed to a bus based communication architecture with a fixed bus capacity. This is a requirement for a highly scalable DBMS server as HypRa (see section 1.1).

The low communication latency is a result of the hypercubic topology. The latency aspect is

		Number of crashed nodes					
		0	1	2	3	4	5
Remaining	Average case	100	93	93	91	90	90
capacity	Worst case	100	93	91	85	78	69

Table 9.1: The communication capacity for a 6-dimensional (64 node) hypercube as a function of crashed nodes. The figures are percentages of the capacity of a perfect hypercube network ([Tor90]).

important for real-time transactions given the distributed transaction model used by HypRa (see section 10.2). The distance between a transaction coordinator and a slave-transaction's node is equal to or shorter than the hypercube dimension d (see section 9.2). The latency aspect of communication is important for transactions bound by real-time response requirements since the communication time may take a significant portion of the total elapsed time.

The operating system (OS) server is assumed to have performance failure semantics and atomic-crash semantics. The OS is local to a node and provides basic process-, segmentation- and event-management services, i.e. no distributed OS services are provided. The OS server at a node depends-on CPU and memory services at the same node (see figure 9.5). The OS allows for online replacement of DBMS, communication, and OS code in a HypRa system.

A communication server is assumed to have crash/omission/performance failure semantics, i.e. messages may be lost or arrive out of order. These failures are masked by the DBMS servers; see for example the update channel protocol in section 13.4. A communication server depends-on the neighbour communication channels, memory, and CPU servers of its node. In addition it depends-on the OS services provided by the OS server at the node. This is illustrated by figure 9.5.

A communication server masks up to $d - 1$ concurrent crashed neighbour communication channels at a node, i.e. a node is available for communication as long as at least one of its communication channels has not crashed. Since the smallest cut in a hypercube is around one node, $d - 1$ fault-tolerance is provided for the communication to a node.

The high connectivity of the hypercube topology gives many independent message routing paths. The HypRa communication design uses **extended e-cube routing** ([Tor90], called table routing in [PB90]) to handle crashed nodes and communication channels. Simple e-cube routing assumes a perfect hypercube, preserves message sequencing, avoids deadlock and distributes the traffic uniformly over the communication network ([AT90]). The extended e-cube routing algorithm handles node and communication channel crashes and is identical to basic e-cube routing for error-free networks. With errors the load becomes skewed and the routing is no longer guaranteed deadlock free ([Tor90]).

Table 9.1 shows the remaining communication capacity for a 6-dimensional (64 node) hypercube as a function of the number of crashed nodes. The table is a result of simulations and shows an acceptable performance degradation. For more details see [HST91a] and [Tor90].

A node or communication channel crash is detected by using an I-am-Alive protocol. A communication server sends an I-am-Alive message to its neighbour communication servers at determined intervals. There is no clock synchronisation between nodes to preserve the high level of isolation between nodes.

The communication servers of a HypRa server are organised into a communication server group. A communication server or a data communication channel crash invokes the activation of availability management service originating at the node detecting the crash. The availability management service is based on the acknowledge-based processor membership protocol ([ASC88]). The new routing tables are produced based on the set of available communication servers and data communication channels.

Exercises

1. (a) Of the shared memory, shared disc, and shared-nothing hardware architectures, which is the simplest to build concurrency control (lock- and deadlock managers) for? (b) Which is the hardest to build commit processing for?

2. (a) Would a DB buffer manager be different for the hardware architectures mentioned in exercise 1? (b) Would a log manager?

3. (a) Why are coarse grained nodes considered to be an advantage over fine grained nodes in a transaction environment? (b) Are there any differences in a join intensive environment?

4. (a) Is RDA an ISO protocol? (b) Is two-phase commit supported by RDA?

5. (a) What are the advantages of fine granularity hardware replaceable units? (b) Are there any disadvantages? (c) What would the advantages be of replacing one node as a unit? (d) How do the current hardware trends influence the granularity of hardware replaceable units?

6. What would the consequences be for depends-on relations if a node is fully self-supplied, i.e. it has its own power supply unit and cooling fans?

7. Can RAID disc technology be applied by HypRa?

8. (a) What are the advantage of a hypercube as compared to a bus? (b) Are there any advantages of a bus over a hypercube?

9. (a) How can a global interval between I-am-Alive messages be established by use of DBMS mechanisms? (b) How does the interval between I-am-Alive messages influence the take-over time after a failure? (c) What is the maximum time a node must wait for an I-am-Alive message before it can decide that the other node has crashed? Assume there is no clock synchronisation between the nodes, and that the interval between the messages is T.

Answers

1. (a) A lock manager and deadlock detection for the shared memory architecture would be the same as in a centralised DBMS and, therefore, the simplest to build. A shared-nothing is like a distributed DBMS and has more complicated deadlock detection than a centralised DBMS. A shared disc DBMS can either have a cache coherence based lock manager, which is more complicated than a lock manager in a centralised DBMS, or it can have the same solution as a shared-nothing architecture with more complicated deadlock detection.

   (b) The commit processing in a shared memory system would be the same as in a centralised DBMS and, therefore, the simplest. Two-phase commit processing is needed in a shared-nothing architecture, which is the most complicated. A shared disc DBMS can use either of these, depending on the DB buffering strategy.

2. (a) A shared memory and a shared-nothing based DBMS would both use the same sort of DB buffer manager. The DB buffer manager of a shared disc DBMS would most probably be different and include a cache coherence mechanism. (b) It is not necessary to build different types of log managers.

3. (a) Coarse grained nodes are less sensitive than fine grained nodes to load skews. (b) No.

4. (a) Yes, it is an application layer protocol which has now become an international ISO/OSI standard (IS). (b) No.

5. (a) Smaller and cheaper units can be replaced as necessary. Economy of scale in larger quantum of fewer different units. (b) More complicated inventory management by stocking a larger number of different units. May need more skilled maintenance people. (c) More power per volume unit and increasing power per money unit makes coarser units like one node the more interesting replacement unit. It is possible to make a HypRa node as indicated in section 9.1 and with its own power supply and 6 Gbyte disc storage in a 4 litre "shoe box".

6. The power supply units and cooling fans would be included in every node but left out of the disaster units (see figure 9.4). Every hardware server in a node would depend-on its power supply and cooling fans. The fans would depend-on the power supply.

7. Yes. Every disc can be a RAID disc. This would increase the disc MTTF.

8. (a) The maximum capacity of a hypercube increases with the number of nodes. A bus has a fixed maximum capacity. A hypercube has graceful degradation when nodes or links fail. (b) A bus has simpler routing algorithms than a hypercube. A bus has lower communication delays than a hypercube. A bus may probably be cheaper.

9. (a) A global interval can be established by a transaction. (b) The interval determines how long to wait before actions to produce a new consistent active set are started. (c) 2T.

Chapter 10

The HypRa DBMS Server Software Design

10.1 The Distributed HypRa DBMS Architecture

A HypRa DBMS server is organised as a **fault-tolerant distributed DBMS** utilising the particular attributes of the HypRa internode communication network (see sections A.2 and 9.6). The services provided by the HypRa DBMS server are according to the ISO-SQL standard ([ISO89]). The distributed HypRa DBMS is organised as a server group with a **DBMS server** at each HypRa node.

The DBMS servers are designed according to the mapping architecture presented in section A.3 with relational, fragment, table, record, and block layers (see figure 10.1). Each layer is implemented by one or more servers. The DBMS server group is constituted of relational- and fragment layer servers. The servers at the table, record, and block layers are local to the node.

An introduction to the detailed DBMS server architecture is presented in [HA89b].

A DBMS server depends-on the services of the communication, the OS, the memory, the CPU, and the disc channel servers at the node. The DBMS software is field online replaceable. Since it is a critical component of the system it is made field replaceable as opposed to customer replaceable to maintain control of the installation.

At least half the DBMS servers must be available for the HypRa DBMS server to be available since communication network partitioning is an assumed failure.

10.2 The Distributed Transaction Model

The HypRa transaction processing is based on a **distributed transaction model** in which the processing is done locally where the data involved in the transaction resides. Each distributed transaction is implemented by a *transaction coordinator* and one or more *slave-transactions* (also called subtransactions or cohorts ([GMA89])), with one and only one slave-transaction per node containing primary replicas of the data involved in the transaction. The distributed transaction model is illustrated in figure 10.3. The transaction model is, in section 13.6, extended with the effects of hot stand-by fragment replicas and the application of the nWAL logging strategy.

The transaction coordinator does not perform database operations. It creates and coordinates slave-transactions and performs query compilation. The slave-transactions may be executed in parallel. A slave-transaction may request services from and create slave-transactions at other nodes, for

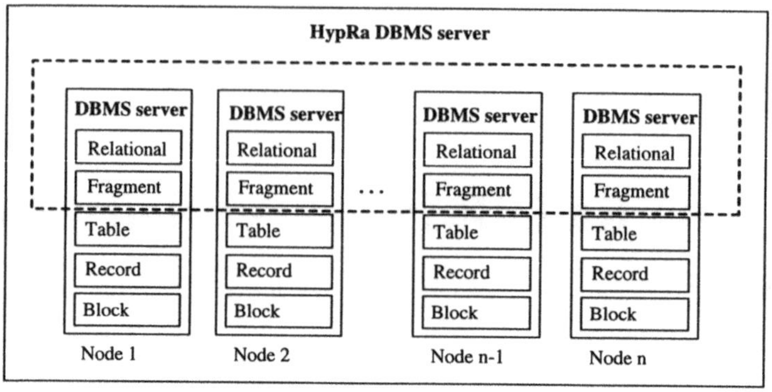

Figure 10.1: The HypRa DBMS server is implemented by a server group (dashed lines) of DBMS servers, one at each node. A DBMS server is layered into a relational-, fragment-, table-, record-, and block layer. The servers constituting the server group are contained at the fragment and relational layers. Servers at the table, record, and block layers are local to a node.

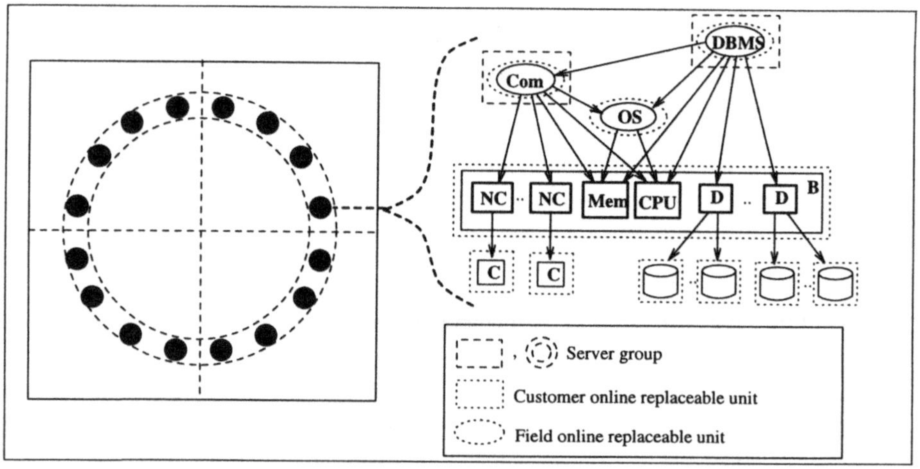

Figure 10.2: A DBMS server depends-on the communication (Com), the operating system (OS), the memory (Mem), the CPU, and the disc channel servers (D) at the node it resides. The DBMS servers constitute a server group. DBMS servers are field online replaceable.

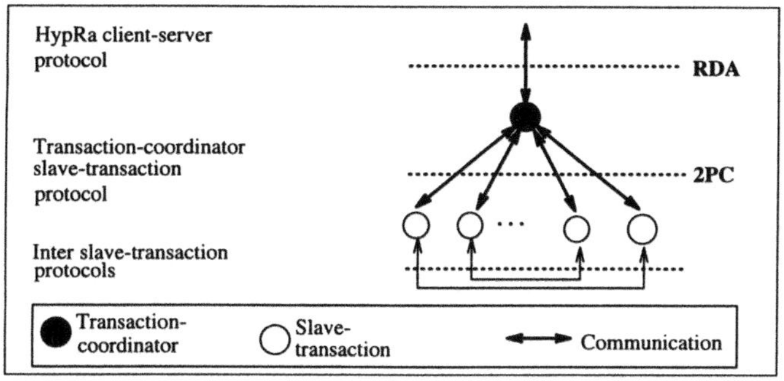

Figure 10.3: The distributed transaction model, with one transaction coordinator and one or more slave-transactions, one and only one at each node, storing primary replicas of data involved in the transaction.

example as a result of updating the primary key of a tuple causing it to move to another node.

Atomic transaction commit is obtained by use of the *presumed-abort two-phase commit protocol* ([ML83]) with the transaction coordinator as commit coordinator.

10.3 Concurrency Control in the HypRa Server

The transaction concurrency control is based on well-formed strict two-phase locking (see section A.9). A distributed locking scheme is adopted in which the locks relating to data stored at a node are managed at the node to provide fault-tolerance with respect to lock management. This is as opposed to a centralised lock management that introduces a critical server ([CP86], [WGAK89]).

Deadlock detection local to a node is done independently by the lock manager at the node. Global deadlock detection is assumed to use a dynamic snooper-based global deadlock detection mechanism where all locks potentially involved in a global deadlock are collected at a node and deadlocks are detected and resolved ([Sto79]).

A semantically rich set of locks is supported, including delta locks (see section A.5). Fine-granularity locking of tuples or groups of fields within a tuple is supported ([ARH+90]). The combination of the semantic richness and fine-granularity of locking requires the recovery manager to handle multiple concurrent DB state changing operations to a tuple.

10.4 The Nested Transaction Model

A nested transaction concept is used within the DBMS server to obtain consistent internal states and correct state transitions in the internal servers of the DBMS (see section A.8).

In the nested transaction model, a transaction server may request services from servers it depends-on, implemented by *synchronous* or *asynchronous* subtransactions. A subtransaction may again request subtransaction implemented services. An example where a synchronous subtransaction is used is when an update query is performed within a transaction containing several queries. By performing the update query as a subtransaction, it can be undone if it fails without aborting the transaction as a whole.

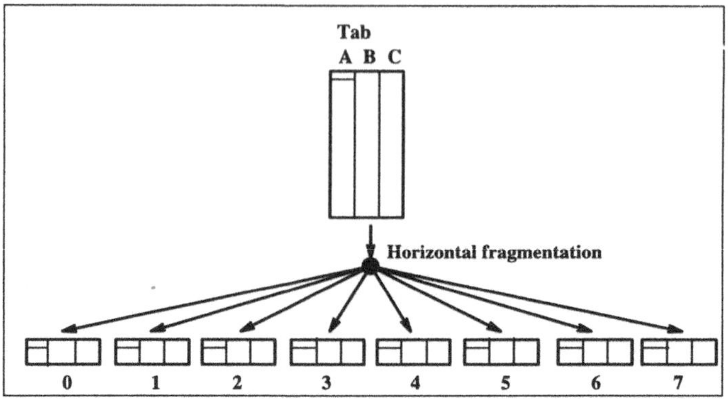

Figure 10.4: Horizontal fragmentation of the relation *Tab* into 8 fragments. The attribute A is the primary key of the relation. The fragmentation is based on a hash-function on the primary key.

An asynchronous subtransaction may be *termination coordinated* with its parent transaction, or allowed to have *independent termination* from the parent. An example where an asynchronous subtransaction with independent termination is used is when inserting an index record into the index part of a B-tree file as part of splitting a data block ([HSAG90]). An example where an asynchronous subtransaction termination coordinated with the parent is used is when index-tuples are inserted into indexes as a result of inserting a tuple into a table.

The result of a committed subtransaction is *persistently independent* of the parent. An example of a persistently independent subtransaction is allocation of data blocks to a file representing a table. If the allocation subtransaction commits and the parent transaction aborts, the result of the subtransaction is not rolled back.

Synchronous, termination coordinated, persistently independent subtransactions correspond to *nested top-level transactions* ([RM89]). Asynchronous, termination non-coordinated, persistently independent subtransactions correspond to independent top-level transactions. In the remainder of this book a subtransaction will correspond to a nested top-level transaction if not explicitly otherwise stated. *Nested top-actions* are introduced in section 13.11 to avoid the overhead of activating subtransactions ([ML89]).

10.5 Buffer Management

The buffer management system of HypRa is adapted to a mixed work load of transactions with traditional response time requirements, transactions with soft real-time requirements, and complex queries. A buffer management system is local to a node.

The HypRa DBMS buffer management system is a very large traditional DBMS buffer management system where the main memory buffer structure reflects the disc structure. The buffer manager is extended with services to lock soft real-time response required data in main memory to avoid disc accesses in real-time transactions. The buffer manager also provides services for query processing subtransactions with dynamically extensible main memory work space ([HSAG90]).

A main memory DBMS, where the complete database is stored in main memory and the main memory structure differs from the disc structure, is a buffer management alternative which is not feasible in HypRa. A HypRa DBMS server is required to handle data volumes with data reference

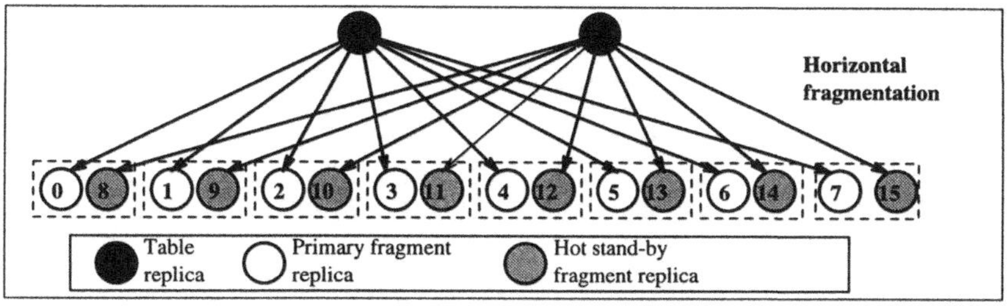

Figure 10.5: A single fault-tolerant relation *Tab* with two replicas horizontally fragmented into 8 fragment groups, with two fragment replicas in each fragment replica group.

rates that impedes a main memory DBMS from being a cost effective alternative ([Bra89c], [GP86], [GR88], [CKS91]).

A buffer management system is local to a node, i.e. it contains only blocks stored on discs connected to the node. This supports node isolation at the block layer. The HypRa approach contrasts with a distributed buffer management system with a buffer cache as proposed in [CSTJ89] and [HB91].

The choice of a traditional buffer management system enables HypRa to use traditional recovery methods as opposed to main memory DBMS oriented recovery methods ([SGM90], [Son89], [Eic89], [LC87], [GK85b]).

10.6 Data Distribution

The HypRa DBMS server is internally a distributed DBMS where the DB is partitioned over the nodes. The DBMS relational and fragment layer servers at the nodes constitute a server group able to mask every single DBMS server failure, online repair of up to a specified number of failures, gradual data unavailability with respect to further failures, and fast restart from failures.

The data distribution determines the relation and index fragmentation and replication, and the allocation of replicas to nodes. See section A.2 for a presentation of distribution terminology.

Every relation is **horizontally fragmented**, i.e. complete tuples are distributed over the nodes. The number of fragments of each relation corresponds to the number of nodes. The fragmentation of a relation *Tab* on the nodes of an 8-node HypRa server is illustrated in figure 10.4. Updates to primary fragment replicas within a transaction are tightly synchronised based on the distributed transaction model presented in section 10.2.

The **replication strategy** is defined for each replica. Two replicas per relation are assumed in this chapter unless explicitly otherwise stated. There is loose synchronisation between the replicas of a relation. One of the replicas is the primary replica and the other(s) the hot stand-by replica(s). There is a corresponding fragmentation of the replicas of a relation. The resulting fragment replica groups have single fault-tolerance with respect to availability. Figure 10.5 illustrates the fragment replica groups of the relation *Tab* with two replicas. The fragmentation and replication information is kept as part of the HypRa dictionary on a per-relation basis.

The replica **allocation strategy** guarantees that two replicas of a tuple are never dependent on the same software or hardware servers. This is fundamental with respect to DB availability fault-tolerance. The fragment replicas of a fragment replica group are stored at nodes within different disaster units, since nodes in different disaster units never depend on common servers. When a

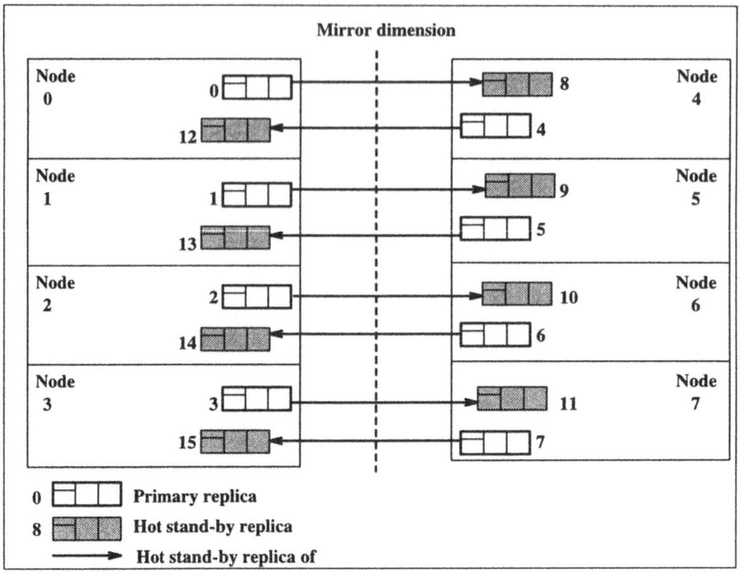

Figure 10.6: Two replicas are defined for each fragment of the relation *Tab*, a primary fragment replica and a hot stand-by fragment replica (shaded). One primary fragment replica is stored at each node. The hot stand-by of a primary fragment replica is stored at the neighbouring node across the mirror dimension. The mirror dimension is one of the fire-wall dimensions of the hypercube.

node containing the primary replica of a fragment fails, the failure is masked by the hot stand-by taking its place. Since the primary and the hot stand-by are stored at different nodes in different disaster units, any single node or single disaster unit failure can always be masked.

One of the hypercube dimensions which is also a fire-wall dimension is chosen as the **mirror dimension** for each relation. The hot stand-by replica is stored at the neighbouring node of the primary fragment across the mirror dimension to induce low communication cost for maintaining the hot stand-by replica. Figure 10.6 illustrates the allocation of the same relation as is fragmented in figures 10.4 and 10.5. Each primary fragment has its hot stand-by fragment across the mirror dimension. It is a consequence of the allocation strategy that every node contains both a primary and a hot stand-by fragment replica for different fragments.

The fragmentation of a relation is hash-based on its primary key if externally accessible attributes are contained in the primary key (see section A.4). If the primary key contains only internally accessible attributes (see section A.4), the fragmentation is round robin. In the latter case no externally defined primary key or unique group ([ISO87]) is defined. The fragmentation policy provides exact knowledge of the node at which a tuple is stored if the access is based on the primary key or through an index. If the access is not based on the primary key, and no index is used, all nodes must be searched for the tuple.

The dictionary relations are fragmented like ordinary relations, but with another replication and allocation strategy. The number of replicas per fragment equals the number of nodes, i.e. **total replication**. There is one primary replica per fragment. One replica of a fragment is allocated to each node. The primary replicas of any two different fragments of a relation are allocated to different nodes. There is tight synchronisation within the fragment groups based on the two-phase commit protocol (see section 10.2). See also [HST+91b] for non-blocking dictionary updating

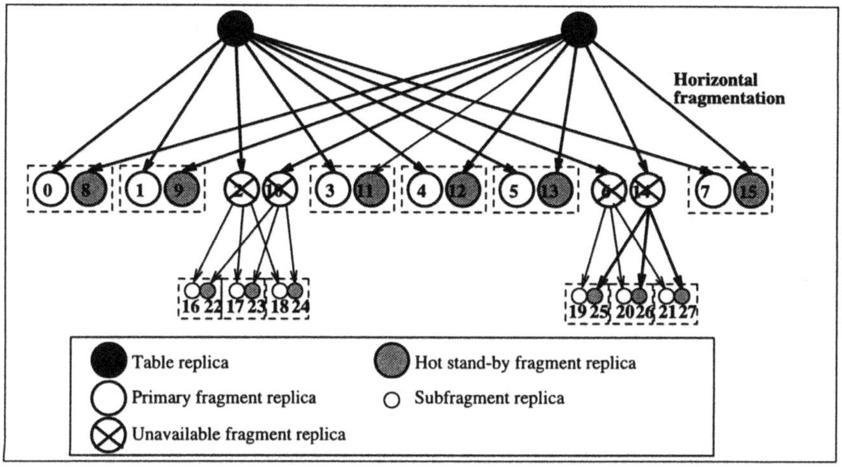

Figure 10.7: The fragment replicas in the group consisting of replicas 2 and 10 are subfragmented into three new fragment replica groups with two fragment replicas in each group. The same refragmentation is applied to the fragment replica group consisting of replica 6 and 14.

transactions.

The hash based horizontal fragmentation and replication method gives an evenly distribution of data over nodes. The data distribution determines the distributed transaction execution. The data distribution is therefore also the basis for transaction work load distribution among nodes. By providing powerful nodes, uneven transaction work loads within certain limits can be handled.

The distribution of query work load over nodes is partially based on the distribution of the data involved in the query and partially on the query and sorting algorithms used ([Bra84], [DG85], [Bra87], [BG89], [DGS+90], [Bra90]).

10.7 Dynamic Reconfiguration of Data as a Mechanism for Repairing Faults

HypRa performs **automatic non-blocking online repair** of single node failures and single fragment replica failures. A new replica is automatically produced without blocking the involved fragment, while the system is online, for each unrecoverable fragment replica resulting from a node or fragment replica crash. While the repair takes place, the system is prone to multiple failure. If two replicas exist for each fragment, and a fragment replica is unavailable, the system is prone to partial DB availability if the other fragment replica fails while the repair takes place. After the repair is completed, the system is again single fault-tolerant.

The dynamic and non-blocking replication of fragment replicas that takes place when repairing replica unavailability provides a means to compensate for hardware failures in software. It also provides the foundation for periodic and planned maintenance versus corrective manual maintenance, and thereby a reduction in maintenance cost ([Gra86]). This repair capability of HypRa introduces a fault-tolerance aspect only partial available in commercial DBMSs.

When one fragment replica of a relation becomes unavailable, the fragment becomes refragmented. (See section A.2 for terminology and introduction to subfragmentation.) The fragment is horizontally fragmented into a collection of subfragments with two replicas of each subfragment. Figure 10.7 illustrates the refragmentation of the fragment replicas 2, 10, 6, and 14 of the relation *Tab*. The involved fragments are subfragmented into three subfragments each. Two replicas are produced per subfragment.

One subfragment replica produced per fragment is allocated to each of the available nodes on the side of the mirror dimension in which the failed node or failed fragment replica resides. The other replica in a subfragment replica group is allocated to the node across the mirror dimension. Figure 10.8 illustrates the distribution and allocation of subfragment replicas while the repair from the crash of node 2 is under way. A take-over has made replica 10 a primary replica since the original primary (2) is unavailable as a result of the failure. The fragment replicas 6 and 10 are each refragmented into three subfragments with two replicas of each subfragment. The subfragments are allocated one per node over the nodes at the same side of the mirror dimension as the failed node 2. The matching subfragment replica is allocated to the node across the mirror dimension.

The subfragment replica allocation strategy maintains the fault tolerance level of each subfragment as presented in section 10.6, because both the node the primary and the node the hot stand-by replica of a leaf-fragment is located to must fail for a leaf-fragment to be unavailable. This is independent of the level of subfragmentation. The allocation of one subfragment replica on each of the available nodes on the side of the mirror dimension in which the failed node or failed fragment belongs is done to distribute the added transaction work load by entering additional data to a node, over as many as possible nodes to constrain the added burden on each node.

The refragmentation replica production is done as a subtransaction for each fragment with a global system based coordination to limit the number of fragments under concurrent refragmentation. The non-blocking replication algorithms are based on relational algebra algorithms (see [Wed91] for an introduction).

When the replication is completed, the subfragments on the same side of the mirror dimension as the originally primary replica for the fragment takes over as the primary replicas for the fragment. Their matching subfragments across the mirror dimension takes over as the hot stand-by replicas for the fragment. When the take-overs are completed, the fragment replicas that have been the primary replicas during the replication (6 and 10) are taken out of operations. Figure 10.9 illustrates the fragment allocation after the replication is completed. Node 6 is then taken out of DBMS operations. If a later non-recoverable failure occurs among the nodes on their side of the mirror dimension, then the fragment replicas on the failed node become replicated in this unused node.

Further crashes may appear after the repair has taken place and may cause a subfragment to be further refragmented. The same policies as for a first level subfragment with respect to fragmentation, allocation, and replication are then used. Data for each subfragment are kept in separate tables to reduce the read and write data volumes when a replica is built.

Section 12.5 presents a subfragment concatenation policy which is used when a non-recoverable node becomes restarted again after maintenance.

10.8 Gradual Reduction of Fragment Availability

A fragment crash, i.e. when the primary and the hot stand-by fragment replicas are crashed, results in **partial** DB availability (see section 2.2). The crashed fragment becomes unavailable, but all the other fragments of the relation are still available. A fragment crash results in omission failures only for those transactions trying to access tuples belonging to the failed fragment, i.e. resulting in a higher abort rate for these transactions. Access based on the primary key, or mapped through an index to a fragment other than the unaccessible fragment, is provided.

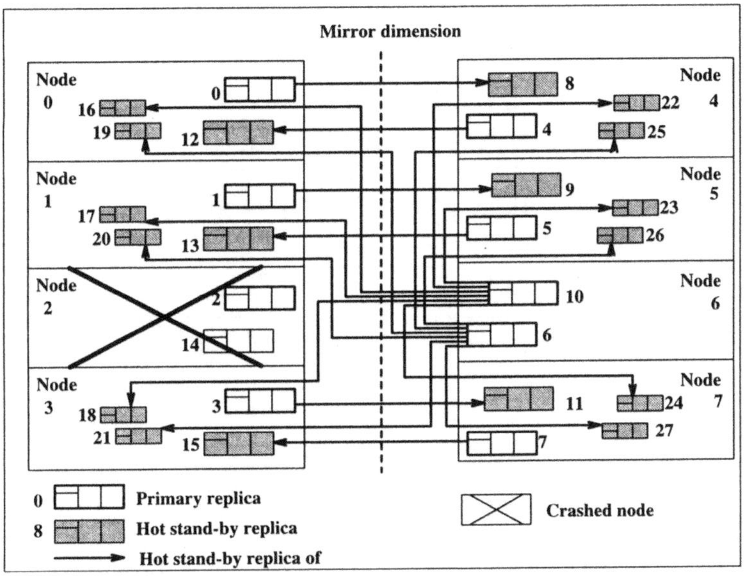

Figure 10.8: Production and allocation of subfragment replicas to compensate for the failure of node 2. Fragment replicas 6 and 10 are refragmented into three subfragments with two replicas of each subfragment. The subfragment replicas are allocated one per node over the nodes at the same side of the mirror dimension as the failed node, and the matching subfragment replica is allocated at the node across the mirror dimension. This allocation is done to distribute the added transaction work load on each node, and to preserve the fault-tolerance level per fragment.

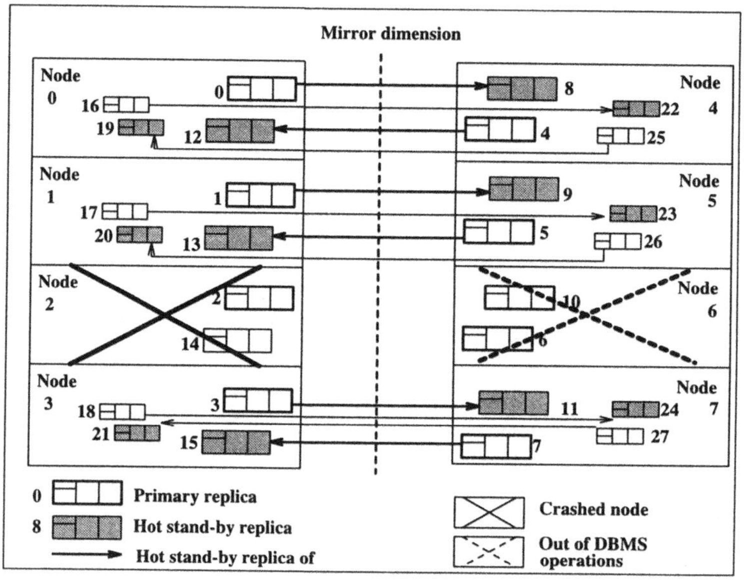

Figure 10.9: The allocation of fragments after the subfragmentation illustrated in figure 10.8. The subfragments allocated to nodes at the same side of the mirror dimension as the original primary replica for the fragment have become primary replicas. The subfragments allocated to nodes at the other side of the mirror dimension have become hot stand-by replicas. All replicas allocated to node 6 are taken out of operations.

A gradual reduction of data availability is also provided for subfragments as well as for fragments. If all replicas of a subfragment, or the fragment replicas containing the subfragment, have crashed, the subfragment has crashed. The gradual reduction of data availability as a result of fragment crashes is opposed to a policy where the entire relation becomes unavailable if any of its fragments crashes ([GMA89]).

Exercises

1. (a) What are the advantages of the presumed-abort two-phase commit protocol? (b) Propose further improvements of the two-phase commit protocol.
2. (a) Why is a centralised lock manager not used in the HypRa approach? (b) Name some advantages and disadvantages of the snooper-based global deadlock detection mechanism. (c) Propose some other global detection mechanisms.
3. (a) Give two examples of the use of nested top-actions. (b) Give two examples of the use of nested top-level transactions.
4. Why is the buffer manager given the ability to lock data in main memory?
5. (a) Propose an improvement of the hash-based fragmentation method for small relations. (b) Give a survey of fragmentation methods.
6. (a) Can two different relations have different number of replicas? (b) What would the effect be of fragmenting the hot stand-by replicas over all nodes across the mirror dimension?
7. What is the effect of using spare nodes instead of overcapacity on each node on reconfiguration after a node failure?
8. What is the relationship between software repair and hardware faults?
9. (a) Work out a dictionary structure for the HypRa fragmentation and replication method. (b) How would you distribute and replicate this information?

Answers

1. (a) In case a slave does not respond, it is assumed to have aborted. This simplifies the protocol logic. (b) A read transaction needs no phase two. The same is true when only one participant does DB state changing operations.
2. (a) A centralised lock manager has no fault-tolerance unless multiple replicas of the lock server are used. A central lock server does not increase with the number of nodes and will therefore become a bottleneck as the number of nodes grows. (b) The deadlock detection mechanism does not increase with the number of nodes and will eventually become a bottleneck. (c) Use the deadlock detection method used in system R*. Think up a hash-based deadlock detection method that increases almost linearly with the number of nodes.
3. (a) To split a bottom level B-tree block. To allocate blocks to a file. To allocate a transaction identifier, a file identifier, a fragment identifier or a replica identifier. To manage overflow in some hash-based access methods. (b) To split a higher level B-tree block. To merge two higher level B-tree blocks. To determine the set of available nodes. To reset the I-am-Alive message interval.
4. To make sure data stay in main memory regardless of the frequency of use.

5. (a) Hash the table over a subset of the nodes instead of over all nodes. (b) Mirroring, chained declustering and interleaved declustering (see [BG88], [CK89], and [HD89]).

6. (a) Yes. (b) The load after a node crash is spread over N/2 nodes instead of being concentrated on one node as in the HypRa replication method.

7. No refragmentation during repair, which gives simpler algorithms. You may eventually run out of spare nodes.

8. Enough HW resources must be available to maintain the service level during and after the repair. The hardware resources thereby limit the number of software repairs.

9. The problem is left as an exercise for the students.

Chapter 11

The Location and Replication Independent Tuple Recovery Strategy

This chapter presents the Location- and Replication Independent tuple recovery (**LRI**) strategy; a tuple recovery strategy in which the location and replication aspects of tuples are hidden from the tuple operation log.

The LRI strategy provides **location independent** tuple recovery. Undo and redo recovery of a tuple from tuple log records is independent of the tuple's location at recovery time relative to its location at log record production time. As a consequence the LRI strategy provides tuple recovery that is both logical to blocks (see section 7.3.1) and logical to tuples within blocks ([GR88]). This is not supported by any of the previously presented recovery approaches (see chapter 7, for example). Tuple recovery is also independent of which fragment and fragment replica a tuple is contained in and which node the fragment replica is allocated to.

The LRI strategy also provides **replication independent** tuple recovery. A tuple log record can be used to redo or undo recover any replicas of the tuple to which the log record is related. Therefore a log record resulting from a tuple operation to a primary tuple replica can be applied to recover any replicas of the same tuple, including its hot stand-by replicas.

HypRa uses the non-blocking fragment replica production policy to avoid threatening the availability of soft real-time transaction services during the execution of fragment replication transactions. (See [HST+91b] for an introduction to fuzzy non-blocking replication.) The LRI strategy is required in order to perform non-blocking dynamic replication of fragment replicas, because it allows production of fuzzy fragment replica snapshots combined with tuple redo recovery catch-up to make a current image of the produced fragment replica. A fuzzy snapshot replica is independent of the access method, record, or block layers of the originator fragment replica. The location independent capability of the LRI strategy is therefore needed when recovery is done to the new fuzzy produced tuples because their locations are different from those of their originating tuples. The replication independence capability of the LRI strategy is required because catch-up uses the log records produced to the originating tuples to produce a current image of the new replica.

The LRI strategy allows the non-blocking replication policy to produce a horizontally *subfragmented fragment replica* (see section A.2). The subfragmentation is used to distribute evenly the added work load of another fragment replica over multiple nodes. The LRI strategy also allows the non-blocking replication policy to produce a *concatenated fragment replica*, i.e. the produced fragment replica is a new replica that is a concatenation of a collection of horizontally fragmented subfragments. A concatenated fragment replica is produced for example when a node is restarted and takes back the fragment replicas it contained before it crashed.

11.1 The Tuple State-Identifier Policy

This section presents the **tuple state-identifier** policy. The tuple state-identifier policy is used if a tuple state-identifier field is connected to a tuple. The tuple state-identifier reflects the state of the tuple, i.e. the sequence of tuple oriented DB operations that have been executed to the tuple (see sections A.5 and 5.4). The use of the tuple state-identifier policy is required when using non-blocking fragment replica production combined with subfragmentation (see [HST+91b]).

HypRa implements each fragment replica by a table. A table contains no more than one fragment replica. The HypRa DBMS server architecture locates the concurrency control and recovery servers as in the table oriented server architecture (see figure 8.1). The tuple oriented DB operations reflected in the tuple state-identifiers are therefore table datamodel operations (see section A.5). The table oriented server architecture ensures that concurrency control is done to the tuple oriented DB operations (see section 7.1). The table oriented server architecture logs the serialised sequence of executed tuple oriented DBMS operations. *Operational logging is applied.*

HypRa manages replication at the fragment DBMS layer and not at lower DBMS layers. Since a relation is horizontally fragmented, the atomic unit of replication is the tuple. Different fragment replicas of the same fragment can have different levels of subfragmentation. A hot stand-by replica can be subfragmented as compared to its primary fragment replica and a primary replica can be subfragmented as compared to its hot stand-by replica (see figures 10.7, 10.8 and 12.4).

The implementation of a fragment replica by lower DBMS layers is mostly autonomous at the node to which the fragment is allocated ([ÖV91]). The fragment replicas are implemented by different tables. The choice of blocks used to implement a table, the block sizes used, and the data structure within a block are selected independently by the local block, record, and table servers at the node in which the table is stored. A consequence of this lower DBMS layer autonomy is that independent maintenance of both hardware and software can be done locally to a node. Hardware and software server heterogeneity at DBMS layers below the fragmentation layer are allowed among the nodes. The tuples contained in one block in one fragment replica may be spread at multiple blocks in another replica of the same fragment. This is a consequence of the lower DBMS layer autonomy and the possible different subfragmentation levels of different replicas of a fragment.

An alternative to the approach taken by HypRa with replication managed at the fragment layer and lower layer autonomy is to manage replication at the fragment and block DBMS layers. A block is in this approach the atomic unit of distribution. Every replica of a given fragment must be replicated at the block DBMS layer. The same logical block size must be used for every replica of a block. If a primary block replica is allowed to be larger than its hot stand-by replica block, then a block split may be done to the hot stand-by replica which is not done to the primary replica. This must be avoided because the sequence of operations to the two block replicas would no longer be equivalent. If, on the other hand, the hot stand-by block replica is larger than the primary block replica when a take-over takes place and the original primary is to be recovered from the produced log, then a block split may happen to the original primary block that was not executed to the current primary. This must also be avoided because the operation sequence to the two block replicas would no longer be equivalent. It can therefore not be decided autonomously at a node which block sizes to support. Since the same operation sequences must be applied to a primary and a hot stand-by block replica, the same access methods must be used to the different tables implementing replicas of a given fragment. Synchronisation must therefore be managed among the access method servers. The consequence of this approach is low node autonomy at lower DBMS layers.

If the block replication approach is combined with non-blocking fragment replica production, the fragment produced must replicate the blocks of the original replica. If subfragmentation is used, every subfragment must contain every block of the original replica. The filling degree of these

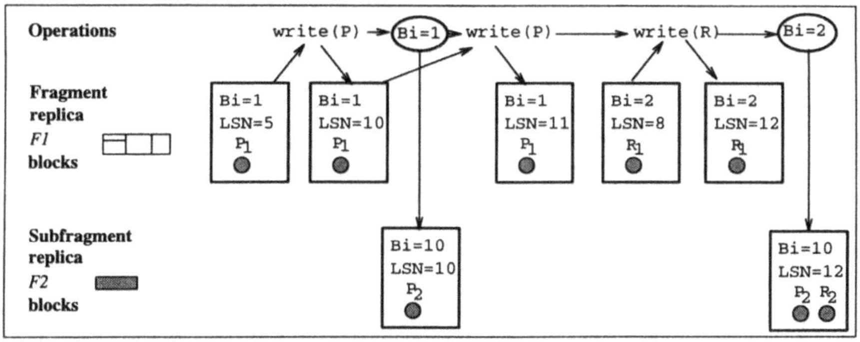

Figure 11.1: Case which illustrates an inconsistent DB state resulting from use of block state-identifiers together with production of a fuzzy subfragmented fragment replica. The inconsistency occurs because the block state-identifier of block $B10$ indicates that the tuple write operation to P, executed after the snapshot of block $B1$ is taken, is reflected in $B10$. The inconsistency occurs because the block state-identifier of the original block in which the snapshoted tuple is stored is applied to the block in the produced subfragment into which the tuple replica is inserted. This block may also contain tuple replicas originating from tuple replicas contained in different blocks.

blocks may therefore be very low if the number of subfragments is large. Non-blocking production of concatenated replicas is ruled out because tuples from different blocks could need be required to be located at the same block in the concatenated fragment replica. Because of these constraints, the number of fragments of a relation will, in practice, be decided when the relation is created and remain unaltered, as far as non-blocking fragment replica production is concerneded, over its lifetime. Since efficient and flexible dynamic subfragmentation and concatenation are fundamental in HypRa to obtain load distribution after a fragment or node failure or a node restart, this approach is not used.

The fragment replication policy combined with the non-blocking replica production policy requires use of the tuple state-identifier policy. This is a consequence of the fact that the tuple and not the block is the atomic unit of replication. *A tuple replica will be stored within one block* (see section 5.3.1). The replicas of the tuples originally stored in one block may, in the produced fragment replica, be spread at multiple blocks and tuple replicas originally stored in different blocks may be stored in one block. This occurs for instance when a new replica of a fragment is subfragmented, and *the subfragmentation criteria is a hash function on the primary key* which is the subfragmentation criteria used by HypRa. This may also occur if the new fragment replica uses different block sizes than the original replica.

The following case demonstrates that inconsistencies can occur if block state-identifiers are used in combination with dynamic non-blocking replication of a fragment and with subfragmentation of the produced fragment replica. The case is illustrated by figure 11.1. The tuples P and R both belong to fragment F. (F_1 and F_2 are replicas of F. They contain P_1, R_1, and P_2, R_2, respectively.) Block $B1$ contains P_1 and block $B2$ contains R_1. Another replica of the fragment F is produced by the non-blocking dynamic fragment replication policy. The produced fragment is subfragmented with F_2 as one of the new subfragments. The fuzzy snapshot part of the fragment replication produces the tuple replicas P_2 and R_2 which becomes part of F_2 and stored in the same block $B10$.

The replica production transaction only locks a block while replicating the tuples it contains to minimise its threat to transaction service availability. The last operation done on $B1$, before the replica production transaction locks the block and replicates its tuples, is a tuple write to P_1 which updates the block state-identifier to 10. The block state-identifier of the block into which P_2 is inserted ($B10$) is set to the same value as the state-identifier of the block in which the replica was contained. This is done because all operations with a lesser or equal state-identifier value are reflected in P_2. The block state-identifier value must therefore be set to this value to reflect this fact. A write operation is executed to P_1 which updates the state-identifier of $B1$ to 11. A write operation is then executed to R_1 which updates the state-identifier of $B2$ to 12. Then $B2$ is locked by the replication transaction. A replica of R_1 is made. The state-identifier value of $B10$, into which R_2 is inserted, is set to 12 since R_2 reflects the effect of all operations with a less or equal state-identifier value. This causes DB inconsistency. The state-identifier of $B2$ now indicates that all operations with an LSN lesser than or equal to 12 have been executed to the tuples contained in that block. It therefore indicates that the write operation with LSN value 11 have been executed to P_2, which is not correct. This operation is missing from P_2 because it was executed after the replication of the tuples contained in $B1$ was completed. Block state-identifiers can therefore not be used in combination with non-blocking fragment replica production and subfragmentation.

If tuple state-identifiers had been used instead of block state-identifiers, the inconsistency would have been avoided. The state-identifier would then only indicate which operations had been executed to a tuple and not to a block. The state-identifier value 10 would have been connected to the tuple replica P_2 indicating only which tuple operations that were reflected in the tuple. Similarly, the state-identifier value 12 would have been connected to R_2, reflecting the tuple operations executed to that tuple replica.

The inconsistencies are caused by using a state-identifier scope larger than the granularity of the unit of atomic distribution. By making the state-identifier scope lesser than or equal to the units of atomic distribution, inconsistencies of this type are avoided. We term this the **atomic distribution rule**.

If blocks had been the unit of atomic replication, the tuple oriented DBMS operations could have been reflected in the block state-identifiers, i.e. tuple state-identifiers could have been avoided. The state-identifier scope of the block state-identifiers would then equal the unit of atomic distribution and the atomic distribution rule would have been obeyed.

If dynamic non-blocking replica production is combined with dynamic non-blocking *vertical* subfragmentation, the unit of atomic distribution would be a field, except for the fields being part of the primary key. Since the primary key is part of every vertical subfragment, the group of fields constituting the primary key is an atomic unit of distribution. To obey the atomic distribution rule, a state-identifier have to be connected to each field in every tuple outside the primary key, and one state-identifier would have to exist for the primary key group.

HypRa applies the tuple state-identifier policy to every table. The tuple state-identifier policy is not used to index-tuples, since access methods are local to a node. Operations on index-tuples are combined with access method block granularity locks (see section 7.1).

11.2 The Primary and Hot Stand-By Tuple Replica Synchronisation Policy

A primary fragment replica contains primary tuple replicas whereas a hot stand-by fragment replica contains hot stand-by tuple replicas. Tuple state-identifiers are connected to both the primary and the hot stand-by tuple replicas. Tuple oriented DBMS operations executed to a hot stand-by tuple replica are reflected in its state-identifier just as tuple oriented DBMS operations executed to a primary tuple replica are reflected in its state-identifier.

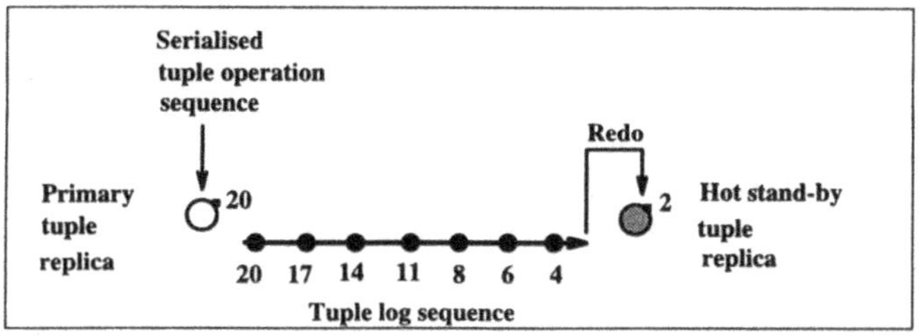

Figure 11.2: A tuple state-identifier is connected to both primary and hot stand-by tuple replicas indicating which tuple operations have been executed to the tuple replica. Tuple operations are executed as deferred redo operations to hot stand-by tuple replicas, based on the log produced by the operations in the primary tuple replica.

A hot stand-by and a primary tuple replica in the same or equivalent states need to have the same state-identifier values. This is required by the non-blocking fragment replica production policy. During the catch-up phase of a non-blocking fragment replica production transaction, it must be possible to determine whether an operation is already reflected in the new tuple by looking at its state-identifier value.

The requirements are met if the operations executed to a hot stand-by tuple replica are redo tuple operations executed in the log produced order to the primary tuple replica. The log production order to a tuple is the same as the execution of tuple operations to the primary tuple replica. The execution sequence of the redo operations is therefore the same as the sequence of the tuple operations to the primary tuple replica. Since the tuple operations are redone to the hot stand-by tuple replicas, they will not be executed if the state-identifier indicates that the operation is already reflected in the tuple replica. This execution policy of tuple operations to a hot stand-by tuple replica is indicated in figure 11.2.

One sequence of tuple operations that is equivalent to the complete sequence of state-changing tuple operations to a primary tuple replica, is a log to which a log compression policy has been applied. The log compression policy applied by HypRa is presented in chapter 14. Applying the log compression policy would require log aggregation to be done over a given time interval to gain a reduction of redo work as compared to a complete redo. HypRa does not allow a hot stand-by tuple replica to lag far behind the primary replica as this would increase the take-over time in case of a fragment or node failure. The redo operations to a hot stand-by replica can therefore not be aggregated over a time interval and then executed.

Another sequence of tuple operations, equivalent to the complete sequence of state-changing tuple operations, is a sequence where all tuple operations belonging to aborted transactions are left out. Not executing tuple operations belonging to aborted transactions would cause delaying operations from being executed to hot stand-by tuple replicas until after the transaction has terminated, i.e. a deferred update policy is applied (see section 6.8). Since the semantically rich locking model is supported by HypRa (see section A.9), operations by committed transactions may have to wait even beyond the commit of the transaction to be redo executed to a hot stand-by replica. If some delta operation by another active transaction precedes a delta operation belonging to a committed transaction, then the committed delta operation cannot be executed because the state-identifier of the tuple would indicate that the delta operation of the still active transaction is also reflected in the tuple. The state-identifier would be increased to a larger value than the state-identifier value when connected to the log record of the delta operation of the still active transaction. The delta operation of the active transaction would therefore not be executed when its transaction commits. The result is an inconsistent DB state. See also section 7.9.2 for comparison.

The delay effect would increase the take-over work compared to the situation if every state-changing tuple operation is executed. The state of replicated tuples produced by a non-blocking replication transaction may reflect operations belonging to transactions which later abort. Complete redo must therefore be performed to such transactions regardless of whether they commit or abort. This further complicates the redo execution policy to a hot stand-by tuple. To avoid possible take-over delays and added complexity involved in trying to avoid redoing operations belonging to aborted transactions, HypRa executes every state changing tuple operation, executed to the primary tuple replicas, to the hot stand-by tuple replicas.

A consequence of this log based synchronisation policy between primary and hot stand-by tuple replicas is that tuple operations other than those executed at the primary replica are not allowed to be reflected in the tuple state-identifier of a hot stand-by tuple replica. Therefore tuple operations executed as part of subtransactions that are local to a node cannot be reflected in the tuple state-identifiers. Tuple operations involved in, for example, block splits cannot be reflected in the tuple state-identifiers since block splits are local to a node. If, on the other hand, the tuple operations executed as part of a block split to a block containing hot stand-by tuple replicas are reflected in the tuple state-identifiers of the moved tuple replicas, then some later tuple operation to the primary replica can be given the same state-identifier value. The same state-identifier value to the primary and the hot stand-by replica of the same tuple no longer reflects the same state. This is shown in section 11.4. When such an operation is attempted to be redo executed to the hot stand-by tuple replica, its state-identifier value indicates that the operation is already reflected in it. The operation is therefore not redone, which causes a DB inconsistency. To avoid these inconsistencies HypRa uses the multi-level state-identifier policy (see section 11.4).

Serialisation of tuple operations is done to the primary tuple replicas (see section 8.1). If a transaction is required to be aborted to resolve a deadlock, the necessary sequence of undo operations is executed to the primary tuple replicas to compensate for the effects of the transaction and the CLRs reflecting the undo operations are entered into the tuple log. The undo operations are redone to the hot stand-by tuple replicas based on the CLRs so that the effects of the transaction are also compensated for in the hot stand-by tuple replicas. Since the sequence of tuple operations executed to hot stand-by tuple replicas is serialised, no deadlocks that are not detected among the primary replica tuple operations, will occur among these operations. This execution policy maintains the state-identifier synchronisation between the primary and the hot stand-by replicas of a tuple also during transaction abort processing.

The redo execution of tuple operations to hot stand-by tuples may activate a subtransaction that fails because, for example, it runs into node internal resource constraints. If an insert operation is attempted and a subtransaction is activated to split the block as the block is full and no free blocks are available at the node, then the subtransaction will fail. Since hot stand-by operations may be executed *deferred*, i.e. after the transaction is committed (see chapter 13), these situations cannot be handled by aborting the top-level transaction. Such situations can not be handled by executing additional tuple operations to hot stand-by tuples than those to be reflected in the tuple state-identifiers, because this can lead to inconsistencies of the same type as mentioned above. These problems will be returned to in chapter 13.

11.3 The Primary Key Update Policies

This section focuses on updating the primary key fields of a tuple (see also section 7.5.6). The **delete/insert tuple replica** policy is applied if the primary key of a tuple replica is updated, and this is logged as a delete followed by an insert tuple operation.

Updating the primary key of a tuple replica may cause the tuple to migrate to another block since the new primary key value may fall outside the primary key range of the block in which it is contained. The operation will then involve two blocks. A node failure may occur where redo is required for both of the involved blocks, i.e. the operation was not done to either. To use block autonomous recovery (see section 7.6.4) which is used by HypRa, the single-block policy (see section 5.3.1) must be followed which requires the delete/insert tuple replica policy to be followed when the do operation moves the tuple to another block.

The delete/insert tuple replica policy must unconditionally be used when updating the primary key of a primary tuple replica if a hot stand-by replica exists for the tuple. Even though the primary key update does not cause the primary tuple replica to be moved to another block, the redo execution of the update to a hot stand-by tuple replica may cause it to be moved to another block. Since the tuple operations executed to a hot stand-by tuple replica, and logged in its state-identifier, are redoing exactly the same operations as those done to the primary tuple replica, the execution to the primary tuple replica must be prepared for a block move to be involved during any redo execution of the operation. HypRa therefore applies the delete/insert tuple replica policy when the primary key of a tuple is updated.

11.4 The Multi-Level State-Identifier Policy

This section demonstrates that block state-identifiers must be used in combination with tuple state-identifiers when the HypRa DBMS server architecture is applied (see section 8.1). A **multi-level state-identifier policy** is used if the tuple state-identifier policy is combined with the block state-identifier policy so that tuple state-identifiers are connected to tuples, and block state-identifiers are connected to blocks.

The tuple oriented DBMS operations that are mapped from relational operations are reflected in the tuple state-identifiers (see sections 11.1 and 11.2). The recovery of these operations is required to be location- and replication independent. The operations executed at lower DBMS layers are local to a node and cannot be reflected in the tuple state-identifiers even if they are tuple oriented DBMS operations. It will be shown that inconsistencies may occur if non-location- and non-replication independent operations are reflected in the tuple state-identifiers. The DBMS server internal layer architecture requires operations performed by the access method server and at the block DBMS layer to be logged as part of block splitting and block flush operations. These lower layer DBMS operations can, on the other hand, be reflected in the block state-identifiers because a block is local to a node.

A block split/merge operation is local to a node. This is an effect of replication at the fragment DBMS layer. In case of a fragment replica failure, the block split/merge operations executed to a fragment replica are not of interest when producing another replica of the fragment. Block split/merge operations are therefore not reflected in tuple state-identifiers, but they may be reflected in block state-identifiers. Tuple insert and delete operations executed as part of a split/merge subtransaction cannot be reflected in the tuple state-identifiers because these tuple operations are local to a node. If such tuple operations were reflected in the tuple state-identifiers, it would lead to situations where the tuple state-identifier of a primary and a hot stand-by replica of the same tuple reflects different tuple replica states. This may lead to DB inconsistencies, as illustrated in the following case.

A tuple replica $P1$ is inserted into a primary fragment replica. Its tuple state-identifier value is 10. A write operation is then executed to an existing primary tuple replica $Q1$ so that its tuple state-identifier is updated to 11. At the hot stand-by fragment replica, the redo execution of the insert operation leads to a block split. The block split causes the hot stand-by replica of the tuple replica $Q1$ to be moved to another block. As part of the block split, a tuple operation is executed to the hot stand-by replica of $Q1$ which updates its tuple state-identifier to 11. When the redo write operation is attempted to the hot stand-by replica of $Q1$, its tuple state-identifier indicates that the operation is already reflected in the tuple replica. A DB inconsistency has occurred.

The inconsistency is a result of tuple operations done to a hot-standby tuple replica that is not a redo of an operation done to the primary tuple replica. The same state-identifier value connected to a primary and a hot stand-by replica of the same tuple does not reflect the same tuple state. The hot stand-by replica is allowed to reflect a state different from the primary replica state with the same state-identifier value. If on the other hand the tuple operation as part of the block split is not reflected in the block state-identifier, the inconsistency is avoided.

The multi-level state-identifier policy is used by HypRa. The location and replication independent tuple operations are reflected in the tuple state-identifiers. The logged operations of DBMS layers below the fragment layer are reflected in the block state-identifiers.

11.5 Conclusion

The location and replication independent tuple recovery provided by the LRI strategy removes the remaining obstacle in the recovery approaches presented in Part III to support non-blocking fragment replication with subfragmentation. Non-blocking fragment replication with subfragmentation is required to perform online non-blocking fragment repair (see section 2.6), online non-blocking index production, and online non-blocking alter table and online non-blocking relation redistribution as presented in [HST+91b].

The LRI strategy provides a foundation for the log distribution strategy presented in chapter 12 because a log record for a tuple operation can be replicated and used to maintain the consistency between primary and hot stand-by tuple replicas located at different nodes.

Exercises

1. (a) Why does scheduling information need to be reflected in the log distribution? (b) What kind of scheduling information needs to be reflected in the log distribution?

2. Are the following tuple state-identifier policies location independent? Assume single-level fragmentation. (a) The tuple state-identifier is local to a tuple. Every tuple operation increments the tuple's state-identifier by one. (b) The tuple state-identifier is composed of the fragment identifier of the fragment in which the tuple is contained and a counter which is local to the tuple. The counter is incremented by one for every tuple operation executed to the tuple. (c) There is one tuple state-identifier counter in each node. A tuple operation sets the tuple's state-identifier to the node's state-identifier counter value and increments this counter by one. (d) The tuple state-identifiers are composed of the node identifier and a counter incremented as in c.

3. Would the policies in exercise 2 be location independent if multi-level fragmentation was assumed instead of single-level fragmentation?

4. Are the following tuple state-identifier policies replication independent? Assume that block split/merge operations are not reflected in the tuple state-identifiers. Assume also the use of single-level fragmentation. (a) The tuple state-identifier is local to a tuple replica. Every tuple operation to a tuple replica increments its state-identifier by one. (b) The tuple state-identifier is local to a primary tuple replica. The state-identifier values of the hot stand-by replicas are based on state-identifier values in the tuple log records. (c) The tuple state-identifier is composed of the fragment identifier of the fragment in which the tuple is contained and a counter which is local to the tuple as in a. (d) Same as c, but with the state-identifiers of

the hot stand-by tuple replicas updated as in c. (e) There is one tuple state-identifier counter for each node. A tuple operation sets the tuple's state-identifier to the node's state-identifier counter value and increments this counter by one. (f) The tuple state-identifiers are composed of the node identifier and a counter which is incremented as in b.

5. Would the policies in exercise 4 be replication independent if multi-level fragmentation was used instead of single-level fragmentation?
6. Would the policies in exercise 4 be replication independent if block split/merge operations are allowed to be reflected in the tuple state-identifiers and the distribution synchronisation is handled at the fragment layer?
7. Would the policies in exercise 4 be replication independent if block split/merge operations are allowed to be reflected in the tuple-identifiers and the distribution synchronisation is handled at the block layer?
8. (a) Propose a scheme in which only block state-identifiers are used and in which the block state-identifiers are location and replication independent. (b) Do you see any disadvantages to the scheme?
9. Propose a scheme that is location and replication independent based on logical blocks or mini pages.
10. Which conditions must be fulfilled for state-identifiers to be clock based (time-stamps)?
11. Assume that two fragments located at the same node are joined. The involved fragments are read locked during the join operation. How would you handle the state-identifiers of the resulting fragment?
12. Assume that two hot stand-by fragment replicas at the same node are joined. How would you handle the state-identifiers of the resulting tuples if read locks are not used and the resulting tuples are to be kept continuously updated based on the updates of the original tuples?
13. Analyse the effects of main memory databases on multi-level state identifiers.

Answers

1. (a) Scheduling information is reflected in the log distribution to maintain the same scheduling of tuple operations for the hot stand-by tuple replicas as for the primary tuple replicas. (b) The sequence of tuple operations must be maintained for each replica of the tuple. The sequence of tuple operations by a transaction to a tuple must be maintained for each replica of the tuple.
2. (a) Yes. (b) Yes. (c) No. Inconsistencies may occur if a tuple is moved to another node where the next state identifier which is to be used at the node is smaller than the last state-identifier reflected in the tuple. (d) No.
3. (a) Yes. (b) Yes, if the subfragments of a given fragment are given larger fragment identifier values than the parent fragment, and a fragment concatenated from its subfragments is given a new larger fragment identifier than any of the concatenated subfragments. (c) No. (d) No.
4. (a) Yes. (b) Yes. (c) Yes. (d) Yes. (e) No. (f) No.
5. (a) Yes. (b) Yes. (c) See exercise 3.b. (d) Yes. (e) No. (f) No.
6. (a) No. (b) No. (c) No. (d) No. (e) No. (f) No.

7. (a) Yes. (b) Yes. (c) See exercise 3.b. (d) Yes. (e) No. (f) No.

8. (a) Fragments are replicated at the block level. The blocks allocated to two different replicas of the same fragment have the same block identifiers and the same block sizes. When a block belonging to the primary fragment replica is split or merged, the same event happens to the hot stand-by replicas of the block. (b) Block identifiers should not be based on physical block numbers because of problems in masking block failures. The same block identifier may appear in multiple fragment replicas on a node after a vertical fragmentation of a fragment. Subfragmentation may lead to nearly empty blocks.

9. Logical blocks are one way to avoid some of the problems indicated in exercise 8. Instead of keeping the block sizes equal between nodes, the logical blocks are of equal size. A physical block is composed of multiple logical blocks. A logical block is split when full and merged as needed according to the access method policy. All operations to a logical block are reflected in the state-identifier of the block. When a primary logical block is split, all hot stand-by replicas of the block must also be split. Find a way to handle physical blocks when they get full.

10. The resolution of the clock must be fine enough for each tuple operation to be given a unique time-stamp state-identifier. There must be clock synchronisation between the nodes with a maximum drifting for the clocks of two nodes. All time-stamp state-identifiers generated after a take-over must be newer than all the time stamps generated before the take-over.

11. Since the fragment is read locked during the join operation, there are no concurrent write operations taking place. The resulting tuples reflect all executed state changing operations. The newly produced tuples have also broken the link to the original tuples. We can therefore assign a separate state-identifier to the resulting tuples. The initial state-identifier value assigned to a resulting tuple is assigned the same way as to any inserted tuple in a fragment.

12. Both of the state-identifiers of the two involved tuples must be kept attached to each of the tuples resulting from the join. Later operations will update the corresponding tuple state-identifier.

13. We leave the answer to this exercise open and only give some hints. A main memory database will not involve discs. Blocks as they are traditionally used will therefore no longer exist. The problems for which multi-level state-identifiers are used disappear. On the other hand, the introduction of large cache-lines may reintroduce the block concept.

Chapter 12

The Log Distribution Strategy

This chapter presents the log distribution strategy. The log distribution strategy determines how the log is fragmented, replicated, and allocated to nodes. It also determines the log record identification policies and the tuple identification policy.

A tuple log contains log records in which tuple operations are reflected, tuple operations which are also reflected in tuple state-identifiers. The same fragmentation, replication, and allocation policies are applied to the tuple log relating to a relation as to the relation itself. The log distribution policy therefore clusters the tuple log so that the fragment replica is dependent on the same node as the fragment replica resides to perform transaction failure recovery. The log necessary to perform the take-over is clustered on the same node as the hot stand-by fragment replica. This provides the basis for fast take-over by a hot stand-by fragment replica as primary replica, in the case the primary replica fails. A tuple log fragment replica only contains log records of one fragment replica.

The data and log fragmentation and allocation policies also enable fast and non-blocking fragment replica production. A minimal data volume is scanned when replicating a fragment because the fragment replica and its tuple log are read only once. Selective fragment replication, i.e. a fragment replica can be replicated independently of other fragment replicas, is also possible under the distribution policy applied.

Tuple log record identifiers are unique and monotonously increasing within a fragment log so that the fragment global log sequence is maintained. The tuple log record identifiers are also unique and monotonously increasing across a subfragmentation or fragment concatenation. The tuple log sequence is therefore maintained by the tuple log record identifiers across node and fragment replica failures. The tuple log record identifiers are therefore used as tuple state-identifier values. A tuple is uniquely identified during redo recovery by the combination of its primary key and tuple state-identifier, and uniquely identified during normal and undo processing by its primary key.

12.1 The Log Distribution Policy

This section presents the log distribution policy, i.e. how the tuple and node internal logs are fragmented, replicated, and allocated. The recovery approaches presented in Part II are all based on discs as the stable log storage (see section 4.4). All these approaches use node global logs, meaning that all log records produced at a node are entered into one log (see section 4.4.1). The node global log policy is used because it gives low disc I/O log overhead and short transaction commit processing delays (see sections 5.3.4 and 5.3.7).

HypRa uses a stable main memory logging policy (see chapter 13). A log record is stably stored when two replicas of it are stored in main memory, and each replica is at a different node that belongs to a different disaster unit (see section 9.5 and chapter 13). For higher levels of fault tolerance, more than two log record replicas can be used. The number of log record replicas is independent of the number of fragment replicas, but will for the purposes of this book be the same. A two replica model will illustrate the principles involved (see also section 8.1). The stable main memory logging policy removes the disc log I/Os involved in transaction commit processing. HypRa can therefore apply a log fragmentation strategy without inducing any transaction commit disc I/O penalty.

Stable main memory logging induces a higher message and communication volume per executed transaction as compared to using disc logging. A TPC-B transaction will use in total 42 messages with stable main memory logging if all the in total eight primary and hot stand-by tuples involved are located on different nodes. Instruction distribution and two-phase commit represents in this case four messages per involved node. In addition comes two messages from the primary to the hot stand-by transaction controller as part of the commit processing. Finally does each primary tuple contribute one log and one log acknowledge message as a consequence of the main memory logging policy. The stable main memory policy will in this case increase the number of messages per transaction will close to 20%. This has been concluded as acceptable in HypRa.

A node global log is fragmented into one **node internal log** and multiple **tuple fragment logs**. A node internal log contains the log records relating to the DBMS layers local to the node. The operations logged in the node internal log are all reflected in the block state-identifiers (see section 11.4). A tuple fragment log contains log records for tuple oriented DBMS operations relating to one fragment. These operations are therefore reflected in the tuple state-identifiers. *The number of fragment logs is equal to the number of fragments.*

There exists one primary and one hot stand-by replica of every node internal log. The primary replica is allocated to the node where the log records are produced. The hot stand-by replica is allocated to a node in another disaster unit. The protocols used to synchronise the primary and the hot stand-by internal log replicas are presented in chapter 13. Figure 12.1 illustrates the replication and allocation of internal logs. The primary internal log of node 2 is allocated to node 2. The hot stand-by replica of this log is allocated to node 6. Node 2 and 6 belong to different disaster units so that the two replicas have independent failure modes. The hot stand-by internal log replica kept at node 6 will be used to recover the internal DBMS layers at node 2 when it is restarted after a node failure.

Two replicas are maintained for every tuple fragment log (see figure 12.1). The primary tuple log fragment replica and the primary fragment replica for each fragment are allocated on the same node. This is also the case for a hot stand-by log fragment replica and a hot stand-by fragment replica. This is done to obtain clustering. During transaction failure recovery processing, the required log is available at the node. During normal redo processing to the hot stand-by replica, the log is also available at the node. The primary fragment replica and the primary log fragment replica therefore have a common failure mode, as do the hot stand-by fragment replica and the hot stand-by log fragment replica. Because the primary replica and the hot stand-by replica of both data and log are located in different disaster units, they have independent failure modes. After any single failure at least one replica of the data and the necessary log to recover a replica of the fragment will be available. If the primary fragment replica, the primary fragment log replica, or the node they are allocated to fails, the hot stand-by replica has sufficient log to perform a consistent take-over as the primary replica. If the hot stand-by replica, the hot stand-by log replica, or the node they are allocated to fails, the primary replica is still available.

HypRa requires fast online non-blocking replication of a failed fragment replica to maintain the availability fault tolerance level of a fragment (see section 10.7). The mapping of one (sub)fragment replica to one table, independently of whether it is a primary or a hot stand-by replica, or of the size of the fragment replica, limits the data volume to be read during the fragment replica production

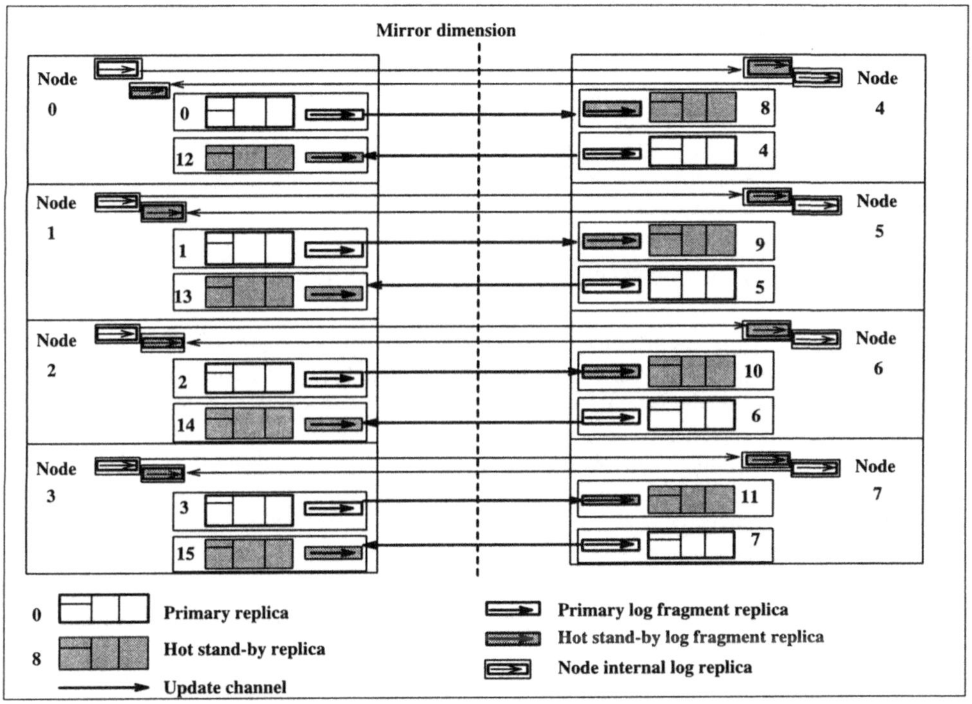

Figure 12.1: Two replicas and two tuple log replicas exist for each fragment of the table *Tab* (see figures 10.4, 10.5, and 10.6). The primary fragment replica and the primary tuple log fragment replica for a given fragment are allocated to the same node. The hot stand-by fragment replica and the hot stand-by tuple log replica for a given fragment are also allocated to the same node. Two replicas are defined for each node internal log. The primary node internal log replica is allocated to the node itself and the hot stand-by is allocated to a node in another disaster unit.

to only the data being replicated. By applying log fragmentation similarly, only tuple log records relating to the fragment need to be read during the replica production. The process is therefore sped up compared to the situation if a global node log policy had been applied. In the case of a global node log, log records relating to multiple fragments would have had to be read.

To maintain the availability fault tolerance level after an unrecoverable node crash, fast replication of all fragments stored at the failed node must be performed (see section 2.4.4). In addition to fast fragment replication, transaction service availability must be provided during replication processing. Since selective fragment replication can be performed, the number of fragments concurrently under replication can be restricted. Each fragment and its log is read once independently of the sequence of replication. This could also be used to support priorities on the sequence of fragment replication.

The node internal log is kept separately from the tuple fragment logs because it contains log records that are local to a node. Since a block, over time, can be used by different fragment replicas, the node internal log should not be further fragmented into different fragment replicas. The node internal log could be fragmented to different discs so that one internal log is maintained per disc. In HypRa one internal log per node is used (see section 12.6).

12.2 The Tuple Log Record Identification Policies

This section presents and evaluates tuple log record identification policies. A tuple log record identifier must satisfy a number of requirements. A **tuple log record identifier** must uniquely identify a tuple log record within a fragment log replica. Only one tuple log record identifier may be used for each tuple log record, in order to restrict the log record data volume overhead and complexity. Furthermore, the **tuple global log sequence** must be maintained for each tuple. The definition of the term (see section 4.4.1) is modified to accomplish dynamic non-blocking tuple replication, i.e. the node global log sequence is substituted with a global log. Finally, a **global tuple log fragment sequence** must be maintained for each tuple log fragment replica to provide low overhead and simple checkpoint WAL undo maintenance.

The *logical* log record identification policy is used (see section 4.4.2). A tuple log record replica may, over its lifetime, be relocated within a tuple log fragment replica as a result of the use of main memory logging (see chapter 13). Since only one log record identifier is assumed to be used for each tuple log record, and non-blocking fragment replication is used, a primary and a hot stand-by replica of the same log record must have the same log record identifier value. This can only be done with the logical log record identifier policy.

The tuple global log sequence gives the production sequence of tuple oriented DB operations to a tuple. The global tuple log sequences must be maintained to provide consistent recovery processing after a node crash. During a node crash recovery, redo of tuple operations reflected in a tuple state-identifier must be executed in forward order relative to their original execution sequence to the tuple replica, in order to avoid the occurrence of DB inconsistencies (see section 6.7.1). Since the primary fragment replica containing the primary replica of a tuple may change over the tuple's lifetime, the log records in the tuples log sequence can have been produced by multiple tuple log fragment replica servers.

One log record to a tuple may have been produced before the primary fragment replica to which the tuple belonged failed. Another log record to the same tuple may have been produced after the primary take-over following the failure and is therefore produced while another replica is the primary replica for the fragment. The production order of these tuple log records must be maintained across the failure because they might both be needed in a later node crash recovery.

A **tuple local LSN** is an LSN that is unique to a tuple instance. The tuple local LSN reflecting the insert of a tuple is given an initial value. The tuple local LSNs reflecting the following state changing tuple operations to the tuple are monotonously increased by one each relative to the previous state changing tuple operation to the tuple.

Multiple tuples can exist over time with the same primary key value even though two tuples with the same primary key value cannot concurrently exist within a relation (see section A.4). The tuple log record identifiers must therefore be guaranteed to be unique even if multiple tuples over time have the same primary key value. Because of this a tuple log record identifier made from the combination of the primary key and a tuple local LSN cannot be used. This combination is not guaranteed to be unique. Another tuple may have existed within the time span of the redo work with the same primary value and the same number of operations executed to it. During a potential redo execution, the operations to the two different tuples can be mixed, leading to DB inconsistencies.

A global tuple sequence is maintained if tuple log record identifiers are composed of the primary key, a surrogate key, (see section A.4) and a tuple local LSN. This policy avoids the confusion caused by multiple tuples with the same primary key value because of the inclusion of a surrogate key per tuple instance. On the other hand, this policy does not maintain the global log sequence of the fragment replica log because tuple local LSNs are used. To maintain the global log sequence another log identifier must be added. Since only one tuple log record identifier is preferred to be used per tuple log record, this policy is not used by HypRa.

The global log sequence for a tuple log fragment replica is maintained if the tuple log records entered into a tuple fragment log replica are given unique and monotonously increasing LSNs. HypRa uses the fuzzy checkpoint policy (see section 4.7.4 and chapter 13). The penultimate checkpoint position will therefore indicate that all log records entered the log replica before the production of that checkpoint are guaranteed to be reflected on disc. To maintain one checkpoint log position per checkpoint for each log replica, the global tuple log fragment sequence must be maintained for each tuple log fragment replica. If a global log sequence is used, the LSN of the last log record entered the log before the checkpoint is the only data required to hold the checkpoint position. If only tuple log sequences were maintained one checkpoint position had to be held per tuple sequence which introduces an unacceptable checkpoint data volume overhead.

A global log sequence for a tuple log fragment replica will maintain the tuple log sequences within one log, but not necessarily between logs. The log records relating to one tuple are given unique and monotonously increasing log record identifiers since this is so for all log records entered a log replica. It will, in section 12.3, be shown that the tuple log sequences can be maintained implicitly by global log sequences by some synchronisation when the primary replica for a fragment is shifted. HypRa therefore uses global tuple log fragment sequences preserving the tuple global log sequences within one log.

12.3 The Tuple Log Record Identification Policy Used at Hot Stand-By Replicas

The log record identification policy applied to primary tuple log fragment replicas maintains the global log sequence within the log, i.e. the production order of tuple oriented DBMS operations executed to the primary fragment replica.

The primary log records are sent through an **update channel** to a hot stand-by tuple log fragment replica server (see section 13.4). The log record replicas are sent in their production order from the primary tuple log fragment replica server to the corresponding hot stand-by tuple log fragment replica server. An update channel provides a reliable transport service so that messages are not lost or damaged, or their sequence altered ([Sta85]). The log records are therefore received by the

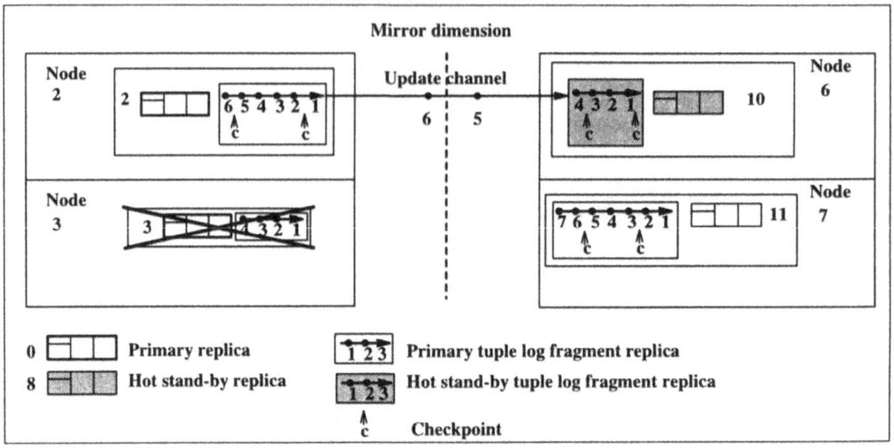

Figure 12.2: The log record identifier given to a log record by the primary tuple log fragment replica server is kept at the hot stand-by replica. See fragment replicas 2 and 10. An update channel (see section 13.4) connects a primary and a hot stand-by tuple log fragment replica and delivers the log record replicas in their production order. See the update channel connecting fragment replicas 2 and 10. Independent checkpointing is done to each log replica. After a primary take-over, the new primary log server produces log record identifiers that are larger than the last log record identifier received before the take-over. See fragment replicas 3 and 11, where a primary take-over has made fragment replica 11 the current primary.

hot stand-by log fragment replica server in their production order. The hot stand-by log record replicas are entered into the hot stand-by tuple log fragment replica in monotonously increasing log record identifier order.

The redo execution of tuple operations to the hot stand-by fragment replica is done in monotonously increasing log record identifier value. This preserves the execution order of tuple operations reflected in tuple state-identifiers at the hot stand-by fragment, so that it is the same as the execution order to the primary fragment (see figure 12.2).

This combination of log record identifiers, which maintain the global log sequence at the hot stand-by tuple log replicas, with an execution policy that follows the global log sequence simplifies checkpointing to the hot stand-by fragments. A checkpoint position can be produced for a hot stand-by log fragment replica in the same way as for a primary log fragment replica, by remembering the log record identifier of the last log record entered into the log before the checkpoint is taken. This is also illustrated in figure 12.2. Because of the hot stand-by capability, the WAL undo rule is guaranteed to be fulfilled. A replica of the log record exists at the primary side.

When a **primary take-over** is executed, a hot stand-by fragment replica changes its role from hot stand-by to primary (see section 14.1). It was shown in section 12.2 that tuple log sequences must be maintained across changes of primary fragment replicas. If the global log sequence for a tuple log fragment is maintained across a take-over, the tuple sequences are also maintained. In order to maintain the global log sequence across the take-over, the log record identifiers produced at the new primary replica must all be larger than the largest stable stored log record at the previous primary replica. A non-stable log record and its DB effect at the previous primary will be lost in the failure. If originally one hot stand-by replica existed, the requirement is met if the log record identifier, assigned to the first log record produced at the new primary fragment, is larger than the record identifier of the last log record it received before the take-over. In addition, the log records

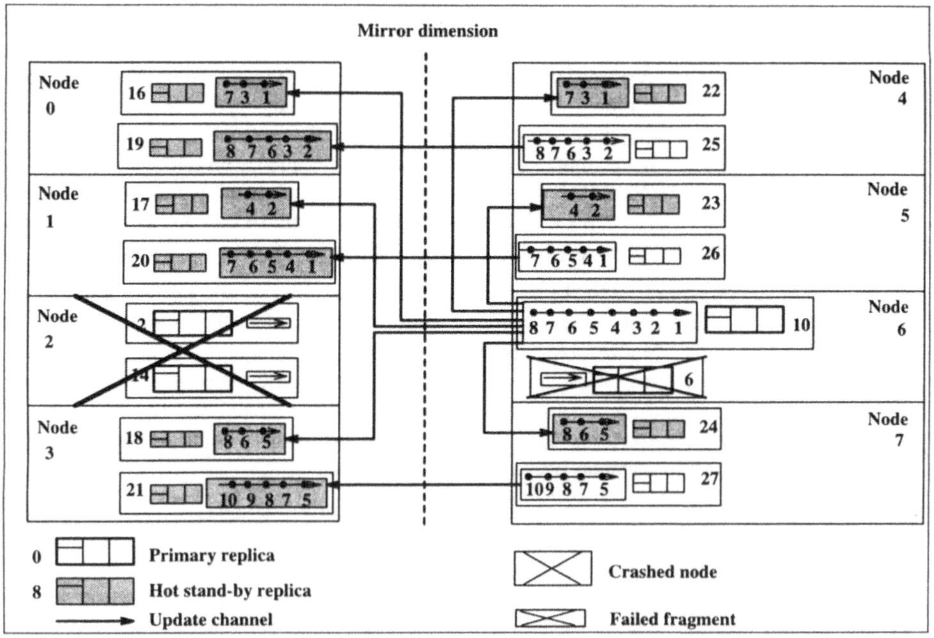

Figure 12.3: Fragment replica 10 is under subfragmentation and two replicas have been produced. Fragment replica 6 has been subfragmented and two replicas have been produced with subfragment replicas 19, 20, 21, 25, 26, and 27 being the result. When the subfragmentation is completed, 25, 26, and 27 became primary replicas and fragment replica 6 is taken out of operations.

produced at the new primary replica are unique and monotonously increasing. HypRa uses one hot stand-by fragment replica. This synchronisation of log record identifiers at take-over is simple and inexpensive. This policy is illustrated in figure12.2.

An alternative policy to one of synchronising the LSNs produced by the new primary fragment replica server with those produced at the previous primary fragment server, is to compose the log record identifiers from the combination of the fragment replica identifier and the LSN. This requires making the hot stand-by fragment replica identifiers larger than the current primary fragment replica identifier, so that the log record identifiers produced at the new primary would be larger than all the log record identifiers produced before the take-over. If a subfragment concatenation is executed, the fragment replica identifier of the resulting replica must be larger than the replica identifiers of all the original fragment replicas. The LSN can then after the take-over be given an initial value independent of its previous value. This policy would require more data overhead per log record than the previously presented LSN synchronisation policy because the fragment replica identifier needs to be included in the tuple log records in addition to the LSN. HypRa uses the synchronisation oriented record identifier policy presented in the previous paragraph.

12.4 The Log Subfragmentation Policy

A fragment replica produced by non-blocking replication can be horizontally subfragmented (see section 10.7). The newly produced subfragments take the role of hot stand-by replicas before eventually changing role to primary replicas. Each of the produced subfragment replicas has its own hot stand-by tuple log fragment replica so that only log records relating to the subfragment replica are entered into its log (see figure 12.3). An update channel is established from the primary log replica to each of the subfragment replicas. A tuple log record replica is sent to one and only one of the subfragment replicas as a consequence of the horizontal fragmentation. The log records are sent in the order in which they were produced from the primary replica to their destination hot stand-by tuple log subfragment replica server. The global log sequence at a hot stand-by subfragment log will therefore be maintained by the global log sequence produced by the primary log fragment server. The LSNs of the hot stand-by log record replicas are unique and monotonously increasing. The redo execution of log records at the subfragment replicas is in increasing log record identifier value, i.e. in the original production order of the log records (see section 12.3).

In the event of a primary take-over, the same protocol as presented in section 12.3 is applied to log record identifier production. The first log record identifier produced by the new primary replica server is larger than the identifier last received by the previous primary or larger than the log record identifier of the last received log record, increased by the maximum number of outstanding log records. The produced log record identifiers are in addition monotonously increasing. In the case of a primary take-over where the hot stand-by replica of the current primary replica is subfragmented, all the subfragments becomes primary replicas.

Since the log record identifiers produced by a primary tuple log subfragment replica server are independent of the log record identifiers produced by the other primary tuple subfragment log servers, the same log record identifier may occur in multiple subfragment logs (see figure 12.3). This presents no problems since, as a result of the horizontal fragmentation, one tuple is never a member of more than one subfragment and therefore never a member of more than one subfragment produced from the same primary fragment replica. The tuple log sequences are therefore preserved even if the same log record identifier occurs in multiple tuple log subfragment replicas.

The subfragmentation policy allows multiple levels of subfragmentation, i.e. a subfragment can again be horizontally subfragmented. Fragment concatenation is presented in section 12.5.

12.5 The Fragment Concatenation Policy

Subfragment replicas are concatenated when reallocated to the node to which they originally belonged before the first fragment or node failure caused its subfragmentation. When a failed node is restarted it takes back the fragment replicas that originally were located at that node. If the fragments became subfragmented while a node was failed, they are concatenated again when located back to this node. This is done so as to maintain a manageable number of subfragments.

During concatenation, the resulting fragment replicas become hot stand-by replicas. Log record replicas belonging to different fragment replicas being concatenated may have the same log record identifiers (see section 12.4). If these logs had been concatenated the original log record identifiers would not have been unique and the resulting log would have multiple log sequences. Therefore one global log sequence is maintained per fragment replica log of the concatenated fragment replicas in order to avoid these problems. One tuple fragment log replica is therefore created for each of the fragment replicas which are being concatenated to maintain only one global log sequence per log. Log records of different fragment replicas which are being concatenated are therefore kept separate. This is illustrated in figure 12.4. In this way the normal checkpointing and redo execution policy can be applied asynchronously to each log. The tuple fragment log replicas for the fragment replicas being concatenated are removed when the log garbage collection have removed all their containing log records.

When a hot stand-by take-over is done so that the concatenated fragment replica becomes operational, a new tuple log replica is created for the fragment. The first log record entered into the new

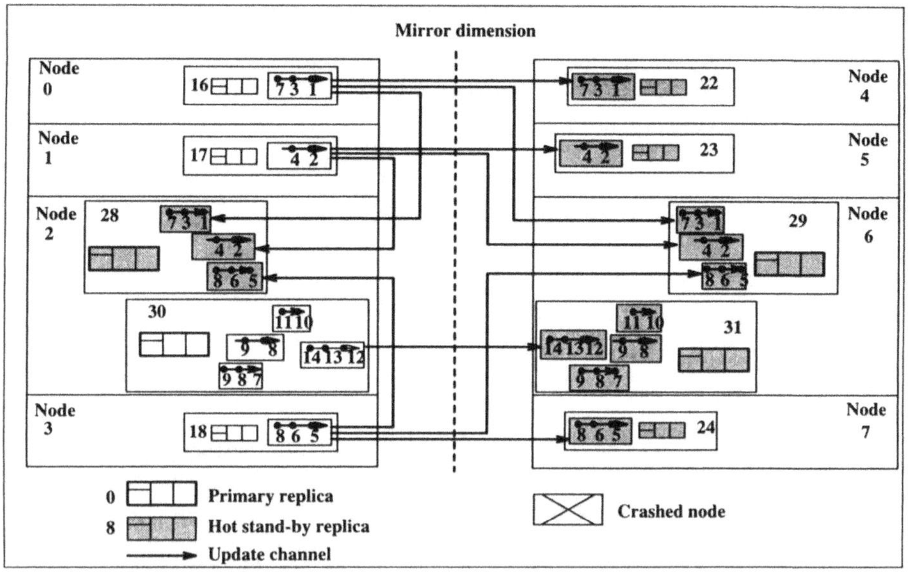

Figure 12.4: Subfragment concatenation. Two concatenated replica, 28 and 29, of the fragment replicas 16, 17, and 18 are under production. The fragment replicas 30 and 31 are the result of a previous concatenation.

log has a larger LSN value than the last log record in all of the hot stand-by logs for the fragment replica. This policy maintains the tuple global log sequences because a log record contained in the new concatenated log will have a larger LSN value than the last log record relating to the tuple contained in the hot stand-by logs. This is illustrated in figure 12.4 where all the log records in the new tuple log replica have an LSN value larger than all the log records in the hot stand-by logs.

12.6 The Node Internal Log

The node internal log uses stable main memory logging. This is done so as to obtain fast subtransaction commit processing. Transaction service availability is thus not threatened by subtransaction commit processing.

HypRa uses one node internal log for each node. Each node internal log maintains a node global log sequence. The BPK/BPK combined identification policy is used for all log records entered into an internal log (see section 7.3.1). The access-method operations are not required to be location and replication independent because they are local to a node. The split/merge operations are physical to blocks and logical within blocks. The link- and upper/lower border records are given fixed index positions in a block (see section 7.5). The block identifier is therefore sufficient as both the redo and undo identification concept for split/merge operations. Because of the block granularity AM locks, index-tuples are never moved during an action consistent block split/merge subtransaction. This avoids any undo block transparency requirements for index-tuple operations. If a split/merge subtransaction fails, the index-tuples will be inserted into the same block as originally contained them. The identification policies for access method operations are therefore block non-independent and the BPK/BPK combined identification policy is used.

Two replicas exist for every node internal log. The primary replica is located at the node for which the log is the internal log. The hot stand-by replica is located at a node in a different disaster unit. An update channel connects the primary and the hot stand-by replicas of an internal log (see figure 12.1). The hot stand-by internal log records are not used as basis for redo execution during normal operations, because the operations are internal to a node.

12.7 The Tuple Identification Concept Policies

This section presents the tuple identification concepts used in tuple log records produced by DB state changing tuple operations logged in tuple log fragment replicas and reflected in tuple state-identifiers. The tuple identification concept determines how the tuple operated on by a tuple operation is uniquely referred to in the tuple log record which is produced (see section 7.3.1).

The tuple log records use the **primary key (PK)** *undo identification* policy to obtain block independent tuple undo recovery processing (see section 7.3.1). As a consequence of the tuple log fragmentation, the primary key requires no further qualification since a tuple log will only contain log records relating to one fragment. The PK undo identification policy is required because the action consistent block split/merge policy is applied and in order to allow the non-sequential undo recovery policy to be applied (see sections 7.6.7 and 14.2.3). The PK undo identification policy is also required because of the fragment and log replication policy (see section 11.2). The CLR produced based on a non-CLR are used to compensate both the primary and the hot stand-by replicas of the tuple. The compensation operation based on a CLR will therefore be redone to the hot stand-by tuple replicas. The undo identification concept of the non-CLRs and the CLRs must therefore be prepared to access both primary and hot stand-by tuple replicas.

The tuple *redo identification* concept must be block independent as the redo identifier is used to both the primary and hot stand-by tuple replicas. A primary and a hot stand-by tuple replica are contained in different tables. Two tables never share a block concurrently. The redo identifier can therefore not be based on the block identifier. Since a tuple replica can only be accessed through the block identifier or through the primary key based access method, and the block identifier cannot be used, the primary key (PK) is included in the redo identification concept. A tuple log fragment replica only contains log records related to one fragment. The primary key therefore does not require any further scope qualification.

The tuple global log sequence is maintained in the tuple log fragment sequences presented in section 12.2 and maintained with respect to subfragmentation and fragment concatenation in section 12.4 and 12.5. A **global tuple state-identifier** policy is used if the tuple state-identifiers reflect the tuple global log sequences. The unnecessary redo work, caused by confusion between an old and a new tuple with the same primary key value when the local tuple state-identifier policy is used, is avoided with the global tuple state-identifier policy. This is a consequence of the fact that the primary key and state-identifier combination is unique, which is not the case when the local state-identifier policy is used.

Tuples are dynamic data objects. When a tuple is deleted, its tuple state-identifier is deleted with it. If tuple operations had been reflected in block state-identifiers, the state-identifier would exist independently of the existence of the tuple. It can therefore be determined if an operation is executed to the block independent of the existence of the tuple. Such is not the case when tuple state-identifiers are used. This is illustrated by the following case. A write operation has been executed to a tuple replica. The write is followed by a delete operation. Both operations are reflected in the stable DB before a node crash occurs. At restart it cannot be determined from the tuple state-identifier if the write operation was executed or not because the tuple does not exist. It will be shown in chapter 14 how the semantics of the tuple operations are combined with the existence or non-existence of a tuple replica in order to handle these situations.

12.8 Conclusion

The log distribution strategy presented in this chapter showed how tuple fragment and node internal logs are fragmented, replicated and allocated to nodes to maintain the consistency between the primary and hot stand-by replica of tuples and the single fault tolerance level during normal operations. The log distribution strategy also showed how consistency between primary and hot stand-by tuple replicas can be maintained during log subfragmentation and log fragment concatenation.

To provide soft real-time transaction services (see section 1.1) disc accesses must be avoided in transaction commit processing (see section 2.6). The problem is addressed in chapter 13 in combination with write-ahead logging rules and two-phase commit processing involving both primary and hot stand-by tuple replicas.

Exercises

1. (a) Why are node internal logs needed in addition to the tuple logs? (b) What would be the effect of merging the node internal log with fragment logs? (c) Propose other ways of organising the information kept in the node internal log.

2. (a) Why are node internal logs replicated at two nodes on opposite sides of the fire wall? (b) What would be the consequences of not replicating the node internal log?

3. (a) Propose a logging method where the node internal log is kept local to a node. The fault-tolerance should be the same as if the log was replicated at two nodes except for the consequences of site failures. The method should support soft real-time transactions. (b) What is the effect of the proposed method on node crash recovery?

4. Assume that the tuple state-identifiers are composed of the fragment identifier of the fragment to which the tuple belongs and a counter part that is local to the fragment. (a) Propose a log record identification policy that maintains the global tuple log fragment sequence and the tuple global log sequence. (b) Evaluate the policy compared to alternative policies.

5. Assume the same tuple state-identifier policy and tuple log record identifier policy as in exercise 4. Propose a policy for tuple log record identifiers which will handle subfragmentation.

6. Assume the same tuple state-identifier policy and tuple log record identifier policy as in exercise 4. Propose a policy for handling fragment concatenation.

7. Assume that one tuple log is maintained per node instead of per fragment. Propose a state-identifier policy and a log record identification policy based on this assumption.

8. How does the use of local tuple counters as state-identifiers influence fragment concatenation?

9. (a) Why is the tuple redo identification concept required to be block independent? (b) Why is the tuple undo identification concept required to be block independent? (c) Why do relation, fragment or table identifiers need to be included in the log records if tuple state-identifiers are local to a tuple and all log records are kept in one log at each node?

10. Develop a policy that makes it possible to recover from multiple site failures within approximately 100 hours.

Answers

1. (a) The node internal logs are needed to keep log information relating to the node internal layers. The separation simplifies different replication policies. (b) The tuple log record identifier could not be based on the tuple state identifiers. (c) The node internal log could be fragmented by blocks.

2. (a) To obtain two replicas which fail independently. (b) Since the node internal log of a node is kept in volatile memory, a node crash would corrupt the node's internal log. Every node therefore would have to be reloaded after a crash instead of being recovered based on their own data.

3. (a) Store the node internal log in two independent RAM modules with battery backup at the node. The response time will be reduced compared to logging at two different nodes. The fault-tolerance level is maintained. (b) A node becomes independent with respect to recovery of its internal layers.

4. (a) Let the tuple state-identifier after-images become log record identifiers. The fragment identifier makes the log record uniquely belong to one fragment. The counter part produces log record identifiers that are unique within the primary fragment replica. The tuple global log sequence is therefore maintained. The local counter maintains the tuple global log sequence. (b) An alternative is to add a tuple log record identifier to each primary tuple log record replica. The tuple log record identifier can be produced locally for each primary log fragment by use of a counter. This policy would require a somewhat more costly testing to obey the undo and redo rules.

5. The fragment identifier is the most significant part and the counter the least significant part of the tuple log identifiers. When subfragmenting a fragment, let every resulting subfragment be assigned a larger fragment identifier than the original fragment. Every log record produced after the subfragments gets a larger tuple log record identifier than those produced before the take-over. The tuple global log sequence and the tuple log fragment sequence are both maintained.

6. See the answer to exercise 5. The fragment identifier of the concatenated fragment is unique and larger than the fragment identifiers of any of the subfragments involved in the concatenation.

7. We propose a collection of state-identifier and tuple record identifier policies that are independent of each other. The state-identifier policy uses a counter that is local to each primary tuple replica. This state-identifier policy maintains the tuple global log sequence. The log record identification policy uses a counter that is local to the node.

8. There is no need to keep separate logs for each of the involved subfragments over a period of time. The reason for this is that the state-identifiers are independent of the actual fragment to which the tuple belongs.

9. (a) Redo can be done to a tuple replica which is located in another block than it was when the corresponding do operation was executed. (b) Undo can be done to a tuple replica which is located in another block than it was when the corresponding do operation was executed. (c) A primary key is unique within a relation, fragment, or table. Since log records for multiple relations are kept in the same log, two log records with the same primary key value may belong to two different relations. For this reason, an additional identifier to the primary key is needed to distinguish the log records.

10. The exercise is left as a project for the students.

Chapter 13

The Neighbour Write-Ahead Logging Strategy

This chapter presents the neighbour write-ahead logging (**nWAL**) strategy. The nWAL strategy determines how stable log storage can be obtained by logging in the main memory of nodes located in different disaster units.

The main reason for using the nWAL strategy is to avoid the commit processing delays encountered with traditional logging strategies and thereby support transaction services with soft real-time response requirements. During two-phase commit processing the traditional logging strategies impose a delay of at least one disc I/O at each node where the DB has been updated, and a delay of at least one additional disc I/O at the node containing the transaction coordinator (see sections 10.2, 5.3.4, and 5.3.7). The traditional logging strategies therefore introduce a minimum response time limit on transactions performing DB updates. This limit is significant when the data accessed by an update transaction is located in main memory. Logging to a neighbour node instead of to disc will, in a HypRa system, be more than one order of magnitude faster than disc logging (see [AT90] and [Tor88]). The nWAL strategy will therefore remove the disc-bound transaction response time constraint.

The use of neighbour logging introduces modifications to the WAL undo and redo rules, and to the log garbage collection rules presented in section 4.4.4 and 4.4.5 respectively. The modifications are the result of replacing discs with stable main memory. In addition, dual stable log storage is used to meet the DB consistency requirement for single media failure. The inclusion of hot stand-by parts in the two-phase commit protocol, i.e. *2-Safe* execution ([MTO91]), causes the use of multi-level two-phase commit processing. The use of the nWAL strategy with the log distribution strategy gives rise to a new log main memory overflow handling policy and new log garbage collection policies. As a consequence of the multi-level logging policy, dynamic access methods are used to store the disc parts of the tuple fragment log replicas.

A log record replica is not allowed to be stored in a log replica before sufficient space is guaranteed for the log record replica and the potential CLR replica. In addition, a transaction is not allowed to commit before sufficient space is allocated at the hot stand-by fragment replica.

A nested top-level transaction model is used by HypRa (see section 10.4). Log sequences are maintained for each log replica. A separate transaction log is used. The fuzzy checkpointing policy (see section 4.7.4) is applied with a stable main memory checkpoint table containing all checkpoint positions for the log replicas located at a node.

13.1 The Stable Storage Policies

No storage media is completely stable, in the sense of being able to preserve its data content over all types of failures (see section A.8). Storage is **stable** if it has a high mean time to failure (MTTF) for hardware-, software-, and power failures. The requirement for a sufficiently high MTTF to qualify as stable storage has increased over time from months in 1980 to more than ten years in 1990 ([HR84], [GS91]). A **media failure** occurs if a stable storage fails, i.e. its data content or part of data content is permanently lost or damaged.

Traditionally, only inherently non-volatile storages have qualified as stable storage (see [BHG87] and section 2.3.3). They represented the storage technologies with the longest MTTF. Magnetic discs, tapes, and optical discs are inherently non-volatile, i.e. their contents are preserved after a power failure or node crash. Main memory is, on the other hand, volatile, because its contents are lost in case of a power failure or a node crash (see section 2.3.2).

Gradually, over the last few years, volatile memory in combination with uninterruptible power supplies (UPS) has obtained an MTTF that is comparable to the inherently non-volatile memories (see e.g. [CKKS89]). This is due to the improved hardware MTTF and the wide use of UPSs ([GS91]). A **stable volatile medium** is therefore a volatile medium that is equipped with its own self-contained power supply that will retain data and permit the transfer of data, before any is lost, to an inherently non-volatile medium after the failure of external power (see [Gra91]). A UPS is in this context not considered an external power source.

HypRa uses UPSs (see section 9.3). In the presence of an external power failure the content of main memory logs and ongoing block flush operations are completed without data being lost or damaged. An external power failure therefore does not imply a node crash but only a **controlled node stop**. The content of the DB buffers is assumed to be lost or corrupted after such a controlled node stop. The DB buffers are therefore not stable storage, so the undo and redo WAL rules are not required to be obeyed before the effect of a DB operation is reflected in the DB buffers (see section 13.2). Controlled node stops and node crashes are assumed to be followed by primary take-overs to maintain fragment availability (see section 2.4.2).

Redo recovery may be required when a node is restarted after a controlled node stop because it is not guaranteed that the complete DB buffer is flushed before a controlled node stop and because operations may have been executed after the take-over. Undo recovery may be required to node internal fragments, log tables, and higher levels of access methods because the take-overs have not affected these node internal layers and because their stable block replicas may reflect effects of internal transactions which were active when the controlled stop occurred. Undo recovery is not executed to the location- and replication independent fragment replicas, because the take-overs make all these fragment replicas recover into hot stand-by roles.

A block flush operation is completed before a controlled node stop occurs, which means that media failures caused by incompletely written disc blocks are avoided.

A HypRa node crash implies a media failure of the stable volatile storage if the main memory content either cannot be flushed, is lost, or corrupted. If the CPU or bus fails, the main memory content cannot be flushed to non-volatile media during the failure ([Gra91]). This is a media failure. If the main memory or the UPS fails, the main memory content is lost which is also a media failure.

A disc read failure that is not masked by a repeated read is a media failure. An ongoing physical block write operation by a disc drive is not necessarily assumed to be atomic. A block may be composed of multiple physical blocks. A flush operation is therefore not necessarily atomic, i.e. it can be partially completed. A node crash may therefore also cause a disc block failure because the ongoing flush operations when the node crashes are either not completed done or are not done at all.

To maintain the DBMS **consistency** requirement (see section 2.2) after the failure of stable storage, either another online replica of the fragments and logs kept on the failed storage, or an archive replica of the failed fragments with redo logs must exist. To meet the *availability* part of the DBMS reliability requirement (see section 2.2) after a persistent storage failure, another replica of the failed fragments and the failed logs must exist online. Meeting the availability requirement will therefore also fill the consistency requirement, but not necessarily the other way around. If the requirements for DB consistency are stronger than for transaction service availability, they can be met by providing an archive DB and an archive redo log. The archive DB and redo log do, however, not meet the availability requirement for a higher availability DBMS class ([GS91]).

HypRa maintains two replicas of every fragment and every log. The replicas are always kept in stable storage with independent failure modes. The DB consistency requirement is met because there are two stable replicas. The availability requirement is also met because fast take-over is provided in combination with fast node and fragment replica failure recovery, and online non-blocking replication of both data fragment replicas and log fragment replicas.

13.2 The Neighbour Write Ahead Log Policy

The use of dual stable log storages with independent failure modes requires some minor modifications to the WAL rules as presented in section 4.4.4. Those rules assumed the storage of each log record part in a single stable storage. The rules presented here provide single fault-tolerance to media failures (see section 2.3.3).

- **Undo nWAL rule**
  An undo log record part must be written to two stable storages with independent failure modes before the effect of the state changing DB operation is allowed to be reflected in the stable storage DB.

- **Redo nWAL rule**
  A redo log record part must be written to two stable storages with independent failure modes before the transaction commits.

Further generalisation of the rules to handle k-fault-tolerance to media failures is obtained by substituting two replicas with $k + 1$ replicas (see section 1.3.3).

In HypRa, a log record replica is sent over an update channel and stored in the hot stand-by log replica. The sender always receives acknowledgement that the hot stand-by log record replica has been received and entered into the hot stand-by log replica. A block containing tuples belonging to a primary fragment replica cannot be flushed to disc before the most recent tuple operation and the most recent node internal operation to the block are both acknowledged as being contained in the hot stand-by and the primary log replicas. This is a consequence of the multiple state-identifier policy and the fact that the tuple operations and node internal operations are logged in different logs. If a block contains, for example, only index-tuples it is sufficient to verify that the log record from the last node internal operation to the block is stably stored in both the primary and the hot stand-by node internal log replica.

Since a block only belongs to one fragment replica at a time, the stable storage of tuple log records relating to one block can be verified to one tuple log fragment, except during subfragment concatenation when multiple tuple fragment log replicas may relate to a block. A hot stand-by log record must be stably stored before the redo of the original operation to the hot stand-by fragment replica is reflected in the stable hot stand-by tuple replica. The primary log replica is then already stably stored. The undo nWAL rule is therefore followed in both the primary and the hot stand-by execution of the operation. Acknowledgement is included in the update channel protocol.

HypRa follows the requirements of the redo nWAL rule. A hot stand-by slave-transaction is not allowed to respond *yes* to a prepare-to-commit (PTC) request before all log records produced by the slave-transaction, or internal node subtransaction coordinator, sending the prepare-to-commit request are received and logged. By this procedure, every log record produced by a transaction is stably stored in two stable storages with independent failure modes before a transaction commits. The redo nWAL rule is therefore fulfilled.

13.3 The Neighbour Write-Ahead Log Garbage Collection Rules

The nWAL strategy modifies the log garbage collection rules presented in section 4.4.5. They are also modified by the semantically rich locking model (see section A.9), the operational and compensation logging (see section 7.7), and the dynamic tuple operations (see section A.5). The following rules apply to tuple log record replicas. It is assumed that the single CLR policy is used with the no-undo/redo and the log-backchain policies (see section 6.4.1). Partial tuple logging is assumed (see section 7.3.3). The block complete recovery policy is used (see section 7.6.4). It will in the following discussion be specified which of the rules require the block complete and the selective redo policies (see sections 7.6.4 and 7.9.2). Note that these rules specify the earliest time a redo or an undo log record part can be removed. Only a subset of the presented rules are used by HypRa.

- The replicas of a *redo log record part* by a non-CLR produced by a tuple operation O for a tuple X by transaction T_i can be removed if:
  1. T_i aborted; or
  2. the effect of O is reflected in every stable replica of X; or
  3. some later operation either wrote all the fields operated on by O, or deleted X.
- The replicas of an *undo log record part* by a non-CLR produced by a tuple operation O for a tuple X by transaction T_i can be removed if:
  1. T_i committed; or
  2. T_i aborted and two stable replicas of the CLR for O exist; or
  3. T_i aborted and some later transactions either wrote all the fields operated on by O, or deleted X.
- The replicas of a CLR produced by a compensating tuple operation O for a tuple X by transaction T_i can be removed if:
  1. Some later operation either wrote all the fields operated on by O, or deleted X; or
  2. the effect of O is reflected in every stable replica of X.

When the redo part of a non-CLR is removed, the log record identification and the primary key fields contained in the log record must remain. The redo part of the non-CLRs replicas of an aborted transaction can be removed independently of whether the operation is reflected in the stable tuple replicas. If, during the redo recovery work after a node crash, the effect of the log record is reflected in the tuple replica, the redo log record part is not needed. If, on the other hand, the effect of the operation is not reflected in the tuple replica before the node crash, the operation does not need to be redone if the block complete and the selective redo policies are both used. The block complete policy removes the possibility that inconsistent intermediate stable states of the block containing the tuple occur as an effect of multiple node crashes. Either a stable tuple replica is completely recovered, or it is found as it was before the first of the multiple node crashes. When the selective redo policy is applied, the redo is not needed for the operations belonging to aborted transactions, if the operations are not reflected in the tuple. A stable tuple state that is equivalent to the situation if both the redo operation and the corresponding undo operation were executed is produced, and the consistency of the tuple state-identifier is preserved. It is therefore possible to remove the redo part of the log records belonging to aborted transactions only if the block complete and the selective redo policies are both used. If these policies are not used together, this rule cannot be applied.

The redo part of the two replicas of a log record is not removed before the effect of the operation is reflected in every stable replica of the tuple. This policy always makes it possible to recover a fragment replica after a node crash based on the log. As long as at least one stable tuple replica lacks the effect of the operation, the two log record replicas must exist. If a node containing the stable tuple lacking the effect of the operation crashes and, as part of the crash, corrupts one log replica, the other log replica still exists when the node is recovered. The effect of the operation can then be applied to the tuple replica. Single fault-tolerance is maintained to a log record by this policy, independently of to what degree it is reflected in the corresponding tuple replica. This is termed the **log preservation** policy.

An alternative policy which is not reflected in the rules above is the **one-replica** policy, in which the redo part of a log record replica is removed when the operation is reflected in the stable tuple replica at the same node as the log replica. If the one-replica policy is used, recovery from a node crash may require tuple replication because the necessary log is not kept. This happens when a node crashes after the redo part of the log record replica at the other node is removed, since its effect is reflected in the corresponding stable tuple, but it is removed before the effect is reflected in stable tuple at the crashed node. When the crashed node is recovered, no log record replicas exist to recover its tuple replica. On the other hand, a stable tuple replica containing the effects of the operation exists. The DB consistency is also preserved when the one-replica policy is applied. In practice, when a node is recovered it cannot be determined on an individual basis which tuples have to be reproduced. Therefore all the fragments at the node have to be reproduced during the node crash recovery. When a crashed node is recovered, the one-replica policy will require production of another replica of all its fragments. To provide fast node crash recovery, HypRa applies the log preservation policy.

If some operations following O wrote all fields involved in O, then the after-image for these fields exists as the before-image in the log records for this write operation. The redo part of the log record replicas for O can therefore be removed. The write operation of the fields can be spread over multiple write operations. There is no requirement that the write operations are committed. An eventual compensation operation will reset the before-image value. A later delete operation will contain the before-image value of every field of the tuple and therefore those affected by O. The redo parts of the log record replicas can be removed in this case also. This does not apply to delta operations, since operational logging is used. The log record therefore does not contain the before-image. The operation O cannot be followed by an insert operation of a tuple with the same primary key value as X unless a delete operation is between O and the insert, since no two tuples are allowed to exist simultaneously with the same primary key value. The use of this rule requires the use of the block complete and selective redo policy. If a node crashes and the effect of O is not reflected in the stable replica of the tuple at the crashed node, it is not necessary to redo O during recovery if the block complete and selective redo policies are both used.

The undo part of all the log record replicas of a committed transaction can be removed because the undo part is only required to roll the transaction back. Since it is committed it will never be rolled back.

Because of the use of the no-undo CLR policy, the CLR replicas do not keep any undo parts by themselves. When the redo CLR policy is applied, the redo part included in a CLR corresponds to the undo part of the non-CLR the CLR is compensating. Therefore when all replicas of the CLR for a non-CLR are stably stored, the undo part of the non-CLR can be removed. Since the CLRs for a transaction are produced before the transaction terminates, the undo log record parts can be removed for aborted transactions. The redo CLR policy used to obtain this effect is easily applicable: an undo log record part can be removed when the transaction is terminated.

If the no-redo CLR policy is used, the undo part of the corresponding non-CLR cannot unconditionally be removed when a CLR for O is produced because it acts as its redo part. The removal rules for the redo part of a non-CLR replica will therefore apply to the undo part of the corresponding non-CLR when O is substituted with the compensation operation for O. If the compensation operation for O is reflected in every replica of X, the undo part of the non-CLR can be removed according to the log preservation policy. This rule is applied to node internal subtransactions because of their short lifetime (see section 13.9).

If the one-replica policy is applied, the undo log record part can be removed when the effect of the compensation operation is reflected in the replica of X at the same node. The undo log record part can therefore also be removed when some later transaction has written all fields operated on by the compensation operation, or deleted the tuple. This requires the use of the block complete and selective redo policies.

13.4 The Update Channel Protocol

An update channel connects one primary log replica server to one hot stand-by log replica server. (See figure 12.2 for an illustration.) An update channel is *connected* when the primary/hot stand-by log replica pair is established and is *disconnected* when one of the log replicas is deleted. If the replicas switches primary/hot stand-by roles the direction of the update channel becomes the opposite. Log record replicas are sent as messages across an update channel from the primary log replica server to the hot stand-by log replica server (see chapter 12). An update channel provides a reliable transport service, ensuring that messages are not lost, duplicated, or damaged, and do not arrive in altered sequence ([Sta85]).

An update channel sends the sending primary log server acknowledgement of the log records received and entered its hot stand-by log replica. The acknowledgement is based on the log record identifiers. When a log record is acknowledged, all log records sent to a hot stand-by log server with a lesser or equal log record identifier value are guaranteed to be received by the hot stand-by log server and stably stored in its hot stand-by log. The primary log server ensures that the primary log record replica is stably stored before the log record is sent to the hot stand-by log server.

The error control and routing used by the update channel protocol is outside the scope of the book. The update channel protocol can be layered on a protocol using any flow control and rate control policies to inform the sender of the current state of the buffers of the receiver ([SW90]).

The buffering policy for log records to be sent across an update channel must obey the undo and redo nWAL rules and should also be compatible with the requirement for fast take-over in case of a node or fragment failure. The more buffering done by the sender, the more take-over redo work may be required when a primary fails and its hot stand-by takes over as primary. This happens because the hot stand-by may have a lag as large as the buffer size of operations behind the primary. The last group of operations received by the hot stand-by must be redo executed before the hot stand-by role is changed to primary. Given the very strict availability requirement for HypRa, fast take-over is given priority over minimising the logging induced communication cost. The primary log server therefore uses a **force-send** policy to send a log record message, i.e.

log records are sent as soon as possible from the primary server to the hot stand-by server. The force-send policy is adopted to minimise how long a hot stand-by fragment replica can lag behind the primary fragment replica. The take-over redo work and the take-over delay are minimised by this policy. Independently of the buffering applied by the primary log replica sender, buffering can also be applied by the hot stand-by log server to reduce the number of acknowledge messages. It is assumed that an acknowledgement is given for each message, i.e. no buffering is applied.

If the requirement for fast take-over is less demanding, buffering of log records can be done by the primary log server. Buffering can then be applied to acknowledges so that only one acknowledge is given for each group of log records. This would reduce the number of log messages sent across the update channel. If the cost per message dominates the cost by message size, a buffering policy will impose smaller log communication cost than the force-send policy ([Ask89a], [AT90], [Tor90]). The buffering policy presented in sections 5.3.5 and 5.3.6 for disc logging can also be used when the nWAL strategy is applied. This buffering policy would not impose any further commit processing delay than the force-send policy would, if the receive-commit commit processing policy is used, i.e. a hot stand-by slave-transaction is willing to commit when the log records are stably stored in the hot stand-by logs (see section 13.5). If the space-reserve commit policy is used, the buffering policy will induce commit processing delays when a PTC (see section 13.2) request is received before the necessary processing of the deferred operations belonging to the transaction is completed on the hot stand-by side. A group-commit oriented buffering policy can also be applied by the primary log replica server. This policy may further reduce the number of log messages sent, and cause more delays of the transaction commit processing because more buffering is done at the sender side (see section 5.3.7).

The update channel flow control policy must maintain the undo nWAL rule. A log record must, in addition to being stored in stable volatile storage at the node in which it is produced, also be acknowledged as stably logged at another node in another disaster unit, before a stable primary tuple replica is allowed to reflect the effect of the operation. Since a log record is stably stored in the primary log before the log record is sent and it is stably stored in the hot stand-by log before it is acknowledged, a block containing tuples can be flushed when the most recent tuple and internal node operations are acknowledged (see section 13.3). A block will normally stay in the DB buffers after a state changing tuple- or node internal operation is executed to it for longer than the time it takes for the most recent tuple and internal operations to the block to be stably stored. This occurs regardless of the buffering policy used since it is also assumed for disc logging (see section 5.3.5). The rationale behind neighbour logging is to have smaller logging delays than by disc logging. The neighbour logging will therefore not normally delay block flush operations. Since the force-send policy is used by the sender and the receiver acknowledges each message, no forcing needs to be done as part of the prepare-to-commit processing.

13.5 The Deferred Execution Policy

Tuple operations are executed as redo operations to hot stand-by fragment replicas (see section 11.2). The update channel is maintaining the execution order for all primary state changing tuple operations at the hot stand-bys. By performing redo executions in the same order as log records are accepted received by an update channel redo execution to a hot stand-by tuple replica corresponds to the execution order to the primary tuple replica. The hot stand-by schedule therefore becomes the same as the primary schedule for state changing tuple operations. Read operations will not normally be allowed to hot stand-by fragment replicas. (See also [HST+91b] for allowing read operation). The hot stand-by redo execution will therefore not introduce any new conflicts and possible deadlocks. It is therefore not required that redo tuple operations must have been executed before a transaction commits, i.e. a deferred execution policy can be applied. A **deferred execution policy** is applied if tuple operations to hot stand-by fragment replicas are allowed to be unexecuted at the transaction commit time.

A fragment replica is opened to primary transactions when a primary take-over is completed. Care must be taken to avoid introducing inconsistencies during the take-over. Inconsistencies may occur if new primary tuple operations can be executed before a deferred operation. This is illustrated by the following case. Transaction T_{11} updates field A of a tuple. The resulting hot stand-by log record is sent across the update channel. The transaction commits without the hot stand-by tuple operation being executed. A primary take-over occurs. Transaction T_{20} then updates field B of the same tuple as transaction T_{11}. When the deferred redo operation is tried executed the tuple state-identifier indicates that the operation is already executed. The consequence is that the update by transaction T_{11} is lost. If on the other hand, the deferred operation had been executed first the inconsistency had been avoided.

The resulting schedule after a primary take-over is consistent if it is equivalent to the state if all the deferred hot stand-by tuple operations had been executed before the new primary tuple operations. This is the effect if all the hot stand-by redo operations are either completely executed or their locks have set before any operations belonging to the primary transactions are executed to a tuple replica. The primary take-over processing must therefore at least include setting tuple locks for all deferred hot stand-by tuple operations before the fragment replica is opened for primary processing. The deferred operations must then still be executed in their received order but this is done concurrently with primary operations.

A limit must be set on the time interval to execute a take-over to preserve the DBMS availability requirement. A limit is therefore set on the number of concurrent deferred operations to a node. The more deferred operations that must be handled, the more time spent before a fragment replica can change its role to primary. For the same reason, constraints are imposed on space allocation to avoid the possibility of subfragmentation of the fragment replica during a take-over processing. If a subfragmentation must be performed before a fragment replica can change its role to primary, the fragment may be unavailable for up to several minutes.

Before an operation to be logged is reflected in the DB buffer, sufficient space should be reserved so that both the non-CLR and a potential CLR for the operation can be logged. If space is reserved for the non-CLR but not for the CLR, a situation may occur where a failed transaction cannot be rolled back because sufficient space is not available for its CLRs. If this is not guaranteed a tuple will stay unavailable until more space is provided to the fragment replica log. By reserving sufficient logging space for both the do and the potential undo processing, this type of unavailability is avoided. Since the single CLR policy is used, the non-CLR and the corresponding CLR data volume can be calculated from the non-CLR log record. The data volume required by the possible CLR is independent of multiple node failures, which is not the case with the recursive CLR policy (see section 6.4.5).

A state changing tuple operation is not allowed to be executed to the primary tuple replica unless sufficient stable log space is available in the primary log replica for both the produced log record and an eventual CLR for the operation. The hot stand-by log replica is not allowed to acknowledge the operation before it has reserved sufficient log space for the non-CLR and the potential CLR for the operation. If such space is not available, it sends a non-acknowledge reply for this log record. If the primary log server receives a non-acknowledge for a log record, the transaction fails and is rolled back. The CLR for the non-acknowledged log record is not sent to the hot stand-by log replica server because the non-CLR is not present in the hot stand-by log replica. An operation that is non-acknowledged will never be reflected in any stable memory replicas. A node crash will therefore not introduce any inconsistencies. The log sequence is maintained in the hot stand-by log because the next log record will also have a larger log record identifier value than the previous when the CLR is left out. This is called the **log-space-reserve** policy.

An alternative policy is to use an additional **debit/credit scheme** based on the available log space at the hot standby log. A hot stand-by log server informs its primary log server of its added credit when stable log space is released or when the hot stand-by log server is allocated more stable storage. Either the primary log server debits the allocated stable log storage as a log record or a CLR is produced. HypRa uses the log-space-reserve policy and not the debit/credit based policy. The log-space-reserve policy isolates the internal level aspects of the nodes since the available space situation for the node containing a hot stand-by log is not spread to other nodes.

Two stable log record redo replica parts of every log record produced by the transaction must exist at transaction commit time (see section 13.2). It must also be guaranteed before transaction commit that the execution of the deferred operations will not be aborted. An abortion would destroy the ACID properties of the transaction (see section A.8). A hot stand-by server, compensating for an operation that is not compensated for by the primary server, may make some hot stand-by tuple replica state-identifiers inconsistent and must therefore be avoided (see chapter 11). If a failure occurs during the execution of a deferred operation, the operation will be redone to reflect its effect in the tuple but it will never be undone. A redo execution will not cause an inconsistent state-identifier value.

The transaction ACID properties are not violated by aborts caused by deadlocks between deferred tuple operations. Deadlock during redo execution between deferred tuple operations will never occur as the operations are executed in their original production order to the fragment. The serialised execution sequence is preserved (see chapter 11) and tuple locks are therefore not needed among the deferred operations. The transaction ACID properties are neither threatened by concurrency aspects of subtransactions nor the concurrency aspects between subtransactions and top-level transactions. By careful design of node internal subtransactions, deadlocks are avoided between the subtransactions, and between subtransactions and top-level transactions. A subtransaction and a top-level transaction will, for example, never access the same tuples. The necessary requirement for a hot stand-by slave-transaction to preserve the DB consistency requirement at transaction commit time, is that all the operations from the slave-transaction requesting the PTC are stably logged. Then the operation will be executed some time in the future. This is called the **receive-commit** policy.

The execution of deferred operations may encounter stable storage limitations. A deferred insert operation, for example, may cause a block to be split. The block split subtransaction will fail if no more unused blocks are available. This possibility can be avoided by not committing a transaction before all deferred operations have reserved the necessary space required to complete the operation. The recursive action consistent block split/merge policy is used so that a tuple requesting space will never require more than one block to complete the transaction (see section 7.5.1). The block is needed in case the block containing the tuple needs to be split. Because an action consistent access method is the result of the block split only one block needs to be reserved. This policy is called the **space-reserve** policy. The space-reserve policy prevents a subfragmentation from being activated during a take-over (see section 14.1).

During a take-over one redo operation could encounter storage limitations if the space-reserve policy was not used. As a consequence, none of the following redo operations in that fragment could be executed until the storage limitations was removed. This is an effect of the sequential execution policy. Since these operations cannot be executed, the fragment cannot be made available. Since the node is full, the fragment or some other fragment must be subfragmented to release space at this node. In order to provide fast take-over in HypRa, subfragmentation must be avoided during a take-over. HypRa therefore adopts the space-reserve policy.

13.6 The nWAL Distributed Transaction Model

This section presents the distributed transaction model including transaction coordinators, slave-transactions, and the hot stand-by aspects of the distributed transactions. See section 10.2 for an introduction to the HypRa distributed transaction model.

There exists a **hot stand-by slave-transaction** group at each node. The hot stand-by slave-transactions are involved in the distributed transaction commit processing. Their effect on the distributed transaction model is the introduction of a three-level acyclic commit processing graph contrary to the two level tree presented in section 10.2. The multi-level presumed abort two-phase commit protocol is used ([ML83]).

Each node contains a primary and a hot stand-by **transaction log** in addition to the logs presented in chapter 12. The primary transaction log replica at a node contains the primary replica of the log records produced as part of the two-phase commit processing done at the node. A hot stand-by log record replica exists for those primary log records kept in the primary replica which require replication to meet the consistent DB state requirement. An update channel connects a primary transaction log to its hot stand-by transaction log. The only log records replicated in the hot stand-by log are the log records produced by the transaction coordinators. A **hot stand-by transaction coordinator** group exists in connection with a hot stand-by transaction log. If the node containing the transaction coordinator crashes or the primary transaction log fails, a hot stand-by transaction coordinator becomes the new transaction coordinator to terminate the transactions affected.

When a slave-transaction receives a PTC request from the transaction coordinator, it must first verify that the hot stand-by slave-transactions at the nodes to which it has sent hot stand-by log records are willing to commit. A PTC request is sent to each of the hot stand-by slave-transaction servers. If log buffering is used by the primary log replica servers, and a buffer contains log records for the committing transaction, the buffer must be force-sent (see section 13.4). The PTC request sent to each hot stand-by slave-transaction must contain the log record identifier of the last log record sent to the hot stand-by log replicas at the node the PTC is sent to. This is done to verify that all the hot stand-by log records intended for the node are received. An alternative policy is to wait until an acknowledgement has been received for each of these log records before the PTC is sent. The latter policy will delay the commit processing compared to including the log record identifiers in the PTC request, as a PTC request may be tagged to the last operation request from the transaction coordinator. A two level commit-processing cannot be used because a hot stand-by slave-transaction must be informed of which log records are the last for the transaction and the hot stand-by slave-transactions do not know the identity of the transaction coordinator. This is known by the slave-transactions but not by the transaction coordinator.

When a hot stand-by slave-transaction receives a PTC, it can decide if the node is willing to commit that part of the transaction originating from the sender slave-transaction. Multiple slave-transactions may have sent PTCs to the same hot stand-by slave-transaction as an effect of sub-fragmentation. The commit processing graph is therefore acyclic but not necessarily a tree. A hot stand-by slave-transaction will respond to each PTC request originating from different slave-transactions within the same transaction. It may respond to a PTC request with an abort regardless of its previous responses to other PTC requests by the same transaction. If it has responded to a PTC request with an abort, it will respond with an abort to the eventual following PTC requests for the same transaction.

A hot stand-by slave-transaction will not respond to a PTC request with a *yes* before all the hot stand-by log record replicas involved are stably stored and storage resources are reserved for all the deferred operations according to the space-reserve policy (see section 13.5). If the storage resources are not available, the hot stand-by slave-transaction will respond with an abort. The hot stand-by slave-transaction will not unilaterally start aborting the transaction because the CLRs are produced from the primary fragment log servers. The hot stand-by slave-transaction will log its decision in the node's primary transaction log unless it is not already logged by a previous reply to an earlier PTC request. The logged decision is not replicated.

When a slave-transaction has received all replies to its PTC requests within the specified time-limit, all hot stand-by slave-transactions have replied *yes*, and the slave-transaction itself decides *yes*, it logs the decision in its primary transaction log and sends a *yes* reply to the transaction coordinator. The logged decision is kept locally in its primary log, i.e. it is not replicated. If one or more of the hot stand-by slave-transactions has replied with an abort, the slave-transaction itself decides to abort, or a time-out has occurred, then the slave-transaction sends an abort message to the transaction coordinator, logs the abort decision in the local primary transaction log, and starts to roll the transaction back.

The transaction coordinator behaves almost the same as the slave-transactions. It logs its decision in the primary transaction log at the node. This log record is replicated. The replication is done to guarantee that at least two replicas of the commit decision exist until the last of the participants replies that the transaction is *done*. The decisions made by lower level participants in the commit processing are implicitly known at the next higher level. Their decisions therefore do not need to be explicitly replicated. No decisions other than the transaction coordinators' are required to be logged as replicated to meet the consistency requirement. If the transaction coordinator fails, a hot stand-by transaction coordinator at the node the hot stand-by transaction log is located becomes the transaction coordinator to terminate the transaction. The location of the hot stand-by tuple fragment and node internal logs is included in the fully replicated dictionary, see [HST$^+$91b]) and [HST91a]. The location of the new transaction coordinator after a node crash is therefore known by all the participants.

13.7 The nWAL Transaction Model

The nWAL transaction model supports transactions and subtransactions as discussed in section 10.4. A subtransaction is a **node internal transaction**, i.e. it is used to perform operations that are local to a node. An example of a subtransaction is a block split subtransaction. Transactions and subtransactions, except for subtransactions which are nested top-actions (see section 13.11), are given identifiers in a HypRa system that are unique throughout.

The transaction log sequences for both transactions and subtransactions are maintained independently for each log replica (see figure 13.1). By maintaining one log sequence per log replica, a transaction can be undone asynchronously to each primary log replica (see section 14.2.2). For long transactions, this policy may speed up transaction recovery, compared to a sequential transaction failure recovery (see sections 7.8 and 14.2.1). An alternative policy would be to maintain one primary and one hot stand-by transaction sequence per transaction per node. This would make fragment replica asynchronous transaction failure recovery impossible. Log aggregation and selective log aggregation can be used during transaction recovery (see sections 7.8 and 14.2.3).

The transaction log sequences are maintained locally per log replica regardless of whether the replica is primary or hot stand-by. The log sequence maintained by a primary tuple fragment log replica does not necessarily correspond to the log sequence in the hot stand-by tuple fragment log replica, because a hot stand-by fragment replica can be subfragmented or concatenated compared to its primary fragment replica. The previous log record replica of a primary log record replica may, relative to the corresponding hot stand-by log record replica, be located in another log replica at another node. The original previous log record must therefore be replaced with the actual previous log record in the hot stand-by log. The transaction previous log record identifier is therefore removed from the log record when it is sent to a hot stand-by tuple fragment log. A slightly more optimal policy is to remove the previous log record identifier only when the fragmentation of the

TransactionTab

TransId	Status	ParentTransId

TransLogRecTab

TransId	LogId	NoNC	UnV	LogRecId

RedoTab

LogId	ReV

SavePoints

TransId	LogId	SavePtId	NoNC	UnV	LogRecId

Figure 13.1: The nWAL transaction model. The transaction table (TransactionTab) maintains the transaction status (Status) and the parent relation between transactions (ParentTransId). The transaction log record table (TransLogRecTab) maintains the log record identifier of the last log record replica (LogRecId) for each log replica (LogId) entered for each transaction (TransId). In addition, it maintains the number of non-compensated non-CLRs (NoNC) produced by the transaction for the log and the undo log volumes (UnV). The redo table (RedoTab) maintains the redo log volume for each log since the last checkpoint (ReV). The savepoint table (SavePoints) maintains the savepoints defined for each transaction, the number of non-compensated non-CLRs produced before the savepoint (NoNC) to the log, and the corresponding undo log volume (UnV).

primary and the hot stand-by logs differ. A transaction table must be maintained for every log regardless of which of these two policies is used. It must be known in case of a take-over which logs a transaction is active to and the transaction's last entered log record replica in each of these log replicas.

The relation between a subtransaction and its parent transaction is maintained in the transaction table (see figure 13.1). No parent relations are maintained in the transaction logs. A parent relation is maintained so that the parent transaction can be undone if a subtransaction fails. The transaction table also maintains the transaction status (see figure 13.1). This information about a transaction is maintained at every node where the transaction is executing.

In case a subtransaction fails, its parent transaction can be undone in parallel with the failed subtransaction. Deadlocks during undo between a subtransaction and its parent are avoided even when the recovery is done asynchronously between the two. A subtransaction will never request a lock during recovery that may conflict with the parent transaction. A subtransaction will hold only AM locks in a table implementing a non-internal fragment replica. It will never hold any tuple locks in such fragment replicas. The parent transaction will not hold an AM lock on a block on which a subtransaction is requested to perform operations. A parent transaction will not hold any AM lock on any other block which its subtransaction might access. The subtransaction may request tuple locks in node internal tables. These tables are never accessed by top-level transactions. Therefore undo operations belonging to the parent transaction can be executed in reverse transaction sequence concurrently with undo operations belonging to the subtransaction.

Savepoints are supported for both transactions and subtransactions. Savepoints are local to a transaction or subtransaction and are maintained by a specific main memory structure (see figure 13.1). Each savepoint is given a unique identifier within the transaction. Savepoint structures are not logged. Partial transaction recovery is presented in section 14.2.4. The hot stand-by logs are not informed of the savepoints because they will never use the savepoints. In case of a take-over an active transaction will be aborted. Therefore savepoint information is kept only by the transaction coordinator and the slave-transactions.

A primary start-transaction log record replica is entered into the transaction log at the node where the transaction coordinator is located when a transaction or subtransaction is started. The log record is replicated. In case a subtransaction is started, the log record will also indicate which transaction is its parent.

13.8 The nWAL Checkpointing Policy

The introduction of the neighbour write-ahead logging strategy involves changes to the node global checkpointing strategy presented in section 4.7. The modifications are also partially a result of the multi-level state-identifier policy and the log distribution strategy (see section 11.4 and chapter 12).

HypRa uses the penultimate fuzzy checkpointing policy with modification to the production of checkpoint log records (see section 4.7.4). A checkpoint is global for a node and used to restrict the redo work after a node crash or a controlled node stop. Checkpoints are produced autonomously at a node. The interval between two checkpoints at a node is set globally by a transaction so that the same checkpointing interval is applied by all nodes.

The checkpoint policy provides the basis for garbage collection of redo log record parts. A redo log record part is removed when it is older than the penultimate checkpoint for both the primary and the hot stand-by log replica. Then the effect of the log record is guaranteed to be reflected in both of the stable tuple replicas. (See the nWAL garbage collection rules in section 13.3.) The archiving aspects of the log are not included in the book.

The multiple online log replicas, which are a result of the nWAL logging strategy, imply modifications to the information necessary to maintain a checkpoint. When a node is fast recovered from a controlled node stop, or from a node crash, the log records missing or lost from the recovering node are supplied from the other replica of the logs. Only redo recovery is applied to the non-internal fragment replicas because a take-over has been executed after the failure. It is therefore not necessary to produce a snapshot of the active transaction table for each checkpoint because the recovery manager does not need to decide which log records to compensate. This is all done by the primary replica server. Only the current transaction table is needed to produce log records for the active and in-doubt transactions to be able to later take over as the primary replica (see section 14.3.8). For node internal transactions, the hot stand-by transaction log contains all the needed transaction status information to perform the recovery. If fast node crash recovery is not successfully applied to a node, then another replica is produced of the fragment replicas stored at the node. In this case the fragments where another replica has been produced are restarted by producing another replica at the node by the online non-blocking fragment replica production method ([HST+91b]).

A **checkpoint server** exists at every node. It is responsible for executing checkpoint transactions. The actions involved at a node when executing a checkpoint transaction correspond to those presented for the penultimate checkpoints in section 4.7.4. Every DB buffer block replica is inspected. A block is locked by an AM read lock while it is inspected and possibly flushed. If the block is dirty and has not been flushed to disc since before the last checkpoint, it is flushed. The double block flush logging policy is used as block write operations are not guaranteed to be crash atomic (see section 7.4.1) and entered into the node internal log for each flushed block. The double block flush logging policy is also used during normal block flushing.

A **checkpoint table** is kept in stable volatile storage (see section 13.1) at every node. The checkpoint table contains a tuple for every log replica at the node. It also contains a tuple for every log replica related to a log stored at the node by being either its pair hot stand-by or its pair primary log replica. A checkpoint tuple contains a field for each checkpoint position required to be kept plus one additional field and the corresponding number of fields containing the redo log volume produced since the previous checkpoint. The oldest checkpoint position kept is the one where it is guaranteed that all older log records are stored on disc. Updates to the checkpoint table are not logged. Updates are done circularly so that the additional field is overwritten. In this way the undo rule is obeyed. If log records older than the fourth oldest log records are guaranteed to be on disc, five fields are required. Since the checkpoint table is stored in stable main memory, it is written to stable non-volatile storage in case of a controlled node stop.

Checkpoint log records cannot be included in the tuple fragment log replicas. The hot stand-by log replicas require the log records they contain to originate from the primary log replica server to avoid DB inconsistencies (see chapter 11). Since checkpoint production is local to a node and not synchronised between a primary and a hot stand-by log replica, the checkpoint log records cannot be entered into the hot stand-by logs. Therefore, separate checkpoint log streams are required, and the checkpoint tables are used.

At that point during the execution of a checkpoint transaction when all dirty blocks are written to disc, the checkpoint server updates the local checkpoint table for all the local log replicas and sends a message informing each of the checkpoint servers containing a log replica pair for some of the log replicas at the node about the new checkpoint positions. The checkpoint servers receiving such a message update their checkpoint table correspondingly and acknowledges. Two-phase commit processing is not required for these updates since the involved log replica server keeps more log records than necessary in case an update is lost. No information is therefore lost.

A **block flush log record** (start-BFR) is written to the internal log and acknowledged before a block is flushed according to the double block flush logging policy (see sections 7.3.5 and 7.4.1). A block flush log record contains the block identifier and the block state-identifier value of the block. The block state-identifier indicates which operations logged in the node internal log have been executed to the block. The block flush log record also contains a *recovery-type* field indicating if the log block is a higher level block (see section 7.5.1), a block belonging to a log table, a block belonging to a node internal fragment replica, or a block belonging to a non-internal fragment replica. If the block is a higher level block, the block flush log record will contain the block identifier of the lesser index-tuple in the block.

The tuples contained in a block will always belong to the same fragment replica. They will therefore all be related to the same tuple fragment log. The redo execution to hot stand-by fragment replicas is done according to the production sequence of the log records. Therefore, when a block is flushed, all tuple operations for the fragment replica relating to those tuples contained in the block which have a lesser or equal log record identifier value than the largest tuple state-identifier value connected to a tuple in the block, are reflected in that block. It is therefore only necessary to log the largest tuple state-identifier value to reflect the stable state of the primary key interval of tuples stored in the block. The block flush log record therefore, in addition to the block identifier and the block state-identifier, contains the fragment replica identifier, the upper and lower border records (see section 7.5.2), and the larger tuple state-identifier value to reflect the tuple state of the block.

If the block belongs to layers whose operations are logged in the node internal log, the recovery type field indicates that. The block flush log records therefore contain information relating to both the internal DBMS layers and the fragment layer. The information is grouped together because it is used at the same node. In case of a node crash, the fragment layer information is used to force all blocks containing the tuples within the intervals of the blocks to be flushed to disc and to replicate these tuples at a node within another disaster unit so that DB consistency is preserved for these tuples. During fast restart of the failed node, the internal layer information is used to replicate the content of the blocks that are potentially corrupted.

To reduce the node crash recovery work, the set of dirty blocks can be written as part of the node checkpoints (see section 5.7.6). An alternative to this policy is to write a log record when a non-dirty block in the DB buffers becomes dirty, i.e. to produce a **dirty block log record**. A dirty block log record contains the same fields as a block flush log record (see above). This dirty block log policy is used by HypRa. Therefore the set of dirty blocks is not written as part of a checkpoint. The set of dirty block log records produced after the penultimate checkpoint, where a later committed block flush log record does not exist, determines all blocks containing tuples potentially requiring redo processing.

13.9 The Main Memory Log Overflow Policy

This section presents the handling of main memory log overflow. Since some long-lived transactions may produce very large log volumes, the main memory logging must be combined with a disc overflow policy to avoid situations where some transactions threaten to overflow the stable main memory with log records. During normal situations the log records produced by a transaction need not be written to disc before garbage collection. The neighbour write-ahead logging strategy will thus also give a significant reduction in the log induced disc I/O work load in addition to the significant reduced commit processing delays.

The checkpoint policy is used to determine when the redo log record parts can be garbage collected and to determine how long a redo log record part should be kept in main memory to avoid writing it to disc. The effect of all operations with log records older than the penultimate checkpoint in both the primary and the hot stand-by log replicas is reflected in both of the stable DB replicas. The redo log record part of these log records can therefore be garbage collected (see section 13.3). If log records are kept in main memory until this rule is followed, then only the undo log record parts for the log records belonging to those transactions that are still active must be written to disc. The undo log record parts of aborted transactions do not need to be written to disc because CLRs have been produced containing redo parts with information compensating for these undo parts. If transactions have terminated before their log records are evaluated to be written to stable storage, then their undo log record parts need not be written to disc. If the bulk of transactions have a smaller response time than the checkpoint intervals kept in main memory, then a log record when evaluated to be written to disc belongs to an already terminated transaction and its undo log record parts can be avoided written to disc.

The HypRa DBMS must primarily meet the requirements for soft real-time transaction services with strict response times, where the maximum transaction work load is given and the system can be dimensioned after these requirements (see section 1.1). It is reasonable to assume that four or more checkpoint intervals of log records can be kept in main memory and that this interval exceeds the typical transaction response time. Therefore most log records will not need to be written to disc. The overflow mechanism for tuple fragment log replicas will primarily be used to handle the volume of undo log record parts produced by long lived transactions.

Because checkpoints are produced locally to a node and only with uniform interval, and because clock synchronisation is not applied between the nodes, the interval between checkpoints for two nodes may drift up to a checkpoint interval. A node must be prepared to keep log records produced over three complete checkpoints in main memory to avoid writing redo log parts to disc. Since new log records are produced and log records between the fourth and the third previous checkpoint are evaluated for disc write, the log space for four checkpoint intervals should be available.

The fragmentation of the node global log into the node internal log and multiple tuple fragment log replicas is used when designing the log overflow mechanism to allow ordinary concurrent access methods (see section 7.5.1) to be used to contain overflow log records. Traditionally log records have been stored in non-dynamic disc structures ([HL86]). The main memory log overflow policy uses one **log table** implemented by a concurrent access method for each tuple log replica to contain overflow log records (see section 7.5.1). In case of a concatenated fragment replica, multiple log tables may temporarily exist (see section 12.5). The maintenance of these access methods uses subtransactions in combination with AM locks. The subtransaction operations on a log table are logged in the node internal log replica. The primary key of a log tuple is its log record identifier. The log records are written to disc in increasing primary key value order. Overflow log records are buffered in a block and flushed to disc when the block is filled. The double block flush logging policy is used also for log blocks (see section 7.4.1). The block is appended to that part of the bottom layer of the access method which contains the most significant log tuples. The recursive action consistent block split/merge policy is also applied to the log tables when blocks are merged (see section 7.5.1). The index-tuples resulting from appending a log block to an access method are handled by independent node internal transactions. A log record is never removed from the main memory log before it is acknowledged as written to disc.

An *ephemeral logging* policy is used when garbage collecting the log tables. See, for example, [Kee91] for an alternative implementation of an ephemeral logging policy based on non-dynamic disc structures. Garbage collection is executed in the form of subtransactions moving non-garbage undo log record parts from one block into a block containing log records with smaller log record identifiers. These subtransactions are logged as block split/merge subtransactions. One subtransaction compacts only one block. The duration of each subtransaction is therefore short. The garbage collection starts from a log record determined by the ephemeral logging policy. The start point is determined so that garbage collection is done most frequently in the part of the log table where the garbage collection has the greatest effect, i.e. among the undo log records of the newer transactions. The garbage collection traverses the log records from the start point to the log record with the oldest checkpoint value kept in the checkpoint table for the log replica (see section 13.8). AM locks are used to handle conflicts between transactions, maintaining higher levels of the access method. The use of AM locks also makes it possible to execute multiple garbage collection transactions concurrently. A garbage collection transaction will not conflict with the transaction writing the log record parts to disc, since it will stop before it comes to the block involved in such a write. When a log record part is moved from one block to another as part of garbage collection, this is logged similarly to a block merge operation in the node internal log.

The **node internal transactions** are designed so that node internal logs and tuple fragment log replicas for node internal fragments will not overflow. The subtransactions are all designed with short response times. Their response times do not exceed a checkpoint interval and they are guaranteed to be rolled back at the speed of their normal processing. The duration of an internal transaction will therefore never exceed two checkpoint intervals. Their produced log records will therefore be fully kept in main memory even if they fail at any time during their execution. Log records older than the penultimate checkpoint can therefore be garbage collected. In addition, an upper bound exists for the log volume produced between two checkpoints. An internal transaction must lock the space required to log an operation and the potential CLR before an operation is executed. A hot stand-by internal log replica is allocated sufficient blocks so that it can be written to non-volatile storage in case the node containing the primary log replica crashes or performs a controlled stop. These block write operations are not logged.

13.10 Dynamic Replication to Preserve DB Consistency

A node crash may cause the loss or corruption of parts of one replica of multiple logs and one replica of multiple tuples. This represents a threat to the consistent DB state requirement because only one replica is left of some log records and tuples. If another node failure occurs before another replica of these log records and tuples is produced, an unrecoverable condition can be the result in parts of the DB. It is assumed in this section that stricter requirements exist for consistency than for availability. Priority is given to automatic corrective online repair to preserve the consistent DB state requirement over transaction service availability (see section 10.7). Priority is therefore also given to fast replication of the log records and tuples where only one replica exists after a node crash.

After a node crash, the content of both the node's volatile and its stable main memories is lost or corrupted (see section 13.1). As a consequence, only one replica exists for parts of the node internal log and for parts of the tuple fragment logs located at the crashed node. In addition, only one replica exists of the replicated part of the transaction log kept at the failed node. Finally, only one replica exists of those checkpoint tuples that are located at the failed node. A node crash may also cause ongoing block flush operations to become only partially completed, so that the logical content of these blocks are corrupted. Only one replica may therefore exist of the tuples located on those blocks. Priority can then be given to producing another replica of those log parts and the potential tuples where only one replica exists.

Another replica of the hot stand-by node internal log replica for the failed primary node is produced at another node in the same disaster unit as the failed node. When this is completed, the original consistency fault-tolerance level of the internal log of the failed node is reestablished. The new internal node log replica can be flushed to disc because it will not be needed until the failed node starts to recover. The internal log is analysed to determine which tuple intervals are affected by the node crash. The internal log is scanned in reverse order. When a start-BFR which is not matched by an already encountered commit log record is encountered, a block is found that may contain lost or corrupted tuples. These block identifiers are aggregated for each fragment replica. When the scanning is completed, one transaction is started per fragment where such blocks are found. The transaction is responsible for producing two replicas of the tuples in the given primary key intervals for these blocks. The replicas are subfragmented according to the subfragmentation strategy for the corresponding fragments. These tuple replicas represents the nucleus of the later potentially produced complete replicated fragments. When the analysis is completed, the hot stand-by node internal log will not be needed until the node is starts to recover. It can therefore be flushed to disc and its main memory be released. Another replica of the primary internal log for the node with its hot stand-by internal log at the failed node is also produced. The new hot stand-by internal log takes-over for the one which was lost.

A replica of those parts of the logs belonging to the node internal fragments of the failed node after the penultimate primary checkpoint is produced at the same node as the new replica of the internal log is produced. By sending the internal logs to the same node, the fault intensity is preserved. When the redo operations are executed to the hot stand-by internal table replicas, the logs are flushed to disc. They will not be needed again until the crashed node starts to recover. Another log replica is also produced for the internal tables that have lost their hot stand-by tuple fragment logs. They are sent to the same node as the new hot stand-by internal log for the node.

Two replicas are produced of the part of the tuple fragment log produced after that checkpoint at which it is guaranteed that all older log records at the failed node are stored on disc. These replicas are subfragmented according to the subfragmentation strategy for the fragment. They therefore represent the nucleus of the log parts later potentially to be produced to maintain the availability requirements. Also included in producing these log replicas is replication of the checkpoint tuples for these logs. The log records produced after a node crash for a fragment are kept until the complete replication of the fragment is done. The log is kept so that a failed node can be restarted from the log until another replica exists. This policy does not influence the main memory overflow policy (see section 13.9).

13.11 Block Split and Merge

The block split and merge policy presented in this section is adapted to suit the multi-level state-identifier policy (see section 11.4). The semantics of the split/merge operations are exploited to reduce the log volume and the number of log records compared to the block split and merge policy presented in section 7.5.3. A block split or merge is executed by a subtransaction. To reduce the overhead involved in activating another transaction, subtransactions performing a block split/merge at the bottom level of access methods are nested top-actions. This is obtained by the use of backchain log records introduced with partial transaction roll backs (see section 14.2.4).

The compensation logging strategy is applied to the node internal logs. The no-undo/no-redo CLR policy is used as this policy produces the least log volume. It is combined with the log-backchain policy (see section 6.4.1). Due to the short duration of the internal subtransactions all of the garbage collection complications of the no-redo policy is avoided (see section 13.3). A log record older than the penultimate checkpoint can be unconditionally removed because it belongs to a terminated transaction and its effect is reflected in the stable DB.

A block split/merge operation is physical to a block as it updates the border records and link pointer of the block. The BPK/BPK combined identification policy must therefore be used for the split/merge operations (see section 7.3.1). The split/merge operations are combined with AM locks. The original tuples contained in the block being split can therefore also be preserved after the split operation is completed. If the subtransaction aborts and the split operation is compensated for, only the border values and link pointer must be reset. The old tuples and their index entries are preserved. This can also be obtained for the block from which the tuples are moved in combination with a block merge operation. The original tuple replica in that block can be kept until the subtransaction terminates. By exploiting the semantics of the split/merge operations, the tuples moved in a block split or merge subtransaction need not be logged as deleted because they are still contained in the original block (see [ML89]).

The tuples moved to the new block as in case of a block split, or to the other block as in case of a block merge, must be logged. This logging is required in order to prevent inconsistencies of the kind where tuples are over-written in the original block, but not reflected as inserted into the stable replica of other block before a node crash occurs (see section 7.5.4). There are alternative policies that can be chosen to avoid such inconsistencies (see for example section 7.5.8). The moved tuples can be logged as insert tuple operations in the node's internal log. An alternative policy is to integrate the logged tuples into the split/merge operation for the new/other block. Since the no-undo/no-redo CLR policy is used for node internal transactions, the operations cannot be logged as undo-delete operations. An undo-delete log record will in this case not contain the inserted tuple.

The **nested top-action** policy presented in [ML89] is combined with the transaction-backchain CLR policy (see section 6.4.1). The transaction-backchain policy can not be used to indicate which non-CLRs are compensated because non-sequential node crash and transaction failure recovery policies are applied (see section 7.7). The nested top-action policy can on the other hand be combined with the use of backchain log records (see section 14.2.4). A nested top-action is indicated to be completed by a backchain log record, and will therefore not be undone in case the transaction aborts. Nested top-actions are used by HypRa in combination with backchain log records when splitting a bottom level block.

13.12 The Global Undo Space Reservation Policy

This section presents the global undo lock (**GUL**) policy which provides sufficient free space globally at a node during execution of undo-delete tuple operations as part of a transaction roll back. The GUL policy is an alternative to the ZSL policy presented in section 7.5.6. The ZSL policy reserves the space required to reinsert tuples deleted by a transaction within the current blocks of an access method, so that block splits are avoided during transaction undo processing. The GUL and the ZSL policy are called the **undo-space-reserve** policies.

The GUL policy allows block splits to occur during transaction undo, node crash undo, and controlled node stop undo recovery processing. Since a block split is done by a split/merge subtransaction, the subtransaction must be guaranteed the necessary resources to complete successfully and to avoid abortion as a result of a deadlock. These requirements are similar to those required by the deferred execution policy (see section 13.5). They can also be obeyed similarly. Sufficient data space is reserved to prevent aborts during roll back processing, and the design of the block split/merge subtransactions is deadlock free.

The data space requirement of a potentially reinserted tuple could be met by reserving one free block per deleted tuple per transaction. For each tuple deleted, a block unit is reserved since an undo-delete may eventually require the block to be split. As the recursive action consistent block split/merge policy is used, the space requirement can be constrained to one block. This is a simpler space reserving policy than the ZSL policy since only one block lock counter is required per transaction. The reserved unit is coarser, but a block will only be reserved over the duration of the transaction. When a transaction commits, all reserved blocks are released. When a transaction completes undo processing, the remaining unused blocks are released. On the other hand, this policy might cause a node to run out of available free blocks in case a transaction performs multiple tuple deletes.

An alternative policy would be to apply zombie space locks and reserve a block only in case the available free space in a block is not sufficient to hold the current zombie tuples located to the block. When a tuple is inserted into a block, the block is tested to see if the remaining free space in the block can keep the zombies related to it. If not, a block is reserved globally within the node. When a transaction terminates and its zombie locks are removed, a check is made to see if the block a zombie is related to has enough free space for the remaining zombie tuples sent to the block, or if removing a zombie can release a reserved block. If so, a reserved block is released. This is called the GUL policy. The GUL policy makes it possible to merge blocks even if the resulting block does not contain sufficient free space for the zombies located to the block.

The GUL policy is not relevant for index-tuples since AM block locks and the BPK undo identification policy are used by the tuple operations to index-tuples. HypRa applies the ZSL policy to node internal fragment replicas. Because sufficient free space is kept in the current blocks of the access methods to store reinserted tuples as a result of rolling back the active transactions, the block allocation server does not need to be available during undo recovery of the internal fragment replicas. The GUL policy is assumed to be applied to non-internal fragment replicas.

13.13 Conclusion

This chapter has presented the effect during normal operations of the combination of the location and replication independent tuple recovery (LRI) strategy, the log distribution strategy, and in particular the neighbour write-ahead logging (nWAL) strategy. By applying the neighbour write-ahead strategy the last remaining requirement to support soft real-time transactions (see sections 2.6 and 1.1), i.e. the avoidance of disc accesses during transaction commit processing, are fulfilled.

The next chapter presents the effect of the combination of the LRI, the log distribution, and the nWAL strategies to the take-over recovery, the transaction recovery, and the fast node crash recovery strategies. The transaction recovery and the fast node crash recovery strategies are based on the non-sequential recovery strategies presented in chapter 7.

Exercises

1. Assume that logging is done to discs, which is traditional. The time critical transaction path is the longest execution path before a non-dialogue transaction can respond to the client. What is the minimum number of disc accesses in the time critical transaction path induced during commit processing at (a) a primary transaction slave, (b) a hot stand-by transaction slave, (c) a primary transaction coordinator, and (d) a hot stand-by transaction coordinator?

2. Explain the differences between the 2-Safe policy and the 1-Safe policy.

3. (a) Propose a policy that makes it possible to base the recovery after a controlled node stop on the content of the database buffer. (b) Propose two methods for checking the integrity of the database buffer after a node crash. (c) Propose a method for checking the integrity of individual log records.

4. (a) What are the consequences of the proposals made in exercise 4 on recovery after a controlled node stop? (b) What are the consequences on node crash recovery?

5. Assume a database buffer of 80M bytes with 8K byte blocks and 100 byte tuples. Further assume that integrity checksums are connected to each block. A disc access is assumed to take 10 milliseconds and we assume the use of a 40 MIPS processor. Estimate the speedup of recovery after a controlled node crash based on the methods presented in exercise 4 as compared to a traditional recovery after a controlled node stop. Assume that the normal speedup effect of the database buffer must be reestablished before the server is considered available.

6. Assume that an integrity checksum is connected to each tuple. (a) Extend the nWAL logging strategy with internode integrity checking at tuple level. (b) How can self-correction be obtained based on the strategy proposed in a?

7. Reformulate the nWAL (a) undo and (b) redo rules so that the node internal log is also covered by the rules.

8. Assume that each hot stand-by slave transaction knows the number of tuple log records it is supposed to receive through the update channels leading to the node in which it is located for the transaction. Which simplifications of the two-phase commit protocol can this be used to obtain?

9. Make the same assumptions as in exercise 9. (a) Propose a modification of the two-phase commit protocol so that the hot stand-by transaction slaves are communicating with the primary transaction coordinator directly instead of through the primary transaction slaves. (b) What are the consequences of the modification on transaction execution delay caused by the two-phase commit protocol?

10. Make the same assumptions as in exercise 9. Propose changes to the two-phase commit protocol that give further reduction in transaction processing delays caused by the two-phase commit protocol as compared to those developed in exercise 10.

11. What are the effects of the one-replica policy on (a) recovery after a controlled node stop, (b) recovery after a node crash?

12. What are the consequences of the receive-commit policy on (a) commit processing, (b) take-over processing, (c) controlled node stop recovery, and (d) node crash recovery.

13. Propose a policy for allocating hot stand-by transaction coordinators to nodes as compared to the location of the primary transaction coordinator.

14. (a) What are the consequences of maintaining one primary transaction log sequence per transaction at each node? (b) How would you, in this case, handle the hot stand-by transaction log sequences?

15. (a) Why is log space for 4 checkpoints needed? (b) How much log space is needed for the node internal log in terms of intervals between checkpoints?

16. (a) Propose a method for fuzzy global checkpointing. (b) How can a global transaction consistent database image be produced from a fuzzy global checkpoint?

17. What are the consequences of assuming atomic block flush operations?

18. Propose another implementation of ephemeral logging.

19. Assume that logs are replicated before the data in case a node crashes. (a) How will this influence the fault-tolerance level? (b) Which parts of the logs need to be replicated?

20. Assume that the operations on tuples involved in a block split/merge operations are logged as tuple operations. Propose an undo and a redo identification policy for the log records reflecting these tuple operations.

21. Assume that every primary fragment replica has one hot stand-by replica that is subfragmented into 4 subfragments. Further assume that tuple state-identifiers are based on counters that are local to the primary tuple replicas and reflected in the hot stand-by tuple replicas. How can a take-over be performed, based on this approach?

Answers

1. (a) One. (b) One. (c) One. (d) One.

2. If the 1-Safe policy is applied, a commit response is sent to the requester after the primary replicas have committed the transaction. If the 2-Safe policy is applied, a commit response is sent to the requester after both the primary and the hot stand-by replicas have committed the transaction.

3. (a) Since a tuple state changing operation is assumed to lock a block for the duration of the operation, integrity checksums cannot be placed on coarser granules than blocks. Place integrity checksums on blocks. Tell the recovery module the start location of the database buffer and the block size. Check the integrity at recovery time block by block. (b) The first method is presented in a. The second method is to place integrity checksums in tuples and record index tables instead of in blocks. (c) Include the checksums in the log records. Test the hot stand-by side during redo execution to see if the before-image checksum in the log record equals the current checksum of the hot stand-by tuple replica. Check also that the after-image checksum in the log record equals the new produced checksum in the tuple.

4. (a) If the database buffer is undamaged, no disc accesses are needed for the recovery. (b) None.

5. We assume that significant recovery time is used to reestablish the effect of the database buffer. The time to read the number of involved blocks into main memory in case disc based recovery is used is estimated to be approximately the same as the disc access time for the blocks. The access time is $\frac{80M \cdot 0{,}01}{8K} = 100$ seconds. We assume that one instruction is used per byte to check the consistency of a tuple if main memory based recovery is applied. The checking then takes approximately $\frac{80M}{40M} = 2$ seconds.

6. (a) The before- and after-image of the integrity checksum for the tuple is included in the tuple log records. During redo execution, the current checksum for the hot stand-by replica of the tuple is checked against the before-image checksum in the log to see if they are the same. After the redo operation is executed, the new checksum is compared with the after-image checksum in the log record to see if they are equal. An error has occurred if the checksums differ. (b) Use two hot stand-by replicas. Use a majority vote to determine the correct replicas.

7. (a) An undo log record part must be written to two stable storages with independent failure modes before the effect of the state changing DB operation or state changing access method operation is allowed to be reflected in the stable storage DB. (b) A redo log record part must be written to two stable storages with independent failure modes before a transaction or a transaction or nested top-action commits.

8. The hot stand-by slaves can respond ready to the primary slaves without the primary slaves needing to send an explicit request to hot stand-by slaves. This will, in addition to the protocol simplification, reduce the number of communication messages per transaction.

9. (a) The primary transaction coordinator sends prepare-to-commit requests directly to all slaves. All slaves respond directly to the primary transaction coordinator. (b) This removes the delay caused by the hot stand-by slaves responding indirectly through the primary slaves.

10. All slaves belonging to a transaction respond to a prepare-to-commit request from their primary transaction coordinator to their hot stand-by transaction coordinator. This removes the request from the primary coordinator to the hot stand-by coordinator. This further reduces the commit processing delay and the number of messages involved in commit processing.

11. (a) Since the log is not kept after the operation is reflected in the stable tuple at a node, some of the log records produced after the controlled node stop relating to tuples at the stopped node may have been sent to garbage. The node must therefore normally be loaded with data after a controlled node stop. (b) The node must normally be loaded with data again.

12. (a) Less work needs to be done on the hot stand-by side before it responds as ready. (b) More work needs to be done during a take-over since less work is done to the outstanding operations. A node may be completely filled with data during the take-over processing. This may cause the need for refragmentation during a take-over. (c) None. (d) None.

13. Allocate, for example, the hot stand-by transaction coordinator at the node across the mirror dimension from the primary transaction coordinator.

14. (a) More log volume must be scanned during a refragmentation. More log volume may have to be scanned during a take-over. (b) Build them on the hot stand-by side based on the log streams received.

15. (a) Two consecutive checkpoint intervals are needed in the normal case. In addition, the process of writing log records belonging to long duration transactions to disc may need an additional checkpoint interval. In addition to this, a primary and a hot stand-by checkpoint may drift up to one checkpoint interval. (b) Two. No internal transaction spans multiple checkpoint intervals.

16. (a) Run the global fuzzy checkpointing as a distributed global transaction. Connect an active transaction list to the global checkpoint either at the start or at the end of the checkpoint at each node. (b) For all transactions that committed during the checkpoint production at each node, determine if they are to be reflected in the transaction consistent checkpoint or not. Base the analysis on the active transaction table and the transaction log produced during the checkpoint production.

17. Block flush logging does not need to be done.

18. Apply, for example, the ideas in [Kee91] and [KD93].

19. (a) The method will reduce the time window in which the system is vulnerable to a double failure when the stable data at the crashed node is undamaged. The fault-tolerance level will therefore be improved. (b) The node internal log for the crashed node must be replicated. The three last checkpoint intervals of the tuple replica logs for fragments located at the crashed node must be replicated.

20. Block and primary key identification.

21. The hot stand-by replicas can monotonously produce log record identifiers that are larger than the last received from the crashed primary. There is no need to introduce a hole in the sequence because the tuple state identifiers are local to each tuple.

Chapter 14

The Recovery Strategies

This chapter presents the HypRa recovery strategies. The non-sequential recovery strategy introduced in chapter 7 is combined with the multi-level state-identifier policy (see section 11.4), the log distribution strategy (see chapter 12), and the neighbour write-ahead logging strategy (see section 13). The non-sequential recovery strategy is applied to obtain recovery work load reduction and recovery processing speed up compared to sequential recovery strategies (see chapter 6).

Primary and *hot stand-by take-over* processing policies are presented. A *primary take-over* occurs when a hot stand-by fragment takes over the role of primary as a consequence of a deliberate swap of fragment roles, a primary fragment replica failure, a controlled node stop, or a node crash. A *hot stand-by take-over* occurs, for example, when a recovered fragment replica is restarted as a hot stand-by replica. The primary take-over policy in HypRa gives priority to minimising fragment unavailability.

Three different *transaction failure recovery* policies are presented. The policies differ with respect to whether sequential or non-sequential undo recovery is done to or between the involved fragments. A slave-transaction can choose a recovery policy autonomously considering the undo recovery work and the resources allocated to transaction recovery at the node.

The presented *node crash recovery* strategy is used for fast recovery. A fragment is *fast recovered* if another replica of the fragment has not been produced by the non-blocking fragment replication policy before the fragment recovery is started. Both fast node crash recovery and fast restart after a controlled node stop use the non-sequential recovery policy to fully exploit any possible inherent CPU and I/O recovery work parallelism to obtain work load reduction and speed up. If new replicas of a crashed fragment replica have been produced before the fragment recovery is started, the online non-blocking fragment replication policy is used to recover the fragments at their original node ([HST+91b]). The log parts required to perform a fast recovery have been removed when the new fragment replicas' production was completed.

The policy used by HypRa to supervise the restart of a node and to restart the communication server and OS server (see chapter 9) at a node are not presented in this book (see [HST91a], [HST+91b], [Hva91b], [HS90], and [Wed91]). The policy used by HypRa to determine the consistent set of available nodes is indicated in section 9.6.

14.1 The Take-Over Strategy

This section presents **take-over** policies. A **primary take-over** is executed when a hot stand-by fragment replica changes its role to become a primary fragment replica. A **hot stand-by take-over** is executed when a primary fragment replica changes its role to become a hot stand-by replica or a recovered fragment replica becomes the hot stand-by replica for the fragment. When the term take-over is used without further qualification, it refers to a primary take-over.

A primary fragment replica crash causes a fragment to be unavailable until the primary take-over processing has opened the new primary replica to transaction processing. A node crash or controlled node stop similarly causes the fragments with their primary replicas at the failed node to be unavailable until the corresponding primary take-overs have opened the new primary fragment replicas. Fast primary take-over must therefore be provided to avoid threatening the availability of soft real-time transaction services.

A primary take-over will normally include both redo and undo recovery work. The redo recovery work comprises the execution of the deferred operations to the hot stand-by fragment replica involved in the take-over. The undo recovery work comprises the compensating undo operations for the transactions active to the fragment involved in the take-over. A primary take-over may therefore induce a massive abort of active transactions which may represent a threat to the availability of soft real-time transactions.

A **redo/undo primary take-over** policy is applied if the fragment involved in a primary take-over stays unavailable during both the redo and the undo recovery work. If locks are not maintained during the normal redo processing on a hot stand-by fragment replica, either the redo/undo primary take-over policy must be applied or else the fragment stays unavailable while locks are set on the data objects requiring recovery work. A consistent DB cannot be provided before the completion of all redo and undo work to the fragment, or before the completion of the lock setting. The redo/undo primary take-over policy therefore does not impose any bounds on the undo work involved in a primary take-over because of the arbitrary number of log records that can have been produced by a transaction. A maximum fragment unavailability caused by a primary take-over cannot be guaranteed if the redo/undo take-over policy is used. The redo/undo primary take-over policy is not acceptable for a DBMS providing continuous availability.

A primary take-over uses the redo-undo sequentialisation policy. The redo execution of the outstanding deferred operations is done in increasing log record identifier sequence. The take-over redo work can also use a non-sequential policy based on log aggregation. The redo log record parts for the outstanding deferred operations are aggregated on the involved tuples. Block complete redo processing can be applied and combined with I/O and CPU parallelism (see non-sequential undo take-over processing). The sequential redo take-over policy is applied by HypRa because of the small number of outstanding deferred operations. Therefore no significant gain would be obtained by applying a non-sequential redo policy.

The primary take-over undo work can be done *sequentially*. The hot stand-by tuple fragment log is scanned sequentially in reverse order, and when a non-compensated non-CLR belonging to one of the transactions to be aborted is encountered, a CLR is produced and a compensating undo operation is executed. A *transaction asynchronous* take-over undo work policy can be applied. The transactions to be aborted are then rolled back asynchronously for the involved tuple fragment log replica and each transaction is rolled back sequentially within the tuple fragment log replica (see also section 7.6.3). A *non-sequential* undo work policy can also be applied and combined with a non-sequential redo take-over work policy. The undo log record parts for the transactions to be aborted are aggregated per involved tuple. Since all log records belong to the same fragment, no fragment aggregation is done. The undo processing can use the block complete policy. The I/O processing can be done in parallel for the blocks to which the tuples requiring undo work are located. The CPU processing can be done in parallel over the tuples requiring undo work (see section 7.6). The choice of take-over undo recovery work policy to a fragment depends on the undo work load as when executing a transaction recovery (see section 14.2).

A **no-undo primary take-over** policy is applied if the fragment involved in the take-over processing becomes available before the undo recovery work is executed. A partial fragment availability is therefore provided during the undo take-over work. To support the no-undo take-over policy, locks must either be maintained on the hot stand-by fragment replicas during normal deferred execution or set during the take-over to the data objects requiring undo processing. Locks maintained during the normal deferred execution do not determine the execution sequence to the hot stand-by fragment replica (see section 11). The locks are removed either when the transactions to be undone complete aborting, or when the take-over undo work completes, depending on the undo recovery work policy used. If the transaction asynchronous undo work policy is used, the locks belonging to a transaction are removed when the transaction completes recovery to the fragment. If the sequential undo policy is applied, the locks are removed when the undo work is completed. If the non-sequential undo policy is used locks can either be removed when the undo work is completed or when it is completed to the tuples in a block. If locks are maintained during normal deferred executions to hot stand-by fragment replicas, a **hot stand-by lock** policy is applied.

The no-undo take-over policy combined with the hot stand-by lock policy imposes a strict and very low bound on the take-over undo work to be done while a fragment is unavailable. If the no-undo take-over policy is not combined with the hot stand-by lock policy, setting the locks might involve disc accesses if some of the affected transactions were active before the third last checkpoint (see section 13.8). Therefore no upper bound can in this case be given on how long the undo take-over work causes a fragment to be unavailable. If the transaction was active before the third last checkpoint and is still active when the take-over is executed, then some log records to be scanned may be kept on disc (see section 13.9) and the fragment may stay unavailable for the duration of disc accesses. An active transaction usually locks only a fraction of a fragment. If some transactions have locked the complete fragment, the availability of the fragment becomes the same as if the undo take-over policy was used.

A **no-redo primary take-over** policy is applied if the fragment becomes available before the redo processing is executed. To provide a consistent fragment replica, the deferred operations on the fragment must have set their locks before the fragment becomes available. If an upper bound on the number of deferred operations on a fragment exists, a maximum redo work imposed fragment unavailability can be determined for both the redo and the no-redo take-over policy. The execution of a deferred operation may cause disc I/O or a block split. The no-redo policy, on the other hand, uses no disc accesses and block splits during the time interval a fragment is unavailable.

Only one replica is available when a primary take-over is executed to a fragment for which two replicas originally existed (see section 8.1). A **multiple take-over** must therefore be prevented, i.e. a take-over required within a take-over. If a multiple take-over occurs the fragment becomes unavailable until another replica of the fragment has been produced or one of the failed replicas has been recovered and restarted. If a multiple take-over occurs, no bounds exist on the possible unavailability of a fragment caused by a primary take-over. Again this threatens the availability of soft real-time transaction services. The space-reserve policy guarantees that there will always be sufficient space available to execute the outstanding deferred operations to a hot stand-by fragment replica (see section 13.5). To prevent the primary take-over redo work from causing a multiple take-over, the space-reserve policy is used. To prevent multiple take-overs from occurring during primary take-over undo work, sufficient space must also be reserved for a potential undo of an operation. If the undo-space-reserve policy is used, this requirement is met (see section 13.12).

HypRa uses the no-redo/no-undo primary take-over policy combined with the hot stand-by lock policy to minimise the fragment unavailability imposed by primary take-over. To provide the same degree of availability at the new primary fragment as at the failed one, the same lock granularity is used for hot stand-by fragments as for primary fragment replicas. HypRa includes the locking information in the log records sent over the update channels (see [HST+91b]). HypRa also applies the space-reserve and an undo-space-reserve policy to avoid multiple take-overs.

When a **hot stand-by take-over** is executed to an available primary fragment replica, no redo or undo work is involved. A hot stand-by take-over can be combined with a primary take-over for another replica of the same fragment. The transactions active to the fragment are aborted as a consequence of the take-over. A fuzzy take-over policy is presented in [HST+91b] which avoids aborting transactions when a primary and a hot stand-by replica of the same fragment swap their roles. Hot stand-by take-over processing after a fragment recovery is presented in section 14.3.9. The fuzzy take-over policy is used by HypRa in combination with soft HW and SW maintenance (see [HST+91b]).

14.2 The Transaction Failure Recovery Strategy

The transaction failure recovery strategy determines how a failed transaction is recovered. Three transaction recovery policies are presented; the sequential-, the fragment replica asynchronous-, and the non-sequential transaction failure recovery policy.

The **sequential** transaction failure recovery policy is an adaptation of the transaction failure recovery policy presented in section 6.6.2 for use with the log distribution strategy (see chapter 12). The **fragment replica asynchronous** transaction failure recovery policy exploits the possible CPU and I/O asynchronous processing during transaction recovery, which is a consequence of the log distribution strategy combined with maintenance of transaction log sequences local to each log replica (see section 13.7). The **non-sequential** transaction failure recovery policy is an adaptation of the non-sequential transaction failure recovery policy presented in section 7.8.2 for use with the log distribution strategy.

The transaction failure recovery policy to be used is determined autonomously by each slave-transaction for each log replica. Therefore different transaction recovery policies can be used for different nodes where the transaction has been active and for different log replicas within a node. The choice of transaction undo policies is based on the number of non-CLRs and the undo log record part volume produced by the transaction to each log replica. This information is kept in the transaction log record table (see section 13.7).

The transaction failure recovery policies are also used when partially rolling back a transaction to a given savepoint (see section 13.7).

14.2.1 The Sequential Transaction Failure Recovery Policy

The sequential transaction failure recovery policy rolls back a transaction sequentially to each log replica and sequentially between the primary log replicas. A subtransaction is rolled back before any of its parent transactions.

A transaction is rolled back in reverse order to each primary log replica to which the transaction has been active at the node by its slave-transaction server. The local transaction chain for a primary log replica is followed and for each non-compensated non-CLR, a CLR is produced and a compensation operation is executed. The CLRs are sent across an update channel to the matching hot stand-by log (see sections 13.4 and 13.5). A list of which non-CLRs are non-compensated can be maintained in a temporary table for each log replica containing the set of compensated non-CLRs which are not yet reached. It can also be made by the use of block log records without temporary tables (see section 14.2.4).

The transaction failure recovery is done sequentially between the primary log replicas at a node. A slave-transaction performs recovery to one and only one primary log replica at a time. The slave-transaction can recover the primary tuple fragment logs affected by the transaction in any order, because all log records relating to a tuple are located in only one primary tuple fragment log replica. Recovery to a tuple will therefore be done in reverse order per tuple regardless of the recovery order between the primary tuple fragment logs (see section 6.6.1).

A node internal transaction never executes tuple operations that are logged in a tuple fragment log to tuples contained in a block to which it also executes operations that are logged in the node internal log. This requirement is part of the node internal transactions semantics. A node internal transaction can therefore undo recover the primary node internal log and the primary tuple fragment log replicas it has has been active to in any order.

A subtransaction that fails causes its parent transaction or parent transactions, if it has multiple levels of parents, to fail recursively (see section 10.4). A sequential recovery policy can be applied between a subtransaction and its parent transactions, i.e. a subtransaction is completely recovered before any of its parent transactions start to roll back. This policy provides a parent transaction with an action consistent access method during its recovery, because a subtransaction that updated the access method is undone before the transactions using the access method. The asynchronous parent-subtransaction recovery policy (see section 14.2.2) could also have been applied between a subtransaction and its parent transactions.

During a transaction failure recovery, an undo-delete tuple operation will require free space in the block into which the tuple is reinserted. If an undo-space-reserve policy is used, such space is available at the node and the execution of the operation will not cause a take-over to be initiated. Primary take-overs caused by lack of space during undo processing are therefore prevented. The GUL policy may cause block split/merge subtransactions to be activated during undo processing (see section 13.12).

14.2.2 The Fragment Replica Asynchronous Transaction Failure Recovery Policy

The fragment replica asynchronous transaction failure recovery policy uses sequential recovery for each primary log replica and asynchronous recovery between the primary log replicas. The policy also uses asynchronous recovery between a subtransaction and its parent transactions.

A slave-transaction may have produced log records in multiple primary log replicas at a node. Since a tuple will never be a member of multiple primary fragment replicas concurrently, the recovery can be done asynchronously between the primary fragment replicas affected by the transaction. (See also section 14.2.1, where the same argument is used to allow recovery to be done in any order between primary fragment replicas.) A subtransaction can recover the operations logged in the primary node internal log concurrently with the recovery of the tuple fragment logs. This is a consequence of the semantics of subtransactions. They never perform tuple operations logged in a primary tuple fragment log to tuples located in a block to which they also perform operations which are logged in the node internal log. There is therefore no need to perform the recovery to the node internal log in any particular order relative to the recovery of the primary fragment replicas for a subtransaction in order to preserve a consistent undo recovery.

The maximum CPU parallelism achievable per slave-transaction is one undo operation concurrently in execution per primary log replica. The maximum obtainable I/O parallelism per slave-transaction is one disc access per primary log replica. This is an improvement compared to the sequential transaction failure recovery policy where only one undo operation is executed at a time and maximum one disc I/O is in progress per slave-transaction. A **selective fragment replica asynchronous transaction failure recovery** policy uses asynchronous recovery to some but not all of the primary log replicas affected by the slave-transaction. The level of parallelism can therefore be adjusted to the resources given to the slave-transaction, with the sequential transaction failure recovery policy as the lowest level of parallelism.

The **asynchronous parent-subtransaction** policy allows a parent transaction to be recovered concurrently with its subtransactions. This can be allowed because a subtransaction will never access a tuple accessed by any of its parents. A subtransaction holds a write AM lock until the block is completed recovered. A parent transaction will not be given access to a tuple located in a block before its subtransaction has completed its recovery because of the write AM lock it holds. A parent transaction will, as a result of the locking policy, be provided with action consistent blocks. The node internal recovery is completed for each block before the tuple recovery is started, because only one subtransaction can set a write AM lock on a block and thus need recovery of the block after a transaction failure. The recovery of the primary fragment replica where it conflicts with an AM lock held by a subtransaction in recovery, is delayed until the recovery of the subtransaction is completed and the lock released. The recovery of the other primary fragment replicas to which the slave-transaction was active are unaffected by this delay. The asynchronous parent-subtransaction policy may therefore improve the level of CPU and I/O parallelism relative to the sequential policy presented in section 14.2.1. It will also, at its lowest level, provide the same I/O and CPU parallelism as the sequential transaction failure recovery policy.

14.2.3 The Non-Sequential Transaction Failure Recovery Policy

The non-sequential transaction failure recovery policy uses the dedicated DB buffer policy and the log-aggregation policy (see sections 7.6.1 and 7.6.2). The block complete- and block autonomous recovery policies are also used (see section 7.6.4). The undo processing is therefore dictionary independent (see section 7.3.2). Since the action consistent block split/merge policy is used, this policy is an adaptation of the non-sequential transaction failure recovery policy introduced in section 7.8.2.

The undo parts of the node internal log records are aggregated per block by the block identifier contained in their undo identification concept, maintaining the log sequence to each block. The aggregation is done per block because the node internal log contains split/merge operations that are physical to blocks and must therefore be aggregated per block. This aggregation corresponds to the aggregation of undo log record parts by split/merge subtransactions illustrated in figure 7.5. The undo log record parts aggregated per block are all produced by node internal transactions. Disc I/O is never involved when aggregation from the node internal log is performed because of the short duration of the internal transactions (see section 13.9).

The undo log record parts from the primary tuple fragment log replicas are aggregated per fragment replica and, within a fragment replica, per tuple. The transaction log sequence is maintained to each tuple. Figure 7.5 illustrates this aggregation when the table identifier is replaced with the fragment replica identifier. As a consequence of the log distribution policy no fragment identifiers are needed when the undo log record parts are aggregated per fragment replica (see section 12.1). This aggregation is already present in the primary tuple replica logs. The aggregation per tuple is based on the PK undo identification concept (see section 12.7).

The aggregation can be done asynchronously between the involved primary tuple fragment log replicas to obtain CPU parallelism during the aggregation. The CPU parallelism is a consequence of the log distribution policy. The CPU parallelism is an improvement relative to the non-sequential transaction failure recovery policy presented in section 7.8.2, where the aggregation is done sequentially to the node global log. The aggregation may involve disc I/O since a transaction may have a lifetime that is longer than the log part kept in main memory. As a consequence of the log distribution policy, I/O parallelism can be obtained during the aggregation since one disc access can concurrently be in progress for each log fragment. The aggregation from the primary node internal log can be done concurrently with the aggregation from the primary tuple fragment log replicas.

The block complete policy is followed when recovering a block (see section 7.6.4). The block aggregated undo processing is completed for a block and the AM lock removed before the tuple aggregated undo processing for the tuples contained in the block are started. The tuple locks held by the recovered tuples contained in the block are removed when these tuples are recovered. The node internal operations are therefore undone first for a block because they are the last

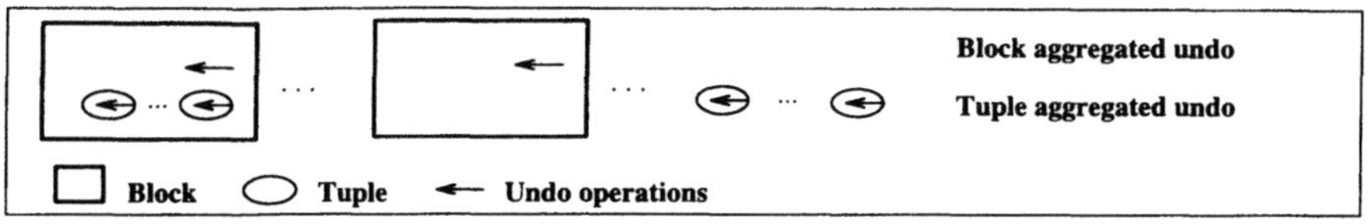

Figure 14.1: The non-sequential transaction failure recovery policy performs block aggregated undo recovery from the primary node internal log before it performs the tuple aggregated undo operations from a primary tuple fragment log replica. The block aggregated undo work can be done asynchronously between blocks. The tuple aggregated undo work can be done asynchronously between the tuples. Block and tuple aggregated undo work may be required for a block. Block aggregated undo work may be required for a block without any undo work for tuples contained in the block. Undo recovery may be required for tuples where no recovery is needed for the blocks which contain them.

operations executed to the block before the transaction failure and must therefore be the first to be recovered (see section 7.6.7). This policy provides the tuple aggregated undo operations with consistent blocks. The recovery processing is done asynchronously between blocks. Tuple aggregated recovery to tuples within a block and between tuples located in different blocks can be performed asynchronously (see figure 14.1). For some blocks, both block and tuple aggregated undo processing must be done. When a tuple requiring undo processing is outside the blocks requiring block aggregated undo recovery, the primary key based access method is used to access the tuple during the undo recovery. The structure of the access method can be used to obtain optimised access to these tuples (see section 7.8.2).

A **selective non-sequential transaction recovery** policy uses the non-sequential transaction recovery policy for some but not all fragment replicas. This policy can be applied if the transaction recovery has sufficient main memory to aggregate the node internal undo log record parts and the undo log record parts for some but not all primary fragment log replicas. The memory required to aggregate the undo log record parts from a log replica is included in the transaction log record table (see figure 13.1). When the block aggregation is completed, it can be determined which fragment replica a block will belong to after the recovery. This is determined from the last split/merge operation to the block. The block complete policy is applied to the blocks that belong to fragments recovered by non-sequential recovery. Groups of fragment replicas are aggregated and recovered in parallel until all fragment replicas where the non-sequential recovery policy is to be applied are recovered. This policy provides less parallelism than the non-sequential recovery policy but it will never reaccess a block during the transaction recovery. The selective non-sequential policy can also be combined with selective the fragment replica asynchronous fragment recovery policy (see section 14.2.2).

14.2.4 Partial Transaction Roll Back

The transaction failure recovery policies presented in sections 14.2.1, 14.2.2, and 14.2.3 can all be used when performing a partial transaction rollback, i.e. when rolling back a transaction to a given savepoint. The savepoint table (see figure 13.1) tells which log records to roll back to in each primary log replica to complete a partial transaction rollback. The savepoint table also tells the undo log record volume and the number of non-compensated non-CLRs produced before the savepoint in the log by the transaction.

When the partial roll back is completed a **backchain log record (BLR)** is produced. A BLR contains the log record identifier of the next log record to be undone in the local transaction chain for the primary log replica. In case of a transaction failure or a partial transaction roll back, all non-CLRs spanned by a BLR are already compensated. A BLR replica is sent across the update channel to the hot stand-by log replica. If the hot stand-by fragment replica is subfragmented, a BLR replica is sent to all the hot stand-by replicas for the primary log replica.

BLRs are used to avoid the need for temporary tables to hold the log record identifier for the not yet encountered non-CLRs which are compensated during a full or partial transaction failure recovery. The recovery policy used for the log records spanned by a BLR does not influence the consistency of the BLR because the sequencing of CLRs compared to the non-CLRs are kept within the log records spanned by a BLR. The use of BLRs serves the same purpose as the use of the transaction-backchain CLR policy with respect to partial transaction roll back and transaction failure recovery (see sections 6.4.1 and 7.7).

14.3 The Fast Node Crash Recovery Strategy

The fast node crash recovery strategy presented in this section is used by node crash recoveries which are attempted before online non-blocking replication of the fragment replicas stored at the recovering node is performed (see also section 2.4.3). The fast recovery strategy is an adaptation of the non-sequential node crash recovery strategy presented in section 7.9 combined with the LRI and the log distribution strategies.

The recovery processing after a node crash gives priority to preserving the consistent DB state requirement (see section A.8) and reestablishing the availability of fragments whose primary replicas have become unavailable, rather than to the fast recovery of the crashed node. A fast recovery is therefore not started before the primary take-over processing has made the new primary fragment replicas available. When the no-redo/no-undo or redo/no-undo take-over policy is applied, fast recovery can be performed concurrently with the part of the take-over processing done after the new primary replicas have become available (see section 14.1).

When two replicas exist of each fragment, only one replica of each involved fragment is available while a fast recovery takes place. A fast recovery is integrated with the following hot stand-by take-overs to transform a recovered replica into an available hot stand-by fragment replica. For those fragment replicas that originally were primary replicas, a fuzzy take-over is executed after the hot stand-by take-over is completed to make them reestablish their original role ([HST+91b]). A fast recovery after a controlled node stop is performed similarly to a fast recovery from a node crash.

14.3.1 The Recovery Work Order and Sequentialisation Policies

This section presents the effects of the LRI and the log distribution strategies on redo and undo recovery work order and on redo and undo sequentialisation policies.

Node internal operations are logged in the node internal log (see section 12.6). The set of index-tuple and tuple operations logged in the internal log is the complete set of state changing tuple operations presented in section A.5. Partial tuple logging is used (see section 7.3.3). As a consequence the redo work must be done in *forward order* for the node internal log. This follows from the analysis presented in section 6.7.1, which is based on the operational logging of delta operations. If delta tuple operations are excluded, the forward redo order must still be retained if partial tuple logging is applied. If the reverse redo order was used in combination with partial tuple logging, the effect of a write operation that was followed by a later write to the same tuple, but where the first write operation wrote a field not written by the last operation, could be missing from that field. The redo work relating to the node internal log must be done in forward order to each *block* because of the use of the BPK redo identification concept, block state-identifiers, and coarse granularity locks (see section 7.6.5). Between blocks, any redo work order can be applied.

The undo work relating to the node internal log must be done in *reverse order* (see section 6.7.1). The undo work to, for example, an index-tuple replica must be done in reverse order for the same reasons as undo work must be done in reverse order to records when the compensation recovery approach is applied (see section 6.6.1). Since a node internal log contains a mix of log records produced by tuple operations and physical block operations, the undo work must be done in reverse order per *block*. The *redo-undo sequentialisation* policy must be used for the recovery resulting from the node internal log because the compensation recovery policy is used. This follows from the analysis presented in section 6.7.2.

The redo work resulting from log records in a primary tuple fragment log must be done in *forward order*. This is again a consequence of the use of delta tuple operations and partial tuple logging (see section 6.7.1). Since a tuple is the scope of tuple operation logging, the scope of locking, and the scope of the tuple state-identifiers, the tuple operations reflected in the redo work must be done in forward order to each *primary tuple replica* (see section 6.7.1). The redo work can, on the other hand, be done in any sequence between the primary tuple replicas.

Undo recovery work resulting from log records in a primary tuple fragment log must be done in *reverse order*. This is discussed in section 6.6.1 for records and record operations. This will be the same for tuples and tuple operations. The undo work must be done in reverse order per *tuple* but can be executed in any sequence between tuples (see section 5.6.2). The *redo-undo sequentialisation* policy must be used for each tuple because the compensation policy is used (see section 6.7.2).

The recovery resulting from the node internal log must be completed to a block before the recovery resulting from a tuple fragment log for any tuple contained in the block is started. This is called the **internal-distributed** synchronisation policy. The internal-distributed synchronisation policy gives the tuple based recovery action consistent blocks. The internal-distributed synchronisation policy may cause internal log based recovery redo operations to be executed to a different block state than the original do operation. The consequences of this is analysed in section 14.3.2. The redo recovery of a split/merge subtransaction must precede the tuple based recovery to a block. The blocks involved can be found at recovery start with, for example, some of the moved tuples missing (see section 7.5.4). This happens when a node crash occurs before the moved tuples are reflected in the stable block replica. The block aggregated redo operations inserting the missing tuples must therefore be executed before the tuple based recovery is started to the block. The undo recovery of a block split/merge subtransaction must also be completed to a block before the tuple based recovery is initiated to the tuples contained in the block. The node crash may have occurred at a time when the border values of the blocks involved indicate that some moved tuples are missing (see sections 13.11 and 7.5.8). The block aggregated undo recovery will reinsert these tuples.

14.3.2 Non-Sequential Redo Recovery Work to a Block

This section presents the effect of the LRI and log distribution strategies on the sequence of redo work to a block. The internal-distributed synchronisation policy may cause redo processing to a block to follow a different execution sequence than the original sequence of operations. The presented policies prevent this from causing inconsistencies during recovery processing.

A consequence of the multi-level state-identifier policy is that the global sequence of operations executed to a block is not reflected in a single state-identifier. Since no node global log is used, the sequence of state changing operations executed to a block is not maintained in a single log. It is therefore not possible to ensure that redo execution to a block will be done in the same sequence as the original execution to the block.

Because a tuple operation sets an AM lock on the block containing the tuple, DB state changing tuple operations are executed sequentially to each block. When a node internal operation is reflected in a stable block replica, all preceding node internal and tuple operations to the block are also reflected in the block. When a node internal operation is not reflected in a stable block, then none of the following node internal or following tuple operations are reflected in the stable block.

Because of the internal-distributed policy, a node internal operation may be redone before some tuple operation that was originally executed before it. This happens when the tuple operation is logged in a tuple fragment log, both the node internal operation and the tuple operation are executed to the same block, and neither the tuple nor the node internal operation is reflected in the stable block replica at the time of the node crash. Since the node internal recovery is completed to the block before the tuple recovery, the redo execution is performed in reverse order relative to the original execution.

The semantics of the block split/merge subtransactions can be used to prevent DB inconsistencies from occurring as a result of such altered redo execution sequences. It must be possible to execute a redo-split/merge operation to a *different block state* than the original split/merge operation without introducing inconsistencies. A redo-split/merge operation is executed to a different block state when the block state-identifier indicates that it is not reflected in the block and some of the preceding tuple operations logged in a tuple fragment log are not reflected in the block. During the original execution the effect of the missing tuple operations was present. On the other hand, if a split/merge operation is not reflected in a block then no tuple operations following the split/merge operation are reflected in the block because in that case the split/merge operation would also have been reflected.

A redo-split/merge may therefore be executed to a block containing tuples that a missing reflected delete or undo-insert tuple operation logged in a tuple fragment log, should have removed. These tuples can be removed by the redo-split/merge operation without introducing DB inconsistencies. The tuple cannot have been inserted by an insert or undo-delete tuple operation following the split/merge operation, because then the split/merge should have been reflected in the block state-identifier. When the tuple operations to these removed tuples are later redone, the tuples with the given primary key will not exist and the redo operation will not be executed (see section 14.3.3). The upper/lower border policy is used to determine which tuples should be removed by the redo-split/merge operation (see section 7.5.2). The redo-split/merge operation will delete all tuple replicas with primary key values outside the border interval without logging these deletes.

A redo-split/merge may also be executed to a block state that is missing some tuples because some preceding insert or undo-delete operations are not reflected in the block. If the primary key value of the missing tuple is within the border values of the block as after the split/merge operation, it will also be missing after the redo-split/merge is completed. During the tuple fragment log based recovery a redo-insert or redo-undo-delete operation will be executed to insert the tuple (see section 14.3.3). If the tuple is moved and the block state-identifier indicates that the insert operation which moved the tuple is not reflected in the new block, the redo-insert operation will insert the tuple and the tuple's state-identifier will reflect all the tuple operations logged in a tuple fragment log executed to it preceding the split/merge.

A redo-split/merge may also be executed to a block containing the same tuples as it had when the original split/merge operation was executed, but missing the effect of some state changing non-dynamic tuple operations preceding it (see section A.5). This does not influence the subtransaction redo. The missing tuple operations will be supplied by the tuple based recovery processing.

The redo of a block split subtransaction will not cause any space problems. Tuples are removed from the original block and no tuples are inserted into that block during the redo processing. The tuples inserted into the new block are the same as were inserted during the original execution of the subtransaction. Since the block starts out empty or containing some but not all of the tuples inserted by the subtransaction, the redo fills the block just as much as the original inserts.

The redo of a block merge operation on an empty a block will not cause any space problems since no tuples are moved. If, on the other hand, a block merge subtransaction moves tuples to the other block, redo processing may cause a situation where not enough space is available to reinsert the moved tuples, because some preceding delete or undo-insert operations logged in a tuple fragment log are not reflected in the block. This problem is avoided in HypRa by merging only empty blocks.

14.3.3 The Tuple State-Identifier Policy and Redo Recovery

This section presents the consequences of applying the tuple state-identifier policy on redo recovery. A policy is presented that avoids unnecessary redo work caused by missing tuple state-identifiers of deleted tuples.

The tuple state-identifier policy connects state-identifiers to dynamic data objects (see section A.5). A consequence of this is that a tuple state-identifier is deleted with its tuple replica. If a single-level block state-identifier policy is used (see section 5.4.1), it can be determined whether operations to a tuple replica are reflected in a stable block replica independently of the existence of the tuple replica. If, on the other hand, the multi-level state-identifier policy is used, it cannot be determined from the tuple state-identifier if a tuple operation is reflected in the stable DB if the tuple replica does not exist, because the tuple state-identifier is deleted. This influences the redo recovery policy because it cannot be determined from the tuple state-identifiers alone if a tuple operation is reflected in the stable DB.

The *tuple operations semantics* can be used in addition to the tuple state-identifier value to determine if the effect of a tuple operation is reflected in the stable DB for non-existing tuple replicas ([HS90]). This is called the **semantics redo** policy. The complete redo recovery is assumed to be used, i.e. the redo tuple operations are executed to the same tuple replica state as the original do operation. An insert or undo-delete tuple operation will always precede a write, undo-write, delta, undo-delta, delete, or undo-insert tuple operation to a tuple replica with the same primary key value if no other delete or undo-insert operation occurs in between. If, therefore, an attempt is made to execute a redo-write, redo-undo-write, redo-delta, or a redo-undo-delta operation to a tuple replica and no tuple replica exists with the given primary key value, then some tuple operation following this operation must have deleted the tuple. It can therefore be concluded from the non-existence of the tuple replica that the effect of the tuple operation is already reflected in the stable DB and the operation does not need to be redone. If a redo-delete or an redo-undo-insert is executed and the tuple does not exist, the same conclusion can be drawn. The delete/insert policy prevents inconsistencies from being caused during redo recovery by tuples swapping primary key values (see section 11.3).

A **redo-insert** and a **redo-undo-delete** operation is executed only if the tuple replica with the given primary key value does not exist in the fragment replica. A redo-insert or redo-undo-delete is not executed if a tuple exists with the given primary key value. The existing tuple replica will then have a tuple state-identifier value that is equal to or greater than the log record identifier value of the redo operation.

A **redo-write**, **redo-delta**, **redo-undo-write**, or **redo-undo-delta** operation is executed if a tuple replica exists with the primary key value of the redo log record part and with a smaller tuple state-identifier value. If the tuple does not exist, the redo operation is not executed. This policy makes it possible to use the partial tuple logging policy because write and delta operations are redone and undone only to existing tuples.

A **redo-delete** and a **redo-undo-insert** is executed if a tuple replica with the given primary key value exists and it has a state-identifier value that is smaller than the log record identifier value of the redo operation. If a tuple replica exists with the same primary key value and a larger tuple state-identifier value, the operation has been executed and some later operation has created or recreated a tuple with the same primary key value. No tuple replica will exist with the same primary key value and the same tuple state-identifier value as the one the log record identifier of the redo operation is based on.

The execution of a redo-insert or a redo-undo-delete operation when a tuple replica with the same primary key does not exist, may cause unnecessary redo work. If a later delete or undo-insert is executed to the tuple, it will not have been necessary to redo the operation and the following operations for the tuple replica up to the delete or undo-insert. When the complete redo policy is applied, this type of unnecessary redo work cannot be avoided. The existence of a potential later delete or undo-insert operation is not known when the redo-insert or the redo-undo-delete is executed if no further analysis is done. If the single-level block state-identifier policy had been used, this unnecessary redo work would have been avoided, because the block state-identifiers would have indicated that the operations were reflected in the stable DB. The unnecessary redo work can also be avoided by using the redo compression policy (see section 14.3.4) in combination with log-aggregation.

14.3.4 The Redo Overflow Policies

This section focuses on policies to handle and avoid temporary overflow during tuple oriented redo recovery to a block. Because of the multi-level state-identifier policy and the log distribution strategy, redo processing to a block is not guaranteed to be executed in the same sequence as the original do operations. Temporary overflow may therefore occur during a complete redo recovery.

When the node internal log based recovery to a block is completed, sufficient space is available within the block to reflect the block state as it is after a complete redo processing, i.e. the main memory block state as when the node crash occurred (see section 14.3.2). The free space within the block, on the other hand, may not be sufficient to contain the tuples occurring during some intermediate stage of the tuple redo work. Complete and sequential redo recovery for a tuple fragment log may lead to **temporary overflows**, because it cannot be determined whether an insert or undo-delete operation has been executed for tuples missing during the redo processing (see section 14.3.3). Temporary overflows can not therefore be avoided by applying a sequential redo recovery policy. Temporary overflows can also occur if complete and sequential redo recovery is applied to each tuple and asynchronous redo recovery is applied between the tuples. Overflows may then occur for the same reason as when a complete and sequential redo recovery is applied. In addition, overflows can occur as a consequence of altered redo execution sequence resulting from the asynchronous redo processing between tuples. Tuples that would not exist concurrently within a block if a complete and sequential recovery is applied may, during an asynchronous recovery, temporary exist concurrently.

Temporary overflows would not occur if the complete redo recovery was executed to a block in the same sequence as the operations were originally executed, and all operations were reflected in the block state-identifier (see section 5.7). A possible policy to avoid temporary overflows would be to reflect the location and replication independent tuple operations in the block state-identifiers as well as in the tuple state-identifiers. This policy is not adopted by HypRa because it is only useful during a fast recovery of original primary fragment replicas. The block state-identifiers are of no use during a fast node crash recovery of an original hot stand-by fragment replica, because the hot stand-by tuple operations' block state-identifiers are not present in the primary tuple fragment log. The block state-identifiers are not useful during a non-blocking fragment replica production.

A possible policy to handle temporary overflow during redo fragment replica recovery is to allow block split/merge subtransactions to be activated during the redo processing. This is called the **redo-overflow** policy. The redo-overflow policy requires it to be possible to allocate blocks during the redo recovery. The block allocation server, i.e. the server controlling the block allocation internal fragments (see section 8.1), must therefore be available. If all primary node internal fragment replicas are redo recovered concurrently this requirement is not met, because the block allocation fragments are under recovery and therefore not available (see section 8.1). The primary disc-block allocation fragment replicas must therefore be recovered before all other fragment replicas to make the redo-overflow policy possible. The redo-overflow policy cannot be applied to the primary disc-block allocation fragment replicas. To avoid temporary overflow during redo recovery of the primary disc-block allocation fragments, dynamic tuple operations are not used for these fragment replicas after the initiation transaction that inserted all its containing tuples. These tuples are all of fixed size, and no state-changing tuple operations are executed to such fragments until after two checkpoints after their initiation.

Another policy to handle temporary overflow during redo primary fragment replica recovery is to allow overflowed blocks to be split in main memory. The disadvantage of this policy is that it may lead to main memory recovery overflow. Since it cannot be predicted which blocks will have to be temporarily split, a situation may occur where all blocks currently under recovery have to be split to be completely recovered, and no free block space exists. If some blocks are written back to disc, the block complete recovery policy is compromised (see section 7.6.4). The introduction of a separate overflow disc area would avoid compromising the block complete policy, but would introduce unnecessary disc accesses and wasted disc space.

An alternative temporary overflow handling policy is the **redo compression** policy. This policy compresses the redo log record parts in main memory, so that only one redo operation is executed per tuple during redo recovery. Redo-insert and redo-undo-delete tuple operations do not need to be executed if the tuple is later deleted. This redo operation produces the same tuple replica state as a complete redo recovery would have done, but without going through any intermediate states. The redo compression policy, in addition, uses synchronisation between the redo operations releasing space within a block and the redo operations requesting space from a block, so that the operations releasing space are executed before those requesting space. The synchronisation is within the scope of a block. Because of the use of partial logging, different operations may be the last operation to different fields of a tuple replica. A detailed presentation of the redo compression policy is given in section 14.3.5.

No tuple operations have been executed to the node internal fragments, with their primary replica located at the recovering node, after the node crash. Application of the redo compression policy will therefore produce block states that are equivalent to the block states before the node crash. Overflow is avoided during the redo processing of these fragment replicas. The disc-block allocation server is not needed.

The redo recovery of hot stand-by node internal fragment replicas, original primary tuple fragment replicas, and original hot stand-by tuple fragment replicas may include redo of operations originating from after the node crash. This is a consequence of the take-overs executed after the node crash. Redo recovery to such fragment replicas may therefore cause overflow even if the redo compression policy is applied. The redo compression policy will, on the other hand, restrict the overflow in these cases to only be caused by space required by the tuple operations originating after the node crash.

The main memory space required to aggregate the redo log record parts involved in a fast recovery is known when a fast recovery is executed. The log servers together with the checkpoint servers involved in the recovery knows the redo log volumes from the redo tables (see section 13.7 and figure 13.1) and the checkpoint tables (see section 13.8). The maximum main memory aggregation space required can therefore be calculated before the aggregation starts for each fragment replica involved. Main memory overflow during the aggregation can therefore normally be avoided, or in case enough main memory is not available to handle a single fragment replica, be planned for.

14.3.5 The Redo Compression Policy

The purpose of the redo compression policy is to avoid unnecessary block splits during a redo recovery caused by temporary block overflows.

The redo compression policy produces one redo operation per tuple requiring redo recovery. The produced redo operation is equivalent to the complete redo for the tuple replica. The redo compression policy executes the redo operations which release space within a block before those which request space to avoid overflow during redo processing to a block. When, therefore, the redo compression policy is applied to a block from which all redo operations originate before the node crash, temporary overflows to the block are avoided. The redo compression policy can also be combined with the selective redo policy so that the redo operations produced are equivalent to those under the selective redo policy (see section 7.9.2). Temporary overflows are avoided if the selective redo policy is combined with the ZSL undo-space-reserve policy, and no redo operations originating from after the node crash are involved in the redo recovery (see section 13.12).

The compression of redo log records can be done by scanning the tuple log sequences in either forward or reverse order. The compression can either be combined with the log-aggregation or be executed by a separate main memory log scan after the aggregation is done. Log records can be sent to a fast recovery server in either forward or reverse order. Since undo log record parts for tuple and internal fragment replicas with an available primary replica may have to be logged, and logging is done in increasing log record identifier value, all log records in HypRa are received in forward order (see section 14.3.8). The compression is therefore combined with the aggregation and done in forward order to obtain the main memory preserving effect of the selective aggregation policy (see section 7.9.3). Since logging is not done while aggregating the node internal log, the transaction log, and the primary internal fragment logs, these logs could have been sent and aggregated in reverse production order.

The compression is done on a per field basis since the partial tuple logging policy is assumed to be used (see section 7.3.3). The last operation executed to a field within a tuple replica may be different from the last operation executed to another field of the same tuple replica and therefore reflected in different log records. A tuple operation type is therefore required for each field in a compressed redo log record part. The log record identifier of the last log record is kept with each compressed redo log record. An operation type field is also kept with the compressed redo log record to reflect dynamic tuple operations. The primary key log vector policy is used by HypRa to obtain dictionary independence during redo and undo processing (see section 7.3.2). This vector is kept with the compressed redo log record.

The compression is based on the semantics of the tuple operations and is done in forward order (see also [HS90]). Fields may be added to the compressed redo log record but only one value is maintained per field. The following rules are used when producing the compressed redo log record part.

- If the operation type of the current log record is **delete** or **undo-insert**, set the operation type of the compressed redo log record to this operation type. Remove all fields outside the primary key, and set the field operation type of the primary key fields to NONE.
- If the operation type of the current log record is **insert** or **undo-delete**, set the operation type of the compressed redo log record to this operation type. Update fields, create fields when they do not exist, and set field operation types to the current operation type.
- If the operation type of the current log record is **write** or **undo-write**, keep the operation type of the compressed redo log record. Update all fields to which the operation is performed, create fields when they do not exist, and set the field operation type for the operated on fields to the current operation type.

- If the operation type of the current log record is **delta** or **undo-delta**, keep the operation type of the compressed redo log record. Calculate the new value for all existing fields to which this operation is active, and keep their original field operation types. Create new fields when they do not exist, update their value, and set their field operation types to the current operation type.

A compression policy can also be used to the undo log record parts. The primary argument for using the redo compression policy is its support of temporary block overflow avoidance to fragments where operations are not done after the node crash. An undo compression policy would not avoid overflows during undo processing. The undo operations are not previously executed, so blocks do not necessarily contain space for their results unless some undo-space-reserve policy is used. The undo-space-reserve policies reserve enough space for any sequence of undo processing. Overflows during undo processing are therefore avoided by the undo-space-reserve policies regardless of the use of any undo compression policy.

14.3.6 Recovery Based on the Node Internal Log

The primary node internal log of the recovering node is assumed to be lost (see section 13.10). The fast node crash recovery is therefore based on its hot stand-by node internal log. The location of the hot stand-by node internal log replica is known by the node restart supervisor ([HS90]).

An **update channel** is established between the hot stand-by node internal log replica server and the recovery server at the recovering node. The hot stand-by log is scanned in forward order starting from the penultimate checkpoint, and sent to the recovery server in forward order. All log records contained in this log originate from the recovering node and from before the node crash. The recovery server aggregates the node internal log records per block identifier. The aggregation is done at the recovering node by the recovery server to minimise the added work load at the sender during a node crash recovery. The block log sequence is maintained per block. Selective aggregation is not applied because of the low volume of log records involved. It is therefore assumed that no significant work load and speed up is obtained by selective aggregation. Because of the short duration of node internal transactions, all log records for the active node internal transactions have been aggregated when the log records produced after the penultimate checkpoint are aggregated. It is therefore never necessary to scan the log prior to the penultimate checkpoint in order to obtain log records to terminate a node internal transaction.

The block flush- and dirty block log records produced after the penultimate checkpoint are also aggregated per block identifier in a separate log sequence (see section 13.8). The **potentially-inconsistent** block set is formed. It contains the blocks for which a start-BFR log record is produced but no matching commit-BFR is produced, i.e. the blocks where a flush operation was in progress when the node crash occurred. The **dirty-block** set is also formed, containing the blocks for which a dirty-block log record has been produced after the penultimate checkpoint and no later committed block flush is done. The **recovery-block** set is also formed, containing the blocks for which a dirty-block log record is produced after the penultimate checkpoint.

The primary **transaction log** located at the recovering node and its log records produced after the penultimate checkpoint are also assumed to be lost as well as parts of the log between the third last and the penultimate checkpoint. An update channel is established between the hot stand-by transaction log replica server and the transaction log recovery server, as for the node internal log. The last stably stored log record can be determined from the hot stand-by block flush log records and the checkpoint table (see section 14.3.7). The log records after this point in the hot stand-by transaction log is transmitted to determine the status of the node internal transactions to be recovered. Sufficient main memory is assumed to be available at the node to aggregate the node internal log and the transaction log.

AM locks are set on the blocks in the recovery-block set because they may require node internal recovery. Both node internal redo and undo are restricted to this set of blocks because of the short duration of internal transactions. An AM lock is released when the node internal recovery is completed for a block. An **internal-aggregation** lock is kept while the node internal log and the transaction log are being aggregated.

The node internal recovery can be started when the internal-aggregation lock is released. The **internal-first** policy is used if the node internal recovery is completed to a fragment replica before the tuple fragment log recovery is started. To obtain block complete recovery for a block, the recovery initiated at this stage should include only blocks requiring block aggregated recovery. The recovery of *higher level access method blocks* (see section 7.5.1) and *log table blocks* (see section 13.9) can therefore be started, because no tuple fragment log based recovery will be done to these blocks (see figure 14.2). The recovery-type fields of the block flush log records and dirty block log records are used to determine which blocks are in this category (see section 13.8). The recovery will be done asynchronously between the involved blocks.

The consistency of the blocks in the potentially-inconsistent set is tested before any other recovery work is executed to the block. If the content of a *log table block* is corrupted, the log records within the primary key interval, which corresponds to the log record identifier interval, contained in the block are requested from the current primary log server. The set of log records received is the same as the set of those lost, because no state changing operations are done to a log record after it is produced. Overflow will therefore not occur. The border-, link-, and block state-identifier values of the block are set to the values contained in the block flush log record. No subtransactions are active to such a block because the flush operation sets a read AM lock. No redo is required because the block state-identifier value is set to the last operation before the crash occurred.

If the content of a higher level access method block is inconsistent, the internal-first policy is used for the fragment replica of the index block to reproduce an action consistent access method. When the node internal log based recovery is completed for the fragment, the block with the block identifier included in the block flush log record and pointing to the leftmost block in the next level of the access method is read, and an index-tuple is inserted into the index block under repair for this block (see section 13.8). The link pointer is followed from this block, and index-tuples are inserted until the upper border of the block is equal to or larger than the upper border in the block flush log record. If another inconsistent block is included in the set of blocks attempted to be read to reproduce a consistent block, the fast recovery of the fragment replica has failed. The fragment is repaired by online non-blocking replication.

14.3.7 Recovery of Primary Internal Fragment Replicas

The primary internal fragment log replicas located at a node performing fast recovery from a node crash are assumed to be lost. A node crash has the same effect on the primary internal fragment log replicas as on the primary node internal log replica (see section 14.3.6). A fast node recovery is therefore based on the hot stand-by node internal fragment replicas. The restart supervisor knows the location of these hot stand-by replicas. Recovery of the primary node internal fragments may involve both block aggregated redo and undo work and tuple aggregated redo and undo work, but the recovery is restricted to the blocks in the recovery-block set (see figure 14.2).

No log records have entered the hot stand-by internal fragment logs after the node crash. Only log records produced by node internal transactions at the recovering node are logged in the node internal fragment log replicas. Because of the short duration of the internal transactions, the log records produced after the penultimate checkpoint contain all log records involved in the recovery of a primary internal fragment replica (see section 14.3.6). The recovery of the log tables is therefore not required to be synchronised with the recovery of the node internal fragments.

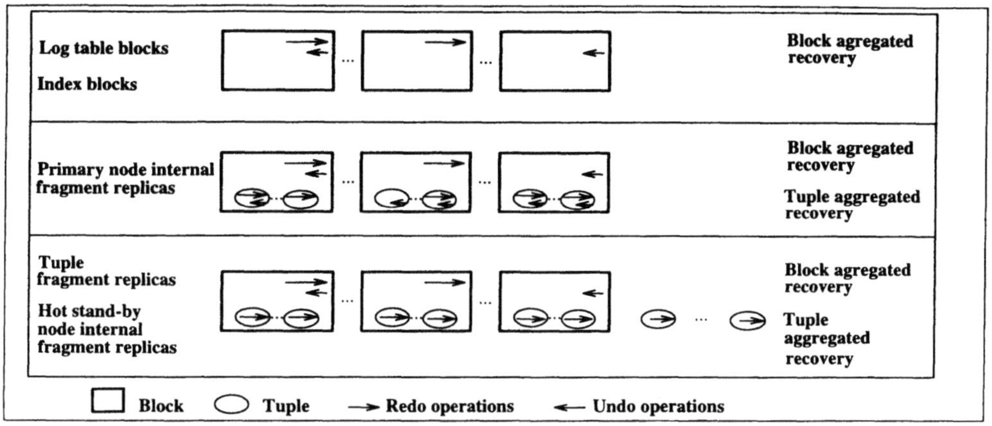

Figure 14.2: Fast recovery involves only block aggregated recovery to higher level access method blocks (index blocks) and log table blocks. Both block aggregated recovery and tuple aggregated recovery may be required for the primary node internal fragment blocks, but block identifier based access is used for all tuples requiring recovery. Both block aggregated redo and undo recovery and tuple aggregated redo recovery may be required for tuple- and hot stand-by node internal fragments. These fragment replicas may also involve the recovery of tuples in which the primary based access methods are used to access the tuples.

An update channel is established from each of the involved hot stand-by internal fragment servers to the recovery server. The log records are sent in forward order for each internal fragment log. The log records are aggregated per internal fragment and per tuple within an internal fragment so that the tuple log sequence is kept for each tuple. The redo compression policy is applied (see sections 14.3.4 and 14.3.5). The selective aggregation policy is not used because of the short duration of the internal transactions (see also section 14.3.6). The aggregation is done concurrently with the aggregation of the node internal log and the transaction log, and it is assumed that sufficient main memory is available to aggregate these logs in addition to the node internal log and the transaction log.

Since only operations originating from before the node crash are involved in the recovery, overflows do not occur during redo recovery of a block. Since the ZSL undo-space-reserve policy is used for primary internal fragment replicas, overflows are also prevented during undo recovery of a block (see section 13.12). The block allocation server is therefore not required to be available during the recovery of a primary internal fragment replica. The compensated non-CLRs are marked during the log aggregation, as CLRs are aggregated. No temporary tables are required to maintain this information (see sections 14.2.1 and 14.2.4).

A tuple redo or undo operation to a tuple contained in a block in the recovery-block set will not use the primary key based access methods but rather the block identifier in order to access the block (see figure 14.2). All the tuples requiring redo or undo recovery are contained within the recovery-block set because of the short duration of the internal transactions. The access methods are therefore not used during the tuple aggregated recovery. The recovery of the node internal fragments can therefore be done regardless of whether their access methods are action consistent.

Since neither action consistent access methods nor an available block allocation server is required when performing the recovery of the primary internal fragment replicas, the recovery can start when the internal-aggregation lock is released (see section 14.3.6). The internal-distributed recovery policy is applied to each block (see section 14.3.1). The AM locks are used to synchronise between the block aggregated and the tuple aggregated recovery to a block (see figure 14.2). The tuple aggregated recovery is not allowed to start before the AM lock is removed from the block.

When an internal fragment log has been sent to the recovery server, the update channel is reversed so that log records are sent from the primary internal fragment log server to the corresponding hot stand-by internal fragment log server. The CLRs produced when compensating for the effects of the internal transactions that were active when the node crashed are logged in the primary internal fragment log at the recovering node and sent to the hot stand-by internal fragment log server, as during normal operations.

A block containing primary replicas of node internal tuples can be in the process of flushing when a node crash occurs. If the block becomes inconsistent because the flush operation was not completed before the node crash, a replica of the tuples limited by the border values of the block is requested from the hot stand-by fragment replica server. The border values are part of the block flush log record (see section 13.8). The state of the tuple replicas received must not precede the aggregated redo log record parts to these tuples. If they do, some operation which is required to be redone could be missing and the redo would produce an inconsistent DB. To avoid such situations, the hot stand-by internal fragment replica server is required to execute the deferred operations before a replica of the requested tuples is produced and sent (see section 13.10). No operations are therefore missing and no redo is required to be done to these tuples. Undo may, on the other hand, be required.

14.3.8 Recovery of Tuple Fragment Replicas and Hot Stand-By Node Internal Fragment Replicas

The parts of the tuple fragment log and the hot stand-by node internal log kept in main memory when a node crashes are lost at the fast node crash recovery which follows. These log replicas may therefore have lost all log record replicas newer than the fourth-last checkpoint before the node crash (see section 13.9). All the tuple fragment replicas and hot stand-by internal fragment replicas undergoing fast recovery have an available primary fragment replica. Take-over has been executed to all the original primary tuple fragment replicas. DB state changing tuple operations may therefore have been executed after the crash to these tuple fragments. State changing tuple operations may also have been executed to the node internal fragment replicas after the node crash because their primary replicas were available. The current primary fragment replicas are all located at the same node, which is a result of the fragment replication and allocation policy (see sections 10.6 and 10.7). This is illustrated in figure 14.3, where node 2 performs a fast recovery. All the available current primary replicas are located at node 6. After a fragment replica is recovered, hot stand-by take-over is executed to the fragment replica to reestablish the original availability fault-tolerance level (see section 14.3.9).

Log records are sent the recovering fragment replicas in forward order. Log records older than the penultimate checkpoint do not need to be redone because they are already reflected in the stable DB and therefore do not need to be aggregated. Undo log record parts newer than the last stably stored log record at the recovering node for the fragment and belonging to non-terminated transactions must be logged so that the recovering fragment replica can later take over as a primary replica and complete the roll back of these transactions in case the current fragment replica should fail before these transactions are terminated.

A new replica of the **transaction table** is produced at the recovering node. This production is performed concurrently with the aggregation of the primary node internal log. An online non-blocking replication is done to the transaction table at the node in which the current primary replicas are located. A new replica of the **checkpoint table** is also formed at the recovering node by non-blocking production based on the checkpoint table at the node containing the primary replicas of

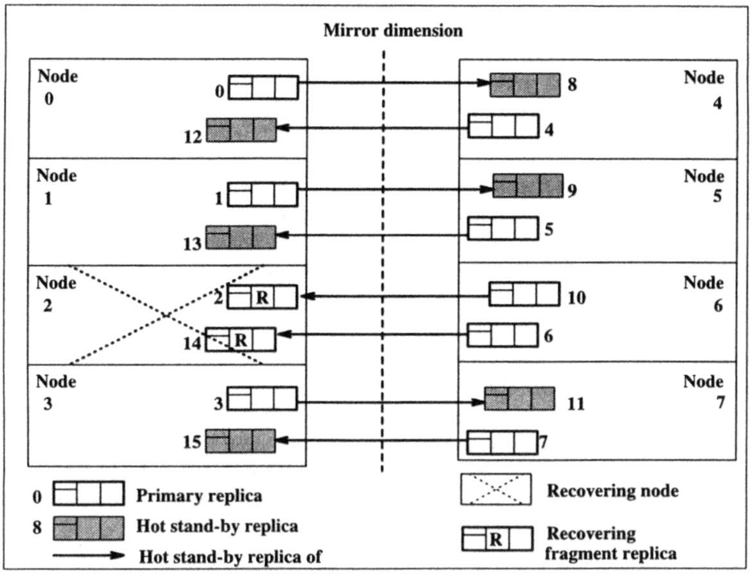

Figure 14.3: Node 2 has crashed and performs a fast node crash recovery. All the current primary fragment replicas for the replicas under recovery are located at node 6. See section 10.6 for a description of the fragmentation and allocation.

the fragments being recovered. If the aggregation of a tuple fragment replica or a hot stand-by node internal fragment replica is started before the transaction table is completed produced, all undo log record parts received are logged. If the aggregation starts before the checkpoint table is produced, all redo log record parts received are aggregated.

An update channel is established for each fragment replica to be recovered. The log records are sent in forward order for each fragment log replica, starting from the first potentially missing log record. This log position can be determined from the block flush log records and the checkpoint table at the node containing the primary replicas and is determined as part of the dynamic replication to preserve the consistent DB state required fault-tolerance level (see section 13.10). The sending of log record replicas can be done concurrently with the aggregation of the node internal log, the transaction log, and the primary internal fragment replica logs, depending on the main memory available. The aggregation starts from the penultimate checkpoint, or if the checkpoint table is under production, from the first log record received by the recovery server. The log records are aggregated per fragment and within a fragment per tuple so that the tuple log sequence is kept for each tuple (see also section 14.3.7). Log records are sent and aggregated until catch-up is reached. When catch-up is reached, the recovery of the fragment replica starts.

Tuple fragment replicas and hot stand-by node internal fragment replicas will usually require block aggregated redo and undo recovery and tuple aggregated redo recovery. Since all these fragment replicas have an available primary fragment replica, the CLRs which compensate for failed transactions are produced by the primary fragment replica servers. Therefore, no tuple aggregated undo work is involved. The block complete policy is used with the internal-distributed policy to each block that requires recovery. The redo-overflow policy is used, which requires the block allocation server to be available during the recovery of a fragment replica. The alternative use of the redo compression policy would also require the block allocation server to be available because operations executed after the crash are involved in the recovery. If the recovery processing is allowed to start before the block allocation server is available, the recovery of some blocks might wait for a split, which could possibly lead to main memory overflow. Tuple redo may affect blocks not in the recovery-block set because operations are executed after the node crash as a consequence of the take-over following the node crash. Because AM locks are used to the blocks requiring block aggregated recovery, the redo processing to these tuples can be done asynchronously with the recovery to the blocks in the recovery-set.

The number of tuple fragment replicas and hot stand-by node internal fragment replicas concurrently under recovery can be restricted by the recovery server so that overflow does not occur during log aggregation. This policy is based on the redo log record volume kept in the redo table (see section 13.7) and maintained in the checkpoint table at the node the primary fragment replicas are located (see section 13.8). This policy is used to provide fast selective fragment replica recovery and can be combined with a fragment recovery priority policy. A fragment replica may require more log aggregation main memory than is available at the recovering node. An overflow policy, as in hash-based algebra operations when a table is too large to be completely stored in main memory, can be developed to handle such situations (see [Bra84], [DG85]). One primary key interval of the fragment replica can be recovered at a time to maintain the block complete recovery and thereby avoid re-reading a block. The overflow log records are temporarily stored on disc at the recovering node. This requires the block allocation server to be available during the log aggregation of such fragment replicas.

Logging of undo log record parts of non-terminated transactions is done for all tuple fragment replicas and hot stand-by node internal fragment replicas during the log aggregation. Logging is also done when compensating node internal transactions which were active at the node crash and during the following normal operations are logged in the node internal log and the primary node internal fragment logs. To avoid log overflow during the fast recovery, checkpointing is done. Checkpointing starts when the internal-aggregation lock is released. Checkpoints are executed to the primary node internal log replica and the primary internal fragment log replicas as during normal operations. If another crash occurs before the recovery based on the node internal log is completed, the hot stand-by node internal log will be added to the already stably stored hot stand-by node internal log replicas. The same is done for the hot stand-by node internal fragment log replicas produced during such a failed fast recovery. When all the node internal based recovery is completed the stable hot stand-by node internal log replicas are removed. This might be at the very end of the fast recovery because block complete recovery is used. The stable hot stand-by node internal fragment log replicas are removed after the second checkpoint because the effect of all redone and undone internal transactions executed before the node crash is then reflected in the stable DB. This is again an effect of the short duration of the node internal transactions.

The checkpoints, for tuple fragment log replicas and hot stand-by node internal fragment log replicas under recovery, are used to move undo log record parts of non-terminated transactions to disc. It is assumed that undo log records stay in main memory for two checkpoint intervals during the recovery before being evaluated to be written to stable storage (see section 13.8). The recovery of the log table for a fragment replica must therefore provide action consistent access to the most significant log table block at the second checkpoint for those fragment replicas starting to recover when the internal-aggregation lock is released. If the log table is not recovered, the log aggregation for the fragment replica is halted by not acknowledging log record replicas sent across the update channel, until the log table is recovered. This checkpointing policy will not introduce inconsistencies, because the complete redo log is kept by the primary fragment replicas until the fast recovery is completed. If another node crash occurs before a fragment replica is completely recovered a possible following fast node crash recovery will restart from the same log position. Which undo log records are stably stored can be determined from the block flush log records so that, during a following fast recovery, these undo log record parts do not need to be resent. When a fragment replica completes its recovery and the last of the blocks involved in the recovery are acknowledged to be flushed, the primary fragment server is informed. The stable hot stand-by log replicas used to perform the recovery are then removed.

A block containing tuple replicas can be in the process of flushing when a node crash occurs. If the block becomes inconsistent because the flush operation was not completed before the node crash, a replica of the tuples within the border values of the block is requested from the current primary fragment replica server. The border values are part of the block flush log record. A fuzzy replica of the primary replica of these tuples are produced. The state of the tuple replicas received may cause the block to be split. The splitting is done by a split/merge subtransactions. Redo recovery may be required to these tuples, since all tuple operations are not necessarily reflected in them.

14.3.9 The Hot Stand-By Take-Over Policy

A hot stand-by take-over recovery makes a recovering fragment replica catch-up with its primary replica so that it can take over as primary replica if the current primary replica fails. The execution to the fragment replica must not lag further behind the primary than is acceptable for a hot stand-by relative to a primary fragment replica before the hot stand-by take-over is done (see section 13.5). If a hot stand-by lock policy is applied (see section 14.1), the current lock set must have been established before the hot stand-by take-over is completed. No transaction abortion is involved when executing a hot stand-by take-over.

The hot stand-by take-over recovery applies sequential recovery to a fragment replica to catch-up the remaining redo operations which originated while a non-sequential fast recovery execution was under way. The hot stand-by take-over recovery can be started when the fast recovery is completed to a fragment replica. The fast recovery can also be executed concurrently with the hot stand-by take-over recovery, if the fast recovery uses locks on those tuples which require recovery. It cannot start before the log aggregation for the fragment replica is completed, because the locks must already have been established. The hot stand-by take-over recovery is halted when it encounters a locked tuple or block and is first restarted when the non-sequential recovery is completed to the block or tuple, and the lock removed. If the redo recovery work load for a fragment replica is small, only a hot stand-by take-over recovery is applied to the fragment replica.

Concurrently with the sequential catch-up processing, a non-blocking fuzzy snapshot of the locks on a fragment is sent to the hot stand-by fragment. The fuzzy lock replication can be done concurrently with the non-sequential fast recovery processing, and locking information can be tagged to the log records for the fragment.

HypRa allows catch-up processing to be done concurrently with the non-sequential fast recovery processing. Locking information is included in the log records. The tuple aggregation structure is organised like the tuple locking structure to make it serve as tuple locks during the fast recovery.

14.4 Conclusion

This chapter presented the HypRa recovery strategies which are based on the non-sequential recovery strategy introduced in chapter 7 combined with the LRI strategy (see chapter 11), the log distribution strategy (see chapter 12.1), and the nWAL strategy (see chapter 13.2). A main goal of the chapter was to provide very fast take-over recovery, fast transaction recovery and fast node crash recovery strategies to maintain the soft real-time transaction service availability across transaction, fragment replica, and node failures. Another main goal was to provide stable main memory logging to avoid disc accesses as part of the commit processing which must be avoided to support soft real-time transaction services.

The HypRa recovery approach (Part III) provides the foundation for non-blocking fragment replication with subfragmentation. The LRI strategy provides redo and undo tuple recovery that are location- and tuple replica independent so that recovery can be applied to other replicas of a tuple located at another node than the tuple the original log record was produced to. The log distribution strategy supports distribution and replication of logs which are required to support subfragmentation. The non-blocking fragment replication strategy is presented in [HST+91b], see also section 10.6 and 10.7.

The HypRa recovery approach does also provides the foundation for online non-blocking maintenance strategies which preserves the transaction service availability during maintenance. The novel methods for online non-blocking DB maintenance presented in [HST+91b] are founded on the strategies presented in the HypRa recovery approach. So are also the novel online non-blocking SW and HW maintenance methods presented in [HST+91b].

Exercises

1. (a) What is the effect of applying the hot stand-by lock policy on a primary take-over? (b) When can locking information be deduced from the tuple log records? (c) When do read locks need to be reflected in the hot stand-by locks?

2. (a) How can disc I/O be avoided during a primary take-over? (b) Are there any advantages in using the no-redo policy in combination with a main memory database?

3. Massive transaction aborts as a consequence of a take-over are a threat to availability. (a) How can savepoints be used to avoid aborting a TPC-B transaction hit by a take-over? (b) How could aborting of transactions with local data-like cursors be avoided when they are hit by a take-over?

4. Propose a roll forward scheme for transactions hit by a primary take-over.

5. (a) Must redo based on the node internal log be done in forward or reverse order? (b) To which granularity is the redo order connected? (c) Must undo based on the node internal log be done in forward or reverse order?

6. (a) Must redo based on a tuple fragment log be done in forward or reverse order? (b) To which granularity is the redo order connected? (c) Must undo based on a tuple fragment log be done in forward or reverse order?

7. Why should the internal-distributed policy be followed?

8. (a) If a block split operation is not reflected in a block, why are tuple operations executed after the block split not reflected in the block? (b) Why do update tuple operations represent no problem during non-sequential redo recovery work to a block?

9. Propose a method to handle non-sequential redo recovery to blocks when block merge operations are allowed to non-empty blocks.

10. (a) Would it be possible to reflect tuple operations in the block state-identifiers in addition to in the tuple state-identifiers? (b) Would this avoid the problems of redoing already reflected operations?

11. What are the effects on the fast node crash strategy of applying an extent based allocation method as compared to a free-block bit mask based method? (For an introduction to extent based allocation see [GR92].)

Answers

1. (a) The no-undo policy can be applied. (b) The locking granularity can be no coarser than a tuple. Range locks, for examples, cannot be applied. (c) If the active transactions involved in a take-over are not to be aborted, the read locks need to be reflected in the hot stand-by locks.

2. (a) By applying the no-redo policy. (b) The redo operations are executed outside the time critical part of a take-over.

3. (a) Make the transaction compiler introduce hidden savepoints in the transaction code. In case of a take-over, roll back to the next savepoint and roll forward from there. (b) Reflect the local transaction data at both the primary and hot stand-by transaction slaves. Use update channels to synchronise the primary and the hot stand-by transaction local data replicas.

4. Introduce one operation identifier for each tuple operation in the transaction code. An operation identifier is unique within a transaction. Reflect the operation identifiers in the tuple log records. Mark which operations have been received on the hot stand-by side based on the operation identifiers. In case of a primary take-over, the hot stand-by slaves could, based on this information, determine exactly which operations are received and which they have to execute to complete the transaction.

5. (a) Forward order. (b) Block. (c) Reverse order.

6. (a) Forward order. (b) Tuple. (c) Reverse order.

7. To provide tuple-based recovery actions with action consistent blocks.

8. (a) If any of the tuple operations had been reflected, the block split operation would also have been reflected. (b) Update operations do not produce tuples or remove them from the block.

9. Do a merge operation if the involved tuples fit into one block. If they do not fit into one block, postpone the merge operation until after the tuple operations to the involved primary key interval have been completed. None of the involved blocks may be written back to disc before both the tuple operations and the block operations have been completed.

10. (a) A tuple operation can be reflected both in the tuple and in the block state-identifier. The block state-identifier value is kept in the corresponding tuple log record at the node, but is removed in the log record sent across to another node. The specific block state-identifier value at the hot stand-by side is included in the log record stored at that node. (b) Yes, because the block state-identifier can be used to determine if the operation has been executed.

11. Recover the access method based on the node internal log. Perform the tuple based recovery from the tuple log. No new block splits may take place before the recovery is completed.

Part IV

Other High Availability DBMS Approaches

Chapter 15

High Availability Approaches

The following chapters present and compare existing high availability approaches, primarily taken from commercial systems. The presentation will use the terminology already established.

The presentation will primarily be restricted to high availability approaches included in or integrated with DBMSs. Solutions based on, for example, transaction processing monitors, ([EMS91], [Enc93], [Mac91]), reliable transaction routing ([DEC93a], [DEC93b]), operating system services ([BBG+89], [SKW92]), and application integrated solutions have therefore been left out (see also [GR92]). We have also restricted the presentation and comparison to approaches that either provide order preserving transaction execution or provide equivalence preserving transaction processing at the hot stand-bys. An *order preserving* solution executes transactions at a hot stand-by in the same order as at the primary. An *equivalence preserving* execution may alter the transaction execution order at the hot stand-by but in such a way that the result is equivalent to an order preserving execution.

We will, in the following sections, discuss some of the most influential strategies when evaluating a hot stand-by approach. The first strategy chooses between the use of symmetric or asymmetric synchronisation protocols between the primary and the hot stand-bys. The second strategy determines which DBMS layer and server an asymmetric synchronisation protocol should be built into. The third strategy chooses between the 2-Safe or the 1-Safe consistency preservation policy.

15.1 The Symmetric Synchronisation Strategy

A synchronisation protocol is symmetric if all participating slave-transactions (see section 10.2) are treated equally. A traditional distributed database two-phase commit protocol is a symmetric synchronisation protocol. An asymmetric synchronisation protocol, on the other hand, assigns different roles to the participating slave-transactions. A primary/hot stand-by approach is therefore asymmetric.

A symmetric two-phase commit policy may have some deficiencies compared to an asymmetric primary/hot stand-by policy in a replicated data environment. One possible deficiency is that it may introduce a *higher percentage of aborted transactions caused by deadlocks*. The deadlocks are caused by competing update operations to hot spot tuples arriving in different sequences at different nodes. A symmetric transaction will launch update operations to all replicas of a tuple in parallel. Closely launched update operations by different transactions destined for the same tuple may be scheduled in different order to the different replicas of the tuple because, for example, the communication delay for different update messages varies. The probability of this type of hot spot deadlocks will increase with larger numbers of replicas. These deadlocks will not occur with an asymmetric synchronisation protocol. The scheduling is then done only to the primary replica.

The communication protocol between the primary and the hot stand-bys ensures that the same schedule is enforced to the hot stand-by replicas as to the primary. Since the scheduling is the same, deadlocks are avoided.

Another potential deficiency with the symmetric two-phase commit policy is that it may introduce *long transaction latencies.* Long transaction latencies occur when there are long distances between the sites involved in a transaction. To obtain a high level of independence between replicas, they may be located far apart. Since a symmetric two-phase commit transaction accesses both replicas in the time critical path of the transaction, messages must cross the distance between the primary and hot stand-by replicas at least twice in the time critical execution path. This deficiency is also inherent in an asymmetric primary/hot stand-by 2-safe policy, since the distance between the sites must be crossed at least twice inside the time critical path of a transaction. The deficiency is avoided if a 1-Safe policy is used, but only as long as the primary replica is local to the client. If the primary replica is remote, the 1-Safe policy would give a similar delay.

Even though none of the evaluated high availability approaches are based on the symmetric two-phase commit policy, it is possible to support high availability in combination with the two-phase commit protocol. The strategy cannot be based on a state-identifier policy if it is combined with a semantically rich locking model. In this case, a state-identifier may not uniquely reflect the sequence of operations executed to multiple replicas of a tuple, because delta operations may have been executed in different sequence to different replicas. Catch-up of a crashed node and repair policies cannot therefore rely on state-identifiers.

The following describes a primary take-over, catch-up, and non-blocking self-repair policy which does not rely on state-identifiers and which can be combined with the symmetric two-phase commit policy. During a primary take-over, all active transactions that have performed state changing operations to the affected data and which are not in the prepare-to-commit state are aborted. Tuple locking is assumed to be used. Since locking is done to all tuple replicas, new transactions reflecting the new set of available fragment replicas can execute in parallel with this undo processing. Catch-up and repair of the failed fragments is assumed to be log based. An asymmetry is therefore introduced which will last either until the failed fragment replicas have caught up or until new replicas have been produced by a repair activity. During later recovery of the failed fragment replicas, a redo-undo recovery is executed. For the transactions that were in the in-doubt state when the replicas became unavailable, the transaction coordinator must be contacted to decide the outcome of the transaction. Those of the in-doubt transactions that are to be aborted can be included in the undo recovery, or separate undos can be executed. After the undo-redo recovery is completed, the catch-up processing can be done by applying the produced log. When the replicas have caught up, a combined primary and hot stand-by take-over can be executed by aborting the ongoing transactions to the involved fragments again before they are all opened to normal symmetric two-phase commit processing.

The production of a new replica of a fragment as part of a non-blocking self-repair can be done by scanning a replica of the fragment in either ascending or descending primary key order. A copy of each tuple is produced and sent to the replica under production. Tuple operations that are executed to that part of the fragment whose primary key value has already been scanned are logged in a side-log and sent in execution order to the replica under production and executed. These tuple operations are not already reflected in the new replica. The tuple operations that are hitting tuples in the primary key range that is to be copied will, as part of the copying, be reflected in the new replica. They are therefore not included in the side-log and shipped.

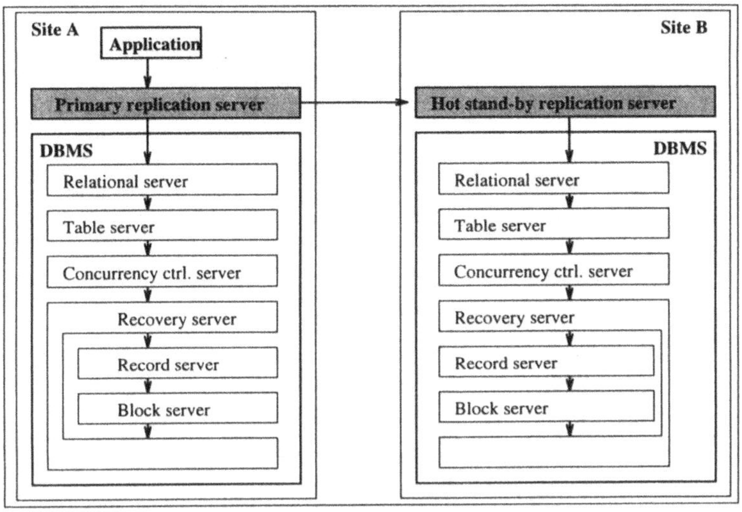

Figure 15.1: The gateway external synchronization policy (G-EXS). The G-EXS policy is combined with the record oriented DBMS server architecture, presented in figure 5.1, and an asymmetric configuration policy. The G-EXS policy can also be combined with any of the other DBMS server arhitectures. The asymmetric replication configuration includes two sites, where one site is the primary and the other site is the hot stand-by. All applications enter a DBMS server through a replication server.

15.2 The Asymmetric Synchronisation Strategy

This section assumes that the asymmetric synchronisation strategy based on a primary/hot stand-by policy is applied. Three different policies for synchronising primaries and hot stand-bys are analyzed. The first policy handles the synchronisation outside the DBMS. This policy is termed the *external synchronisation* (**EXS**) policy. In the second policy synchronisation relies on locking information from the primary. This policy is termed the *locking based synchronisation* (**LCS**) policy. The third policy is based on the log produced by the primary. This policy is termed the *log based synchronisation* (**LGS**) policy.

15.2.1 External Synchronisation Policies

An **EXS** policy is typically used in approaches demanding a low to medium rate of transactions per second, combined with high availability and medium to long response times. Two EXS policies are presented. The *gateway-EXS* (**G-EXS**) policy locates replication synchronisation in a gateway server between clients and the DBMS server. The *trigger-EXS* (**T-EXS**) policy uses a DBMS trigger mechanism to produce replication synchronisation information. The T-EXS policy is used by the Oracle7 Symmetric Replication Facility (see section 17.3) and the CA-OpenIngres/Replicator (see section 17.5) products. An EXS policy can be combined with both a 2-Safe and a 1-Safe transaction execution policy. It is assumed in this section that a 1-Safe policy is used.

The G-EXS policy handles the primary/hot stand-by synchronisation entirely outside the DBMSs. The G-EXS policy is illustrated in figure 15.1. The synchronisation is handled by *replication gateways* located between a DBMS and its applications. The synchronisation information can only

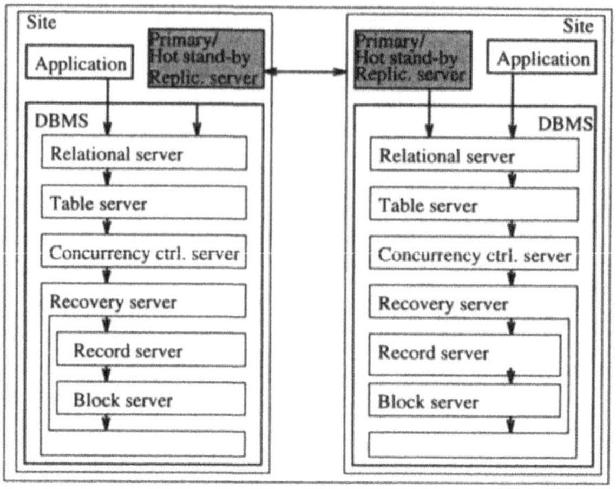

Figure 15.2: The trigger based external synchronisation policy (T-EXS). The T-EXS policy is combined with the record oriented DBMS server architecture (see also figure 15.1) and a symmetric replication configuration policy. Two sites each handle both primary- and hot stand-by replicas of data.

be expressed in terms of transaction operations and the relational datamodel operations since any internal DBMS layers are unreachable. The replication gateways are responsible for executing transactions in the same order at the hot stand-bys as at the primaries.

The replication gateway to which the application requesting the transaction execution is connected, produces a log of the relational operations executed in the transaction. The log reflects the execution sequence of the relational operations. The transaction is given a global transaction identifier which reflects its commit sequence position. The transactions are then executed to the hot stand-by replicas according to their commit sequence for the primary replicas. A simple method to provide transaction sequence numbers is to use a database tuple which manages the global transaction number to be assigned the next transaction. This tuple is read and incremented by every transaction. This introduces a sequential commit processing since every transaction exclusively locks this tuple. To minimise the locking period of the tuple, the replication gateways read and update it at the end of the transaction execution to the primary replicas. Some DBMSs provide sequencer objects which avoid exclusive locking when generating transaction identifiers ([BCFea95]). The equivalent of sequence objects can also be included in the replication gateway by caching a range of transaction identifiers and not using cached values after recovering from a replication gateway crash.

A 1-Safe transaction execution policy can use a symmetric two-phase commit policy to obtain atomic distribution of the relevant operation log parts for a transaction to the hot stand-bys involved in it. Each replication gateway is responsible for executing the hot stand-by operations belonging to a transaction in the proper transaction execution order. A simple method for obtaining the correct execution order for hot stand-by transaction parts is for the replication server to execute the hot stand-by transactions parts strictly sequentially. As an alternative to a 2-Safe shipping policy a 2-Safe policy can be used to include both shipping and execution of deferred transaction parts.

During a primary take-over, a replication gateway server must ensure that all committed and deferred hot stand-by transaction parts have set their locks before the replicas are opened as primaries. The remaining take-over processing can be done after the replicas have become primaries. This includes executing the deferred committed hot stand-by transaction parts, aborting all active hot stand-by transaction parts, and handling all in-doubt hot stand-by transaction parts.

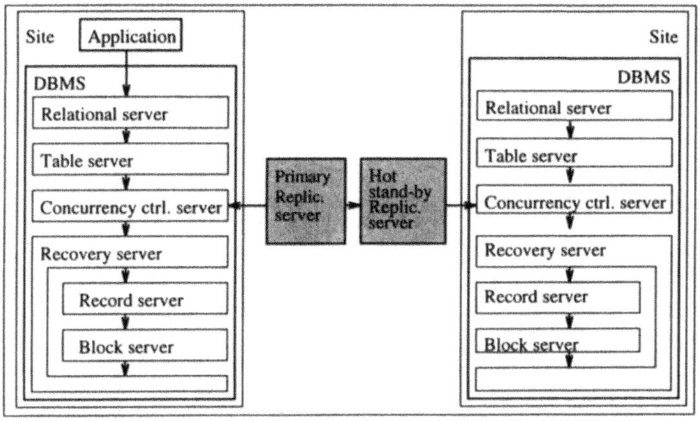

Figure 15.3: The locking based synchronisation policy (LCS). The LCS policy is combined with the compensation oriented DBMS server policy, presented in figure 6.1, and an asymmetric replication configuration policy with one primary site and one hot stand-by site. The LCS policy can also be combined with other DBMS server policies, the symmetric replication synchronisation policy, and multiple sites.

Restarting of some failed replicas will involve a local DBMS recovery followed by a catch-up. A possible non-blocking repair policy could be similar to the repair policy presented in section 15.1 for a symmetric strategy. The only relational operations required to be used this policy would be single tuple operations based on primary key access. Another option is a blocking repair policy.

A T-EXS policy will use DBMS triggers related to the execution of tuple operations to generate a primary transaction log for the executed transactions. The T-EXS policy is illustrated in figure 15.2. This log is kept in dedicated tables and reflects tuple operations. Distribution servers will read these tables and perform 2-Safe shipping of relevant log records to replication servers where the hot stand-by replicas are located. These replication servers are responsible for atomic execution of the transaction parts. The 2-Safe policy may, as an alternative, include both the shipping and the deferred execution take-over, catch-up, and repair can be handled similar to the G-EXS policy.

15.2.2 The Locking Based Synchronisation Policy

The **LCS** policy uses scheduling information from the DBMS lock manager relating to primary fragment replicas as the basis for the primary/hot stand-by synchronisation. The policy has been evaluated as a candidate, but it is not used by any of the products presented in chapter 16 and 17. The LCS policy is illustrated in figure 15.3.

Locking must be done at the same DBMS layer by all involved DBMSs, and the locking granularity of the involved DBMSs must be the same. A replica of a primary operation is sent to the sites with corresponding hot stand-by fragment replicas as soon as the operation has entered its lock(s) into the lock manager. The communication protocol which transmits the operations to the hot stand-bys must keep the sequence of the operations so that the locks can be set in the same sequence at the hot stand-bys. If delta operations to the same locked unit are allowed to bypass each other, a state-identifier policy cannot be used as the basis for take-back and non-blocking repair. A policy similar to the one proposed in section 15.1 can then be used. If bypass is not allowed, a state-identifier based approach can be used.

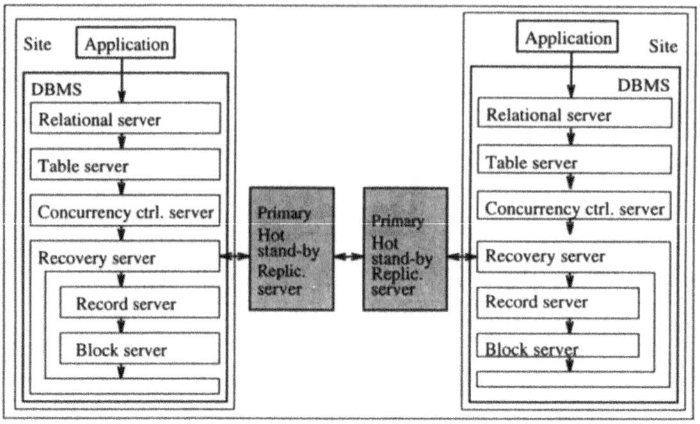

Figure 15.4: The log based synchronisation policy (LGS). The LGS policy is combined with the compensation oriented DBMS server architecture and the symmetric replication synchronisation policy with two sites.

15.2.3 The Log Based Synchronisation Policy

The **LGS** policy uses the DBMS internal log as the basis for primary/hot stand-by synchronisation. The LGS policy is illustrated in figure 15.4. The log reflects the execution sequence of tuple operations to the primary fragments. By using the log as basis for the primary/hot stand-by synchronisation, the same execution sequence can be applied to a hot stand-by replica as to the primary replica.

The main difference between the LCS policy and the LGS policy is that the LCS policy sends the operations to the hot stand-bys earlier. Except for this, the same type of buffering policies of operations/log record replicas sent from primaries to hot stand-bys can be used in combination with both policies.

The HypRa recovery approach is based on the LGS policy. The Tandem Non-Stop and RDF, IBM XRF and RSR, E-Net RRDF, Sybase Replication Server, and INFORMIX-OnLine Dynamic Server products are also based on the LGS policy. All these products have opened up an interface to their logs. This makes it possible to read the generated log and to ship a replica to the hot stand-bys. As a consequence, it is possible to build replication servers which use this interface to extract the synchronisation information. This simplifies the building of a replication server since they can be built outside the DBMSs without altering their internal structure.

15.3 The 1-Safe Consistency Policy

Applications exist where it would be "economically acceptable" to lose a few committed transactions in a disaster as long as the availability of the DBMS services is maintained across the disaster ([KHGMP91]). Other applications can compromise on consistency to obtain reduced response times. Documented examples of applications accepting loss of some committed transactions are automatic teller machine (ATM) networks and airline reservations ([Lyo90]). Examples from telecommunications are location update transactions for mobile telephone users and registration transactions for universal personal telephone (UPT) users ([MP92]).

The 1-Safe strategy executes and commits a transaction at the primary replicas first. Then the transaction is asynchronously shipped and executed to the hot stand-by replicas. In the event of a site crash, this may cause the loss of those transactions that have been committed to the crashed primary site and have not yet been shipped to the hot stand-bys. When the hot stand-by takes over as primary, new transactions will see a state where these transactions are missing and continue the transaction processing from that state. Application specific policies can be developed to minimise the effect of these missing transactions. All the shared-nothing based products presented in chapter 17 support the 1-Safe policy.

An advantage of the 1-Safe strategy over the 2-Safe strategy is a reduced transaction latency. This is a consequence of not involving the hot stand-bys in the time critical execution path of a transaction.

The following set of consistency rules has been defined for 1-Safe policies ([KHGMP90], [KHGMP91], [PG94]):

- **Atomicity**
  If a transaction is executed to 1-Safe hot stand-by replicas, then all its state changing tuple operations are executed to the replicas. Either an entire transaction is installed to the 1-Safe hot stand-by replicas or none of it is installed.

- **Mutual consistency**
  If transaction T_1 and T_2 conflict, and T_1 precedes T_2 to the primary replicas, then T_1 must precede T_2 to the 1-Safe hot stand-by replicas.

- **Local consistency**
  No transaction which depends on missing transactions to the 1-Safe hot stand-by replicas may be installed to the 1-Safe hot stand-by replicas. No transaction may be executed to the 1-Safe hot stand-by replicas if it has directly or indirectly read results produced by missing transactions or if it has performed state changing operations to hot stand-by replicas to which missing transactions have performed state changing operations.

- **Minimum divergence**
  If a transaction is not missing from the 1-Safe hot stand-by replicas or does not depend on missing transactions, then it should be executed to the 1-Safe hot stand-by replicas.

The 1-Safe atomicity property corresponds to the 2-Safe failure atomicity property which is compatible to ACID. The mutual consistency, local consistency, and minimum divergence properties, on the other hand, are specific for 1-Safe approaches. The use of the local consistency property for state changing operations is illustrated in the following case, in which log records for different fragments are assumed to be sent over asynchronous log streams, e.g. independent update channels.

Transaction T_{11} updated attribute *A* of tuple *X* and attribute *B* of tuple *Y* and it has committed. The two tuples belong to different fragments. Transaction T_{12} updated attribute *A* of tuple *X* and committed after T_{11}. Replicas of both transactions are received in their production order at the node where the 1-Safe hot stand-by replica of *X* is stored. Both the corresponding redo operations are executed before the primary replica crashes. The log record reflecting T_{11}'s operation to *Y* did not arrive at the node where the 1-Safe replica of *Y* is located. As a consequence of this missing hot stand-by log record replica, T_{11} can not be atomically installed at the 1-Safe replicas and it must therefore be completely undone. Undoing T_{11}'s operation to *X* wipes out the committed transaction T_{12}'s operation to *X*. The result is an inconsistency. The inconsistency would have been avoided if T_{12} had not been allowed to execute before T_{11} had committed. In this case the local consistency property is obeyed.

15.4 Evaluation Criteria

The product presentation in chapter 16 and 17 is divided into a presentation of products based on the shared disc and a presentation of product based on the shared-nothing hardware architecture. The following evaluation criteria are used for both ([KHGMP90], [BT90]):

- **Unit of replication**
  The unit of replication, i.e. the granularity of the units that can be independently replicated, is analysed for each approach. In HypRa the unit of replication is a fragment. We will find approaches where the unit of replication is a *database*, physical parts of a database like *discs* or *tablespaces*, and approaches where the unit of replication is a *table* or a *fragment*.

- **Unit of take-over**
  The unit of take-over is also analysed for each approach. In HypRa the unit of take-over is a *fragment*, a *node*, or a *site*. We will find that for most of the approaches we have analysed, the unit of take-over is a *site*.

- **Scalability**
  The ability to scale is also analysed for each approach. If a centralised entity is needed, the ability to scale is limited. As a consequence, the use of a *single log stream* or *multiple asynchronous log streams* is vital. We will find here that all products rely on single log streams.

- **Consistency**
  The support of database consistency is analysed for each approach. The consistency properties defined in section 15.3 are used for 1-Safe approaches.

Chapter 16

Shared Disc Approaches

This chapter analyses high availability approaches based on the shared disc hardware architecture. The products we have analysed are Tandem Non-Stop SQL by Tandem Computers and IBM Extended Recovery Facility by IBM.

16.1 The Tandem Non-Stop System

The Tandem Non-Stop System was developed circa 1976 by Tandem Computers. The system represented major contributions to the area of high availability through its systematic use of primary and hot stand-by hardware and software servers and its provision for online manual non-blocking repair of fine-grained hardware units ([Kat78], [Kim84], [Ser84], [Cri90]).

The Non-Stop System is based on the shared disc hardware architecture, i.e. discs are shared between nodes while no main memory is shared. A Non-Stop System is single fault tolerant, i.e. data is kept available regardless of any single disc, disc controller, bus, or processor failure. Tandem uses mirrored discs, which act as disc server groups. Each disc in a server group is connected to two different processors by independent I/O channels ([Kat78]).

Pairs of primary and hot stand-by software servers, also called process pairs, are supported by the Tandem Guardian operating system ([Bar78], [Bar81], [Bor81]). Process pairs are used to mask failures. The primary process and one hot stand-by process in a process pair are allocated to two different nodes so that a node failure or a partial node failure can be masked. The process pair concept is combined with a checkpoint mechanism which is used to synchronise the pair. A primary process sends a checkpoint message to its hot stand-by companion at application determined points. If the primary process fails, the hot stand-by performs a take-over, becomes the current primary, and resumes processing from the last checkpoint. If the hot stand-by process fails, the primary runs on without a hot stand-by.

A Tandem server is assumed to be fail-fast, i.e. the server either functions correctly or stops until it is repaired. When, for example, an inconsistency is detected in a software server, the server is stopped. The process pairs are able to mask Heisenbugs. A Heisenbug that causes a primary server to fail will normally not cause its hot stand-by server to failure. Experience with Tandem has shown that more than 80% of the failures in mature software are Heisenbugs ([Gra86], [Gra90]). Later works have indicated that this figure is as high as 96% ([LI93]).

An I-am-Alive protocol is supported in the Guardian operating system to detect and report crashed nodes and software servers, to support the establishment of a consistent node set after a node crash, and to support the activation of a primary take-over. I-am-Alive messages are broadcasted by a node every second. The waiting time by a node to initiate actions is 2 seconds without receiving

I-am-Alive messages from another node. The consequence is a minimum unavailability time of 2 seconds for the services affected by a failure.

A Tandem Non-Stop system does not support automatic non-blocking repair. The length of time in which a Tandem system is running with a reduced fault tolerance level is dependent on the speed of manual repair. A typical repair time is from 4 to 12 hours. Version upgrades of operating system or DBMS are not allowed to be online and non-blocking. To obtain this, the Non-Stop system must be combined with RDF (see section 17.1).

16.1.1 Encompass and Non-Stop SQL

Encompass is the oldest of the Tandem DBMS products ([Bor84]). Non-Stop SQL is the newest ([BP88]). The systems use mostly the same DBMS internal policies. The description for Encompass also holds for Non-Stop SQL except where otherwise stated.

An Encompass server is composed of a set of DBMS servers. DBMS servers are called disc processes by Tandem. Each DBMS server is implemented as a server group with one primary and one hot stand-by DBMS server, i.e. it is implemented by a type of process pair which is called an I/O process pair. A DBMS server group controls one disc group. The servers of a DBMS server group which control a particular disc group are running on the nodes to which the disc group has I/O channels.

A DBMS server provides the equivalent of table-, record-, and block layer functionality. An Encompass DBMS server provides a tuple-at-a-time data shipping oriented interface while a Non-Stop SQL DBMS server supports a function shipping oriented interface. Every DBMS server maintains its own DB buffer, locks, and log buffer. Stable logging is centralised to one DBMS server group.

Encompass is a distributed DBMS. A relation is horizontally fragmented on key value ranges. One fragment replica is stored in a table which is managed by a DBMS server group. As a consequence, a fragment is stored on a disc group with a replica on each of the mirrored discs in the group. The unit of replication is a fragment. Refragmentation is not supported. Every tuple within a table is required to have a unique key.

Encompass uses the *steal/no-force* DB buffer policy. This is the combination of DB buffer policies that imposes the fewest disc I/O bottlenecks during performance stress (see section 4.6 and 4.9). Encompass also uses the *in-place update* policy. The *penultimate fuzzy checkpointing* (FCP) policy is used. As a consequence, blocks may be flushed during a checkpoint production. Encompass supports the *semantically rich* and *fine grained locking model*. The *WAL* policy is used in combination with tuple logging. All stable logging is done by a single DBMS server. A DBMS server applies a transaction commit oriented log buffering policy, i.e. log records are buffered until a transaction commit log record is received, and then they are sent to the DBMS server performing the stable logging. The DBMS server performing the stable logging uses a group commit policy to minimise the log induced disc I/O. The recursive CLR policy is used (see section 6.4.5) in combination with a *block state-identifier* policy. A crash recovery involves two log passes and a redo-undo sequentialisation of the recovery work. A full redo policy is followed. Undo recovery is performed logically to a block, while redo must be performed to the same block state as the corresponding do operation.

A checkpoint message sent from a primary DBMS server to its corresponding hot stand-by DBMS server contains log records. A primary DBMS server applies the same log buffering policy with respect to its hot stand-by companion as to the DBMS server providing stable logging services. A hot stand-by DBMS server supports a *dedicated DB buffer* policy based on the log records it receives in the checkpoint messages. The dedicated log buffer contains all log records produced after the penultimate checkpoint. The dedicated DB buffer recovery policy is not combined with any log-aggregation policy. A hot stand-by DBMS server, on the other hand, does not maintain a hot dirty block table, support a *hot stand-by lock* policy, or maintain a hot DB buffer.

Primary take-overs performed by Encompass have redo/no-undo characteristics and may involve disc accesses. During a primary take-over, a hot stand-by DBMS server will perform redo recovery starting from the current penultimate checkpoint. A complete redo recovery is performed. Since the penultimate FCP policy guarantees that all older log records are reflected in the stable DB, no older log records are needed in the redo recovery work. As a consequence of the dedicated DB buffer policy, no disc accesses are needed to log data during the redo work. All DB blocks referred to in the log blocks need to be read from disc at least once during the redo recovery to verify if the effect of the operation that produced the redo log record part is reflected in the block. As a consequence of the possible disc accesses, no upper limit can be set on the redo part of a primary take-over.

During the redo recovery work, locks are produced. When the redo recovery phase is completed, all locks held by transactions that were active and in the prepare-to-commit phase at the node crash time have been reset. Tuple locks are deduced from the TPK undo identification policy, but all locks with coarser granularity than tuples must be explicitly logged. When the redo recovery work is completed, all access methods are consistent and all blocks which needed physical redo recovery have been redo recovered. At this time, the DBMS server is opened for transaction execution again. The undo recovery work is done concurrently with the normal transaction processing. The undo recovery work is done asynchronously between the involved transactions.

16.2 The IBM Extended Recovery Facility

The IBM Extended Recovery Facility (**XRF**) is IBM's main shared disc hot stand-by support product. XRF can, when combined with IMS, provide a primary and a hot stand-by IMS DBMS and primary and hot stand-by terminal sessions. The major purpose of IMS XRF is to provide higher availability of IMS online systems to end users compared to traditional IMS systems. In case a primary IMS crashes, the hot stand-by DBMS takes over as the current primary and the hot stand-by session takes over as the primary session so that terminal based transaction services remain available.

CICS provides a DB2 XRF facility ([GR92]).

IMS is presented in subsection 16.2.1, while XRF is presented in subsection 16.2.2.

16.2.1 IMS

IMS is a hierarchical DBMS which is divided into IMS Full Function and IMS Fast Path parts ([IMS84], [IMS85], [IMS86a], [IMS86b], [MHL+89]). Full Function is also called DL/I. Fast Path is further divided into Main Storage and Data Entry. A data block can either be accessed through IMS Full Function, Main Storage, or Data Entry, but never through more than one of these IMS parts. A transaction, on the other hand, can access data under multiple IMS parts. Fast Path applies the no-steal/no-force and Full Function applies the steal/force DB buffer policies (see section 4.6). Main Storage uses the deferred update policy (see section 6.8.1). IMS uses the traditional locking model (see section A.9). Fine granularity record locking is supported by Full Function and Main Storage, while coarse granularity block locking is supported by Data Entry. Data Entry forces blocks which have been updated by a transaction out to disc just after the transaction has committed. Full Function uses the structure preservation locking policy to maintain stable access to records during transaction undo processing (see section 6.5). As a consequence of the steal/force DB buffer policy and the traditional locking model, Full Function blocks will need only undo recovery during a node crash recovery (see section 5.8.2). Data Entry blocks will need only redo recovery during a node crash recovery as a consequence of the combined no-steal/no-force DB buffer policy and the coarse granularity traditional locking policy (see section 4.8). Main Storage blocks will also need only redo recovery during a node crash recovery as a consequence of the combined no-steal/no-force buffer policy, deferred update policy, and record granularity traditional locking policy (see section 6.8.1).

IMS uses record logging. Fast Path uses a block state-identifier policy, while Full Function uses a non-state-identifier policy (see section 5.4). The identification concepts used in log records are a combination of the block identifier and record address within the block of the record which has been operated on (see section 7.3). Full Function log records contain both redo and undo log record parts. Undo log record parts are not included in the log records produced by Fast Path. IMS Full Function uses the repeating CLR policy (see section 6.4.5). Fast Path does not apply any CLR policy during transaction rollback, since, as a consequence of the deferred update policy, no state changes to stable data accessed by Fast Path have been performed by the aborting transaction. Fast Path applies the repeating CLR policy during node crash recovery to mark as compensated all log records produced by the transactions that were in the process of flushing their log records to stable storage when the node crash occurred.

IMS Main Storage data is checkpointed by being flushed alternately to two different files. Either all effects of a committed transaction are reflected in a checkpoint or none are, that is to say, a produced checkpoint is transaction consistent. IMS Full Function and Data Entry use a fuzzy checkpoint policy combined with the dirty block table policy, but do not flush any dirty blocks during checkpoint processing. Data Entry only includes committed dirty blocks in the dirty block table. IMS uses a checkpoint log policy to maintain a stable reference to the last begin-checkpoint log record (see section 4.7.5).

An IMS node crash recovery starts by reading the last checkpointed Main Storage DBs from stable storage into the DB buffer. Node crash recovery uses a dedicated DB buffer policy combined with a log-aggregation policy. The log is scanned once starting from the last checkpoint. Full Function log records are aggregated per transaction and a sequential transaction recovery is applied with asynchronous execution between the transactions. Fast Path log records are aggregated per block and block complete non-sequential recovery is performed to a block. All the Data Entry blocks that were included in the dirty table of the last checkpoint before the node crash are read into DB buffer and placed in the same buffer locations as they had at the checkpoint. All committed operations since last checkpoint will be redone to the Main Storage data. The LSN determines which operations are to be redone to the Data Entry blocks.

16.2.2 XRF

XRF provides an IMS DBMS with a shared disc hot stand-by IMS system which can take over as the primary DBMS if the primary fails ([XRF87a], [XRF87b], [XRF87c], [XRF87d], [XRF87e]). The primary and hot stand-by IMS systems under XRF control may run either on different processors or on the same processor. If the IMS systems run on different processors, XRF can mask a processor, site, and IMS system failure in the primary system. The unit of replaceable hardware is an entire IBM processor. If the IMS systems run on the same processor, XRF is only able to mask a failure in the primary IMS system. XRF only supports single fault-tolerance, because a primary IMS DBMS may have only one hot stand-by replica. XRF supports 2-Safe synchronisation with no 1-Safe option.

The unit of replication handled by XRF is entire databases. The main stable data structures shared between a primary and a hot stand-by IMS system are, in addition to the replicated databases, the IMS log and the IMS checkpoint log. IMS XRF can maintain two replicas to obtain single fault-tolerance for all the shared data structures. Single fault-tolerance for the shared data structures is maintained also after a primary take-over by the hot stand-by IMS system.

XRF supports an I-am-Alive protocol between a primary and a hot stand-by IMS system. The protocol can be based on the log, the checkpoint log, explicit messages, or on a combination of these. The interval between two I-am-Alive interactions is given in seconds with a default interval of one second and a maximum interval of 99 seconds. The take-over activation period is at least twice the interval between I-am-Alive interactions. As a consequence, a take-over will cause an IMS system unavailability of at least two seconds. A take-over can be activated manually in addition to being activated automatically.

When it starts, a hot stand-by IMS system opens all the databases which were open at the primary IMS system. The hot stand-by system uses a dedicated DB buffer policy in combination with a log aggregation policy. The use of these policies minimises the disc accesses to the log during a primary take-over. A hot stand-by IMS replica, on the other hand, does not maintain a hot stand-by DB buffer.

The log is scanned in forward direction by the hot stand-by system at regular intervals, starting from the first log record produced after the previous scan and continuing until the end of the log is detected. After a node crash, a scan must be done to fetch the last log records produced by the primary system. The aggregation is done in a similar manner as during normal node crash recovery. The Full Function log records are aggregated per transaction. Full Function log records for a transaction are removed when the commit log record for the transaction is encountered, because Full Function blocks never require redo recovery after a node crash. The Fast Path log records are aggregated per block. Data Entry log records aggregated to a block and belonging to committed transactions are removed after the block has been flushed to disc.

The hot stand-by IMS also maintains a dirty DB block table which is extended to also track the dirty DB buffer blocks. XRF requires that a hot stand-by system has the same number of DB buffer blocks as the primary system. The blocks accessed by state changing Full Function operations are deduced from the block identifiers included in the log record identification concepts. A commit log record is used to make all Full Function blocks accessed by a transaction non-dirty.

An implicit double block flush logging policy is used for Data Entry blocks. This is a consequence of the fact that all Data Entry blocks accessed by state changing operations are flushed immediately after the transaction that executed the operations commits. The commit log record serves as an implicit start flush block log record. All update log records are piggybacked with the blocks that are in the process of being flushed when the log record is produced. When a block is no longer marked as in the process of being flushed, the block is no longer dirty with respect to that transaction. The blocks are then removed from the dirty table, unless some update log record by the block has been received after the transaction arrived. If an update log record with another block in the same DB buffer block is received, we know that the previous block has been flushed and this block is removed from the dirty table.

When a primary IMS crash is detected, all block flush operations by the crashed system are blocked to avoid introduction of state-failures in the stable data structures. The last log records produced are scanned and aggregated so that all log information needed during the primary take-over is in main memory. If an overflow occurs, the log is read from disc.

An equivalent to a write lock is set on all blocks that potentially need redo or undo recovery, i.e. the blocks in the dirty block table. These locks are kept until the primary take-over recovery is completed to prevent new transactions from executing concurrently with the take-over recovery and performing operations to these blocks. The locks on potentially dirty Data Entry blocks are needed to let a redo operation be performed to the same block state as the do operation was executed. The locks on the dirty Full Function blocks are needed to maintain effect of structure preserving locking during the recovery. Locks are also set on every Full Function record that needs recovery. The aggregated Full Function log records are used as the basis for this lock setting. These locks are released as normal during transaction rollbacks.

Main Storage databases start to be read into the DB buffer from the last checkpoint dump file in parallel with the other primary take-over activities. A Main Storage database is kept unavailable until the reading is completed. This is caused by the fact that no hot stand-by DB buffers are maintained at the hot stand-by IMS system.

Transaction processing is started at the new primary IMS when all recovery related locks have been set. The effect of this policy to Full Function and Data Entry data is close to the no-redo/no-undo policy, because transaction processing is resumed without waiting for any redo or undo recovery work. The duration of unavailability for Full Function and Data Entry databases is the period when the remaining log part is scanned and locks are set. A significantly longer unavailability period is imposed on Main Storage data because Main Storage databases must be read from disc before transaction processing is resumed.

Transactions which are aborted as a consequence of a primary take-over are rescheduled for execution after their rollback is completed.

Chapter 17

Shared-Nothing Approaches

This chapter analyses high availability approaches based on the shared-nothing hardware architecture. A main advantage of the shared-nothing approach is that two shared-nothing sites with two replicas of a replication unit can provide a high degree of failure isolation with respect to software failures and environmental disasters, e.g. fires, floods, avalanches, and land slides. The sites can also be managed independently, which provides a high degree of isolation from operator errors.

The products analysed in this chapter are: Remote Duplicate Database Facility by Tandem; Remote Recovery Data Facility by E-Net Corporation; Sybase Replication Server by Sybase Inc.; Oracle7 Symmetric Replication Facility by Oracle Inc.; CA-OpenIngres/Replicator by Computer Associates; and INFORMIX-OnLine Dynamic Server by Informix Software Inc. High availability approaches used by some telecom switch internal DBMSs are also presented. Finally some academic research works are presented.

17.1 The Tandem Remote Duplicate Database Facility

The Tandem Remote Duplicate Database Facility (**RDF**) is primarily intended to mask disaster failures ([Gue91], [Lyo90], [GMPH90]). RDF can also be used to avoid system unavailability in connection with system software upgrades, hardware changes, hardware platform migration, and site migration.

The unit of replication is either a *database* or a *disc volume* used by a single database. RDF allows one primary and one hot stand-by replica of each replicated unit. RDF also allows multi-level hierarchical replication so that a hot stand-by unit acts as a primary for the next-level hot stand-by. The replication configuration policy can be symmetric or asymmetric. A *symmetric replication configuration* policy allows both primary and hot stand-by replication units at a site. An *asymmetric configuration* policy allows only either primary or hot stand-by replication units at a site.

The failure unit is a site. A non-maskable failure by any part of a site will therefore cause a take-over, which will affect all replication units allocated at the site.

RDF supports both 1-Safe and 2-Safe synchronisation between a primary replication unit and its corresponding hot stand-by replication unit. RDF works by copying the master log produced relating to primary replication units. This log is record oriented and contains the before- and after-image of the records which have been operated on. The master log is kept at one node per site, and is copied in blocks by an RDF Extractor server after it is flushed to disc. The Extractor requests a copy of the log block which immediately follows the last one copied. If it reaches the end of the log, it waits before requesting the next log block. The log records are analysed and sent to a receiver server at the site where the corresponding hot stand-by replication unit is allocated.

The log record replicas are sent in a single stream from one site to another site. This restrains the scaling ability of RDF. A log record may be sent while the transaction is active. The log records received at the site where the hot stand-by replication unit is located are flushed to disc. When there is no traffic between two sites, I-am-Alive messages are exchanged.

The redo work on the hot stand-by side is executed as record operations based directly on the operation code in the log records. This redo work can be done in parallel by allocating up to one redo executer (Updater) server per database file in each disc volume. The redo record operations for a transaction are executed when a commit log record for the transaction has been received. Log records for aborted transactions are not sent to the hot stand-by site from the site where the primary replicas involved in the transaction are located. RDF supports transaction consistent read from the hot stand-by replica units. When RDF executes a transaction in 2-Safe mode, the transaction is not committed before all its log records have been acknowledged as received and stably stored at the hot stand-by site.

A primary take-over must be initiated manually. At a primary take-over, the redo policy is followed. Undo processing is avoided since no transactions are executed to hot stand-by data before they are committed. A typical primary take-over time is indicated to take on the order of minutes ([GR92]). When an original primary site restarts, it will catch up based on the log produced while it was unavailable. When it has caught up, it becomes a hot stand-by site. It may take back its original primary role through a process which potentially causes unavailability. The current primary site stops accepting new transactions. When all transaction processing has stopped, the sites switch roles and the transaction processing is resumed. A typical unavailability of less than 5 seconds is indicated during such a role switch ([Lyo88]).

The primary and the corresponding hot stand-by replication unit must be fully synchronised when RDF is started. RDF supports manual online non-blocking repair of a crashed site. A fuzzy replica of the current primary replica of the involved data must be produced. This fuzzy replica then needs to be transported to the site under repair and then installed. Then the log which has been produced since the fuzzy dump production started is sent to the repairing site and applied. Repair from a site crash may take several hours. RDF does not support automatic online repair.

17.2 The E-Net Remote Recovery Data and Log Apply Facility

Remote Recovery Data Facility (**RRDF**), Log Apply, and Shadow Database Facility are products by E-Net ([ENE93a], [ENE93b], [ENE93c], [ENE93d], [ENE93e], [ENE94], [Luc93]). The products are primarily directed towards IBM mainframe environments. RRDF is intended to mask loss of log caused by a primary site failure. Log Apply works with RRDF and supports 1-Safe replication for DB2 databases. Shadow Database Facility works with RRDF and supports 1-Safe replication for IDMS databases. RRDF uses the LGS policy.

17.2.1 Remote Recovery Data Facility

RRDF provides hot stand-by replication of log records produced by DB2, IMS, IDMS, CPCS, Adabase, and SuperMICR databases. A replica of the primary log records is shipped to a hot stand-by site. The replication policy is 1-Safe and restricted to connecting two sites. All hot stand-by log records produced must be stored at a single site. Both a symmetric and an asymmetric replication configuration policy can be supported by using two independent RRDFs at the sites.

RRDF assumes that the DBMS uses disc as the stable log media. When a block containing primary log records is flushed to disc, another copy of the log records is produced in RRDF's main memory buffer. The hot stand-by log records are sent to the hot stand-by site by use of RRDF's own proprietary protocol on top of VTAM/SNA. The protocol uses buffering on the sending side. The log records are sent in buffer unit groups. The protocol can be combined with log compression and encryption. The hot stand-by log records are immediately flushed to disc at the receiver site as the buffer units arrive. An acknowledgement is sent back when a log unit is stable stored. A buffer unit can be reused when an acknowledgement is received indicating that its hot stand-by log records are stably stored at the other site.

If the communication or the hot stand-by site becomes unavailable, RRDF supports mass storage of log records at the site in which the primary log records are located. After recovery, the newly produced hot stand-by log records are sent, starting with the oldest log record. No mechanism exists for the use of an alternate site if a hot stand-by site becomes unavailable for an extended period.

If we compare the delay imposed by RRDF with the HypRa update channel in production of a hot stand-by log record at a site other than where the primary log record is located, we see that RRDF uses a significantly longer time. This is caused by three factors. First, RRDF delays the sending of a log record to the other site until the log block the primary log record replica is located in is flushed to disc because it is filled up or is forced to disc because of transaction commit processing. The HypRa update channel uses the force-send policy, which sends a copy of a primary log record as soon as the primary log record is produced. Secondly, RRDF imposes an additional delay by performing its own buffering at the sending site in addition to the log buffering done by the DBMS. Thirdly, RRDF imposes a disc access at the receiver site to obtain stable storage of a hot stand-by log record. Both the space-receive policy (which is applied by HypRa) and the receive-commit policy assume that stable storage is obtained when the hot stand-by log record is stored in main memory at a site with independent failure mode. A typical delay reported by ENET for production of a hot stand-by log record at another site by RRDF is one second.

The unit of replication is either an entire database or all the tables belonging to the same database and stored at the same named physical storage area (tablespace). The failure unit is either a site, a database, or a tablespace. RRDF supports 1-Safe synchronisation between a primary and a hot stand-by site. A typical take-over time for RRDF is on the order of minutes.

Log Apply uses RRDF to produce and send hot stand-by log records to the hot stand-by site. Redo execution, in connection with DB2, is done by transforming each log record into SQL statements which are executed to the hot stand-by database replica. Redo operations are collected for a transaction until the commit record is received. Redo execution is done in batches, where each batch contains one or more committed transactions. One batch is executed as one hot stand-by transaction in which the dependencies between the included transactions are maintained. The dictionary at the hot stand-by site is used to translate the attribute identifiers in the log record to attribute names. Four static SQL statements are prepared for each table: Lock Table, Insert, Update, and Delete. To perform the transformation the primary key (unique key) is needed in every log record. To obtain the primary key, including for delete log records, both the undo and the redo log record parts are sent to the hot stand-by site. Log records are sorted on tablespaces and up to one redo executer can be allocated to each table space to obtain parallel redo execution. RRDF also supports a log compression policy to each tuple by further sorting the log records on tuples and maintaining the log sequence within each tuple.

RRDF supports online blocking repair of a site where some data is lost as a consequence of a crash. An image copy of a table space at the current primary site can be produced and installed at the recovering site. RRDF sets a read lock while the image copy is produced. The log produced after the image copying is applied to the recovering site. RRDF supports read access from the hot stand-by site. Integrity references are not consistently maintained as a consequence of the redo execution policy. RRDF also handles schema modifications to a limited degree.

17.3 Oracle7 Symmetric Replication Facility

Oracle7 supports replicated data based on both the *shared-nothing* and the *shared disc* architectures. The shared-nothing architecture is handled by the Oracle7 Symmetric Replication Facility ([Pea95a], [Pea95b], [BCFea95], [FKea95], [Bob92]). The shared disc architecture is handled by the Oracle7 Parallel Server. Both replication policies provide the 1-Safe policy. Oracle7 also supports symmetric 2-Safe replication ([BCFea95]). High availability can be based on Oracle7, but this will require that components to obtain high availability are built into the applications. Oracle7 Symmetric Replication Facility uses the T-EXS policy.

The symmetric replication facility provides both the *update-anywhere peer-to-peer* replication policy and the *update-anywhere two-level hierarchy* replication policy ([Gol95]). The peer-to-peer replication policy handles two or more sites, where each site is running an Oracle7 server with the symmetric replication facility. The peer-to-peer policy is called *N-way replication* by Oracle. The N-way replication only allows replication of complete tables, where each replicated table is replicated at all sites. Replicated tables are organised in replicated schemes, all tables are not required to be replicated in a replicated scheme.

A peer-to-peer replicated transaction originates at a given site and can perform tuple operations to all replicated data at that site. The transaction is then replicated in deferred fashion to all the other peer sites through a 1-Safe policy. The originating site is responsible for the replication. The peer-to-peer policy may cause persistent inconsistencies resulting from non-equivalent transaction schedules at the different peer sites. Non-equivalent transaction schedules may, for example, result from different propagation times for the deferred transactions to different peer sites (see [Gol95]). The symmetric replication facility provides for detection and resolution of some classes of potential inconsistencies.

The update-everywhere two-level hierarchy policy allows updatable snapshot tables to be replication connected to one master table each. A master table can be a peer table but cannot itself be an updatable snapshot table. An updatable snapshot table can either be a replica of a complete table or a replica of a fragment from a single table. All updatable snapshots at a given site have their master tables at the same site. Originating transactions performed to updatable snapshots are 1-Safe forwarded to the connected master site. Updatable snapshots are refreshed periodically from the master table. The symmetric replication facility supports read-only snapshots in addition to updatable snapshots.

The symmetric replication facility has to build its own log separate from the Oracle internal log. The DBMS internal log maintains the undo and the redo log as separate logs. The undo log is a block log maintained for each transaction. It therefore cannot be deduced from an undo log block whose tuple it reflects an operation to. Oracle7 uses the undo log to support multi-version concurrency control ([BCFea95]). The undo log for a transaction is deleted when the transaction terminates or shortly afterwards if the older version of a block kept in the undo log has been read by a concurrent transaction. The undo information therefore may not necessarily exist when the symmetric replication facility needs it. A redo log record contains the portion of a page modified by a tuple operation in addition to a block status identifier. Redo log records are not connected to the producing transaction. The symmetric replication facility therefore may not be able to deduce the required redo information from these redo log records.

Every originating transaction executed to peer-to-peer replicated tables produces one tuple log record per state changing tuple operation. These log records are in addition to and separate from the Oracle internal log records. The log records are produced by triggers fired in connection with the execution of a state changing tuple operation. The log records are inserted into a log table under full transactional management. Each log record contains a complete before- and after-image of the tuple for update operations, a complete before-image for the delete operations, and a complete after-image for insert operations. The effect of this log production strategy is that every replicated state changing tuple operation becomes two tuple operations to two different tables. This may significantly increase the work in the time critical part of a transaction, which may in turn increase transaction response time and reduce system throughput.

Every replication transaction is given a unique identifier when it starts. The transaction identifier is allocated from an Oracle7 sequence. Oracle7 sequences support a concurrency control policy which avoid exclusive locking as part of obtaining sequence values ([FKea95]). The transaction identifier is included in each log record produced by the transaction. The symmetric replication facility requires that a primary key is specified for all peer-to-peer replicated tables. The identification of the tuple replica to execute a logged state changing tuple operation at the other peer sites is based on the primary key. The consistency of the tuple is checked before the tuple operation is executed. If an inconsistency is detected, a conflict resolution method can be activated. When an originating transaction commits, a unique transaction number is given to each replica of the transaction which is to be executed in deferred fashion at the other sites. These identifiers are also allocated from Oracle7 sequences to avoid commit bottlenecks. The transaction replicas are then entered into the queue of deferred transactions at the originating site. The deferred transaction job queue at a site will be checked for the presence of waiting deferred transactions to be sent to other sites at regular intervals. Oracle7 allows a minimum interval of one second and a maximum interval of 3600 seconds. The waiting deferred transactions are sent to another site if that site is available, otherwise they will be held and attempted to be sent next time the job queue is checked. Log records are shipped in one stream from the originating site to another site. A two-phase commit is used to ensure that transactions are shipped atomically. When the transactions have been received at the receiving site, they are executed in strict serial order in increasing transaction identifier order. This ensures that transactions are executed in their originating order. This execution policy may constrain the throughput at the remote sites, since transactions that originally were executing concurrently will be executed back to back.

When a state changing operation is executed to the master table for an updatable snapshot, a trigger is fired and an entry is produced in a snapshot log table for the master table. The entry contains the site local surrogate key for the actual tuple in addition to a time stamp for the operation. When the snapshot is refreshed, the log table is used to determine which tuples on the master need to be shipped to produce a consistent refreshed snapshot. Transactions which perform state changing operations to updatable snapshots are handled as transactions to peer tables. The resulting deferred transactions are shipped and executed at the site where the master tables are located as deferred transactions to peer tables.

The symmetric replication facility supports data definition (DDL) and maintenance operations on replicated data. One site is defined as the maintenance master site and all maintenance must originate from that site. The maintenance master site must be available in order to perform DDL and maintenance operations. Most DDL and maintenance operations are system blocking, i.e. all transaction execution to all replicated tables on all sites are stopped and all deferred transactions are shipped and executed at their remote sites before a maintenance operation is allowed to be executed.

Oracle7 does not support any I-am-Alive protocol or take-over policies. The system does not maintain a consistent image of which sites are available. When a site has been recovered, it will be sent all transactions which were deferred while it was unavailable. Oracle7 supports manual system blocking repair of tables in which all sites are unavailable for state changing operations during the repair.

17.4 The Sybase Replication Server

The Sybase replication server is primarily intended for management of replicated data ([Pub95c], [Pub95a], [Pub95b], [Pub95d]). All replication is based on the 1-Safe policy. High availability can be obtained with the Sybase replication server as basis, but this will require that additional functionality is included in the applications. Sybase uses the LGS policy.

The Sybase replication server supports the *primary/hot stand-by* replication policy. The unit of replication is a horizontal or vertical fragment of a table. A specific language is provided for distribution management and the information is kept in a distribution dictionary. Fragmentation predicates can be constructed from attribute identifiers from the relation under fragmentation. One primary and one or more hot stand-by replicas are allowed for each fragment. The primary fragment replicas of a relation can be allocated to different sites. Multiple hot stand-by replicas can be maintained for each fragment. The Sybase replication server also supports multi-level hot stand-by replicas, so that a hot stand-by replica may serve in the role of a primary replica for the next-level hot stand-by replica.

A site may store primary data, hot stand-by data, or both. There is one *replication server* per site. The replication server uses the information kept in the distribution dictionary. There is, in addition to the replication server, one *log transfer manager* per site when a Sybase DBMS server is used. DBMS servers other than Sybase are accepted, but these DBMSs must support log transfer managers. A replication server can use multiple log transfer managers at one site. A log transfer manager reads the log records produced by the DBMS server at the site where it is located. The log is scanned in production order at regular intervals, starting from the first log record produced after the last scan and continuing to the end of the log. The log transfer manager sends a replica of the read log records to the replication server to which it is connected.

The replication server buffers all log records for a transaction in production order until the transaction commit record is received. The replication server may store the received log record replicas on stable storage. A log record must contain a complete before-image of the operated on tuple. The after-image can either be complete or include, at a minimum, only the modified attributes. If the transaction aborts, its log records are ignored by the replication manager.

When a transaction has committed, the replication manager prepares deferred replicas of the transaction to be shipped to sites where the hot stand-by data is located. A full replica of a log record is included in the deferred transaction for a site if a horizontal hot stand-by fragment replica is located at the site and the log record will be applied to a tuple replica located in that fragment. A vertical fragment replica of the log record is included if there is a matching vertical fragment at the site.

Log records are shipped one transaction at a time from a site. Outbound transactions may be stably stored at a replication server. A checkpoint policy is used for stable storage to limit the number of lost transactions in case of a site or replication server crash. The Sybase replication server provides stable storage and a forward routing facility when a deferred transaction is shipped to its destination site. The deferred transaction may therefore hop from one replication server to another several times before reaching its destination replication server.

Deferred transactions from each originating replication server will arrive at the destination server in their commit order. A destination replication server receives all log records belonging to one transaction from one originating replication server before receiving any log records of the next transaction. Transactions from one originating replication server are executed in strict serial order to the DBMS that the destination replication server is serving. Transactions from different originating replication servers may be executed in parallel.

The Sybase replication server supports asynchronous store and forward procedure execution based on the deferred transaction handling system. Only read transactions are allowed on hot stand-by replicas. An automatic take-over policy is supported for DBMS server failures. There is no automatic support for a primary or hot stand-by take-over policy in case of a site failure. A hot stand-by database can be changed manually to a primary database and a primary database can be changed manually to a hot stand-by database. Application switch-over is left to the applications. An I-am-Alive function is supported, making it possible for an application to test the availability of a site.

The Sybase replication server supports atomic blocking online self-repair of replicated units. Only the replication unit(s) under repair are blocked during the repair activity. In addition, a manual non-atomic non-blocking self-repair policy of replication units is provided. This policy may cause transactions to be executed to a replica twice.

17.5 The CA-OpenIngres/Replicator

The CA-OpenIngres/Replicator supports data replication based on the *shared-nothing* architecture ([Ing93]) and employs a 1-Safe policy. The CA-OpenIngres/Replicator runs on CA-OpenIngres/Server release 6.4/04 or later. A 2-Safe policy is provided by the CA-OpenIngres/Star product, of which CA-OpenIngres/Replicator is independent. High availability can be achieved based on CA-OpenIngres/Replicator if additional components are supplied by the applications. CA-OpenIngres/Replicator uses the T-EXS policy.

The CA-OpenIngres/Replicator supports the update-anywhere peer-to-peer replication policy, the update-anywhere multi-level hierarchy policy, and a primary/hot stand-by policy. In addition, a snapshot replication policy is provided where order preserving execution of hot stand-by transactions is not necessarily guaranteed.

The CA-OpenIngres/Replicator allows replication of entire databases, tables, and horizontal and vertical fragments based on a single table. Replication units are grouped in Consistent Distributed Data Sets (CDDS). A CDDS can be distributed over multiple databases. An originating transaction may involve primary data on multiple databases. If multiple databases are involved in an originating transaction, a two-phase commit protocol is used to obtain its atomic execution. A 1-Safe policy is used to execute the transaction in deferred fashion to peer and hot stand-by replicas of the data at the next hierarchical level. The transaction coordinator is located at the site where the transaction coordinator of the original transaction was located. A deferred transaction is executed atomically and uses a two-phase commit protocol if multiple databases are involved. In case of multi-level replication, a site at a given level serves as the originator for the next level of replication.

The update-anywhere peer-to-peer policy may cause persistent inconsistencies ([Gol95]). Inconsistencies may also be caused by multiple propagations of a transaction to a site along different replication paths. This may cause the same transaction to be executed more than once to the same replica. CA-OpenIngres/Replicator supports mechanisms for detection and handling of some classes of inconsistences. Inconsistencies are detected when an insert tries to produce two tuples with the same primary key value, a delete is attempted on a non-existing tuple, and updates are tried on tuples that do not exist or do not correspond to the before-image. The conflict resolution mechanism is based on a priority scheme. Conflicts and aborted transactions are logged and reported.

The CA-OpenIngres/Replicator builds its own log. When a transaction starts, it is given a unique transaction identifier. Additionally, a transaction performing a state changing operation to a tuple will insert a tuple into three different tables to log the operation. The before-image of the tuple, together with the transaction identifier and the operation identifier within the transaction, are logged in the *shadow table* for the table to which the tuple operated on belongs. In addition, a tuple is inserted into an *archive table* for the table to which the tuple operated on belongs. The archive tuple identifies the transaction and operation within the transaction, together with a unique replication key for the updated tuple. The replication key for a table is defined in the replication schema and it can be the primary key for the table. Each state changing tuple operation by all transactions with their transaction controller at one site is, in addition, reflected by a tuple inserted into an *input queue table*. A deferred transaction performs the same activities with respect to log production at a target site as the originating transaction. This log production policy ensures that any site can be an originator with respect to the next hierarchical level.

A transaction committing at a site activates a Replicator Server server at that site. The Replicator Server starts a transaction that will first request a write lock on the input queue table. This ensures that transactions are treated by Replicator Servers in commit order. A Replicator Server gives each transaction that it handles a time stamp, which reflects the commit order. A Replicator Server produces all operations for a deferred transaction from the originating transaction's entries in the input queue table and from the information in the replication scheme. Each deferred operation produced is reflected in the *distribution queue table*. The transactions' entries are removed from the input queue table before the transaction producing the deferred transaction commits.

The execution of deferred transactions can be activated periodically or on demand. The transaction coordinator for a deferred transaction is located at the site of the deferred transaction log. This may increase the work load on the sites with primary data as compared to managing the execution of deferred transactions at sites where hot stand-by data is located. Transactions originating at a site are executed strictly serially in increasing time stamp order. Within a deferred transaction, operations are executed at the receiving database in their production order.

The CA-OpenIngres/Replicator does not support any I-am-Alive protocol or take-over policies. It supports maintenance operations on the replicated data. Maintenance and data definition operations should be performed in a consistent and stable system state. As a consequence, the entire replication system is blocked during maintenance. To obtain a stable system, all Replicator Servers exclude new client applications from replicated data. The system then waits for all deferred transactions to be executed. When this is achieved, the Replicator Servers are shut down. Repair activities can be performed in the same way as maintenance operations.

17.6 The INFORMIX-OnLine Dynamic Server

The INFORMIX-OnLine Dynamic Server supports the *shared-nothing* architecture ([Inf94a], [Inf94b], [Inf94c], [Inf94d]). It provides both the 1-Safe and the 2-Safe replication consistency policies. High availability support is included in the product. Transparent detection and masking of DBMS site crashes and automatic client switch-over in case of a site crash are provided. INFORMIX-OnLine Dynamic Server uses the LGS policy.

The INFORMIX-OnLine Dynamic Server supports the primary/hot stand-by replication policy. The unit of replication is all data located on one site. All primary replicas at a site must have their hot stand-by replicas on another single site. A site is allowed to contain either primary or hot stand-by data but not both. The INFORMIX-OnLine Dynamic Server is able to mask a site crash and a DBMS server crash. Multi-level hierarchical replication is not supported.

The INFORMIX-OnLine Dynamic Server uses the DBMS internal log as the basis for replication synchronisation. The INFORMIX-OnLine Dynamic Server applies record logging. A log record contains a complete before- and after-image of the tuple which was operated on. A compensation recovery strategy is used with a single CLR policy. The INFORMIX-OnLine Dynamic Server uses the action consistent checkpoint policy. A before-image block log is produced in addition to the record log. When a block gets dirty, a before-image of the block is produced. The log which this produces is flushed to stable storage as part of checkpoint production. The INFORMIX-OnLine Dynamic Server does not use any state-identifier policy. Recovery is divided into three phases. In the first phase, the block before-image log is compared to the last checkpoint applied so that all effects of record operations executed after the last checkpoint are removed. The second and third phases perform a redo-undo recovery based on the record log. The redo recovery applies the complete redo policy. The redo processing starts from the last checkpoint.

A primary site produces a replica of the record oriented log records in its log-buffer into its *data-replication buffer* each time the the log-buffer is flushed to disc. These log records are shipped to the hot stand-by site and entered into its *reception buffer*. The log records are sent in a single log stream between the two sites, which constrains the scaling of a site. The shipping of log records can be either synchronous or asynchronous. The synchronous policy gives a 2-Safe transaction execution. A transaction is then committed by flushing its log records to disc after all its hot stand-by log records are acknowledged to be received at the hot stand-by site. The synchronous policy applies a force-send policy to send a log message after it has been copied into the data-replication buffer. The asynchronous policy gives a 1-Safe transaction execution. It sends all log records in the data-replication buffer to the hot stand-by site when a transaction commits, the buffer is full, or if it times out. The time-out interval can be specified, from one to 30 seconds. Log records are processed in redo mode at the hot stand-by site. The INFORMIX-OnLine Dynamic Server allows parallel redo execution during both site recovery and hot stand-by processing. There can be only one redo thread per table. This will preserve consistency, since the execution sequence is maintained to each tuple.

The INFORMIX-OnLine Dynamic Server maintains an I-am-Alive protocol between a primary and a hot stand-by site. The minimum interval between I-am-Alive messages from a site is one second. A site waits for two missing I-am-Alive messages before any take-over processing is activated. INFORMIX-OnLine Dynamic Server supports an automatic primary take-over policy in addition to manual primary take-over and a non-take-over policy. Locking information is not maintained at the hot stand-by site during hot stand-by execution. The redo/undo primary take-over policy is therefore applied to the entire hot stand-by site. This may cause a long primary take-over time if a large transaction has to be undone during the take-over. Automatic switch-over is supported for clients if the site to which the client is connected, fails. The replication service and I-am-Alive protocol is automatically restarted when a site is restarted. A restarted primary site may either take back its original primary status by not allowing new clients to connect to the current primary or perform a primary take-over when no clients are connected. This policy may cause unavailability. The alternative policies cause an abrupt primary take-over, which in turn causes some aborted transactions.

The INFORMIX-OnLine Dynamic Server does not support a primary/hot stand-by policy for binary large objects (BLOBs) because operations on BLOBs are not logged in the record oriented log. There is no support for online non-blocking repair but, on the other hand, online manual blocking repair is supported.

17.7 The IBM Remote Site Recovery

The IBM Remote Site Recovery (**RSR**) is IBM's main *shared-nothing* hot stand-by product ([BT90], [MTO91] [RSR95]). RSR works with IMS. It is the IMS/ESA version 5 strategic solution to customer remote site recovery requirements. RSR is intended to facilitate recovery in case of lengthy or catastrophic failures. RSR provides remote recovery of all recoverable resources needed to support an application system. These recoverable resources are databases, communication with clients and terminals, and transaction manager message queues and "scratch-pads".

RSR supports 1-Safe replication. Two levels of primary take-over readiness are provided for databases. This makes it possible to adjust the availability insurance cost to the required availability level per database. The *database* readiness level, which is the highest level, corresponds to a hot stand-by support. The *recovery* level, which is the lowest readiness level, keeps a stand-by image of the database and gathers the log at a stand-by site during normal operations. The use of RSR gives a typical primary take-over time of less than one hour at the highest readiness level.

RSR supports IMS Full Function (DL/I) databases, IMS Fast Path Data Entry databases (DEDB), IMS TM message queues, and IMS TM telecommunications network. A site, in RSR terminology, is composed of *subsystems*, e.g. an IMS Data Entry subsystem which manages one or more databases. A subsystem consists of *components*. The smallest unit of replication supported by RSR is a database. A site is either a primary site or a hot stand-by site. Multiple primary sites may share one hot stand-by site. All of the databases at a primary site do not have to be replicated. The unit of failure is an entire site. RSR can be combined with XRF at a primary site so that XRF masks site local failures and RSR masks site failures. RSR allows shared disc architecture for primary subsystems.

RSR uses the LGS policy. The *logger* component of a primary subsystem ships a replica of the log records for the databases it manages to the *log router* component at the hot stand-by system. The logger replicates the log records when a log buffer block is full or before a log buffer block is flushed to disc. The log records are shipped in blocks reflecting their production order. There is a single log stream from a primary subsystem to its hot stand-by subsystem. The log is shipped through the transport manager subsystem, of which there is one at each site.

RSR requires that the block size used by Full Function and Data Entry hot stand-by databases is the same as the block size used by the corresponding primary database. This is a consequence of the block and record address identification concepts used by IMS. A hot stand-by log record must be executed to the hot stand-by replica of the original primary block to preserve consistency during redo processing.

A log router may receive logs from multiple primary subsystems. It copies the received logs to stable storage. The log for each subsystem is maintained separately. Log record blocks for subsystems and databases at recovery readiness level are kept until a primary take-over is completed or until receipt of database images which make the log records obsolete. When a log router detects missing log records from a primary subsystem after a short duration communication or hot stand-by site disruption, it requests the *isolated log sender* component of the primary subsystem to send a replica of the missing log records. This log is shipped in parallel with the normal log shipping.

Log records for a subsystem at database readiness level are sent by the log router in production order to the *tracker* component of the hot stand-by subsystem. A hot stand-by log record is not sent before it is flushed to disc and its primary replica is confirmed to be flushed to disc at the primary subsystem. This ensures that the write-ahead policy is obeyed. Trackers execute asynchronously and may execute in parallel. A tracker receives one sequence of log records at a time. The log router performs checkpointing (milestones) to stable storage to reflect the execution progress and establish a redo execution start point after a hot stand-by subsystem crash. A new sequence is not sent before the previous is acknowledged to be executed by the tracker. The log record garbaging policy is different for Full Function and Data Entry databases.

The Full Function trackers perform redo execution in the order in which log records were received. Log records contain both redo and undo parts. The no-steal/force DB buffer policy, without locking, is applied during redo execution for each execution sequence. A Full Function tracker therefore forces all hot stand-by DB buffer blocks updated by a sequence of redo operations to disc at the end of the sequence. A log record becomes garbage when its transaction is committed and all effects of the log records in the sequence it belongs to have been forced to disc.

The Data Entry trackers perform redo execution based on the log records received and execute the redo operations in the logged sequence. Log records only contain redo parts. The no-steal/force

DB buffer policy with traditional block locking is applied during hot stand-by execution. All log records for a transaction are kept by the log router until the termination log record for the transaction is received. This makes it possible to determine the blocks updated by the transaction if it is to be aborted or when its updated blocks are to be flushed. A transaction may be aborted either because its termination record is aborted or because the primary site crashed before all its log records were received at the hot stand-by site.

RSR supports only manual take-over. A primary take-over applies the redo/undo policy. A hot stand-by replica is not available for read transactions. XRF cannot be applied to hot stand-by subsystems. XRF, on the other hand, can be started after a primary take-over is completed. Manual online blocking repair is supported by RSR based on image copying of databases.

17.8 Telecom Switch Internal DBMSs

Digital switches are monolithic units supporting plain old telephony service (POTS). They have, over time, been given increasing amounts of functionality, e.g., for management of routing, terminals, subscribers and charging. A digital switch typically contains millions of lines of software. It may not be out of service for more than two to three minutes per year, corresponding to availability class five [GR92].

The classical use of switch internal DBMSs is in various types of call routing, where transactions read one record, demand 0.5 to 5 milliseconds response time, and 10 to 10.000 TPS. A typical example is mapping from a phone number to a physical subscriber line. Update transactions are less than 10% of the transaction volume, and demand a response time from 5 to 50 milliseconds. Mobile telephony implies update transactions in the mobile switching centers (MSCs) with 10 to 20 millisecond response time because a user should never experience glitches longer than 100 milliseconds when a mobile terminal is handed over from one MSC to another. Durable connections, which imply crash atomic call status, demand update transactions with response times similar to mobile telephony.

Switch internal DBMSs have barely been documented in the research literature. They have been tailored to meet the needs of routing applications. As a consequence, they support very fast reading of a few records, and most provide dirty read. Some systems are pure main-memory databases, others have background disc support. Update transactions involve write-ahead logging to disc, and the response time is therefore longer than a disc access. The throughput rate for update transactions is rather low. Some systems are centralised, some are parallel. The parallel systems seem to give scalable throughput growth. They differ in availability attention and implementation. Some rely entirely on fault-tolerant hardware, others have implemented fault tolerance in software using multiple loosely synchronised main memory replicas of tables. A hot stand-by replica becomes primary if the primary fails. A hot stand-by replica is available to be read during a primary take-over. Update transactions caught in a primary take-over are typically aborted and restarted. Automatic online repair is supported by some systems. The repair is done by producing a new main memory replica for one that has been lost. The production is based on an existing main memory replica which may be read during the replication. Update transactions which are active to the repaired replica are typically aborted and restarted. Online software upgrade is not normally supported. The relational model is used by most systems.

17.9 Academic Research Work

High availability approaches have attained academic research interest over the last decade ([KHGMP90], [GMPH90], [KHGMP91], [CAP91], [PG94]). The research has focused on applying the 1-Safe strategy to multi-node sites combined with multiple log streams between primaries and hot stand-bys. All the products documented in this chapter, even the multi-node site Tandem product, use a single log stream between a primary and a hot stand-by subsystem or site. This may cause performance bottlenecks, especially for large multi-node sites.

Two policies have been developed for parallel log streams. The first policy is termed the dependency reconstruction algorithm (**DRA**). For a detailed description of DRA, see [KHGMP90] and [GMP90]. The second policy is termed the epoch algorithm (**Epoch**). For a detailed description of Epoch, see [GMPH90]. A performance evaluation of DRA and Epoch policies and a performance evaluation of 1-Safe and 2-Safe strategies are presented in [PG94].

The DRA policy assumes that transactions may involve multiple primary nodes and that a two-phase commit protocol is used locally between a transaction coordinator and its slave-transactions at the primary site. DRA uses the LGS policy, where only redo log record parts are included in the log records sent from a primary to a hot stand-by. DRA assigns a sequence number or *ticket* to each committed primary transaction part generated by one primary slave-transaction. Ticket numbers are assigned in monotonously increasing value locally at a node. They reflect the commit sequence of primary transactions local to a primary node. A ticket counter is maintained for each primary slave. A primary slave-transaction that has executed state changing tuple operations is assigned the next unused ticket number when it receives the commit message from the primary transaction controller and the ticket counter is then incremented. A read-only primary slave-transaction is assigned the next unused ticket number but the ticket counter is not incremented. The ticket number is included in the commit log record which is produced for the primary slave-transaction. A primary transaction controller must include in its commit record a list of nodes where its primary slave-transactions had been executing. The DRA strategy requires that also tuple read operations are logged to maintain the 1-Safe mutual consistency property.

The execution of a hot stand-by transaction includes a hot stand-by transaction controller, hot stand-by slave-transactions and the application of a two-phase commit protocol. A hot stand-by slave-transaction must wait to start execution until all those hot stand-by log record replicas for the transaction which are intended for the node have arrived at the node. When all log records have arrived, the slave-transaction must wait to be allowed to start requesting locks until all hot stand-by slave transactions at the node with a smaller ticket number in their commit log record have requested all their locks. When a hot stand-by slave-transaction has obtained all its locks and executed all its hot stand-by state changing operations, it informs the hot stand-by transaction coordinator that it is ready to commit. When the coordinator has received a ready signal from all participants, it commits the hot stand-by transaction according to the two-phase commit protocol.

The DRA policy guarantees the 1-Safe minimal divergence property if all log records from a node are sent to their hot stand-by nodes in a single stream. If, on the other hand, all hot stand-by log record replicas for a transaction are bundled at the primary transaction coordinator, and the bundle is shipped to the hot stand-by transaction coordinator which then forwards the hot stand-by log records to their respective hot stand-by slave-transactions, minimal divergence is not guaranteed.

The DRA policy only supports mirrored declustering. All hot stand-by replicas for the primary replicas located at a node must be located at a single node. DRA can be extended to handle other declustering strategies by generating tickets for each primary fragment replicas, including a list of fragments with their corresponding ticket numbers in the slave-participant's commit records, and also including the list of involved fragments in the transaction coordinator's commit records. DRA does not handle subfragmentations. It is possible to handle subfragmentation if, in addition to the changes proposed above, a slave-transaction's commit record is shipped to all hot stand-by nodes where a hot stand-by subfragment replica for each involved primary fragment replica is located.

The *Epoch* policy installs state-changing operations at a hot stand-by node in batches called epochs. Delimiters are entered into the logs generated at the primary nodes to ensure that all commit log records for a primary transaction will be in the same epoch. This can be ensured by running a distributed Epoch-coordination transaction that involves all nodes at regular intervals. An Epoch-transaction distributes the next epoch number to all nodes. A node will enter an epoch log record into its log record, reflecting the epoch number, when it receives such an Epoch-transaction message and will also update its current epoch number. The current epoch number at the node where a primary transaction coordinator is located is included in the commit records it sends to its primary slave-transactions. If a hot stand-by node receives a commit record with a higher epoch number than its current epoch number, then an epoch log record is entered into its log and its current epoch number is updated. This is done before the commit record for the involved primary slave-transaction is produced, so that the resulting commit record will belong to the same epoch as the coordinator's commit log record.

An epoch is not evaluated for execution at a hot stand-by node before all hot stand-by nodes have received an epoch with the same epoch number. The synchronisation needed in order to obey this can be obtained by having each hot stand-by node broadcast the receipt of an epoch to the other hot stand-by nodes and having each hot stand-by node keep track of which other hot stand-by nodes have announced their receipt. As an alternative, each hot stand-by node can report its receipt of an epoch to a master. The master must keep track of which hot stand-by nodes have received the epoch. When the master has received the information that all hot stand-by nodes have received the epoch, it can broadcast the receipt of the epoch to all slaves. A slave-transaction will not be started at a hot stand-by node for a given transaction before the epoch containing the commit record for the corresponding primary slave-transaction has been received or the prepare-to-commit record for the primary slave-transaction has been received and the hot stand-by transaction coordinator has received the transaction's commit log record.

The Epoch policy avoids the needs for transmitting read information to the hot stand-by site because there is no need to recreate transaction dependencies during hot stand-by execution. The Epoch policy will involve fewer messages between the hot stand-by nodes than the DRA policy, since there is no two-phase commit processing for each transaction, only for each epoch. The Epoch policy delays hot stand-by transaction execution compared with the DRA policy since a hot stand-by transaction does not start executing before the complete epoch in which its commit information is contained has arrived. The Epoch policy supports mirrored declustering. It does not obey the minimal divergence property.

Part V

Conclusion and Future Work

Chapter 18

Conclusion

To validate the HypRa recovery approach presented in this book, i.e. to evaluate the correctness of the approach and how likely it is that the approach will meet the stated requirements, key parts of the approach have been presented at international conferences ([HST+91b], [HST91a], [HT92]) to obtain both validation by the program committee and evaluation by the conference audience. Other key parts of the approach have been presented to research colleagues at international research institutes and universities ([Hva89a], [Hva91a], [Hva92a], [Hva92b]). Based on the validation given and the depth of the research leading to the approach, we feel confident that we have convincingly argued for the correctness of the recovery approach and that the approach meets the above stated requirements.

The conclusions to be drawn from this research are organised into three sections: i) conclusions drawn from the analysis of existing recovery approaches which meet some but not all HypRa requirements; ii) conclusions from the development of the HypRa recovery approach through which the remaining requirements are met; and iii) conclusions from the development of online non-blocking fragment repair and online non-blocking DB, SW, and HW maintenance which are based on the new features provided by the HypRa recovery approach.

18.1 Lessons Learned from Centralised DBMS Recovery Approaches

The main recovery approaches for centralised DBMSs which have been developed over the last two decades have been systematically analysed according to how well they meet the requirements of the HypRa recovery approach. The final conclusion is that a recovery approach can be constructed from these approaches to meet the HypRa *consistency* and *simple transaction load* requirements, but these approaches have inherent limitations with respect to the *availability* and *transaction response* requirements of HypRa.

The HypRa recovery approach is therefore constructed from strategies and policies inherent in the existing recovery approaches as well as from new strategies and policies developed in Part II. The following summarises the main strategies and policies from the existing approaches used in the HypRa approach, and explains why they are used. The main conclusion is explicitly related to the first five recovery design goals specified in section 2.6:

- **Locking**
  The HypRa DBMS supports *fine granularity* and *semantically rich locking* to meet the very high transaction load requirement. The *compensation recovery* strategy is therefore used. The *action consistent block split/merge* policy is used to limit block lock duration to a fraction of a transaction and to avoid block lock hot-spots. The *fuzzy checkpoint* policy is

used because it imposes very little locking during normal operations, and also sets acceptable restrictions on node crash recovery work.

- **Low overhead and no bottlenecks during normal processing**
  Low logging overhead is obtained by the *partial tuple logging* strategy. The *steal/no-force DB buffer* policy is used because it provides the most flexible DB buffer management policy and supports very large DB buffers without increased overhead. The steal/no-force policy is also applied to split/merge subtransactions to minimise the overhead involved. The *recursive action consistent split/merge* policy is used to remove access method maintenance overhead from the nested top-level transactions in order to meet the soft real-time transaction response requirements.

- **Fast recovery from transaction failures**
  Sequential transaction failure recovery is supported in order to recover a transaction at the same speed as do processing. The *non-sequential transaction failure recovery strategy* is supported for large transactions to recover a failed transaction faster than the do processing.

- **Fast node crash recovery**
  The *non-sequential recovery strategy* is used to speed up node crash recovery and reduce work load. The *single log scan* and *dedicated DB buffer* policies are used to minimise the log disc I/O work load and speed up log scanning. The *log-aggregation, block autonomous*, and *block complete* policies are used to allow asynchronous recovery to blocks and to tuples within a block, to avoid re-accessing blocks, and to access the blocks in a sequence that minimises the disc work load. The *dictionary independent* and the *upper/lower border* policies are applied to obtain block autonomous and complete recovery. The *log-backchain CLR* policy is used to support non-sequential recovery. The *single CLR* policy is used to guarantee a maximum log volume produced during node crash recovery regardless of multiple node crashes.

There are two main deficiencies in the existing recovery approaches. First, the *block state-identifier* policy is used. As a consequence, the existing approaches are unable to support online non-blocking fragment repair with subfragment load distribution and therefore cannot offer very high availability. Second, a transaction involves at least one disc access during its commit processing due to disc based logging. As a consequence, transactions cannot meet the soft real-time response requirement. The *group commit* policy handles the commit processing load resulting from the transaction load, but does not meet the response time requirement.

18.2 Main Contributions from the HypRa Recovery Approach

Recovery strategies have been developed to meet those of the HypRa recovery requirements not met by the existing recovery approaches: very high availability and soft real-time response. In the process, existing strategies have been adapted to compliment the added strategies. A summary of the main contributions is presented in Part III, "The HypRa Recovery Approach".

The HypRa architecture is based on multiple relation replicas, i.e. one primary replica and one or more hot stand-by replicas, in order to provide at least single data fault-tolerance. Every relation is horizontally fragmented and fragment replicas are allocated over the nodes to obtain a fairly even distribution of the work load. Two replicas of a fragment are never located at nodes with a common failure mode. Logs and locks are fragmented and allocated as relation fragments to obtain clustering, work load distribution, and fault-tolerance. Main memory logging is applied so that a log record is stably stored when it is contained in main memory at the nodes in which the log fragment replicas are located. Operations are executed as deferred to hot stand-by replicas and are guaranteed to succeed. HypRa fault-tolerance is based on HW failure detection, SW online failure masking, online fast recovery, and online non-blocking repair.

The HypRa recovery approach is founded on: i) very fast primary take-over to maintain continuous fragment availability in case of a primary fragment replica or node failure; ii) fast node and fragment replica recovery to recover a failed node or fragment, and fast catch up with the current primary; and iii) fast online non-blocking repair to reestablish both the original consistency fault-tolerance level and the original availability fault-tolerance level, within the given time windows, to meet the consistency and availability requirements.

Chapter 11, "The Location- and Replication Independent Tuple Recovery Strategy", introduced the *tuple state-identifier* policy, which makes tuple recovery location and replication independent. This is the founding policy for non-blocking fragment repair and subfragmentation because it allows a log record replica to be used to recover any replica of the tuple regardless of its node, table, or block location. The *multi-level state-identifier* policy is applied to allow node internal operations to be reflected locally to the node.

Chapter 12, "The Log Distribution Strategy", presented log fragmentation and allocation. One log is supported per fragment to limit the log part involved in a fragment failure. The fragment log is replicated with the fragment replica and clustered to the same node as the fragment replica. This replication provides the same fault-tolerance level to the log fragments as to the data fragments. The log is subfragmented when the fragment is subfragmented. A log concatenation policy is provided. The tuple state-identifiers are derived from the tuple log record identifiers so that the sequence of tuple operations is maintained for each tuple. The tuple log record identifiers are global for each log fragment replica, and the tuple log record identifiers of a subfragment are greater than the tuple log record identifiers in the parent fragment log.

Chapter 13, "The Neighbour Write-Ahead Logging Strategy", presented logging policies supporting disc access-free transaction processing so that the soft real-time response requirement is met. This is done by logging in main memory at the nodes in which the primary and the hot stand-by log replicas are located. Deferred operations are involved in two-phase commits and are guaranteed to be executed when a transaction commits. The consistency requirement is obeyed by replicating the log parts and possible tuple replicas lost during a node crash which are determined by use of the *double block flush logging* policy. The redo/no-undo CLR policy is applied to simplify log garbage collection of top-level transactions and the no-redo/no-undo policy to node internal transactions. The *nested top-action* policy is applied to minimise overhead when performing a bottom level block split.

Chapter 14, "The Recovery Strategies", focused on *fast* take-over, fast transaction failure recovery, and fast node crash recovery. The *no-undo/no-redo* primary take-over policy is applied to minimise fragment unavailability during a take-over and thereby to meet the continuous availability requirement. The *fragment replica asynchronous* transaction failure recovery policy is a consequence of log fragmentation and supports faster recovery than sequential recovery because the recovery is done in parallel to the fragment logs. A fast *non-sequential node crash recovery* policy is supported. Selective fragment recovery is supported so that some, but not all, fragments can be recovered at one time.

18.3 Maintaining a Continuously Available Transaction Server

The HypRa recovery approach is used as the foundation for non-blocking DB, SW, and HW maintenance transactions and non-blocking mixed loads of simple transactions and complex transactions. Online non-blocking maintenance of all these aspects is required to support continuous availability. These novel maintenance and transaction methods are presented in [HST+91b]. They are based on the results presented in this book.

Complex transactions are provided with read access to hot stand-by fragment replicas. A concurrency control scheme is developed maintaining consistency between the simple and complex transactions.

Non-blocking maintenance transactions are provided to the data dictionary concurrently with simple transactions. This is also based on multiple hot stand-by dictionary fragment replicas combined with node region serialised commit processing ([Nyg90]) in order to maintain continuous dictionary availability.

A general fuzzy non-blocking fragment replica production mechanism is provided. This is the mechanism used to provide *online non-blocking fragment repair*. The fuzzy non-blocking fragment replica production mechanism is also used to support *soft* customer HW replacements. HW replacements are met by this mechanism without compromising availability and without aborting or delaying active transactions. A *hard* HW replacement is handled as a node crash. Soft SW replacements are similarly handled without aborting transactions by applying a *fuzzy take-over* policy.

Chapter 19

Future Work

We have, to a large degree, directed the research leading to what is presented in this book towards developing a recovery approach meeting, in particular, the telecommunication operational requirements for a DBMS. We are confident that we have convincingly argued for the correctness of the recovery approach and that it meets the telecommunication operational requirements.

To validate the demands for the capabilities provided by the HypRa recovery approach and the non-blocking maintenance mechanisms, the results of this research have been presented to a number of demanding international users of DBMS technology: The Norwegian Telecom, Pacific Bell, AMERITECH, BellSouth, NYNEX, and AT&T. Based on the reactions from these presentations we are confident that we have attacked some of the current major challenges to DBMS technology.

The reactions from these presentations to users have also convinced us that the decision to attack a real world, as opposed to a purely theoretical, problem using scientific methods, was right. Because of the size of the problem, no prototype implementation of the developed recovery approach was possible as part of the Dr.Ing. research.

The next step in developing the HypRa recovery approach is implementation. In order to further validate the correctness of the approach, an experimental prototype of the approach would be necessary. The ClustRa project was started by Telenor R&D in December 1993 to implement a research prototype of HypRa based on off-the-shelf hardware, basic software, and communication technology. The results obtained in the ClustRa project are presented in [HTBH95].

The next step in the validation of the HypRa recovery approach's ability to meet the telecommunication operational requirements is a product prototype implementation in a real setting. From this, the feasibility of the approach can be determined. This work is currently under way (see section 19.2).

19.1 Follow Up Threads

There is a fair number of threads to be followed up from this Dr.Ing. research:

- **Primary take-over**
  A limitation inherent in the HypRa recovery approach is its inability to support *seamless primary take-over*, i.e. to avoid aborting active transactions at a failed node. Since a node failure may cause a massive transaction abort, it may threaten transaction service availability. We have, in later work which was not part of the Dr.Ing. research, developed a seamless primary take-over policy. This policy is derived from the present framework, based on savepoints and more active hot stand-by slave-transaction and hot stand-by transaction

coordinators.

- **Multiple hot stand-by fragment replicas**
  The solution presented in Part III is based on one hot stand-by fragment replica and one hot stand-by log fragment replica, which provides single fault-tolerance. Multiple hot stand-by replicas are needed to provide multi-level fault-tolerance. Multiple hot stand-by replicas will introduce modifications of the update channel protocol. Some hot stand-by replica, other than the one becoming the new primary, could have received a log record replica before the crash that was not received by the replica which became the primary. Synchronisation is required to prevent DB inconsistencies from occurring as a result of this. We have, in later work which was not part of the Dr.Ing. research, developed an update channel protocol that also allows multiple hot stand-by fragment replicas.

- **Vertical fragmentation**
  The presented solution is based on horizontal fragmentation. The framework can be extended to also cover vertical fragmentation and vertical subfragmentation. The tuple state-identifiers must then be connected to fields instead of to tuples. A software RAID technology ([PGK88], [LK91]) with non-blocking repair can be obtained by vertical fragmentation.

19.2 Commercialising HypRa

It has been most interesting to do the research reported in this book. The interesting aspects have been enhanced by the fact that real problems have been attacked. This work has therefore not been done primarily for academic purposes, but to establish the recovery design foundation for the HypRa DBMS.

Telenor R&D have decided to turn the ClustRa DBMS, which started out as a research project in December 1993, into a Telenor internal product by the end of 1996. ClustRa is expected to be used in intelligent network applications.

Bibliography

[ABC+76] M. M. Astrahan, M. W. Blasgen, D. D. Chamberlin, K. P. Eswaran, J. N. Gray, P. P. Griffiths, W. F. King, R. A. Lorie, P. R. McJones, J. W. Mehl, G. R. Putzolu, I. L. Traiger, B. W. Wade, and V. Watson. System R: Relational Approach to Database Management. *ACM Transactions on Database Systems*, 1(2):97–137, June 1976.

[ABF+81] T. Amble, K. Bratbergsengen, A. Frøseth, S.O. Hvasshovd, M. Kongshavn, O. Risnes, and T. Aandalen. Spesifikasjon av ASTRA Databasemaskin. Technical Report ASTRA-notat nr. 41, SINTEF, RUNIT, 1981. In Norwegian.

[AH89] K. Albertsen and S.O. Hvasshovd. The TelSQL Report. Research Report STF14 A88048, SINTEF, RUNIT, 1989.

[ARH+90] O. J. Aske, O. Risnes, S.O. Hvasshovd, K. Bratbergsengen, and T. Sæter. HypRa DBMS Detail Design Volume III: High Level DBMS Software. Research Report STF40 F90133, SINTEF, ELAB-RUNIT, 1990.

[ASC88] A. El Abbadi, D. Skeen, and F. Cristian. An Efficient, Fault-Tolerant Protocol for Replicated Data Management. In M. Stonebraker, editor, *Readings in Database Systems*, pages 259–273. Morgan Kaufmann Publishers, Inc., San Mateo, California, 1988.

[Ask89a] O. J. Aske. Communicating on HC16: A Study of Performance and Methods Used to Communicate in a Hypercubic Network Based on Dual Port RAM. Technical report, Division of Computer Systems and Telematics, University of Trondheim, Norwegian Institute of Technology, N-7034 Trondheim, Norway, 1989.

[Ask89b] O. J. Aske. HypRa Hardware and System Software Overall Design. Research Report STF40 F89201, ELAB-RUNIT, SINTEF, 1989.

[AT90] O. J. Aske and Ø. Torbjørnsen. Communication on HC16 - A Study of Methods and Performance in a Hypercubic Network Based on Dual Port RAM. In *Proceedings of The Fifth Distributed Memory Computing Conference*, volume 2, pages 660–669. IEEE, April 1990.

[Bar78] J. F. Bartlett. A "NonStop" Operating System. In *Proceedings of the 11th Hawaii International Conference on System Sciences*, volume III, 1978.

[Bar81] J. Bartlett. A NonStop Kernel. In *The 8th Symposium on Operating System Principles*, December 1981.

[BBG+89] A. Borg, W. Blau, W. Graetsch, F. Herrman, and W. Oberle. Fault Tolerance Under UNIX. *ACM Transactions on Computer Systems*, 7(1):1–24, February 1989.

[BCFea95] B. Bobrowski, C. Closkey, J. Frazzini, and et al. Oracle7 Server Concepts. Product documentation Part No. A20321-2, ORACLE Corporation, 500 Oracle Parkway, Redwood City, CA, USA, 1995.

[BG88] D. Bitton and J. N. Gray. Disk Shadowing. In F. Bancilhon and D. J. DeWitt, editors, *Proceedings of the 14th International Conference on Very Large Data Bases*, pages 331–338, Los Angeles, California, USA, August 1988.

[BG89] K. Bratbergsengen and T. Gjelsvik. The Development of the CROSS8 and HC16-186 Parallel (Database) Computers. In H. Boral and P. Faudemay, editors, *The 6th International Workshop on Database Machines*, Deauville, France, June 1989. Lecture Notes on Computer Science, 368, Springer-Verlag.

[BG89] B. A. W. Baugstø and J. F. Greipsland. Parallel Sorting Methods for Large Data Volumes on a Hypercube Database Computer. In H. Boral and P. Faudemay, editors, *Proceedings from Sixth International Workshop on Database Machines, IWDM '89, Lecture Notes in Computer Science 368*, pages 127 – 141. Springer-Verlag, June 89.

[BHG87] P. A. Bernstein, V. Hadzilacos, and N. Goodman. *Concurrency Control and Recovery in Database Systems*. Addison-Wesley Publishing Company, Inc., 1987.

[BHW74] K. Bratbergsengen, K. Hofstad, and K. Wibe. *Filsystemer og Databaser*. Tapir, 1974. In Norwegian.

[BJWK+76] K. Bratbergsengen, K. Juul-Wedde, P. Kongshaug, S. H. Kvitsand, and A. Laugen. RA2 - System Description. Research Report STF14 F76040, SINTEF RUNIT, 1976. In Norwegian.

[BK91] N. S. Barghouti and G. E. Kaiser. Concurrency Control in Advanced Database Applications. *ACM Computing Surveys*, 23(3):269–317, September 1991.

[BLRA80] K. Bratbergsengen, R. Larsen, O. Risnes, and T. Aandalen. A Neighbor Connected Processor Network for Performing Relational Algebra Operations. In *The Fifth Workshop on Computer Architecture for Non-numeric Processing*, Pacific Grove, Ca, USA, March 1980. SIGMOD.

[BM72] R. Bayer and E. McCreight. Organization and Maintenace of Large Ordered Indices. *Acta Informatica*, 1(3), 1972.

[Bob92] S. Bobrowski. ORACLE RDBMS: Database Administrator's Guide Volume II, Developer's Release Documentation. Technical Report ORACLE Part No. 6694-70-0592, ORACLE Corporation, May 1992.

[Bor81] A. Borr. Transaction Monitoring in ENCOMPASS: Reliable Distributed Transaction Processing. In *Proceedings of the 7th Conference on Very Large Data Bases*, September 1981.

[Bor84] A. Borr. Robustness to Crash in a Distributed Database: A Non Shared-Memory Multi-Processor Approach. In *Proceedings of the 10th Conference on Very Large Data Bases*, August 1984.

[BP88] A. Borr and F. Putzolu. High performance SQL through low-level system integration. In *Proceedings of ACM SIGMOD International Conference on Management of Data*, Chicago USA, June 1988.

[Bra84] K. Bratbergsengen. Hashing Methods and Relational Algebra Operations. In *Proceedings of the 10th International Conference on Very Large Data Bases*, pages 323–333, 1984.

[Bra87] K. Bratbergsengen. Algebra Operations on a Parallel Computer - Performance Evaluation. In *Proceedings of the 5th International Workshop on Database Machines*, 1987.

[Bra89a] K. Bratbergsengen. The Development of Database Computers. In *SIBUG-89*, Bergen, Norway, February 1989.

[Bra89b] K. Bratbergsengen. The Development of the Parallel Database Computer HC16-186. In *Fourth Conference on Hypercubes, Concurrent Computers and Applications*, Monterey, California, USA, March 1989.

[Bra89c] K. Bratbergsengen. HypRa Databasesystem Realitetsanalyse. Research Report STF40 F89199, SINTEF, ELAB-RUNIT, 1989. In Norwegian.

[Bra90] K. Bratbergsengen. Relational Algebra Operations. In P. American, editor, *Proceedings of the PRISMA Workshop - Parallel Database Systems*, pages 28–47, Nordwijk, The Netherlands, September 1990.

[Bro85] R. C. Brooks. An Approach to High Availability in High-Transaction-Rate Systems. *IBM System Journal*, 24(3/4):279–293, 1985.

[BT90] D. L. Burkes and R. K. Treiber. Design Approaches for Real-Time Transaction Processing Remote Site Recovery. In *The 35th IEEE Computer Society International Conference COMPCON 90*, February 1990.

[CAB+81] D. D. Chamberlin, M. A. Astrahan, M. W. Blasgen, J. N. Gray, W. F. King, B. G. Lindsay, R. Lorie, J. W. Mehl, T. G. Price, F. Putzolu, P. G. Selinger, M. Schkolnick, D. R. Slutz, I. L. Traiger, B. W. Wade, and R. A. Yost. A History and Evaluation of System R. *Communication of the ACM*, 24(10), October 1981.

[CAP91] H. Garcia-Molina C. A. Polyzois. A Generalized Disaster Recovery Model and Algorithm. In *Proceedings of the 4nd International Workshop on High Performace Systems*, September 1991.

[CDD90] F. Cristian, R. D. Dancey, and J. Dehn. Fault-Tolerance in the Advanced Automation System. Research Report RJ7424 (69595) 4/16/90 Computer Science, IBM Research Division, Almaden Research Center, 650 Harry Road, San Jose, California 95120-6099, USA, 1990.

[CGY81] D. Chamberlin, A. Gilbert, and R. Yost. A History of System R and SQL/Data System. In *Proceedings of the 7th International Conference on Very Large Data Bases*, 1981.

[Chr86] B. Christensen. IMS/VS Virtual Storage Management. Technical Report GG24-1750, IBM, March 1986.

[CK89] G. Copeland and T. Keller. A Comparison of High-Availability Media Recovery. In *Proceedings of the ACM SIGMOD Conference*, pages 98–109, Los Angeles, California, USA, June 1989.

[CKKS89] G. Copeland, T. Keller, R. Krishnamurthy, and M. Smith. The Case For Safe RAM. In *Proceedings of the 15th International Conference on Very Large Data Bases*, pages 327–335, 1989.

[CKS91] G. Copeland, T. Keller, and M. Smith. Database Buffer and Disk Configuring and The Battle of yhe Bottlenecks. In *Proceedings of the 4th International Workshop on High Performance Transaction Systems*, September 1991.

[CMI88] Information Processing Systems, Open System Interconnection - Management Information Service Definition - Common Management Information Service. Technical Report ISO/IEC JTC1/SC21 N-2835, ISO/ANSI, 1988.

[Cod70] E. F. Codd. A Relational Model for Large Shared Databanks. *Communication of the ACM*, 13(6):377–387, 1970.

[Cod91] E. F. Codd. Choosing a Relational DBMS Product Today. *The Relational Journal*, 3(5):3–13, Novenber 1991.

[CP86] S. Ceri and G. Pelagatti. *Distributed Databases Principles and Systems*. Mc Graw Hill, 1986.

[Cri85] F. Cristian. A Rigorous Approach to Fault-Tolerant Programming. *IEEE Transaction on Software Engineering*, SE-11(1), January 1985.

[Cri87] F. Cristian. Basic Consepts and Terminology in Fault-Tolerant Computing. In *The 7. International Conference on Distributed Computing Systems, Tutorial No. 2, Highly Avalable Distributed Systems*, September 1987.

[Cri89] F. Cristian. Questions to Ask when Designing or Attempting to Understand a Fault-tolerant Distributed System. Research Report RJ6980 (66517) 8/24/89 Computer Science, IBM Research Division, Almaden Research Center, 650 Harry Road, San Jose, California 95120, USA, 1989.

[Cri90] F. Cristian. Understanding Fault-Tolerant Distributed Systems. Research report, IBM Research Division, Almaden Research Center, 650 Harry Road, San Jose, California 95120-6099, USA, 1990.

[Cru84] R. Crus. Data Recovery in IBM Database 2. *IBM Systems Journal*, 23(2), 1984.

[CSTJ89] K. Cohen, G. Smith, D. Tolkowsky, and K. Jacobs. Oracle for the NCUBE 2 - Technology Overview: The Parallel Server. Technical Report Part Number 50333-0789, Oracle Corporation, July 1989.

[Dat83] C. J. Date. *An Introduction to Database Systems, Vol II*. Addison-Wesley Publishing Company, Inc., 1983.

[Dat84] C. J. Date. *A Guide to DB2*. Addison-Wesley Publishing Company, Inc., 1984.

[Dat86] C. J. Date. *An Introduction to Database Systems, Vol I*. Addison-Wesley Publishing Company, Inc., fourth edition, 1986.

[Dea87] S. Dimmick and et al. ORACLE Database Administrator's Guide Version 5.1. Product documentation ORACLE Part No. 3601-V5.1, ORACLE Corporation, Belmont, California, USA, 1987.

[DEC93a] Dec reliable transaction router (rtr) for openvms, system manager's manual. Technical Report Order Number: AA-PHWHC-TE, Digital Equipment Corporation, Maynard, Massachusetts, USA, September 1993.

[DEC93b] Dec reliable transaction router (rtr) for openvms, application programmer's reference manual. Technical Report Order Number: AA-PHWGC-TE, Digital Equipment Corporation, Maynard, Massachusetts, USA, September 1993.

[DG85] D. DeWitt and R. Gerber. Multiprocessor Hash-Based Join Algorithms. In *Proceedings of the 11th Conference on Very Large Data Bases*, Stockholm, August 1985.

[DGS+90] D. J. DeWitt, S. Ghandeharizadeh, D. A. Schneider, A. Bricker, H. I. Hsiao, and R. Rasmussen. The Gamma Database Machine Project. *IEEE Transactions on Knowledge and Data Engineering*, 2(1):44–62, March 1990.

[DHL90] U. Dayal, M. Hsu, and R. Ladin. Organizing Long-Running Activities with Triggers and Transactions. In *Proceedings of the 1990 ACM SIGMOD International Conference on Management of Data*, pages 204–214, 1990.

[Dim85] C. I. Dimmer. The Tandem Non-Stop System. In T. Anderson, editor, *Resilient Computer Systems*, chapter 10. Blackwell Scientific Publications Professional Books, Oxford, UK, 1985.

[Dou90] B. Dougherty. Industry Viewpoint: Telco's Strategic Importance in Tandem's Success, 1990.

[DP88] M. Darnovsky and K. Paulsell. *System Administration Guide*. Sybase Inc., December 1988.

[EB84] K. Elhardt and R. Bayer. A Database Cache for High Performance and Fast Restart in Database Systems. *ACM Transactions on Database Systems*, 9(4):503–525, December 1984.

[EH84] W. Effelsberg and T. Haerder. Principles of Database Buffer Management. *Transactions on the ACM*, 9(4), December 1984.

[Eic89] M. H. Eich. Main Memory Database Research Directions. In H. Boral and P. Faudemay, editors, *The 6th International Workshop on Database Machines*, pages 251–268, Deauville, France, June 1989. Lecture Notes on Computer Science, 368, Springer-Verlag.

[EMS91] J. L. Eppinger, L. B. Mummert, and A. Z. Spector. *Camelot and Avelon: A A Distributed Transaction Facility*. Morgan Kaufmann Publishers, Inc, 1991.

[Enc93] Encina Monitor Programmer's Guide. Product documentation TP-D130-30.14.4, Transarc Corporation, The Gulf Tower, 707 Grant Street, Pittsburgh, PA, USA, 1993.

[ENE93a] Remote Recovery Data Facility, Technical Overview, Version 2. Technical report, E-Net Corporation, Sansome Street, 20th Floor, San Francisco, CA. 94111, USA, 1993.

[ENE93b] Remote Recovery Data Facility, Operations Guide, Version 2 Release 1. Technical report, E-Net Corporation, Sansome Street, 20th Floor, San Francisco, CA. 94111, USA, November 1993.

[ENE93c] RRDF Log Apply, Program Directory, Version 2, Release 1. Technical report, E-Net Corporation, Sansome Street, 20th Floor, San Francisco, CA. 94111, USA, 1993.

[ENE93d] RRDF, Log Apply Operations Guide, Version 2, Release 1. Technical report, E-Net Corporation, Sansome Street, 20th Floor, San Francisco, CA. 94111, USA, 1993.

[ENE93e] E-NET2 IDMS Shadow Database Facility. Technical report, E-Net Corporation, Sansome Street, 20th Floor, San Francisco, CA. 94111, USA, 1993.

[ENE94] RRDF Log Apply, Benchmark Test, Version 1, Release 2. Technical report, E-Net Corporation, Sansome Street, 20th Floor, San Francisco, CA. 94111, USA, February 1994.

[FCK87] J. C. Freytag, F. Cristian, and B. Kähler. Masking System Crashes in Database Application Programs. Research Report RJ5558 (56647) 3/18/87, IBM Almaden Research Center, 1987.

[FKea95] J. Fee, V. K. Kane, and et al. Oracle7 Server Administrator's Guide, Release 7.2. Product documentation Part No. A20322-2, ORACLE Corporation, 500 Oracle Parkway, Redwood City, CA, USA, 1995.

[Fri90] O. Frieder. Multiprocessor Algorithms for Relational-Database Operators on Hypercube Systems. *IEEE Computer*, 23(11):13–28, November 1990.

[Gaw85] D. Gawlick. Processing Hot Spots in High Performance Systems. In *Proceedings of the IEEE Compcon Spring '85*, 1985.

[GK85a] D. Gawlick and D. Kinkade. Varieties of Concurrency Control in IMS/VS Fast Path. *IEEE Database Engineering*, 8(2), June 1985.

[GK85b] D. Gawlick and D. Kinkade. Varieties of Concurrency Control in IMS/VS FastPath. *Data Engineering Bulletin*, 8(2), June 1985.

[GMA89] H. Garcia-Molina and R. K. Abbott. Reliable Distributed Database Management. *Proceedings of the IEEE*, 75(5):601–620, May 1989.

[GMB+81] J. N. Gray, P. McJones, M. Blasgen, B. Lindsay, R. Lorie, T. Price, F. Putzolu, and I. Traiger. The Recovery Manager of the System R Database Manager. *ACM Computing Surveys*, 13(2), June 1981.

[GMP90] H. Garcia-Molina and C. A. Polyzois. Issues in Disaster Recovery. In *The 35th IEEE Computer Society International Conference COMPCON 90*, February 1990.

[GMPH90] H. Garcia-Molina, C. A. Polyzois, and R. Hagman. Two Epoch Algorithms for Disaster Recovery. In *Proceedings of the 16th Conference on Very Large Data Bases*, 1990.

[Gol95] R. Goldring. Update replication: What every designer should know. *InfoDB*, 9(2), 1995.

[GP86] J. N. Gray and F. Putzolu. The 5 Minute Rule for Trading Memory for Disc Accesses and the 5 Byte Rule for Trading Memory for CPU Time. Technical Report 86.1 PN87615, Tandem Computers, February 1986.

[GR88] J. N. Gray and A. Reuter. Transaction Processing (Version 3 of Slides). Heather Gray, 439 Greenwich St. 8A, San Fransisco, California, USA, June 1988. Foils and 18 videotapes.

[GR92] J. N. Gray and A. Reuter. *Transaction Processing: Concepts and Techniques*. Morgan Kaufmann Publishers, Inc., San Mateo, California, USA, 1992.

[Gra78] J. N. Gray. Notes on Data Base Operating Systems. Research Report RJ2188 (30001) 2/23/78 Computer Science, IBM Research Division, IBM Research Laboratory, San Jose, California 95193, USA, 1978.

[Gra81] J. N. Gray. The Transaction Concept: Virtues and Limitations. In *Proceedings of the 7th International Conference on Very Large Data Bases*, pages 144–154, 1981.

[Gra86] J. N. Gray. Why Do Computers Stop and What Can be Done About It. In *Proceedings of the 5th Symposium on Reliability in Distributed Software and Database Systems*, January 1986.

[Gra87] J. N. Gray. White Paper. Technical report, Tandem Computers, 1987. NonStop SQL Performance.

[Gra90] J. N. Gray. Census of Tandem System Availability Between 1985 and 1990. *IEEE Transactions on Reliability*, 39(4):409–418, October 1990.

[Gra91] J. N. Gray, editor. *The Benchmark Handbook for Database and Transaction Processing Systems*. Morgan Kaufmann Publishers, Inc., San Mateo, California, USA, 1991.

[Gro88] Tandem Performance Group. A Benchmark for Non-Stop SQL on the Debit Credit Transaction. In *Proceedings of ACM SIGMOD International Conference on Management of Data*, Chicago USA, June 1988.

[GS84] D. Gifford and A. Spector. The TWA Reservation System. *Communication of the ACM*, 27(7):649–665, July 1984.

[GS91] J. N. Gray and D. P. Siewiorek. High-Availability Computer Systems. *IEEE Computer*, 24(9):39–48, September 1991.

[Gue91] J. Guerrero. Rdf: An overview. *Tandem Systems Review*, 7(2), October 1991.

[HA88] S.O. Hvasshovd and K. Albertsen. Handling of the Telecommunication System within the TMN. Research Report STF14 A88027, SINTEF, RUNIT, 1988.

[HA89a] S.O. Hvasshovd and O. J. Aske. HypRa Database Management System Functional Specification. Research Report STF40 F89202, SINTEF, ELAB-RUNIT, 1989.

[HA89b] S.O. Hvasshovd and O. J. Aske. HypRa Database Management System Overall Design. Research Report STF40 F89203, ELAB-RUNIT, SINTEF, 1989.

[HA89c] S.O. Hvasshovd and O. J. Aske. HypRa Database System: Functional Specification. Research Report STF14 F89202, SINTEF, ELAB-RUNIT, 1989.

[Hag90] R. B. Hagmann. Rebuilding Database Caches During Fast Crash Recovery. Research Report CSL-90-2 April 1990 P90-00057, Xerox Corporation, Xerox Corporation, Palo Alto Research Center, 3333 Coyote Hill Road, Palo Alto, California 94304, USA, 1990.

[HB84] K. Hwang and F. A. Briggs. *Computer Architecture and Parallell Processing*. McGraw-Hill Book Company, 1984.

[HB91] A. Holman and E. Barton. The Computing Surface - A Platform for ORACLE. Technical Summary X0081-00N101.01, Meiko, Meiko Limited, 650 Aztec Road, Bristol, BS12 4SD, UK, June 1991.

[HD89] H. I. Hsiao and D. J. DeWitt. Chained Declustering: A New Availability Strategy for Multiprocessor Database Machines. Computer Science Technical Report 854, Gamma Database Machine Project, Computer Science Department, University of Wisconsin - Madison, June 1989.

[Hel85a] P. Helland. High Transaction Rates in a Distributed System. In *Proceedings of the International Workshop on High Performance Transaction Systems*, pages 215–228, March 1985.

[Hel85b] P. Helland. The Transaction Monitoring Facility (TMF). *IEEE Database Engineering*, 8(2), 1985.

[HJ84] D. Haderle and R. Jackson. IBM Database 2 Overview. *IBM Systems Journal*, 23(2), 1984.

[HL86] S.O. Hvasshovd and R. Lyseng. The TechRa DBMS Log and Recovery Design Specification. Software Design Specification Report TDB-LOG-1-R2, KVATRO, March 1986.

[HR84] T. Haerder and A. Reuter. Principles of Transaction-Oriented Database Recovery. Research Report RJ4214 (46292) 3/2/84 Computer Science, IBM Research Division, IBM Research Laboratory, San Jose, California 95193, USA, 1984.

[HRA+90] S.O. Hvasshovd, O. Risnes, O. J. Aske, K. Bratbergsengen, and T. Sæter (editor). HypRa DBMS Detailed Design Volume III: High Level DBMS Software. Research Report STF40 F90133, SINTEF, ELAB-RUNIT, 1990.

[HRL89] S.O. Hvasshovd, O. Risnes, and R. Lyseng. Outline of the NORA DBMS Software. Technical report, SINTEF, ELAB-RUNIT, 1989.

[HS90] S.O. Hvasshovd and T. Sæter. HypRa DBMS Detail Design Volume IV: DBMS Support Software. Research Report STF40 F90134, SINTEF, ELAB-RUNIT, 1990.

[HSAG90] S.O. Hvasshovd, T. Sæter, O. J. Aske, and T. Gjelsvik. HypRa DBMS Detail Design Volume II: Basic DBMS Software. Research Report STF40 F90132, SINTEF, ELAB-RUNIT, 1990.

[HST91a] S.O. Hvasshovd, T. Sæter, and Ø. Torbjørnsen. Critical Issues in the Design of a Fault-Tolerant Multiprocessor Database Server. In *Proceedings of the 1991 Pacific Rim International Symposium on Fault-Tolerant Systems*, Kawasaki, Kanagawa, Japan, September 1991.

[HST+91b] S.O. Hvasshovd, T. Sæter, Ø. Torbjørnsen, P. Moe, and O. Risnes. A Continously Available and Highly Scalable Transaction Server: Design Experience from the HypRa Project. In *Proceedings of the 4th International Workshop on High Performance Transaction Systems*, September 1991.

[HT92] S.O. Hvasshovd and Ø. Torbjørnsen. A Process Architecture Supporting Fault-Tolerance in a Parallel Database Server. In *Proceedings of the Nordic Seminar on Dependable Computing Systems 1992*, August 1992.

[HTBH95] S.O. Hvasshovd, Ø. Torbjørnsen, S. E. Bratsberg, and P. Holager. The ClustRa Telecom Database: High Availability, High Throughput, and Real-Time Response. In *Proceedings of the 21st International Conference on Very Large Data Bases*, Zurich, Switzerland, September 1995.

[Hva89a] S.O. Hvasshovd. HypRa a Distributed DBMS on a Shared Nothing Platform. Presentation at the Princeton University, May 1989.

[Hva89b] S.O. Hvasshovd. HypRa Database Management System Overall Software Design. Research Report STF40 F89204, ELAB-RUNIT, SINTEF, 1989.

[Hva90] S.O. Hvasshovd. HypRa Database Management System, The Record Oriented Local Node Based Log and Recovery Study. Research report, SINTEF, ELAB-RUNIT, 1990.

[Hva91a] S.O. Hvasshovd. Fault Tolerance Aspects of a Multiprocessor DBMS. HypRa Technical Report, 1991. Presentation at the Hewlett-Packard Laboratories, September 1991.

[Hva91b] S.O. Hvasshovd. HypRa/TR - A Tuple Oriented Recovery Method for a DDBMS on a Shared Nothing Platform. Presentation at the Data Base Technology Institute, IBM Almaden Research Center, September 1991.

[Hva92a] S.O. Hvasshovd. Introduction to the TeleServe DBMS. Presentation at the Hewlett Packard Laboratories, March 1992.

[Hva92b] S.O. Hvasshovd. The TeleServe DBMS Architecture. Presentation at the Bell Laboratories, March 1992.

[IBM86a] IBM. *IBM DATABASE 2*, March 1986. Document Number SC26-4078-2.

[IBM86b] IBM. *IMS/VS Version 2 Release 1 Data Base Administration Guide*, March 1986. Document Number SC26-4179.

[IBM86c] IBM. *IMS/VS Version2, Application Programming*, March 1986. Document NumberSC26-4177.

[IBM89a] IBM. *DATABASE 2 Version 2, Application Programming and SQL Guide, Release 2*, September 1989. Document Number SC26-4377-1.

[IBM89b] IBM. *DATABASE 2 Version 2, SQL Reference, Release 2*, September 1989. Document Number SC26-4380-1.

[IMS84] IMS/VS Version 1 Release 3: Recovery/Restart. Technical Report GG24-1652, IBM, 1984.

[IMS85] IMS/VS Fast Path Application Design. Technical Report GG24-1684, IBM, 1985.

[IMS86a] IMS/VS Version 2 Release 1: Data Base Administration Guide. Technical Report SC26-4179, IBM, 1986.

[IMS86b] IMS/VS Version 2: Application Programming. Technical Report SC26-4179, IBM, 1986.

[Inf94a] INFORMIX-OnLine Dynamic Server, Database Server, Administrator's Guide, Volume 1, Verion 7.1. Product documentation Part No. 000-7778, Informix Software, Inc., 4100 Bohannon Drive, Menlo Park, CA, USA, December 1994.

[Inf94b] INFORMIX-OnLine Dynamic Server, Database Server, Administrator's Guide, Volume 2, Version 7.1. Product documentation Part No. 000-7777, Informix Software, Inc., 4100 Bohannon Drive, Menlo Park, CA, USA, December 1994.

[Inf94c] Informix Guide to SQL, Tutorial, Version 7.1. Product documentation Part No. 000-7634, Informix Software, Inc., 4100 Bohannon Drive, Menlo Park, CA, USA, December 1994.

[Inf94d] Informix Guide to SQL, Reference, Version 7.1. Product documentation Part No. 000-7632, Informix Software, Inc., 4100 Bohannon Drive, Menlo Park, CA, USA, December 1994.

[Ing93] ASK OpenIngres Replicator User's Guide. Product documentation REP10-9(9)-16200, The ASK Group, Inc., 1080 Marina Village Parkway, Alameda, CA, USA, December 1993.

[ISO87] ISO-ANSI. *Information Processing Systems - Database Language SQL*, 1987.

[ISO88] ISO-ANSI. *IPS OSI Remote Datebase Access*, 1988.

[ISO89] ISO-ANSI. *Information Processing Systems - Database Language SQL with Integrity Enhancement*, 1989. Second edition.

[Jen89] C. S. Jensen. Incremental Implementation Model for Relational Databases with Transaction Time. Research Report R 89-16, The University of Aalborg, Institute for Electronic Systems, Departmen of Mathematics and Computers, Strandveien 19, DK 9000 Aalborg, Denmark, 1989.

[JR89] A. Joshi and K. Rodwell. A Database Management System for Production Applications. *Digital Technical Journal*, (8), February 1989.

[Kat78] J. A. Katzman. A Fault-Tolerant Computing System. In *Proceedings of the 11th Hawaii International Conference on System Sciences*, volume III, 1978.

[KD93] J. S. Keen and W. J. Dally. Performance Evaluation of Ephemeral Logging. In *Proceedings of the 1993 ACM SIGMOD International Conference on Management of Data*, Washington,DC, USA, May 1993.

[Kee91] J. S. Keen. Logging and Recovery in Highly Concurrent Databases. MIT AI Lab, NE43-614, Handout, June 1991.

[KGMC85] J. Kent, H. Garcia-Molina, and J. Chung. An Experimental Evaluation of Crash Recovery Mechanisms. In *Proceedings of the 4th SIGACT-SIGMOD Symposium on Principles of Database Systems*, pages 113–122, 1985.

[KHGMP90] R. P. King, N. Halim, H. Garcia-Molina, and C. A. Polyzois. Overview of Disaster Recovery for Transaction Processing Systems. In *Proceedings of the 10th International Conference on Distributed Computing Systems*, 1990.

[KHGMP91] R. P. King, N. Halim, H. Garcia-Molina, and C. A. Polyzois. Management of Remote Backup Copy for Disaster Recovery. *ACM Transactions on Database Systems*, 16(2):338–368, June 1991.

[Kim84] W. Kim. Highly Available Systems for Database Applications. *ACM Computing Surveys*, 16(1), March 1984.

[KLS90] H. F. Korth, E. Levy, and A. Silberschatz. Compensating Transactions: A New Recovery Paradigm. In *Proceedings of the 16th International Conference on Very Large Data Bases*, Brisbane, Australia, August 1990.

[KVA89] KVATRO A/S. *Techra SQL Reference Manual*, 1989.

[Lap89] J. C. Laprie. Dependability: A Unifying Concept for Reliable Computing and Fault Tolerance. In T. Anderson, editor, *Dependability of Resilient Computers*, chapter 1, pages 1–28. Blackwell Scientific Publications Professional Books, Oxford, UK, 1989.

[LC87] T. J. Lehman and M. J. Carey. A Recovery Algorithm for A High-Performance Memory-Resident Database System. In *Proceedings of the ACM-SIGMOD International Conference on Management of Data*, pages 104–117, May 1987.

[LI93] I. Lee and R. K. Iyer. Faults, Symptoms, and Software Fault Tolerance in the Tanden GUARDIAN90 Operating System. In *Proceedings of the 23rd International Conference on Fault-Tolerant Computing (FTCS-23)*, June 1993.

[LK91] E. K. Lee and R. H. Katz. Performance Consequences of Parity Placement in Disk Arrays. In *Proceedings of the 4th International Conference on Architectural Support for Programming Languages and operating Systems*, pages 190–199, 1991.

[Lor77] R. A. Lorie. Physical Integrity in a Large Segmented Database. *ACM Transactions on Database Systems*, 2(1):91–104, September 1977.

[LSG+79] B. G. Lindsay, P. G. Selinger, C. Galtieri, J. N. Gray, R. A. Lorie, T. G. Price, F. Putzolu, I. L. Traiger, and B. W. Wade. Notes on Distributed Databases. Research Report RJ2571 (33471) 7/14/79 Computer Science, IBM Research Division, IBM Research Laboratory, San Jose, California 95193, USA, 1979.

[Luc93] B. Lucyk, editor. *Advanced Topics in DB2*. Addison-Wesley, 1993.

[Lyn83] N. Lynch. Multilevel Atomicity - A New Correctness Criterion for Database Concurrency Control. *ACM Transactions on Database Systems*, 8(4):484–502, December 1983.

[Lyo88] J. Lyon. Design Considerations in Replicated Database Systems for Disaster Protection. In *The 33rd IEEE Computer Society International Conference COMPCON 88*, 1988.

[Lyo90] J. Lyon. Tandem's Remote Data Facility. In *The 35th IEEE Computer Society International Conference COMPCON 90*, February 1990.

[Lys86a] R. Lyseng. The TechRa DBMS Basic File System Design Specification. Software Design Specification Report TDB-FIL-2-R2.0, KVATRO, 1986.

[Lys86b] R. Lyseng. The TechRa DBMS Bufferpool Administration Design Specification. Software Design Specification Report TDB-BUF-2-R2.0, KVATRO, August 1986.

[Mac91] R. MacBane. The Tuxedo Transaction Processing System. In *Proceedings of the 4nd International Workshop on High Performace Systems*, September 1991.

[Mai83] D. Maier. *The Theory of Relational Databases*. Pitman Publishing Limited, 1983.

[McG77] W. C. McGee. The Information Management System IMS/VS - Part V: Transaction Processing Facilities. *IBM Systems Journal*, 16(2), 1977.

[MET88] METIS A/S. *TORNADO Reference Manual*, 1988.

[MHL+89] C. Mohan, D. Haderle, B. Lindsay, H. Pirahesh, and P. Schwarz. ARIES: A Transaction Recovery Method Supporting Fine-Granularity Locking and Partial Rollbacks Using Write-Ahead Logging. Research Report RJ6649 01/19/89 Computer Science, IBM Research Division, Almaden Research Center, San Jose, California 95150, USA, 1989.

[ML83] C. Mohan and B. Lindsay. Efficient Commit Protocols for the Tree of Processes Model of Distributed Transactions. In *Proceedings of the 2nd ACM Symposium on Principles of Distributed Computing*, 1983.

[ML89] C. Mohan and F. Levine. ARIES/IM: An Efficient and High Concurrency Index Management Method Using Write-Ahead Logging. Research Report RJ6846 08/29/89 Computer Science, IBM Research Division, Almaden Research Center, San Jose, California 95150, USA, 1989.

[Moh90] C. Mohan. ARIES/LHS: A Concurrency Control and Recovery Method Using Write-Ahead Logging for Linear Hashing with Separators. Research report, IBM Research Division, Almaden Research Center, San Jose, California 95150, USA, 1990.

[Moh91] C. Mohan. A Cost-Effective Method for Providing Improved Data Availability During DBMS Restart Recovery After a Failure. In *Proceedings of the 4th International Workshop on High Performance Transaction Systems*, September 1991.

[Mos82] J. E. B. Moss. Nested Transactions and Reliable Distributed Computing. In *Proceedings 2nd Symposium on Reliability in Distributed Software and Database Systems*, 1982.

[MP90] C. Mohan and H. Pirahesh. ARIES-RRH: Restricted Repeating of History in the ARIES Transaction Recovery Method. Research Report RJ7343 02/23/90 Computer Science, IBM Research Division, Data Base Technology Institute, IBM Almaden Research Center, San Jose, California 95120, USA, February 1990. Proceedings of the 7th International Conference on Data Engineering, Kobe, April 1991.

[MP92] M. Mouly and M.-B. Pautet. *The GSM System for Mobile Communication*. Published by the authors, 49, rue Louise Bruneau, F-91120 Palaiseau, France, 1992.

[MTO91] C. Mohan, K. Treiber, and R. Obermarck. Algorithms for the Management of Remote Backup Data Bases for Disaster Recovery. Research report, IBM Research Division, Almaden Research Center, San Jose, California 95150, USA, 1991.

[MTT91] Quantum Product Guide, 1991. Quantum Corporation, 135K CP-ALLPRD991.

[NBC+93] C. Nyberg, T. Barclay, Z. Cvetanovic, J. N. Gray, and D. Lomet. AlphaSort: A RISC Machine Sort. SFSC Technical Report 93.2, Digital San Francisco Systems Center, April 1993.

[Nel90] V. P. Nelson. Fault-Tolerant Computing: Fundamental Concepts. *IEEE Computer*, 23(7):19–25, July 1990.

[Nor83] Norwegian Telecommunications Administration. *Specifications and Technical Requirements for Digital Public Telephone Exchanges*, November 1983.

[Nug88] S. F. Nugent. The iPSC/2 Direct-Connect Communications Technology. In *Proc. of The Third Conference on Hypercube Concurrent Computers and Applications*, volume 1, January 1988.

[Nyg88] M. Nygård. Non-Serializability with Wander-Transactions in Skeleton-Databases. Research Report STF14 A88056, SINTEF, RUNIT, 1988. Dr.Tech. thesis.

[Nyg90] M. Nygård. Varying Degrees of Serialisability. Research report, SINTEF, ELAB-RUNIT, 1990.

[Obe80] R. Obermarck. IMS/VS Program Isolation Feature. IBM Research Report RJ2879, IBM Research Division, IBM Research Laboratory, San Jose, California 95193, USA, 1980.

[Ols90] S. M. Olsen. Traffic Load Estimates. Norwegian Telecom Department of Information Systems, Private communication, 1990.

[ÖV91] M. T. Özsu and P. Valduriez. *Principles of Distributed Database Systems*. Prentice-Hall International Editions, 1991.

[PB90] M. Peercy and P. Banerjee. Distributed Algorithms for Shortest-Path, Deadlock-Free Routing and Broadcasting in Arbitrarily Faulty Hypercubes. In *Proc. 20th Int. Symp. Fault-Tolerant Computing*, June 1990.

[Pea95a] M. Pratt and et al. Oracle7 Server Distributed Systems: Replicated Data, Release 7.1. Product documentation Part No. A21903-2, ORACLE Corporation, 500 Oracle Parkway, Redwood City, CA, USA, 1995.

[Pea95b] M. Pratt and et al. Oracle7 Server Distributed Systems, Volume II: Replicated Data, Release 7.2. Product documentation Part No. A25434-1, ORACLE Corporation, 500 Oracle Parkway, Redwood City, CA, USA, 1995.

[PG94] C. A. Polyzois and H. Garcia-Molina. Evaluation of Remote Backup Algorithms for Transaction-Processing Systems. *ACM Transactions on Database Systems*, 19(3):423–449, September 1994.

[PGK88] D. A. Patterson, G. Gibson, and R. H. Katz. A Case for Redundant Arrays of Inexpensive Disks (RAID). In *Proceedings of the 1988 ACM SIGMOD International Conference on Management of Data*, 1988.

[PLL81] S. B. Yao P. L. Lehman. Efficient Locking for Concurrent Operations on B-Trees. *ACM Transactions on Database Systems*, 6(4):650–670, 1981.

[PRS88] P. Peinl, A. Reuter, and H. Sammer. High Contention in a Stock Trading Database: A Case Study. In *ACM SIGMOD International Conference on Management of Data*, June 1988.

[PS83] R. J. Peterson and J. P. Strickland. Log Write-Ahead Protocols and IMS/VS Logging. In *Proceedings of the 2nd ACM SIGACT-SIGMOD Symposium on Principles of Database Systems*, Atlanta, USA, March 1983.

[Pub95a] Replication Server Technical Publications. Replication Server Administration Guide. Technical Report 32511-01-0101, Sybase, Inc., Sybase Inc., 6475 Christie Avenue, Emeryville, CA 94608, USA, March 1995.

[Pub95b] Replication Server Technical Publications. Replication Server Commands Reference. Technical Report 32410-01-0101, Sybase, Inc., Sybase Inc., 6475 Christie Avenue, Emeryville, CA 94608, USA, March 1995.

[Pub95c] Replication Server Technical Publications. Replication Server Design Guide. Technical Report 35580-01-0101, Sybase, Inc., Sybase Inc., 6475 Christie Avenue, Emeryville, CA 94608, USA, March 1995.

[Pub95d] Replication Server Technical Publications. Replication Server Troubleshooting Guide. Technical Report 35920-01-0101, Sybase, Inc., Sybase Inc., 6475 Christie Avenue, Emeryville, CA 94608, USA, March 1995.

[Ref86] G. Refvik. SIBAS Advanced. Course Handbook, Norsk Data, 1986.

[Reu80] A. Reuter. A Fast Transaction-Oriented Logging Scheme for UNDO-Recovery. *IEEE Transactions on Software Engineering*, SE-6, July 1980.

[Reu84] A. Reuter. Performance Analysis of Recovery Techniques. *ACM Transactions on Database Systems*, 9(4):526–559, December 1984.

[Rhe89] M. Young Rhee. *Error Correcting Codes*. McGraw-Hill Book Company, 1989.

[Ris87] O. Risnes. Database Snapshots: A Mechanism for Replication of Data in Distributed Databases. Research Report STF14 A87069, SINTEF, RUNIT, 1987. Dr.Ing. thesis.

[RM89] K. Rothermel and C. Mohan. ARIES/NT: A Recovery Method Based on Write-Ahead Logging for Nested Transactions. In *Proceedings of the 15th International Conference on Very Large Data Bases*, pages 337–346, 1989.

[RS86] L. Rowe and M. Stonebraker. The Commercial INGRES Epilogue. In M. Stonebraker, editor, *The INGRES Papers*, chapter 3. Addison-Wesley Publishing Company, Inc., 1986.

[RS89] T. K. Rengarajan and P. Spiro. High Availability Mechanisms of VAX DBMS Software. *Digital Technical Journal*, (8), February 1989.

[RSR95] IMS/ESA Administration Guide: System, Version 5, First Edition. Technical Report SC26-8013-00, IBM, April 1995.

[SB91] T. Sæter and K. Bratbergsengen. The impact of high reliability, high capacity database servers on telecommunication systems and services. In *Proceedings of the 6th World Telecommunication Forum, Part 2 (Technical Symposium); Integration, Interoperation and Interconnection: The Way to Global Services*, October 1991.

[SC91] V. Srinivasan and M. J. Carey. Performance of B-Tree Concurrency Control Algorithms. In *Proceedings of the 1991 ACM SIGMOD International Conference on Management of Data*, May 1991.

[Ser84] O. Serlin. Fault-Toelerant Systems in Commercial Applications. In *Tutorial: Fault-Tolerant Computing*, 1984.

[Sev82] D. Severance. A Practical Guide to the Design of Differential Files for Recovery of On-Line Databases. *ACM Transactions on Database Systems*, 7(4):540–565, December 1982.

[SGM90] K. Salem and H. Garcia-Molina. System M: A Transaction Processing Testbed for Memory Resident Data. *IEEE Transactions on Knowledge and Data Engineering*, 2(1):161–172, March 1990.

[SKW92] V. Singhal, S. V. Kakkad, and P. R. Wilson. Texas: An Efficient, Portable Persistent Store. In *Proceedings of the 5th International Workshop on Persistent Object Systems*, September 1992.

[Son89] S. H. Son. Recovery in Main Memory Database Systems for Engineering Design Applications. *Information Software Technology*, 31(2):85–90, March 1989.

[SR84] J. W. Stillwell and P. M. Rader. *IMS/VS Version 1 Release 3 Fast Path Notebook*. IBM, September 1984. Document Number G320-0149-0.

[Sta85] W. Stallings. *Data and Computer Communications*. Macmillan Publishing Company, 1985.

[Sto79] M. Stonebraker. Concurrency Control and Consistency of Multiple Copies of Data in Distributed INGRES. *IEEE Transaction on Software Engineering*, SE-5:188–194, May 1979.

[Sto87] M. Stonebraker. Transparency in Distributed Database Systems. Technical report, Relational Technology International, Alameda, California, USA, January 1987.

[SUW82] J. Strickland, P. Uhrowczik, and V. Watts. IMS/VS: An Evolving System. *IBM Systems Journal*, 21(4), 1982.

[SW90] R. M. Sanders and A. C. Weaver. The Xpress Transfer Protocol (XTP) - A Tutorial. *Computer Communication Review*, 20(5):67–80, October 1990.

[Tan81] A. S. Tanenbaum. *Computer Networks*. Prentice-Hall, Inc, 1981.

[Tec84] Techra User Manual. Technical report, Kongsberg Våpenfabrikk avd. Trondheim, 1984.

[Tor88] Ø. Torbjørnsen. Communication in a Failsoft Hypercube Database Machine. Technical report, Division of Computer Systems and Telematics, University of Trondheim, Norwegian Institute of Technology, N-7034 Trondheim, Norway, October 25 1988.

[Tor90] Ø. Torbjørnsen. Shortest Path Routing in a Failsoft Hypercube Database Machine. In *Proceedings of The Fifth Distributed Memory Computing Conference*, volume 2, pages 839–844. IEEE, April 1990.

[TPP88] J. Tuazon, J. Peterson, and M. Pniel. Mark IIIfp Hypercube Concurrent Processor Architecture. In *Proc. of The Third Conference on Hypercube Concurrent Computers and Applications*, volume 1, pages 71–80, January 1988.

[Tra82] I. L. Traiger. Virtual Memory Management for Database Systems. Research Report RJ3489 5/25/82 Computer Science, IBM Research Division, IBM Research Laboratory, San Jose, California 95193, USA, 1982.

[TW89] D. Taylor and G. Wilson. The Stratus System Architecture. In T. Anderson, editor, *Dependability of Resilient Computers*, chapter 10. Blackwell Scientific Publications Professional Books, Oxford, UK, 1989.

[Ull88] J. D. Ullman. *Principles of Database and Knowledgebase Systems*. Computer Science Press, Inc., 1988.

[VG89] P. Valduriez and G. Gardarin. *Analysis and Comparison of Relational Database Systems*. Addison-Wesley Publishing Company, Inc., 1989.

[Wal84] B. Walter. Nested Transactions with Multiple Commit Points: An Approach to the Structuring of Advanced Database Applications. In *Proceedings of the 10th International Conference on Very Large Data Bases*, pages 161–171, 1984.

[WBEK91] G. Y. Wyatt, A. Barshefsky, R. V. Epley, and M. P. Kaplan. The Evolution of Global Intelligent Network Architectures. *AT&T Technical Journal*, pages 11–25, Summer 1991.

[Wed91] J. Wedvik. Continuous Available DBMSs by the Use of Non-Blocking Fragment Replication Production. Diploma Thesis, December 1991. In Norwegian.

[Wei91] G. Weikum. Principles and Realization Strategies of Multilevel Transaction Management. *ACM Transactions on Database Systems*, 16(1):132–180, March 1991.

[WGAK89] A. N. Wilschot, P. W.P.J. Grefen, P. M.G. Apers, and M. L. Kersten. Implementing PRISMA/DB in an OOPL. In H. Boral and P. Faudemay, editors, *The 6th International Workshop on Database Machines*, Deauville, France, June 1989. Lecture Notes on Computer Science, 368, Springer-Verlag.

[Wil85] D. Wilson. The STRATUS Computer System. In T. Anderson, editor, *Resilient Computer Systems*, chapter 12. Blackwell Scientific Publications Professional Books, Oxford, UK, 1985.

[XRF87a] IMS/VS Extended Recovery Facility (XRF): Technical reference. Technical Report GG24-3153, IBM, April 1987.

[XRF87b] IMS/VS Extended Recovery Facility (XRF): Planning. Technical Report GG24-3151, IBM, 1987.

[XRF87c] IMS/VS Extended Recovery Facility (XRF): General information. Technical Report GG24-3150, IBM, 1987.

[XRF87d] IMS/VS Extended Recovery Facility (XRF): Implementation. Technical Report GG24-3152, IBM, 1987.

[XRF87e] IMS/VS Extended Recovery Facility (XRF): Operation and recovery. Technical Report GG24-3154, IBM, 1987.

Index

Part VI

Appendices

Appendix A

Basic Concepts

The intention of this chapter is to present the basic terminology of the book. This terminology is provided since most of the concepts are presented in other sources with slightly different semantics. The presentations are primarily based on [BHG87], [Nyg88], [Mai83], and [Cri90].

A.1 Datamodel, Database, and Database Management System Concepts

This section presents an introduction to basic datamodel and database related concepts.

A **datamodel** is a mathematical formalism for expressing data and data relationships, data integrity constraints, and operations on data.

A **database** (DB) is a finite set of data items $DB = \{x_1, x_2, ..., x_m\}$. A data item either is atomic or is comprised of a finite set of data items. Each data item has a value. The current value of the items represents the state of the database.

Database operations are operations on DB data items specified in the datamodel and supported by the DBMS.

Figure A.1 illustrates the concepts presented. The DB consists of data items operated on by the database operations. The data items may either be atomic or complex. The data item X_9 is complex, containing the data items X_1, X_2, and X_5. The data items X_7 and X_4 are atomic.

A **database management system (DBMS)** is a collection of hardware and software supporting database- and transaction-operations (see section A.8). A **centralised database management system** is a DBMS where the hardware component is a single autonomous computing node.

For a survey of DBMS technology see [Gra78], [Dat86], [Dat83], and [Ull88].

A.2 Distributed Database Concepts

This section defines basic distributed database concepts. For a more complete introduction to distributed databases, see [CP86] and [ÖV91].

A **centralised database** is a DB where all the data items are stored at one autonomous computing node. A **distributed database** is a DB comprised of centralised DBs.

There are two aspects in the distributed DB concept applied in this book. First there is the obvious

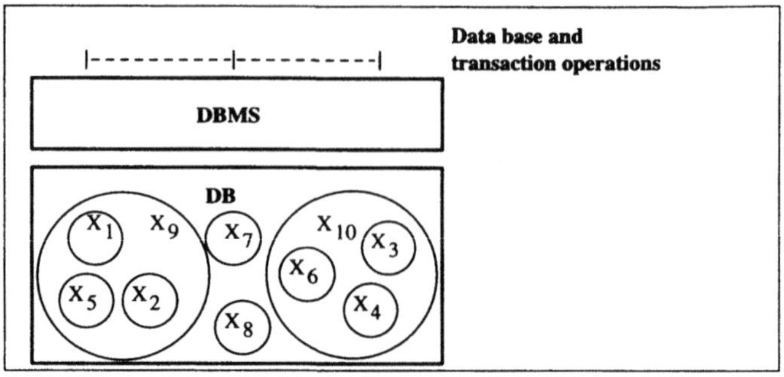

Figure A.1: A database (DB) comprising data items, a Database Management System (DBMS), and its database and transaction operations interface.

aspect of *distribution*. The data items are physically distributed on one or more nodes. The second aspect is the *replication* of data items. One or more replicas may exist of each data item. Both these aspects are illustrated in figure A.2. The data items are distributed among three centralised DBs. Some of the data items are replicated. Two replicas exist of X_9, and three replicas exist of X_8.

A **distributed database management system** is a DBMS which is a collection of centralised DBMSs, a data communication network connecting the centralised DBMSs, and a software component controlling the distribution and replication of data items.

The distribution and replication of data items may be more or less visible to the DBMS users, i.e. more or less transparent ([Sto87], [Ris87]). If complete distribution transparency is provided, data distribution and replication are completely hidden by the distributed DBMS. The external view is as for a centralised DB. Complete distribution transparency is assumed to be provided in this book.

A logical unit in a relational DB is a relation, which is divided into a collection of distribution units called **fragments**. The fragmentation is described in a **fragmentation schema**. Fragmentation may either be single- or multi-level. The fragmentation of a relation is **single level** if only one level of fragmentation is defined ([CP86], [HA88], [AH89]). Fragmentation is **multi-level** if a fragment is again allowed to be fragmented. A subfragmented fragment is called a **parent-fragment**. The relation is the top level parent-fragment. A fragment not further fragmented is called a **leaf-fragment**.

A parent-fragment is **horizontally fragmented** if it is partitioned into subsets of tuples. A parent-fragment is **vertically fragmented** if attribute names (see section A.4) are grouped, the parent-fragment is projected on the attributes in each group, and it is possible to reconstruct the parent-fragment from the fragments. More complex fragmentations may be constructed ([CP86]). This book is restricted to horizontal fragments, except where otherwise explicitly stated.

A fragment is the unit of replication, i.e. the same number of replicas exist for every data item of the fragment. A replica of a leaf-fragment is allocated on one specific node. A fragment is **n-replicated** if n replicas exist for all its data items.

A.3 The DBMS Mapping Architecture

This section presents the DBMS mapping architecture both for centralised and distributed DBMSs. The DBMS is structured into a hierarchy of abstraction layers in which a layer maps from a higher

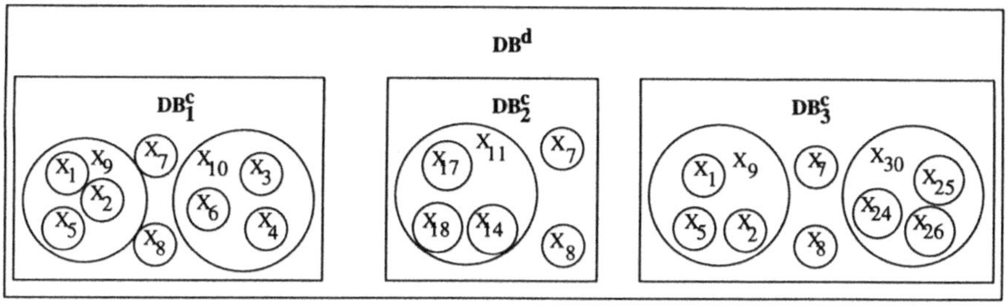

Figure A.2: The distributed database concept. A distributed database is comprised of centralised databases.

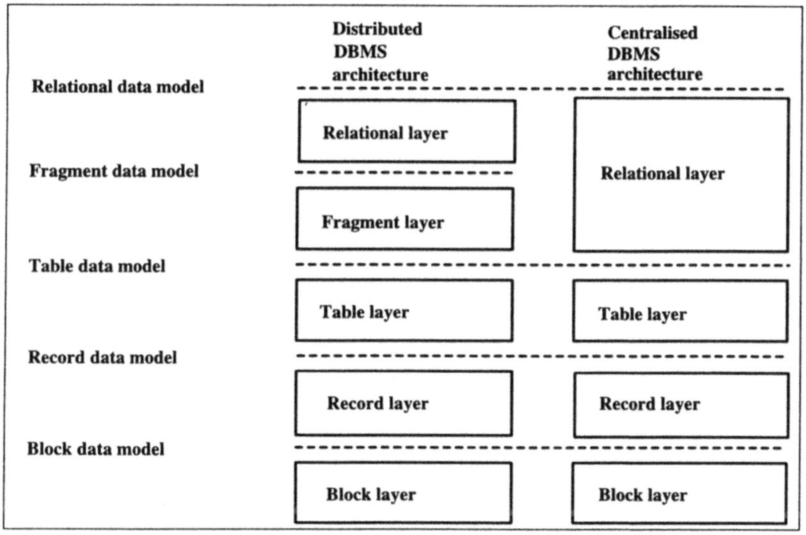

Figure A.3: The centralised and the distributed DBMS reference mapping architecture.

to a lower layer datamodel. A higher level datamodel may provide more complex data items, a larger number of integrity rules, and more powerful database operations. Figure A.3 illustrates the mapping hierarchy.

The **relational datamodel** ([Cod70], [Mai83]) is the datamodel externally visible to the users of the DBMS. The **relational layer** performs, in case of a centralised DBMS, mapping from relations to tables according to the table datamodel, and from declarative relational operations to navigational table operations. In case of a distributed DBMS, the relational layer performs mapping from relations to fragments. The operations supported to fragments are the same as to tables, so the operational mapping are as for tables. Multiple unique keys for a relation are maintained by mapping the relation to a collection of tables each maintaining one unique key. The table maintaining a primary key is called the **primary table**. The tables maintaining non-primary unique keys are called **index tables**.

The semantics of the **fragment datamodel** correspond to the table datamodel. The **fragment layer** supports the mapping of fragments to tables and the allocation of fragment replicas. One

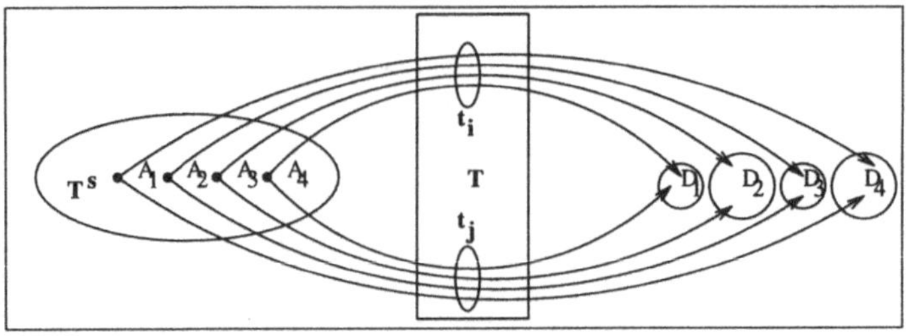

Figure A.4: The table schema (T^s), the table (T), and the tuple (t_i, t_j) concepts.

fragment replica is mapped to one table.

The **table datamodel** is an implementation platform for the relational model. The **table layer** maps tuple operations to record operations. A record is assumed to be contained within a block. The mapping is supported by access methods, for example B-trees. The unique primary key of a tuple is maintained by the use of these access methods. A more detailed definition of the table datamodel is presented in section A.4.

The **record layer** maps operations on uniquely identified records within a block to block operations on the main memory representation of blocks. The mapping is supported by access structures within a block.

The **block layer** is the most basic mapping layer. It performs the mapping from blocks to their physical representations in the main memory and on disc. Block read and write operations (on complete blocks) are mapped to hardware supported operations on the block representations. Unique block identifiers are the only integrity requirements supported and are based on hardware supported block access concepts.

A.4 The Table Datamodel

This section presents concepts related to the table datamodel. The intention of this datamodel is to define an implementation platform for a relational datamodel. The presented model represents a compromise between the easy implementation by a record layer server and the requirements of a complete relational model based on this layer. The model will also be used as a platform for recovery analysis.

A **table schema** T^s is a finite set of **attribute names**, i.e. $T^s = \{A_1, A_2, ..., A_n\}$. To each attribute name A_i is assigned a set D_i $1 \leq i \leq n$ which is its **domain**. A domain is an arbitrary nonempty set.

A **table** T on the table schema T^s is a finite set of functions $\{t_1, t_2, ..., t_m\}$, called **tuples**, from T^s to $D_1 \times D_2 \times ... \times D_n$ with the restriction that for each tuple $t \in T, t(A_i) \in D_i, 1 \leq i \leq n$.

Figure A.4 illustrates the table schema, table, and tuple concepts. A tuple is a function mapping from attribute name to a value in its domain for every attribute name of the corresponding table schema. A table is a set of tuples.

The attribute names of a table schema are divided with respect to external and internal accessibility. The externally accessible attributes are operated on by the database operations. The internal attributes are operated on only by the internal parts of the DBMS itself. This distinction is included in the model because attribute names are traditionally assumed to be externally accessible (see

[Nyg88]). The main reason for including internal attributes into the model is the recovery analysis where for example tuple state-identifiers are fundamental.

The **externally accessible** attribute names A^e of a table T are a nonempty subset of attribute names $\{B_1, B_2, ..., B_p\}$ from its table schema T^s. The **internally accessible** attribute names A^i of a table T are a subset of attribute names $\{C_1, C_2, ..., C_q\}$ from its table schema T^s so that an attribute is either externally accessible or internally accessible, and the union of externally and internally accessible attributes contains all defined attributes: $A^e \cup A^i = T^s$. If $A_i \in A^e$ then $A_i \notin A^i$.

Two key concepts are provided by the table datamodel; the **primary key** and the **surrogate key**. A primary key identifies a tuple uniquely within a table. Only one primary key is allowed to be defined on a table. The primary key concept is the integrity concept provided by the datamodel. The table datamodel provides no concepts like foreign key or null value ([Dat83]).

A surrogate is a DBMS generated value that uniquely identifies a tuple within a table throughout time ([Dat83], [Jen89]). A primary key value identifies a tuple uniquely at a given time, but not necessarily throughout time. A surrogate gives each tuple a unique name within a table.

A **primary key** P of a table T is a subset of attribute names $\{E_1, E_2, ..., E_k\}$ from A^e of T^s with the following properties. For every pair of distinct tuples t_1 and t_2 in T there is an E_i, $1 \leq i \leq k$ such that $t_1(E_i) \neq t_2(E_i)$.

A **surrogate key** S of a table T is a nonempty subset of attribute names $\{S_1, S_2..., S_l\}$ from A^i of T^s so that, for every two tuple t_1 and t_2 of T that exists or has ever existed, $t_1(S) \neq t_2(S)$.

A DB representing data items according to the table datamodel contains the following: each table is represented as a data item. A table contains tuples which are also data items. A tuple contains a collection of **fields**. A field represents the mapping from an attribute name to a value in its domain.

A.5 Table Datamodel Operations

The table datamodel contains the following tuple oriented DB operations: insert, delete, read, write, and delta tuple. The state changing tuple oriented DB operations are: insert, delete, write, and delta tuple. The dynamic tuple operations are: insert and delete tuple. Details of each of the operations are given below. The delta operation corresponds to an increment operation or a decrement operation with negated parameter value, without range tests. The delta operation avoids the need to include both the increment and the decrement operations in the operations set, thereby keeping the operations set to be analysed during the recovery analysis to a minimum without losing the semantics of the increment and decrement operations.

In the description of the operations below, As denote any attribute whereas Bs denote primary key attributes.

The following describes the **insert** operation: *Ins*$(T : A_1 = d_1, A_2 = d_2, ..., A_n = d_n)$. The table T is given with all the attribute names of T^s and a value from the respective domains. If the primary key is unique, the tuple becomes a member of T.

The following describes the **delete** operation: *Del*$(T : B_1 = d_1, B_2 = d_2, ..., B_m = d_m)$. The table T is given with the primary key attribute names and a value for each attribute name in the primary key. If a tuple with the specified primary key is in T, the tuple is removed from T.

The following describes the **read** operation: *Read*$(T : B_1 = d_1, B_2 = d_2, ..., B_m = d_m : A_i, A_j, ..., A_k)$. The table T is given, and the tuple to be read is uniquely identified by its primary key value. In addition the names of attributes to be read are specified. If the primary key uniquely distinguishes a tuple, the values of the specified attribute names are returned.

The following describes the **write** operation: *Write*($T : B_1 = d_1, B_2 = d_2, ..., B_m = d_m : A_i = d_i, A_j = d_j, ..., A_k = d_k$). The table T is given, and the tuple is identified by its primary key value. The attributes to be written into are specified by their name and the new attribute value. If the primary key value specified corresponds to a tuple in T, the attribute values are updated to the new values.

The following describes the **delta** operation: *Delta*($T : B_1 = d_1, B_2 = d_2, ..., B_m = d_m : A_i \triangle d_i, A_j \triangle d_j, ..., A_k \triangle d_k$). The table T is given, and the tuple is identified by its primary key value. The attributes to be operated on are specified by their names and the delta values. If the primary key value specified corresponds to a tuple in T the attribute values are modified by the specified value.

A.6 The Record Datamodel

The **complete record datamodel** contains the following record oriented DB operations: insert, delete, read, write, and delta. The **restricted record datamodel** contains the insert, delete, read, and write record operations. The state changing record oriented DB operations are the insert, delete, write, and delta record operations. The dynamic record operations are: insert and delete record.

Record datamodels use one of the following **record identification policies** to uniquely identify a record within a block.

- **Record index**
  The record is identified by its position relative to other records within the block.
- **Record address**
  The record is identified by the address within the block of the first byte of the record.

The identification of a record within a block may be based on the identification concepts of the table datamodel, i.e. the primary key or the surrogate key, or it may be based on identification concepts of the record datamodel itself, i.e. the record index or record address. The record index identification concept is based on an internal structuring of a block with a pointer array in the block head pointing to each record in the block ([VG89], [ABC+76], [ABF+81], [Dat84], [Lys86a], [MHL+89], [HSAG90]).

The following describes the record operations combined with the record index identification concept. The record index is given by X. A_i is any attribute and d_i associated domain.

The following describes the **insert** record operation: *Ins*($B_i : X : A_1 = d_1, A_2 = d_2, ..., A_n = d_n$). The block identifier B_i uniquely identifies the block into which the record is to be inserted. All the attribute names T^s of the table T to which the record belongs are given with a value from their respective domains.

The following describes the **delete** record operation: *Del*($B_i : X$). The block identifier B_i and the index of the record X within the record are given.

The following describes the **read** record operation: *Read*($B_i : X : A_i, A_j, ..., A_k$). The block identifier B_i and the record index within the block X are given. In addition the names of attributes to be read are required specified.

The following describes the **write** record operation: *Write*($B_i : X : A_i = d_i, A_j = d_j, ..., A_k = d_k$). The block identifier B_i and record index within the block X identify the record to be written into. The attributes to be written into are specified by their name and the corresponding new attribute values.

The following describes the **delta** record operation: *Delta*($B_i : X : A_i \triangle d_i, A_j \triangle d_j, ..., A_k \triangle d_k$). The block identifier B_i and the record identifier within the block X are given. The attributes to be operated on are specified by their name and their delta value.

A.7 The Block Datamodel

This section presents the block datamodel. The datamodel corresponds to the datamodel assumed in e.g. [BHG87].

A **block** B is a mapping from a block-identifier from the set of block-identifiers to a block-value from the set of block-values. A DB is a set of blocks. The only integrity requirement of the block model is the unique name of each block.

A block is assumed to be a fixed sized data item. A block is uniquely identified by a **block-identifier**. The block-identifier is a surrogate, unique within the scope of a DB.

The block datamodel includes the operations read and write block. Dynamic block operations are not included in the block datamodel. The state changing DB operation is write block.

The following describes the **read** operation: *Read*(B_i). The block with block-identifier B_i is read if a block with the block-identifier exists.

The following describes the **write** operation: *Write*(B_i). The block with the block-identifier B_i is written if a block with the block-identifier exists.

A.8 The Transaction Model

This section presents the transaction model and its properties. This transaction model is based on the transaction concept presented in [Gra81].

A **transaction program** contains DB and transaction operations. The **transaction operations** are *commit*, and *abort*. A **transaction** seen from the DBMS user's perspective is an execution of a particular transaction program.

A **transaction** seen from the DBMS perspective is a sequence of DB and transaction operations started by a *start* operation followed by a sequence of DB operations and terminated by either a *commit* or *abort* operation. A transaction is **active** if it is started but not terminated. A transaction is **committed** if it is terminated by a *commit* operation, and **aborted** if it is terminated by an *abort* operation.

The DBMS assumes a transaction to be *an atomic unit* performing a correct DB transformation when executed alone. This is termed the *consistency requirement* ([Gra91]). A consistent transformation means preservation of the integrity requirements among the data items. The DBMS offers the following properties with respect to a transaction:

- **Failure atomic** (*Atomicity requirement* ([Gra81], [Gra91]))
  A transaction is never abandoned when partially completed. If the execution of a transaction is stopped, the effect on the DB is either as though the transaction had not started, or as though it were completed. This is called the *all-or-nothing* property (see [Gra81]). If more than one participant is involved in the execution, the effect of a stopped transaction is either as if no participants had started, or all had completed.
- **Serialisable** (*Isolation requirement*)
  Concurrent execution of transactions do not interfere with each other. For the executed

transactions the result is as if the transactions were executed in some serial order. This is also called the *isolation* ([HR84]) or *one-after-the-other* property ([Nyg88]).

- **Persistent** (*Durability requirement*)
  The effect of a committed transaction will not be lost. The DBMS guarantees that the results of committed transactions survive future failures. This is also termed the *durability* ([HR84]) or *survivability* ([GMA89]) property of a transaction.

The atomicity, consistency, isolation, and durability properties of a transaction are termed the ACID properties ([HR84]).

If the initial state of a DB is consistent, any ACID execution of transactions will produce a consistent DB. This is ensured by the atomicity of the transaction concept, together with the consistency transformation assumption and the isolation requirement. The durability requirement maintains this property over time. These features of a DBMS resemble the requirement of a large group of real world applications. Later in the book, this ACID property is used as the **consistent DB state requirement** when performing recovery actions.

The serialisability property means that the transactions are the *units of concurrency*. The serialisability property is provided by the scheduler or concurrency control server of a DBMS (see section A.9).

The persistency property guarantees that the effect of database operations of committed transactions are never lost, neither as a result of a failure, nor as a result of the recovery after a failure. In this respect the transactions becomes the *units of recovery*.

A transaction may at any time during its execution be aborted, either by the transaction program executing an *abort* operation, or by the DBMS as a result of a failure. The abortion leaves no trace of the effect of the transaction in the DB. Once a transaction is committed, it cannot be aborted. Its effect can only be cancelled by a **compensating transaction** ([KLS90]).

A **non-dialogue transaction** is a transaction in which its output is not seen outside the scope of the DBMS until after it is committed. A precompiled, parameterised transaction is an example of a non-dialogue transaction. Since the output from a non-dialogue transaction is not revealed until after it is committed, a non-dialogue transaction that has been aborted by the DBMS can be automatically reexecuted.

Over the last years intensive research has taken place to extend the transaction concept both with respect to *nesting*, i.e. nested transactions ([Mos82], [Wal84], [RM89], [HS90], [BK91]), and *long-duration transactions*, i.e. transactions spanning hours and days ([DHL90]). This research is motivated by the use of DBMSs in new application areas.

A distributed transaction model is introduced in section 10.2 in the context of the HypRa DBMS. The concept of nested subtransactions are introduced in section 10.2 and will be used internally at a node.

A.9 Concurrency Control Concepts

Extensive surveys of concurrency control methods for both centralised and distributed DBMSs are given in [BHG87].

Concurrency control is assumed to be based on **locking**.

The locking scheme used is required to be:

- **Well-formed**

	Read	Write	Delta
Read	y	n	n
Write	n	n	n
Delta	n	n	y

Table A.1: The compatibility matrix for read, write, and delta locks. A "y" indicate that locks in the corresponding row and column on the same data item are compatible, i.e. they do not conflict. An "n" indicates that they are not compatible, i.e they do conflict.

	Read	Write
Read	y	n
Write	n	n

Table A.2: The compatibility matrix for the traditional locking model containing read and write locks. See table A.1 for terminology presentation.

The lock scheme is well-formed if a data item is locked before it is accessed and the operation is delayed until the lock can be set if the lock tried set is incompatible with an existing lock.

- **Strict two-phased** (strict 2PL)
  The lock scheme is strict two-phased if all locks kept by a transaction is released together when the transaction terminates.

The locking model is called **semantically rich** if *Read*, *Write*, and *Delta* lock types are supported with compatibility as presented in table A.1. The locking model is called **traditional** if the *Read* and *Write* lock types are supported with compatibility as presented in table A.2 ([BHG87]). Locks are **fine grained** if tuples, records, or fields are the unit of locking. Locks are **coarse grained** if blocks are the unit of locking.

Exercises

1. A telecommunication operator plans to provide a simple universal personal telecommunication (UPT) service. Every subscriber is given his own unique logical phone number which is used when calling the subscriber. A *home location register* (HLR) is needed to map a logical phone number to a physical phone number. When a logical number is called the HLR is accessed to look up the corresponding physical number. The telecom operator allows only one logical number to be connected to each physical number at a time. (a) Propose a simple relational data model for HLR. (b) Propose a mapping from the relational data model to tables according to the centralised DBMS architecture. (c) Propose a mapping according to the distributed DBMS architecture when the UPT service is implemented by multiples UPT sites each serving a set of customers.

2. (a) Which layer would a file access method fit into? (b) Would the choice of access method influence the choice of which layer the access method resides in? (c) Which layer does the access method to determine in which fragment a tuple belongs fit into?

3. When a UPT subscriber moves, he keeps his logical phone number. (a) Design a transaction for moving a logical phone number from one physical phone number to another. (b) Using this transaction, develop four scenarios, each violating one ACID property.

4. (a) Introduce a multiplication (*Mult*) operation into the compatibility matrix illustrated in table A.1. (b) Does this operation have any advantages with respect to concurrency? (c) Would the introduction of range tests on delta operations influence the compatibility matrix?

Answers

1. (a) The HLR is a single relation with two columns. The logical phone number of a subscriber is one column and the physical phone number the subscriber is connected to is the other column. Both the logical phone number and the physical phone number are unique columns because only one logical number can be connected to one physical number (see [ISO89]). The logical phone number is chosen as the primary column because the HLR is most frequently accessed on logical phone numbers.

   (b) The HLR relation is mapped to one primary table and one index table. The primary table has the logical phone number as its primary key. The index table has the physical phone number as its primary key. The complete record datamodel and the record index policy are used. The blocks of one table are members of that table only.

   (c) The relation is fragmented horizontally. There is a single level of fragments. The number of fragments corresponds to the number of UPT server sites. There are two replicas of every fragment. There are one set of fragment replicas composed of primary tables and one set of fragments of index tables. Two replicas of different fragments may be allocated on the same node and the two replicas of a single fragment are allocated on different nodes.

2. (a) File access methods fit into the table layer. (b) No. (c) It fits into the fragment layer.

3. (a) The transaction consists of updating the row with the given logical telephone number as the primary unique key with the new physical telephone number.

   (b) *Atomicity:* Only one of the two row replicas becomes updated, i.e. one replica keeps the old committed value and the other gets the new committed value. *Consistency:* The physical phone number becomes incorrectly updated, e.g. by a logical software bug. *Isolation*: The new physical telephone number becomes visible to other transactions before the move is committed. *Durability:* Special Forces vapourises every UPT node.

4. (a) A mult operation is compatible with other mult operations. It is not compatible with other read, write, or delta operations. (b) Increase concurrency and avoid hot-spots. (c) No.

State-of-the-Art zum Thema Statistische Datenbanken

1997. XVIII, 258 S. (Datenbanksysteme; hrsg. von Härder, Theo/ Reuter, Andreas)
Br. DM 118,00
ISBN 3-528-05565-0

Inhalt: Fallstudien aus den Bereichen Klima- und Umweltforschung, Molekularbiologie, Fertigungsqualitätskontrolle, Banken- und Finanzwesen - Modelle zur Unterstützung zeit- und verlaufsbezogener sowie statistischer Auswertungen von empirisch erhobenen Massendatenbeständen - Das SSDB-Modell CROSS-DB (Categorization- and Redundancy-based Optimization of Scientific and Statistical Data Bases)

Das Buch stellt Anforderungen und Lösungskonzepte zur Datenbankunterstützung bei der Verwaltung und Auswertung empirisch erhobener Massendatenanwendungen vor. Es bietet Anwendungsbeispiele aus den Bereichen Banken-/Finanzwesen, beschreibende Statistik, Fertigungsqualitätskontrolle, Molekularbiologie, Klima-/Umweltforschung. Zur Unterstützung dieser Anwendungsbereiche wird ein Modell für ein SSDB-System (Scientific&Statistical Database System) dargestellt, das hinsichtlich Modellierungsflexibilität und Durchgängigkeit auf allen Schemaebenen eines Datenbanksystems deutlich über vergleichbare Ansätze hinausgeht.

Ein besonderer Vorzug dieses Buches ist, dass auch aktuelle Themen wie „Data Warehousing“ und „On-Line Analytical Processing (OLAP)“ behandelt werden.

vieweg

Abraham-Lincoln-Straße 46
65189 Wiesbaden
Fax 0611. 78 78-400
www.vieweg.de

Stand 1.8.99. Änderungen vorbehalten.
Erhältlich im Buchhandel oder beim Verlag.

Retter aus der Informationsflut!

Hartmut Wittig

Intelligent Media Agents

Key technology for Interactive Television, Multimedia and Internet Applications

vieweg

1999. XX, 176 S. mit 63 Abb., 18 Tab.
Br. DM 98,00
ISBN 3-528-05706-8

Inhalt: Intelligente Agenten - Software-Agenten - Programmierung - fuzzy logic

Intelligente Agenten sind die Retter aus der Informationsflut. Sie helfen dabei, wichtige und unwichtige Nachrichten zu unterscheiden. Damit sind sie wegweisend für die Entwicklung künftiger Internet-Systeme. Das Buch beschreibt Grundlagen und die Architektur von intelligenten Medienagenten. Ein durchgängiges Anwendungsbeispiel - der intelligenten Agenten für ein interaktives Fernsehsystem - verschafft ein praxisnahes Kennenlernen der intelligenten Helfer. Einerseits erhält der Leser einen Überblick über die Arbeitsweise eines Agenten. Andererseits gelingt es, wichtige Abläufe am Beispiel des interaktiven Fernsehens detailgenau zu beschreiben und damit den Leser bei der Entwicklung intelligenter Multimedia-Systeme anzuleiten.

vieweg

Abraham-Lincoln-Straße 46
65189 Wiesbaden
Fax 0611. 78 78-400
www.vieweg.de

Stand 1.8.99. Änderungen vorbehalten.
Erhältlich im Buchhandel oder beim Verlag.

GPSR Compliance

The European Union's (EU) General Product Safety Regulation (GPSR) is a set of rules that requires consumer products to be safe and our obligations to ensure this.

If you have any concerns about our products, you can contact us on ProductSafety@springernature.com

In case Publisher is established outside the EU, the EU authorized representative is:

Springer Nature Customer Service Center GmbH
Europaplatz 3
69115 Heidelberg, Germany

Batch number: 10584556

Printed by Printforce, the Netherlands